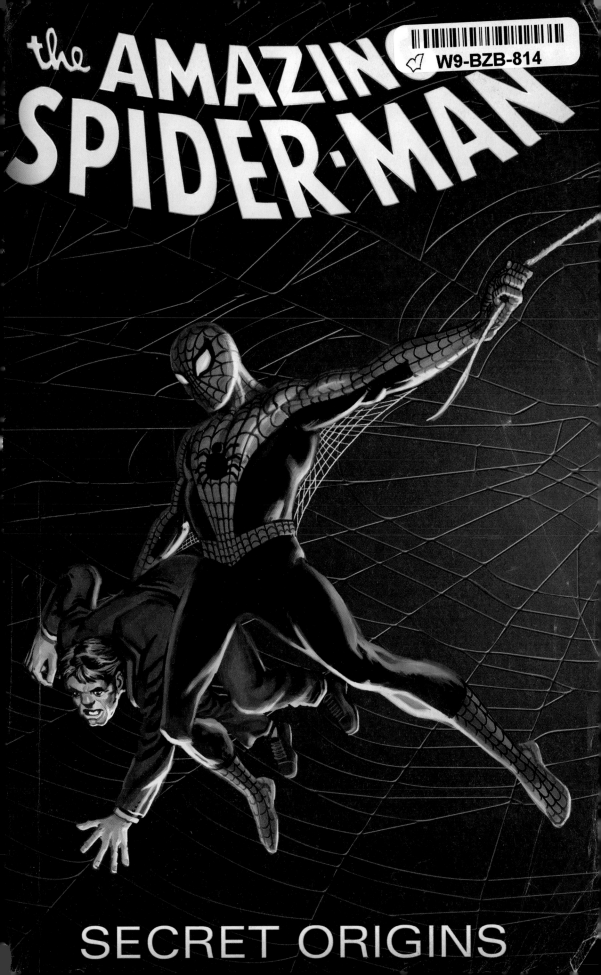

the AMAZING SPIDER-MAN

SECRET ORIGINS

the AMAZING SPIDER-MAN

SECRET ORIGINS

WRITERS: STAN LEE & PAUL JENKINS

PENCILERS: STEVE DITKO, JOHN ROMITA, GIL KANE & MARK BUCKINGHAM

INKERS: STEVE DITKO, JIM MOONEY, JOHN ROMITA & MARK BUCKINGHAM

COLORIST: D'ISRAELI LETTERERS: ART SIMEK, SAM ROSEN & VIRTUAL CALLIGRAPHY'S CORY PETIT

EDITORS: STAN LEE & TOM BREVOORT

OFFICIAL HANDBOOK OF THE MARVEL UNIVERSE BONUS PAGES

HEAD WRITERS/COORDINATORS: JEFF CHRISTIANSEN & MIKE FICHERA

WRITERS: RONALD BYRD, JONATHAN COUPER-SMARTT, MIKE FICHERA, SEAN MCQUAID & AL SJOERDSMA

FOR MORE **SPIDER-MAN** AND MARVEL COMICS CHARACTER PROFILES, PLEASE SEE
THE OFFICIAL HANDBOOK OF THE MARVEL UNIVERSE HARDCOVER/SOFTCOVER SERIES, VOLUMES 1-14.

COLLECTION EDITOR: MARK D. BEAZLEY ASSISTANT EDITORS: ALEX STARBUCK & NELSON RIBEIRO

EDITOR, SPECIAL PROJECTS: JENNIFER GRÜNWALD SENIOR EDITOR, SPECIAL PROJECTS: JEFF YOUNGQUIST

RESEARCH: ROB LONDON LAYOUT: JEPH YORK BOOK DESIGNER: RODOLFO MURAGUCHI

SENIOR VICE PRESIDENT OF SALES: DAVID GABRIEL SVP OF BRAND PLANNING & COMMUNICATIONS: MICHAEL PASCIULLO

EDITOR IN CHIEF: AXEL ALONSO CHIEF CREATIVE OFFICER: JOE QUESADA

PUBLISHER: DAN BUCKLEY EXECUTIVE PRODUCER: ALAN FINE

AMAZING SPIDER-MAN: SECRET ORIGINS. Contains material originally published in magazine form as AMAZING FANTASY #15; AMAZING SPIDER-MAN #6, #8, #82 and #90; SPECTACULAR SPIDER-MAN #27. First printing 2012. ISBN# 978-0-7851-6472-2. Published by MARVEL WORLDWIDE, INC., a subsidiary of MARVEL ENTERTAINMENT, LLC. OFFICE OF PUBLICATION: 135 West 50th Street, New York, NY 10020. Copyright © 1962, 1963, 1964, 1970, 2005 and 2012 Marvel Characters, Inc. All rights reserved. $14.99 per copy in the U.S. and $16.99 in Canada (GST #R127032852); Canadian Agreement #40668537. All characters featured in this issue and the distinctive names and likenesses thereof, and all related indicia are trademarks of Marvel Characters, Inc. No similarity between any of the names, characters, persons, and/or institutions in this magazine with those of any living or dead person or institution is intended, and any such similarity which may exist is purely coincidental. **Printed in the U.S.A.** ALAN FINE, EVP - Office of the President, Marvel Worldwide, Inc. and EVP & CMO Marvel Characters B.V.; DAN BUCKLEY, Publisher & President - Print, Animation & Digital Divisions; JOE QUESADA, Chief Creative Officer; TOM BREVOORT, SVP of Publishing; DAVID BOGART, SVP of Operations & Procurement, Publishing; RUWAN JAYATILLEKE, SVP & Associate Publisher, Publishing; C.B. CEBULSKI, SVP of Creator & Content Development; DAVID GABRIEL, SVP of Publishing Sales & Circulation; MICHAEL PASCIULLO, SVP of Brand Planning & Communications; JIM O'KEEFE, VP of Operations & Logistics; DAN CARR, Executive Director of Publishing Technology; SUSAN CRESPI, Editorial Operations Manager; ALEX MORALES, Publishing Operations Manager; STAN LEE, Chairman Emeritus. For information regarding advertising in Marvel Comics or on Marvel.com, please contact John Dokes, SVP Integrated Sales and Marketing, at jdokes@marvel.com. For Marvel subscription inquiries, please call 800-217-9158. **Manufactured between 3/28/2012 and 4/16/2012 by R.R. DONNELLEY, INC., SALEM, VA, USA.**

10 9 8 7 6 5 4 3 2 1

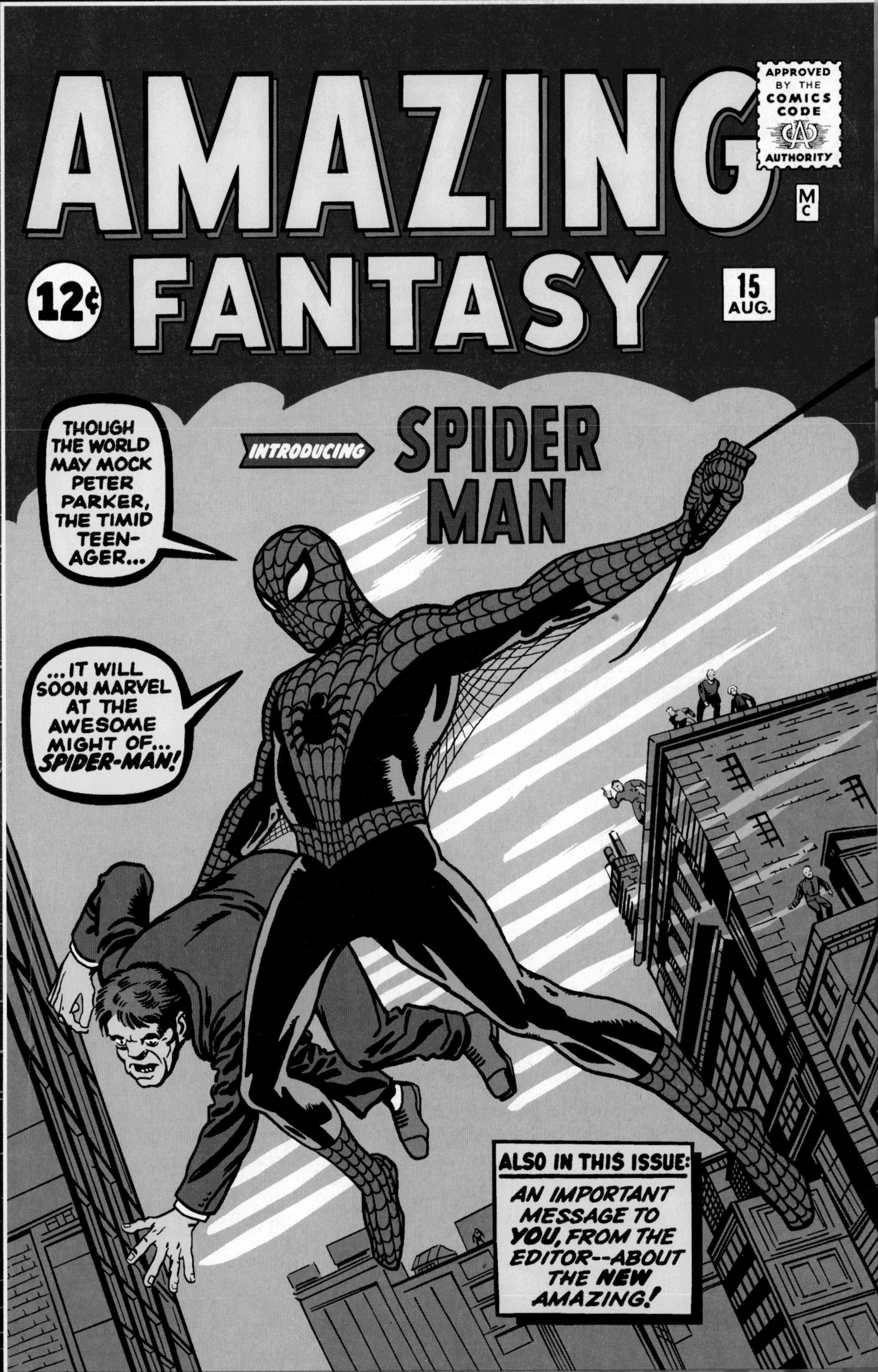

AMAZING FANTASY
APPROVED BY THE COMICS CODE AUTHORITY
MC
12¢
15 AUG.
INTRODUCING SPIDER MAN
THOUGH THE WORLD MAY MOCK PETER PARKER, THE TIMID TEEN-AGER...
...IT WILL SOON MARVEL AT THE AWESOME MIGHT OF... SPIDER-MAN!
ALSO IN THIS ISSUE:
AN IMPORTANT MESSAGE TO YOU, FROM THE EDITOR--ABOUT THE NEW AMAZING!

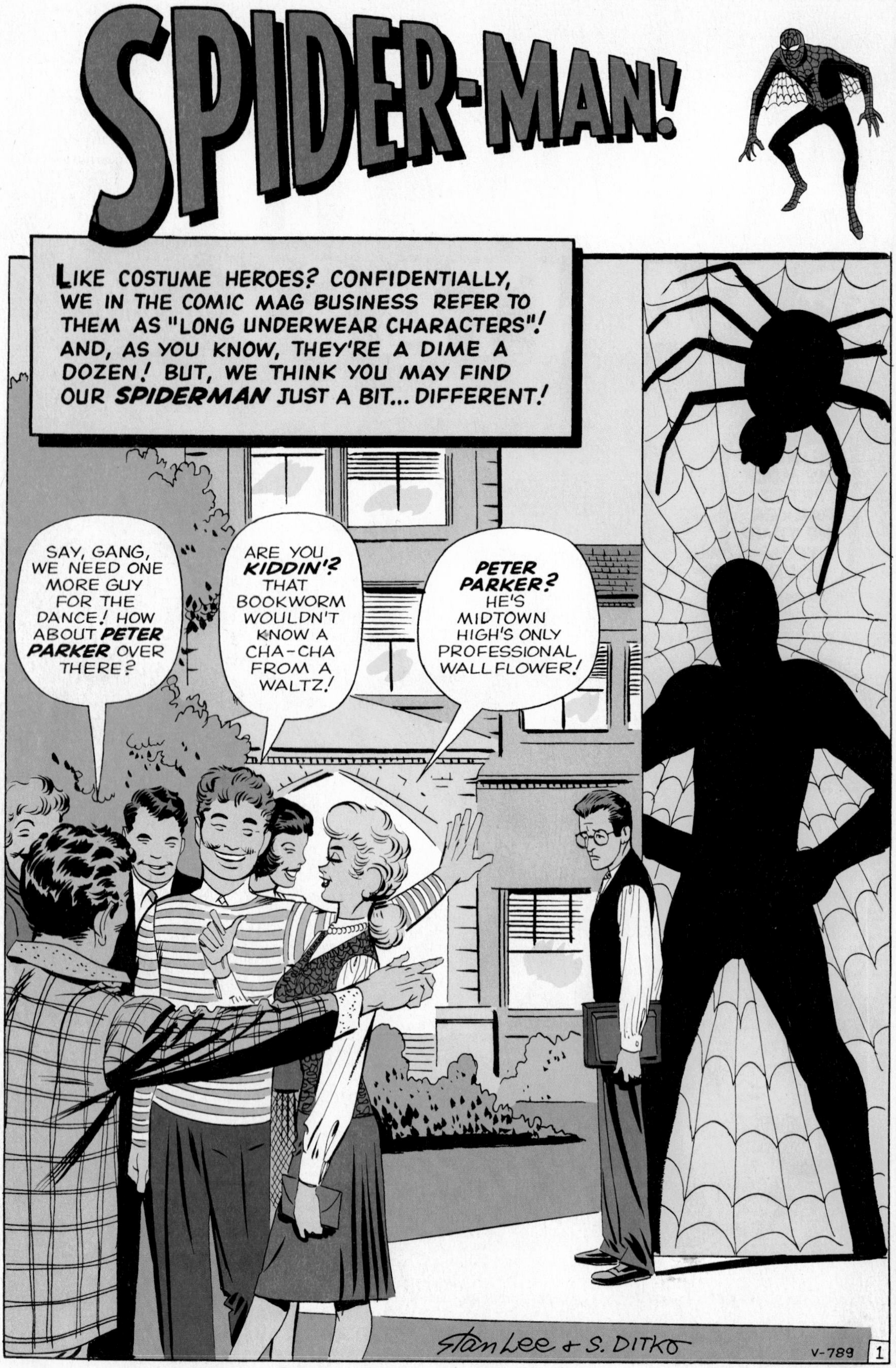
SPIDER-MAN!
LIKE COSTUME HEROES? CONFIDENTIALLY, WE IN THE COMIC MAG BUSINESS REFER TO THEM AS "LONG UNDERWEAR CHARACTERS"! AND, AS YOU KNOW, THEY'RE A DIME A DOZEN! BUT, WE THINK YOU MAY FIND OUR SPIDERMAN JUST A BIT... DIFFERENT!
SAY, GANG, WE NEED ONE MORE GUY FOR THE DANCE! HOW ABOUT PETER PARKER OVER THERE?
ARE YOU KIDDIN'? THAT BOOKWORM WOULDN'T KNOW A CHA-CHA FROM A WALTZ!
PETER PARKER? HE'S MIDTOWN HIGH'S ONLY PROFESSIONAL WALLFLOWER!
Stan Lee + S. DITKO
V-789
1

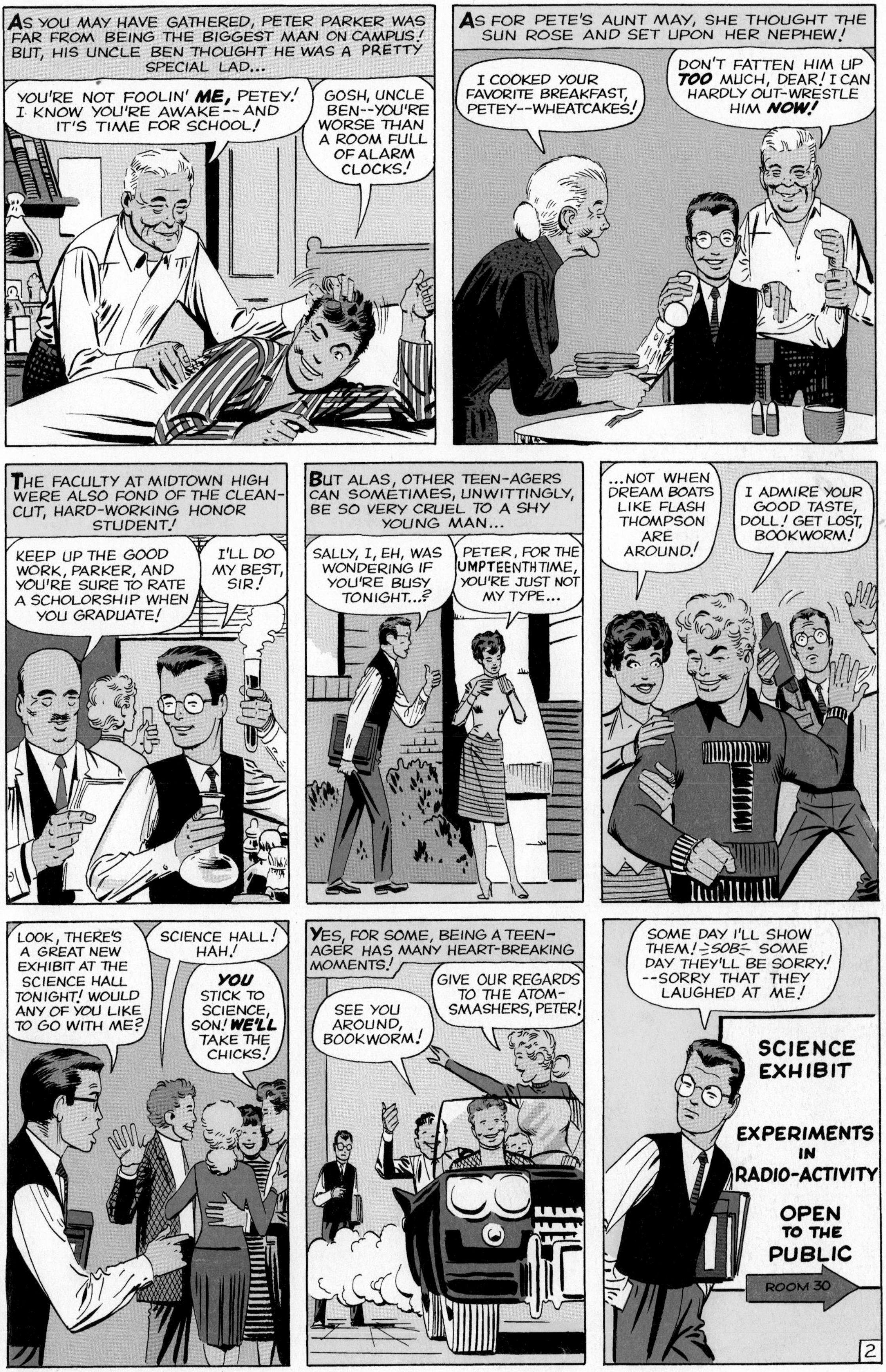
AS YOU MAY HAVE GATHERED, PETER PARKER WAS FAR FROM BEING THE BIGGEST MAN ON CAMPUS! BUT, HIS UNCLE BEN THOUGHT HE WAS A PRETTY SPECIAL LAD...
YOU'RE NOT FOOLIN' ME, PETEY! I KNOW YOU'RE AWAKE--AND IT'S TIME FOR SCHOOL!
GOSH, UNCLE BEN--YOU'RE WORSE THAN A ROOM FULL OF ALARM CLOCKS!
AS FOR PETE'S AUNT MAY, SHE THOUGHT THE SUN ROSE AND SET UPON HER NEPHEW!
I COOKED YOUR FAVORITE BREAKFAST, PETEY--WHEATCAKES!
DON'T FATTEN HIM UP TOO MUCH, DEAR! I CAN HARDLY OUT-WRESTLE HIM NOW!
THE FACULTY AT MIDTOWN HIGH WERE ALSO FOND OF THE CLEAN-CUT, HARD-WORKING HONOR STUDENT!
KEEP UP THE GOOD WORK, PARKER, AND YOU'RE SURE TO RATE A SCHOLORSHIP WHEN YOU GRADUATE!
I'LL DO MY BEST, SIR!
BUT ALAS, OTHER TEEN-AGERS CAN SOMETIMES, UNWITTINGLY, BE SO VERY CRUEL TO A SHY YOUNG MAN...
SALLY, I, EH, WAS WONDERING IF YOU'RE BUSY TONIGHT...?
PETER, FOR THE UMPTEENTH TIME, YOU'RE JUST NOT MY TYPE...
...NOT WHEN DREAM BOATS LIKE FLASH THOMPSON ARE AROUND!
I ADMIRE YOUR GOOD TASTE, DOLL! GET LOST, BOOKWORM!
LOOK, THERE'S A GREAT NEW EXHIBIT AT THE SCIENCE HALL TONIGHT! WOULD ANY OF YOU LIKE TO GO WITH ME?
SCIENCE HALL! HAH!
YOU STICK TO SCIENCE, SON! WE'LL TAKE THE CHICKS!
YES, FOR SOME, BEING A TEEN-AGER HAS MANY HEART-BREAKING MOMENTS!
SEE YOU AROUND, BOOKWORM!
GIVE OUR REGARDS TO THE ATOM-SMASHERS, PETER!
SOME DAY I'LL SHOW THEM! ≥SOB≤ SOME DAY THEY'LL BE SORRY! --SORRY THAT THEY LAUGHED AT ME!
SCIENCE EXHIBIT
EXPERIMENTS IN RADIO-ACTIVITY
OPEN TO THE PUBLIC
ROOM 30
2

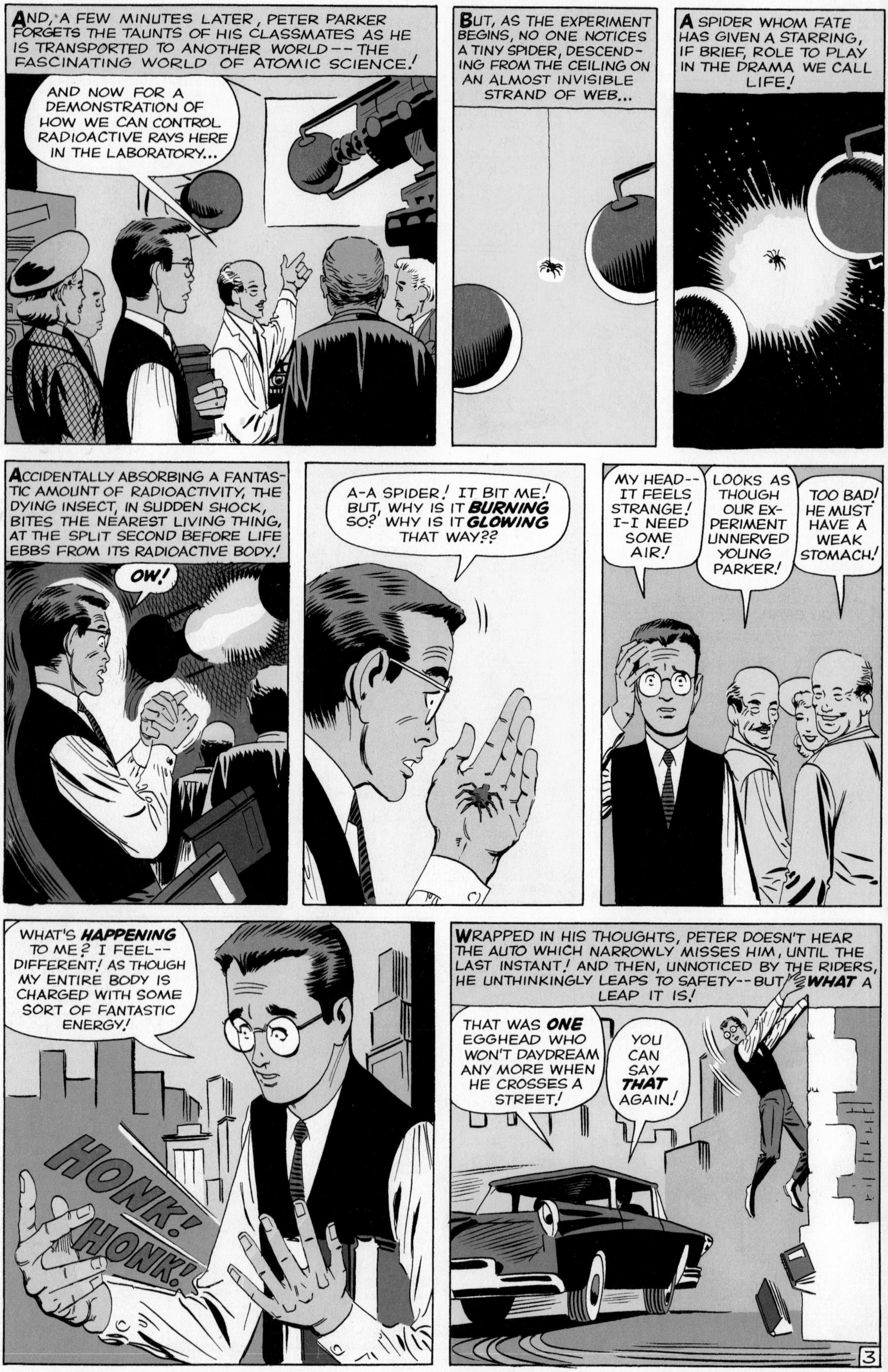
AND, A FEW MINUTES LATER, PETER PARKER FORGETS THE TAUNTS OF HIS CLASSMATES AS HE IS TRANSPORTED TO ANOTHER WORLD -- THE FASCINATING WORLD OF ATOMIC SCIENCE!
AND NOW FOR A DEMONSTRATION OF HOW WE CAN CONTROL RADIOACTIVE RAYS HERE IN THE LABORATORY...
BUT, AS THE EXPERIMENT BEGINS, NO ONE NOTICES A TINY SPIDER, DESCENDING FROM THE CEILING ON AN ALMOST INVISIBLE STRAND OF WEB...
A SPIDER WHOM FATE HAS GIVEN A STARRING, IF BRIEF, ROLE TO PLAY IN THE DRAMA WE CALL LIFE!
ACCIDENTALLY ABSORBING A FANTASTIC AMOUNT OF RADIOACTIVITY, THE DYING INSECT, IN SUDDEN SHOCK, BITES THE NEAREST LIVING THING, AT THE SPLIT SECOND BEFORE LIFE EBBS FROM ITS RADIOACTIVE BODY!
OW!
A-A SPIDER! IT BIT ME! BUT, WHY IS IT BURNING SO? WHY IS IT GLOWING THAT WAY??
MY HEAD-- IT FEELS STRANGE! I-I NEED SOME AIR!
LOOKS AS THOUGH OUR EXPERIMENT UNNERVED YOUNG PARKER!
TOO BAD! HE MUST HAVE A WEAK STOMACH!
WHAT'S HAPPENING TO ME? I FEEL-- DIFFERENT! AS THOUGH MY ENTIRE BODY IS CHARGED WITH SOME SORT OF FANTASTIC ENERGY!
HONK! HONK!
WRAPPED IN HIS THOUGHTS, PETER DOESN'T HEAR THE AUTO WHICH NARROWLY MISSES HIM, UNTIL THE LAST INSTANT! AND THEN, UNNOTICED BY THE RIDERS, HE UNTHINKINGLY LEAPS TO SAFETY--BUT WHAT A LEAP IT IS!
THAT WAS ONE EGGHEAD WHO WON'T DAYDREAM ANY MORE WHEN HE CROSSES A STREET!
YOU CAN SAY THAT AGAIN!
3

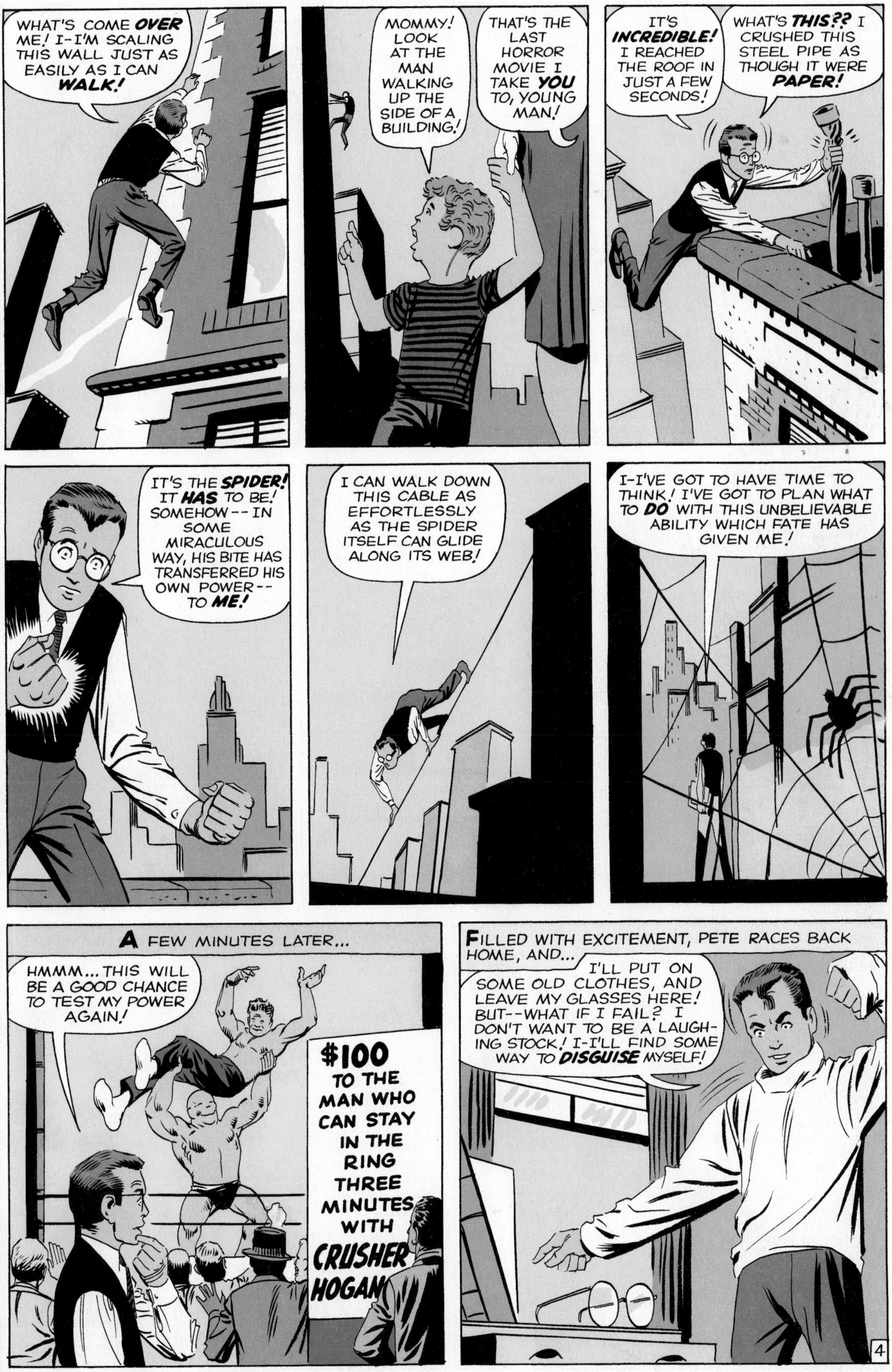
WHAT'S COME OVER ME! I-I'M SCALING THIS WALL JUST AS EASILY AS I CAN WALK!
MOMMY! LOOK AT THE MAN WALKING UP THE SIDE OF A BUILDING!
THAT'S THE LAST HORROR MOVIE I TAKE YOU TO, YOUNG MAN!
IT'S INCREDIBLE! I REACHED THE ROOF IN JUST A FEW SECONDS!
WHAT'S THIS?? I CRUSHED THIS STEEL PIPE AS THOUGH IT WERE PAPER!
IT'S THE SPIDER! IT HAS TO BE! SOMEHOW--IN SOME MIRACULOUS WAY, HIS BITE HAS TRANSFERRED HIS OWN POWER--TO ME!
I CAN WALK DOWN THIS CABLE AS EFFORTLESSLY AS THE SPIDER ITSELF CAN GLIDE ALONG ITS WEB!
I-I'VE GOT TO HAVE TIME TO THINK! I'VE GOT TO PLAN WHAT TO DO WITH THIS UNBELIEVABLE ABILITY WHICH FATE HAS GIVEN ME!
A FEW MINUTES LATER...
HMMM... THIS WILL BE A GOOD CHANCE TO TEST MY POWER AGAIN!
$100 TO THE MAN WHO CAN STAY IN THE RING THREE MINUTES WITH CRUSHER HOGAN
FILLED WITH EXCITEMENT, PETE RACES BACK HOME, AND...
I'LL PUT ON SOME OLD CLOTHES, AND LEAVE MY GLASSES HERE! BUT--WHAT IF I FAIL? I DON'T WANT TO BE A LAUGHING STOCK! I-I'LL FIND SOME WAY TO DISGUISE MYSELF!
4

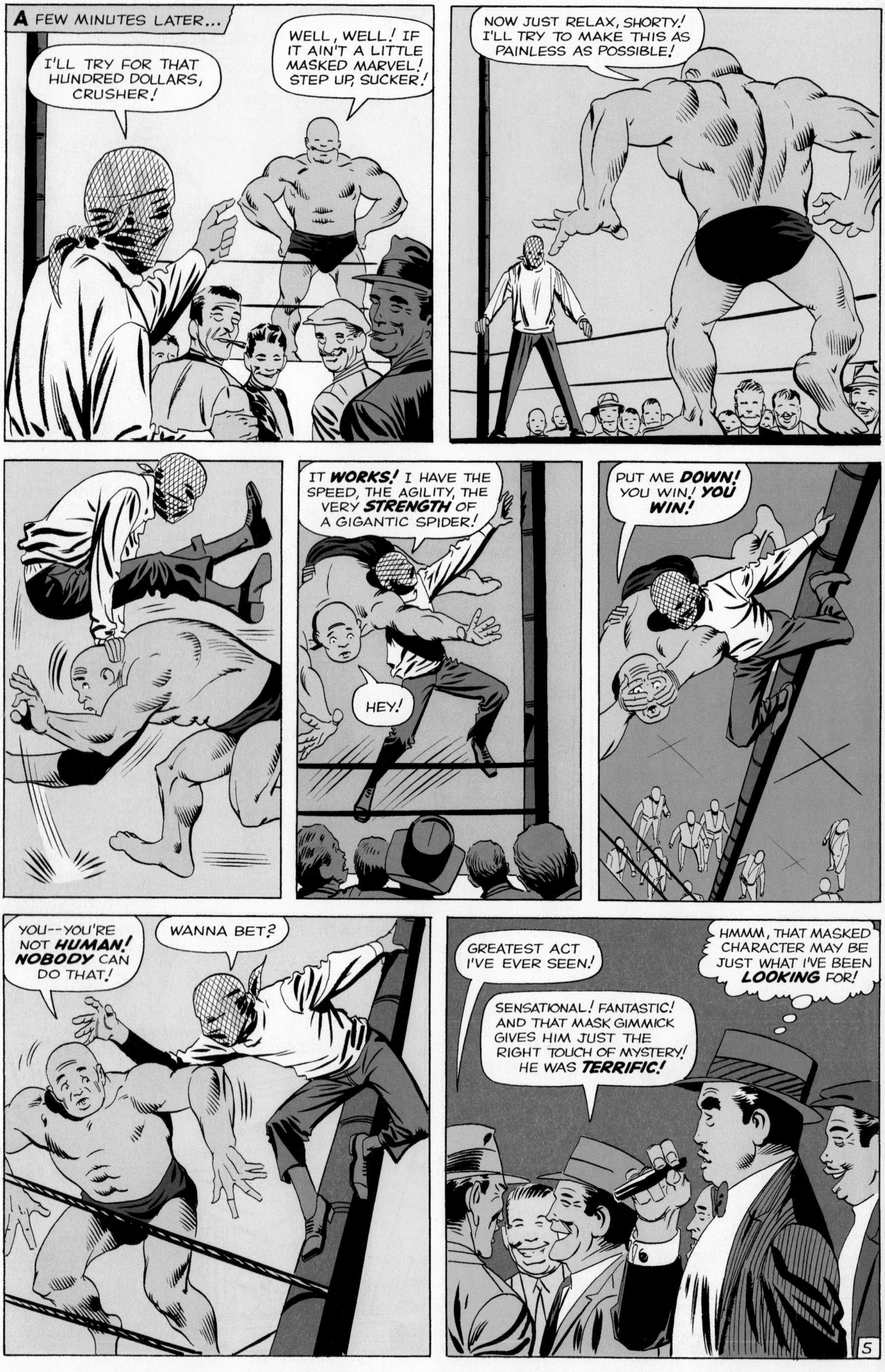
A FEW MINUTES LATER...
I'LL TRY FOR THAT HUNDRED DOLLARS, CRUSHER!
WELL, WELL! IF IT AIN'T A LITTLE MASKED MARVEL! STEP UP, SUCKER!
NOW JUST RELAX, SHORTY! I'LL TRY TO MAKE THIS AS PAINLESS AS POSSIBLE!
IT WORKS! I HAVE THE SPEED, THE AGILITY, THE VERY STRENGTH OF A GIGANTIC SPIDER!
HEY!
PUT ME DOWN! YOU WIN! YOU WIN!
YOU--YOU'RE NOT HUMAN! NOBODY CAN DO THAT!
WANNA BET?
GREATEST ACT I'VE EVER SEEN!
HMMM, THAT MASKED CHARACTER MAY BE JUST WHAT I'VE BEEN LOOKING FOR!
SENSATIONAL! FANTASTIC! AND THAT MASK GIMMICK GIVES HIM JUST THE RIGHT TOUCH OF MYSTERY! HE WAS TERRIFIC!
5

LISTEN, FRIEND, I'M A TV PRODUCER! WITH THAT ACT OF YOURS I CAN MAKE YOU A *FORTUNE!* AND KEEP THE MASK ANGLE -- IT'S GREAT SHOWMANSHIP! HERE'S MY CARD! CALL ME! YOU'D BE A SMASH ON ED SULLIVAN'S SHOW!

THANKS...

LATER, AT HOME AGAIN...

SHOWMANSHIP?? HE HASN'T SEEN *ANYTHING* YET! SINCE I HAVE THE *POWERS* OF A SPIDER, I'LL DESIGN MYSELF A *SPIDER COSTUME!* AND... OH, HI, AUNT MAY!

YOU LOOKED A LITTLE TIRED, PETEY, SO WE BROUGHT YOU SOME CRACKERS AND MILK!

CRACKERS AND MILK! BLESS 'EM-- IF THEY ONLY *KNEW!*

NOW LET'S SEE-- A SPIDER NEEDS A WEB! THIS LITTLE DEVICE SHOULD JUST DO THE TRICK!

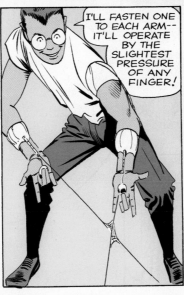

I'LL FASTEN ONE TO EACH ARM-- IT'LL OPERATE BY THE SLIGHTEST PRESSURE OF ANY FINGER!

I'LL NEED A NAME --WELL, GUESS *SPIDERMAN* IS AS GOOD AS ANY! LOOKS PRETTY GOOD, IF I *DO* SAY SO MYSELF!

SO, THEY LAUGHED AT ME FOR BEING A BOOKWORM, EH? WELL, ONLY A SCIENCE MAJOR COULD HAVE CREATED A DEVICE LIKE THIS!

WITH SOME STRONG LIQUID CEMENT AT THE END, I CAN PULL MYSELF UP *ANYWHERE* WITH MY LITTLE WEB!

AND MY COSTUME IS THIN ENOUGH TO WEAR, UNSEEN, UNDER MY STREET CLOTHES!

OKAY, WORLD-- BETTER HANG ONTO YOUR HAT! HERE COMES THE *SPIDERMAN!*

6

PART 2

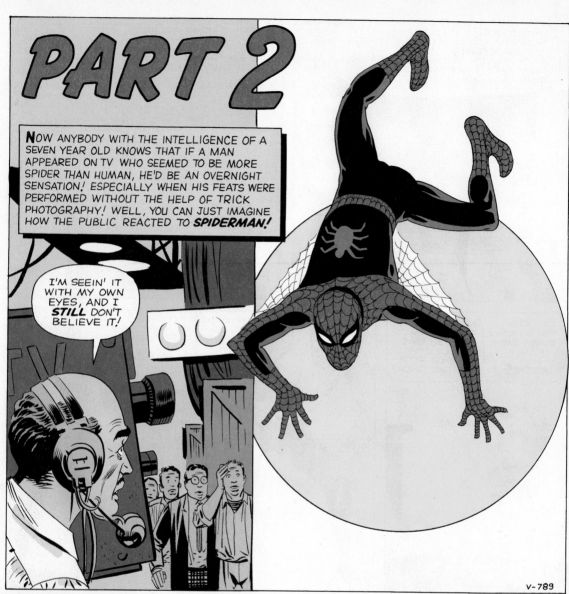

NOW ANYBODY WITH THE INTELLIGENCE OF A SEVEN YEAR OLD KNOWS THAT IF A MAN APPEARED ON TV WHO SEEMED TO BE MORE SPIDER THAN HUMAN, HE'D BE AN OVERNIGHT SENSATION! ESPECIALLY WHEN HIS FEATS WERE PERFORMED WITHOUT THE HELP OF TRICK PHOTOGRAPHY! WELL, YOU CAN JUST IMAGINE HOW THE PUBLIC REACTED TO *SPIDERMAN!*

I'M SEEIN' IT WITH MY OWN EYES, AND I *STILL* DON'T BELIEVE IT!

V-789

SURE THEY LOOK AMAZED, INCREDIBLE, AWE-STRICKEN! WOULDN'T *YOU???*

AFTER ALL, WHEN WAS THE LAST TIME *YOU* SAW A MAN WITH HIS OWN FANTASTIC SPIDER WEB???

OKAY, SPIDERMAN-- CUT! THAT'S ENOUGH! DON'T SHOW 'EM *TOO MUCH!* LEAVE 'EM BEGGIN' FOR MORE!

7

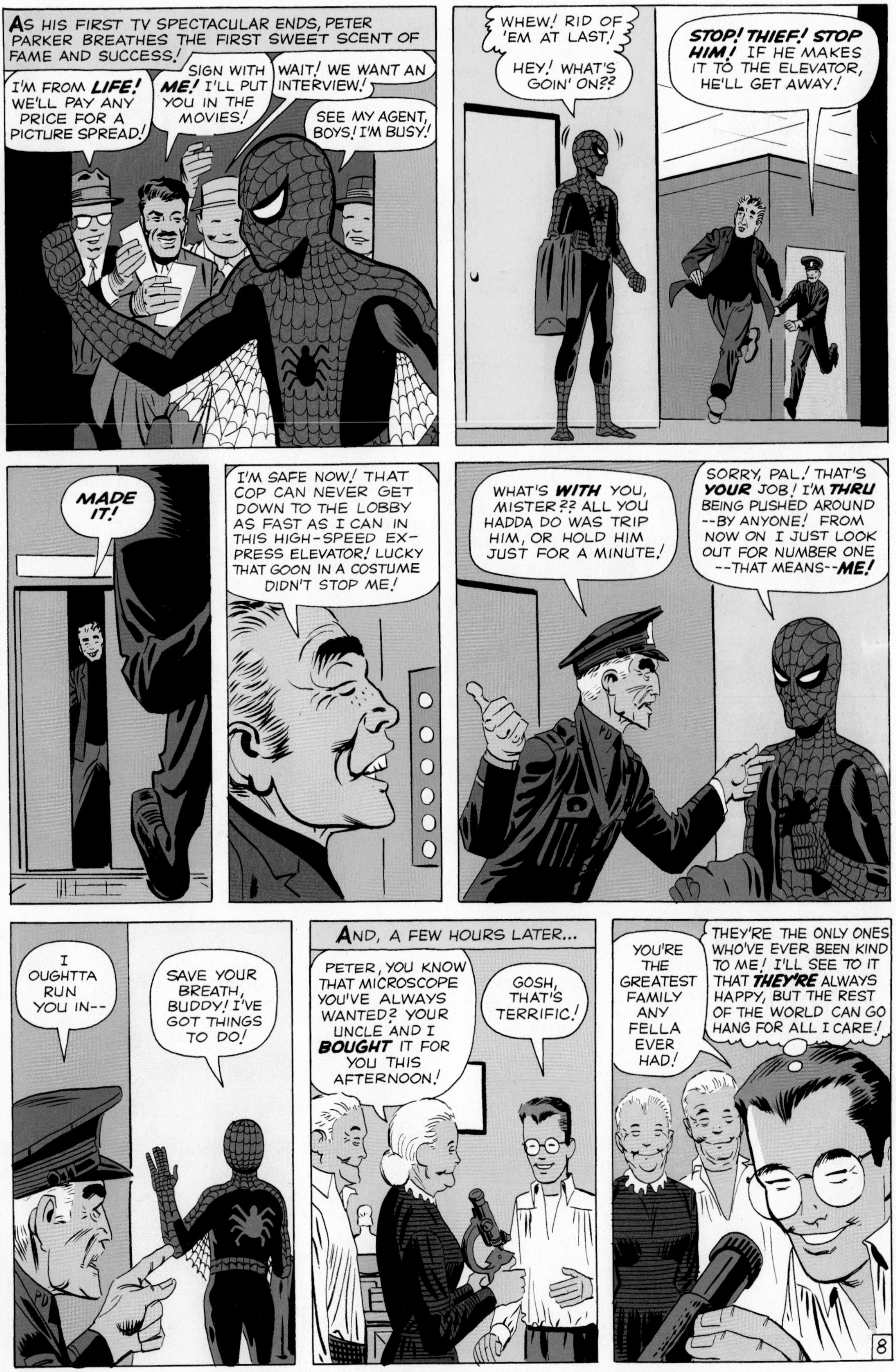

AS HIS FIRST TV SPECTACULAR ENDS, PETER PARKER BREATHES THE FIRST SWEET SCENT OF FAME AND SUCCESS!
I'M FROM LIFE! WE'LL PAY ANY PRICE FOR A PICTURE SPREAD!
SIGN WITH ME! I'LL PUT YOU IN THE MOVIES!
WAIT! WE WANT AN INTERVIEW!
SEE MY AGENT, BOYS! I'M BUSY!
WHEW! RID OF 'EM AT LAST!
HEY! WHAT'S GOIN' ON??
STOP! THIEF! STOP HIM! IF HE MAKES IT TO THE ELEVATOR, HE'LL GET AWAY!
MADE IT!
I'M SAFE NOW! THAT COP CAN NEVER GET DOWN TO THE LOBBY AS FAST AS I CAN IN THIS HIGH-SPEED EX-PRESS ELEVATOR! LUCKY THAT GOON IN A COSTUME DIDN'T STOP ME!
WHAT'S WITH YOU, MISTER?? ALL YOU HADDA DO WAS TRIP HIM, OR HOLD HIM JUST FOR A MINUTE!
SORRY, PAL! THAT'S YOUR JOB! I'M THRU BEING PUSHED AROUND --BY ANYONE! FROM NOW ON I JUST LOOK OUT FOR NUMBER ONE --THAT MEANS--ME!
I OUGHTTA RUN YOU IN--
SAVE YOUR BREATH, BUDDY! I'VE GOT THINGS TO DO!
AND, A FEW HOURS LATER...
PETER, YOU KNOW THAT MICROSCOPE YOU'VE ALWAYS WANTED? YOUR UNCLE AND I BOUGHT IT FOR YOU THIS AFTERNOON!
GOSH, THAT'S TERRIFIC!
YOU'RE THE GREATEST FAMILY ANY FELLA EVER HAD!
THEY'RE THE ONLY ONES WHO'VE EVER BEEN KIND TO ME! I'LL SEE TO IT THAT THEY'RE ALWAYS HAPPY, BUT THE REST OF THE WORLD CAN GO HANG FOR ALL I CARE!
8

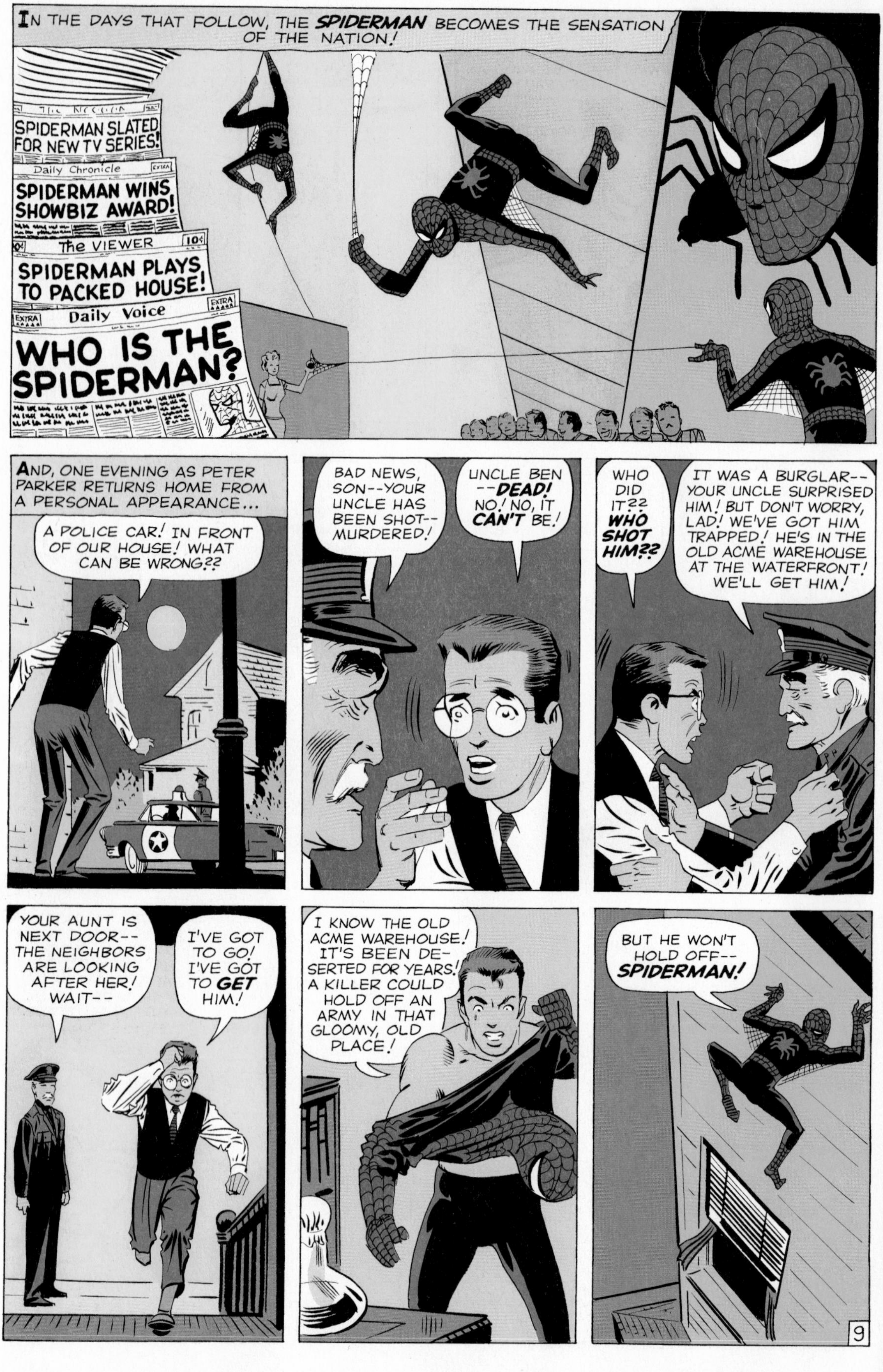

IN THE DAYS THAT FOLLOW, THE SPIDERMAN BECOMES THE SENSATION OF THE NATION!
SPIDERMAN SLATED FOR NEW TV SERIES!
Daily Chronicle
EXTRA
SPIDERMAN WINS SHOWBIZ AWARD!
The VIEWER
10¢
SPIDERMAN PLAYS TO PACKED HOUSE!
EXTRA
Daily Voice
EXTRA
WHO IS THE SPIDERMAN?
AND, ONE EVENING AS PETER PARKER RETURNS HOME FROM A PERSONAL APPEARANCE...
A POLICE CAR! IN FRONT OF OUR HOUSE! WHAT CAN BE WRONG??
BAD NEWS, SON--YOUR UNCLE HAS BEEN SHOT--MURDERED!
UNCLE BEN --DEAD! NO! NO, IT CAN'T BE!
WHO DID IT?? WHO SHOT HIM??
IT WAS A BURGLAR--YOUR UNCLE SURPRISED HIM! BUT DON'T WORRY, LAD! WE'VE GOT HIM TRAPPED! HE'S IN THE OLD ACME WAREHOUSE AT THE WATERFRONT! WE'LL GET HIM!
YOUR AUNT IS NEXT DOOR--THE NEIGHBORS ARE LOOKING AFTER HER! WAIT--
I'VE GOT TO GO! I'VE GOT TO GET HIM!
I KNOW THE OLD ACME WAREHOUSE! IT'S BEEN DE-SERTED FOR YEARS! A KILLER COULD HOLD OFF AN ARMY IN THAT GLOOMY, OLD PLACE!
BUT HE WON'T HOLD OFF--SPIDERMAN!
9

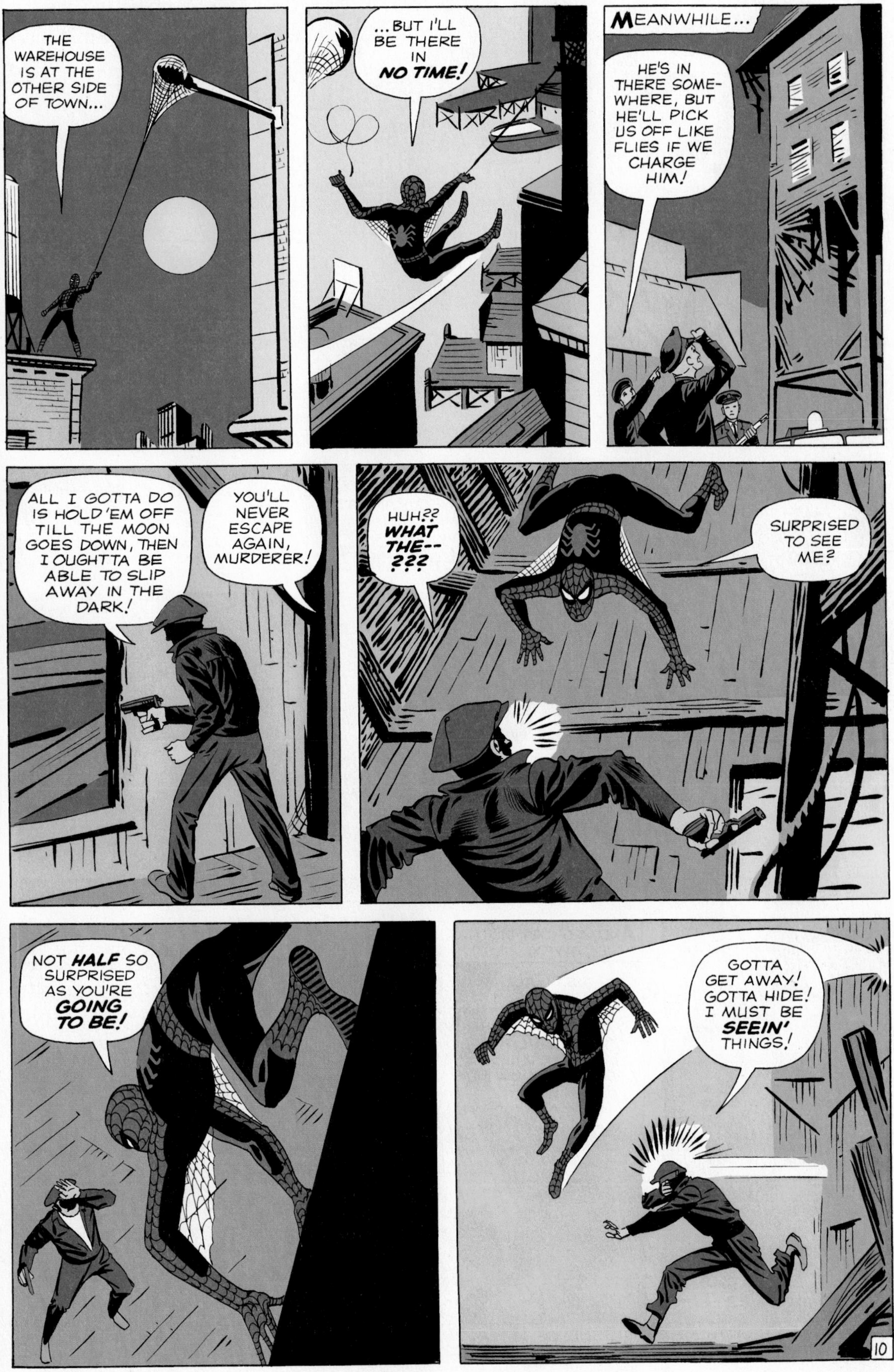
THE WAREHOUSE IS AT THE OTHER SIDE OF TOWN...
...BUT I'LL BE THERE IN NO TIME!
MEANWHILE...
HE'S IN THERE SOMEWHERE, BUT HE'LL PICK US OFF LIKE FLIES IF WE CHARGE HIM!
ALL I GOTTA DO IS HOLD'EM OFF TILL THE MOON GOES DOWN, THEN I OUGHTTA BE ABLE TO SLIP AWAY IN THE DARK!
YOU'LL NEVER ESCAPE AGAIN, MURDERER!
HUH?? WHAT THE-- ???
SURPRISED TO SEE ME?
NOT HALF SO SURPRISED AS YOU'RE GOING TO BE!
GOTTA GET AWAY! GOTTA HIDE! I MUST BE SEEIN' THINGS!
10

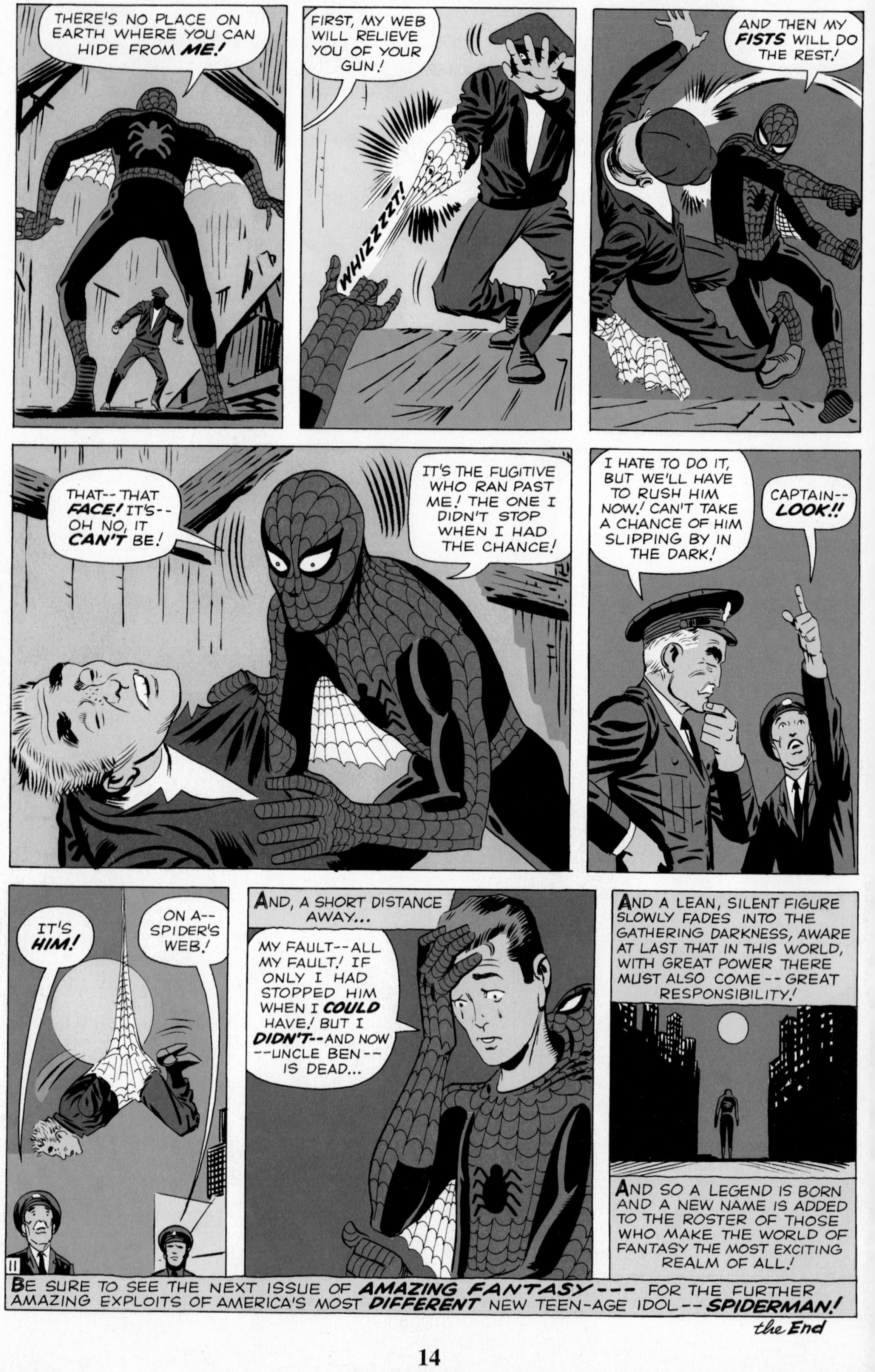
THERE'S NO PLACE ON EARTH WHERE YOU CAN HIDE FROM ME!
FIRST, MY WEB WILL RELIEVE YOU OF YOUR GUN!
WHIZZZZZT!
AND THEN MY FISTS WILL DO THE REST!
THAT-- THAT FACE! IT'S-- OH NO, IT CAN'T BE!
IT'S THE FUGITIVE WHO RAN PAST ME! THE ONE I DIDN'T STOP WHEN I HAD THE CHANCE!
I HATE TO DO IT, BUT WE'LL HAVE TO RUSH HIM NOW! CAN'T TAKE A CHANCE OF HIM SLIPPING BY IN THE DARK!
CAPTAIN-- LOOK!!
IT'S HIM!
ON A-- SPIDER'S WEB!
11
AND, A SHORT DISTANCE AWAY...
MY FAULT--ALL MY FAULT! IF ONLY I HAD STOPPED HIM WHEN I COULD HAVE! BUT I DIDN'T--AND NOW --UNCLE BEN-- IS DEAD...
AND A LEAN, SILENT FIGURE SLOWLY FADES INTO THE GATHERING DARKNESS, AWARE AT LAST THAT IN THIS WORLD, WITH GREAT POWER THERE MUST ALSO COME-- GREAT RESPONSIBILITY!
AND SO A LEGEND IS BORN AND A NEW NAME IS ADDED TO THE ROSTER OF THOSE WHO MAKE THE WORLD OF FANTASY THE MOST EXCITING REALM OF ALL!
BE SURE TO SEE THE NEXT ISSUE OF AMAZING FANTASY--- FOR THE FURTHER AMAZING EXPLOITS OF AMERICA'S MOST DIFFERENT NEW TEEN-AGE IDOL-- SPIDERMAN!
the End

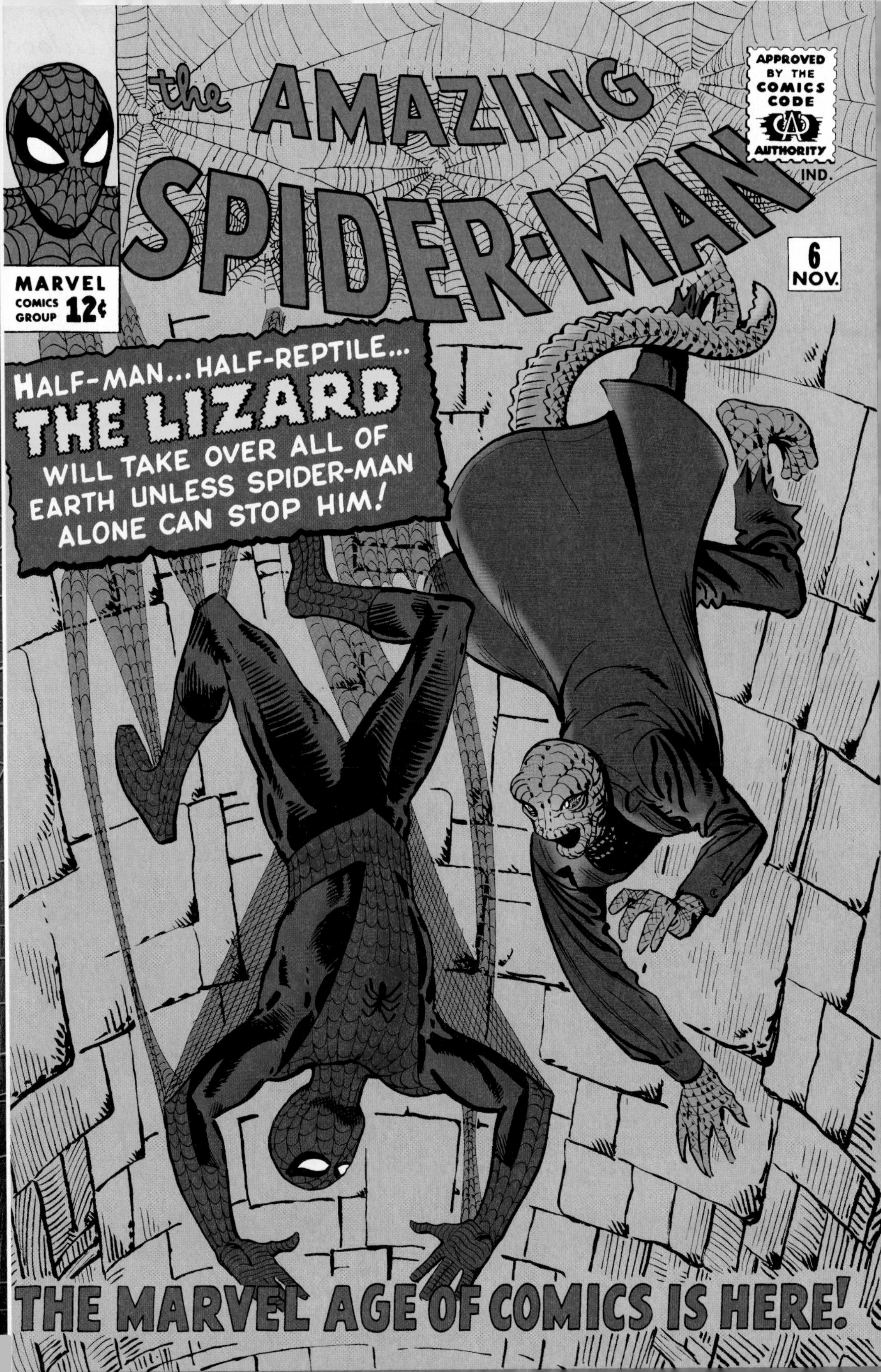
the AMAZING SPIDER-MAN
APPROVED BY THE COMICS CODE AUTHORITY
IND.
6 NOV.
MARVEL COMICS GROUP 12¢
HALF-MAN... HALF-REPTILE...
THE LIZARD
WILL TAKE OVER ALL OF EARTH UNLESS SPIDER-MAN ALONE CAN STOP HIM!
THE MARVEL AGE OF COMICS IS HERE!

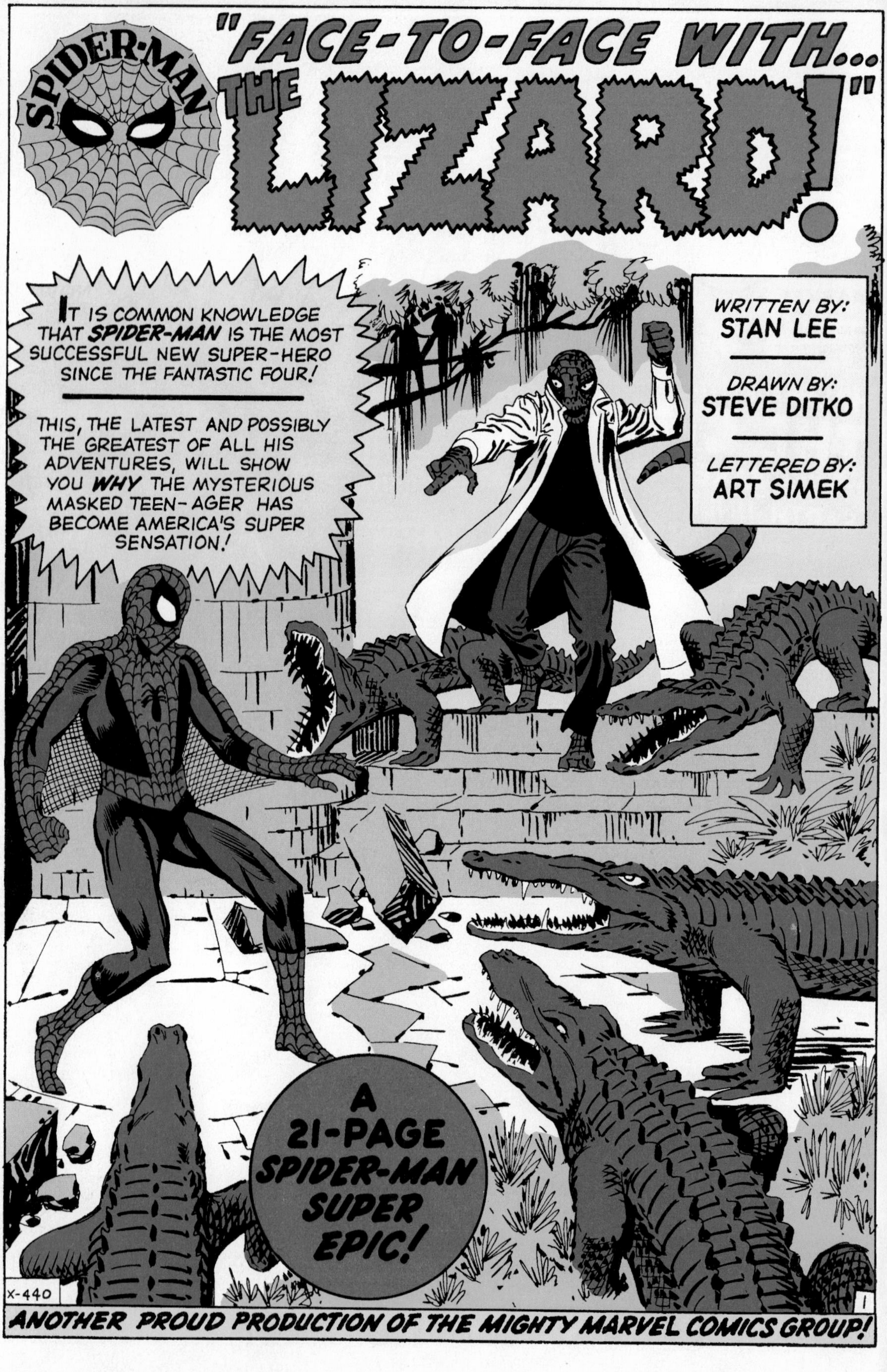

SPIDER-MAN
"FACE-TO-FACE WITH... THE LIZARD!"
IT IS COMMON KNOWLEDGE THAT SPIDER-MAN IS THE MOST SUCCESSFUL NEW SUPER-HERO SINCE THE FANTASTIC FOUR!
THIS, THE LATEST AND POSSIBLY THE GREATEST OF ALL HIS ADVENTURES, WILL SHOW YOU WHY THE MYSTERIOUS MASKED TEEN-AGER HAS BECOME AMERICA'S SUPER SENSATION!
WRITTEN BY: STAN LEE
DRAWN BY: STEVE DITKO
LETTERED BY: ART SIMEK
A 21-PAGE SPIDER-MAN SUPER EPIC!
X-440
1
ANOTHER PROUD PRODUCTION OF THE MIGHTY MARVEL COMICS GROUP!

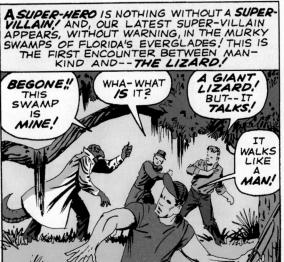

A **SUPER-HERO** IS NOTHING WITHOUT A **SUPER-VILLAIN!** AND, OUR LATEST SUPER-VILLAIN APPEARS, WITHOUT WARNING, IN THE MURKY SWAMPS OF FLORIDA'S EVERGLADES! THIS IS THE FIRST ENCOUNTER BETWEEN MANKIND AND--**THE LIZARD!**

BEGONE!! THIS SWAMP IS **MINE!**

WHA-WHAT **IS** IT?

A GIANT LIZARD! BUT-- IT **TALKS!**

IT WALKS LIKE A **MAN!**

WHATEVER IT IS, IT'S **ATTACKING** US!! I'LL--**LOOK!** BULLETS DON'T STOP IT!

YOU DARE DEFY **THE LIZARD?** YOU'LL **PAY** FOR THAT FOLLY!

HE SNAPPED THAT HUGE TREE AS IF IT WERE CARDBOARD!

RUN! WE'VE GOT TO GET **AWAY** FROM HERE!

FLEE, PUNY HUMANS! THIS SWAMP IS **MINE!** HERE **THE LIZARD** REIGNS SUPREME!

BOY! HE DOESN'T HAVE TO TELL ME **TWICE!**

LIKE WILDFIRE, THE REPORTS OF THE HUMAN LIZARD SPREAD THRUOUT THE EVERGLADES... THE STATE... AND THE ENTIRE NATION!

THEY SAY IT WALKS AND TALKS LIKE A MAN!

BULLETS CANNOT HARM IT!! WHAT IS **IT?** **WHO** IS IT?

IT HAS THE STRENGTH OF A DOZEN BULL-DOZERS!

NOBODY CAN EVER TRACK IT DOWN... NOBODY WOULD **DARE** INVADE ITS DARK DOMAIN!

EVEN AS FAR NORTH AS NEW YORK, THE NAME OF **THE LIZARD** IS ON EVERYONE'S LIPS!

EXTRA! READ ALL ABOUT **THE LIZARD!** EXTRA! EXTRA!

I'D LIKE A PAPER, TOO! BUT I'LL GET IT MY **OWN** WAY!

AND SO, QUIETLY-- SECRETLY-- AMERICA'S MOST MYSTERIOUS SUPER HERO LEARNS ABOUT THE NATION'S NEWEST MENACE FOR THE FIRST TIME!

WHAT KIND OF CORNBALL GAG IS **THIS?** EVERY PUBLICITY-MAD' NUT AND HIS BROTHER TRY TO CHALLENGE ME TO SOMETHING OR OTHER!

EXTRA **DAILY BUGLE** E

THE BUGLE CHALLENGES SPIDER-MAN TO DEFEAT THE LIZARD!

2

WELL, I'LL CHANGE TO PETER PARKER, AND GO SEE MISTER JAMESON! MAYBE HE'LL SEND ME TO FLORIDA TO SNAP SOME PHOTOS OF THAT LIZARD CHARACTER!

A FEW MINUTES LATER, AT THE OFFICE OF THE "DAILY BUGLE"...

YOU'RE OUT OF YOUR MIND, PARKER! I JUST PRINTED THAT "CHALLENGE" HEADLINE TO SELL PAPERS! THE LIZARD IS PROBABLY JUST A PHONY, ANYWAY! I'M NOT PAYING YOU TO WASTE TIME!

BUT IF SPIDER-MAN DOES FIGHT HIM, THINK WHAT A SCOOP WE COULD GET!

DON'T MAKE ME LAUGH! IF THERE REALLY IS A GIANT LIZARD DOWN SOUTH, SPIDER-MAN WILL NEVER TACKLE HIM! HE'D RATHER STAY HERE, FIGHTING TWO-BIT HOODS AND MAKING A REP FOR HIMSELF!

I SHOULD HAVE KNOWN OLD HATCHET-FACE WOULD TURN ME DOWN!

TOO BAD, PETER! I THINK HE SHOULD HAVE SENT YOU TO COVER THE LIZARD STORY! IT MIGHT BE A REAL SCOOP!

THANKS, BETTY! I SURE WISH YOU WERE THE PUBLISHER, INSTEAD OF JUST BEING HIS SECRETARY!

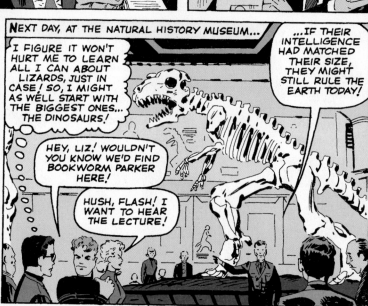

NEXT DAY, AT THE NATURAL HISTORY MUSEUM...

I FIGURE IT WON'T HURT ME TO LEARN ALL I CAN ABOUT LIZARDS, JUST IN CASE! SO, I MIGHT AS WELL START WITH THE BIGGEST ONES... THE DINOSAURS!

...IF THEIR INTELLIGENCE HAD MATCHED THEIR SIZE, THEY MIGHT STILL RULE THE EARTH TODAY!

HEY, LIZ! WOULDN'T YOU KNOW WE'D FIND BOOKWORM PARKER HERE!

HUSH, FLASH! I WANT TO HEAR THE LECTURE!

THEIR HIDES WERE SO THICK THAT IF THEY LIVED TODAY NO GUN SMALLER THAN A CANNON COULD INJURE THEM!

MY SPIDER SENSE IS TINGLING! THOSE TWO MEN COMING IN... IT'S DUE TO THEM!

NO ONE SAW US TAKE THE IDOL'S RUBY! NOW LET'S SCRAM!

THEY LIVED IN OR OUT OF WATER... THEY COULD CRUSH A PRESENT-DAY TANK...

THEY'VE STOLEN SOMETHING! I CAN SENSE IT! HAVE TO FOLLOW THEM!

DON'T LIKE THE WAY THAT KID'S LOOKIN' AT US!

ME, NEITHER! COME ON!

3

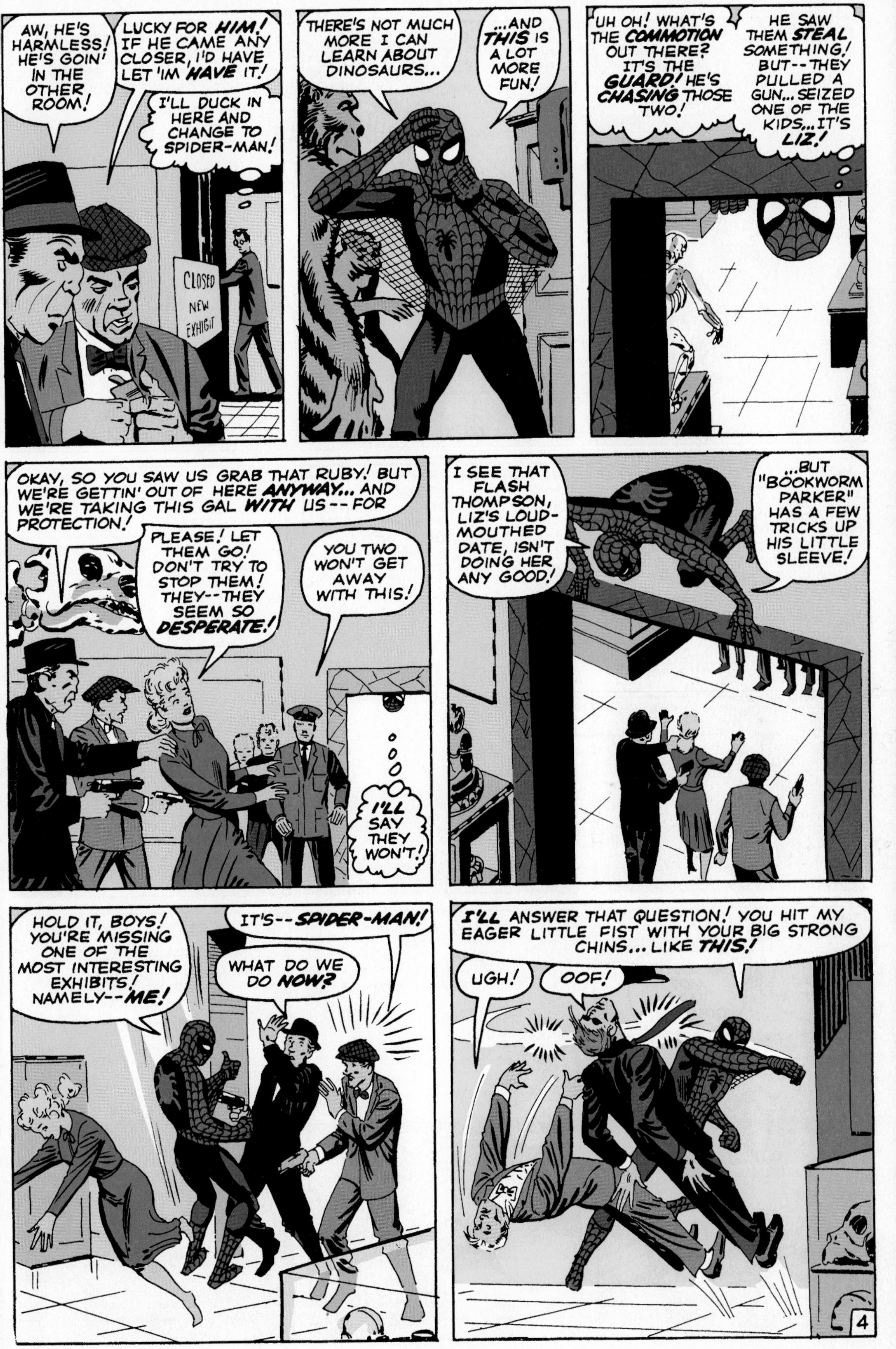
AW, HE'S HARMLESS! HE'S GOIN' IN THE OTHER ROOM!
LUCKY FOR HIM! IF HE CAME ANY CLOSER, I'D HAVE LET 'IM HAVE IT!
I'LL DUCK IN HERE AND CHANGE TO SPIDER-MAN!
CLOSED NEW EXHIBIT
THERE'S NOT MUCH MORE I CAN LEARN ABOUT DINOSAURS...
...AND THIS IS A LOT MORE FUN!
UH OH! WHAT'S THE COMMOTION OUT THERE? IT'S THE GUARD! HE'S CHASING THOSE TWO!
HE SAW THEM STEAL SOMETHING! BUT--THEY PULLED A GUN...SEIZED ONE OF THE KIDS...IT'S LIZ!
OKAY, SO YOU SAW US GRAB THAT RUBY! BUT WE'RE GETTIN' OUT OF HERE ANYWAY... AND WE'RE TAKING THIS GAL WITH US--FOR PROTECTION!
PLEASE! LET THEM GO! DON'T TRY TO STOP THEM! THEY--THEY SEEM SO DESPERATE!
YOU TWO WON'T GET AWAY WITH THIS!
I'LL SAY THEY WON'T!
I SEE THAT FLASH THOMPSON, LIZ'S LOUD-MOUTHED DATE, ISN'T DOING HER ANY GOOD!
...BUT "BOOKWORM PARKER" HAS A FEW TRICKS UP HIS LITTLE SLEEVE!
HOLD IT, BOYS! YOU'RE MISSING ONE OF THE MOST INTERESTING EXHIBITS! NAMELY--ME!
IT'S--SPIDER-MAN!
WHAT DO WE DO NOW?
I'LL ANSWER THAT QUESTION! YOU HIT MY EAGER LITTLE FIST WITH YOUR BIG STRONG CHINS... LIKE THIS!
UGH!
OOF!
4

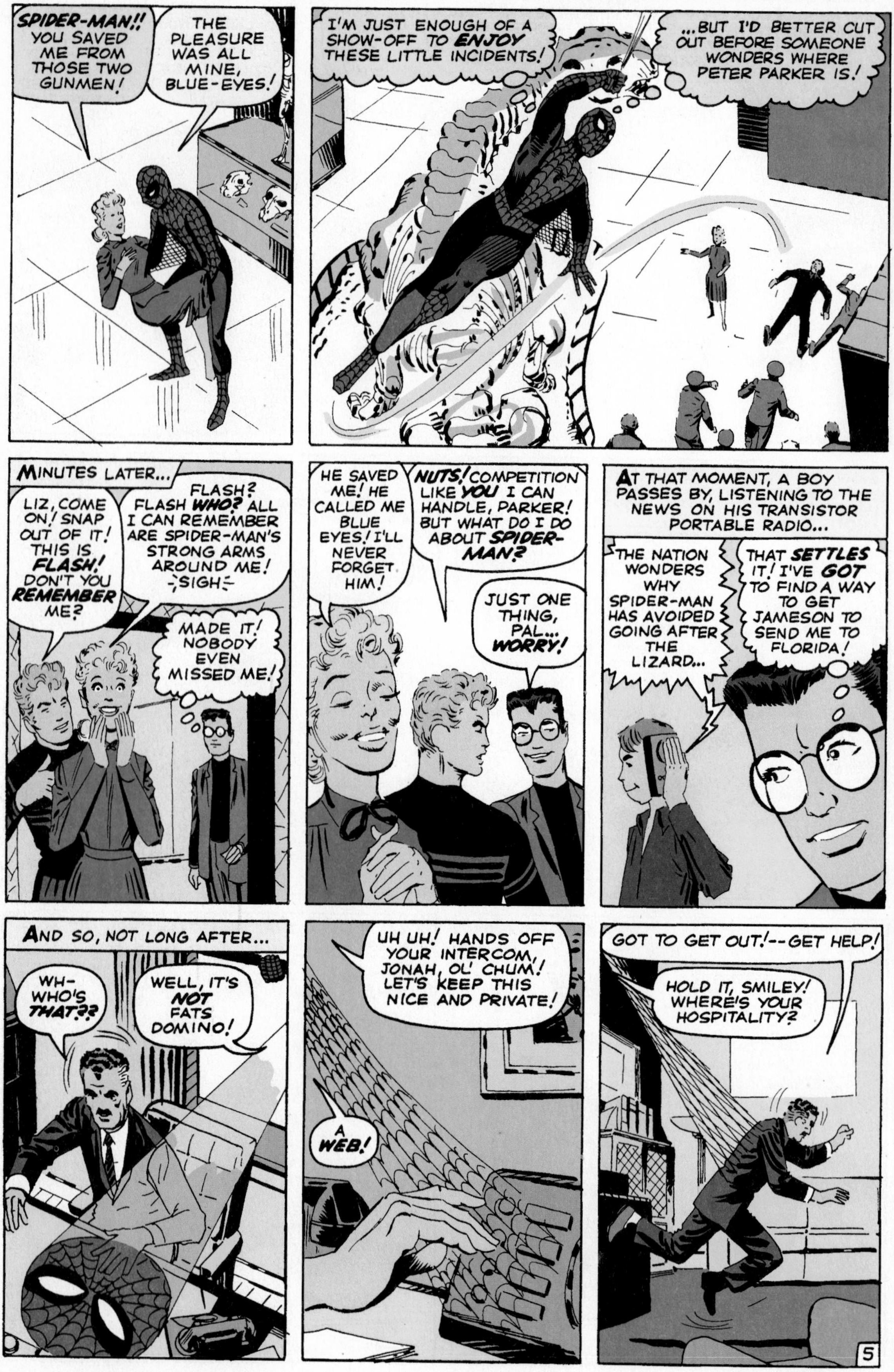
SPIDER-MAN!! YOU SAVED ME FROM THOSE TWO GUNMEN!
THE PLEASURE WAS ALL MINE, BLUE-EYES!
I'M JUST ENOUGH OF A SHOW-OFF TO ENJOY THESE LITTLE INCIDENTS!
...BUT I'D BETTER CUT OUT BEFORE SOMEONE WONDERS WHERE PETER PARKER IS!
MINUTES LATER...
LIZ, COME ON! SNAP OUT OF IT! THIS IS FLASH! DON'T YOU REMEMBER ME?
FLASH? FLASH WHO? ALL I CAN REMEMBER ARE SPIDER-MAN'S STRONG ARMS AROUND ME! -SIGH-
MADE IT! NOBODY EVEN MISSED ME!
HE SAVED ME! HE CALLED ME BLUE EYES! I'LL NEVER FORGET HIM!
NUTS! COMPETITION LIKE YOU I CAN HANDLE, PARKER! BUT WHAT DO I DO ABOUT SPIDER-MAN?
JUST ONE THING, PAL... WORRY!
AT THAT MOMENT, A BOY PASSES BY, LISTENING TO THE NEWS ON HIS TRANSISTOR PORTABLE RADIO...
THE NATION WONDERS WHY SPIDER-MAN HAS AVOIDED GOING AFTER THE LIZARD...
THAT SETTLES IT! I'VE GOT TO FIND A WAY TO GET JAMESON TO SEND ME TO FLORIDA!
AND SO, NOT LONG AFTER...
WH-WHO'S THAT??
WELL, IT'S NOT FATS DOMINO!
UH UH! HANDS OFF YOUR INTERCOM, JONAH, OL' CHUM! LET'S KEEP THIS NICE AND PRIVATE!
A WEB!
GOT TO GET OUT!--GET HELP!
HOLD IT, SMILEY! WHERE'S YOUR HOSPITALITY?
5

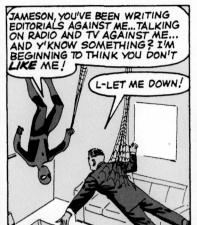

JAMESON, YOU'VE BEEN WRITING EDITORIALS AGAINST ME...TALKING ON RADIO AND TV AGAINST ME... AND Y'KNOW SOMETHING? I'M BEGINNING TO THINK YOU DON'T **LIKE** ME!

L-LET ME DOWN!

WHAT'S THE RUSH? I HAVE A NEWS ITEM FOR YOU! I'M GOING TO **ACCEPT** THE LIZARD'S CHALLENGE! SO, IF YOU WANT TO SEE WHAT I CAN **REALLY** DO, YOU'D BETTER SEND A PHOTOGRAPHER TO FLORIDA TO COVER THE STORY!

AS FOR MY WEB, IT'LL LOOSEN IN A MINUTE AND YOU'LL COME DOWN... **BOY**, WILL YOU COME DOWN!!

THAT DOES IT! NOW, I HAVE TO HOPE HE'S CONVINCED ENOUGH TO SEND PETE PARKER TO FLORIDA-- BECAUSE I HAVEN'T ENOUGH MONEY TO GET THERE BY MYSELF!

SOME SUPER-HERO **I** AM! TOO BROKE TO BUY A PLANE TICKET TO MEET A NEW ENEMY!

MISS BRANT, STOP GAPING AND CALL PETER PARKER! I WANT TO SEE HIM HERE **AT ONCE!** BUT FIRST, PUT SOME SOFT **CUSHIONS** ON THE FLOOR UNDER ME!

Y-YES, SIR!

WHUMP!

OWW!! NEVER MIND THOSE *!?+! CUSHIONS!

TSK! TSK! POOR GENTLE JONAH!

EXACTLY FIVE MINUTES LATER...

PETER! WHERE HAVE YOU **BEEN?** MR. JAMESON HAS BEEN LOOKING **EVERYWHERE** FOR YOU!

NO **WONDER** HE DIDN'T FIND ME! I HAVEN'T **BEEN** EVERYWHERE!

YOU KNOW, BETTY... I'VE BEEN WANTING TO **ASK** YOU SOMETHING...

YES, PETER?

PARKER! GET **IN** HERE!

I'VE DECIDED TO SEND YOU TO FLORIDA AFTER ALL, TO TRY TO GET SOME PICTURES OF THE LIZARD...AND SPIDER-MAN, IF HE SHOWS UP!

THAT'S **GREAT!** WHEN DO I START?

START PACKING **NOW!** WE'RE LEAVING AS SOON AS POSSIBLE!

WE'RE LEAVING--???!

THAT'S RIGHT! IT'S SUCH A BIG STORY THAT **I'M** GOING **WITH** YOU!

6

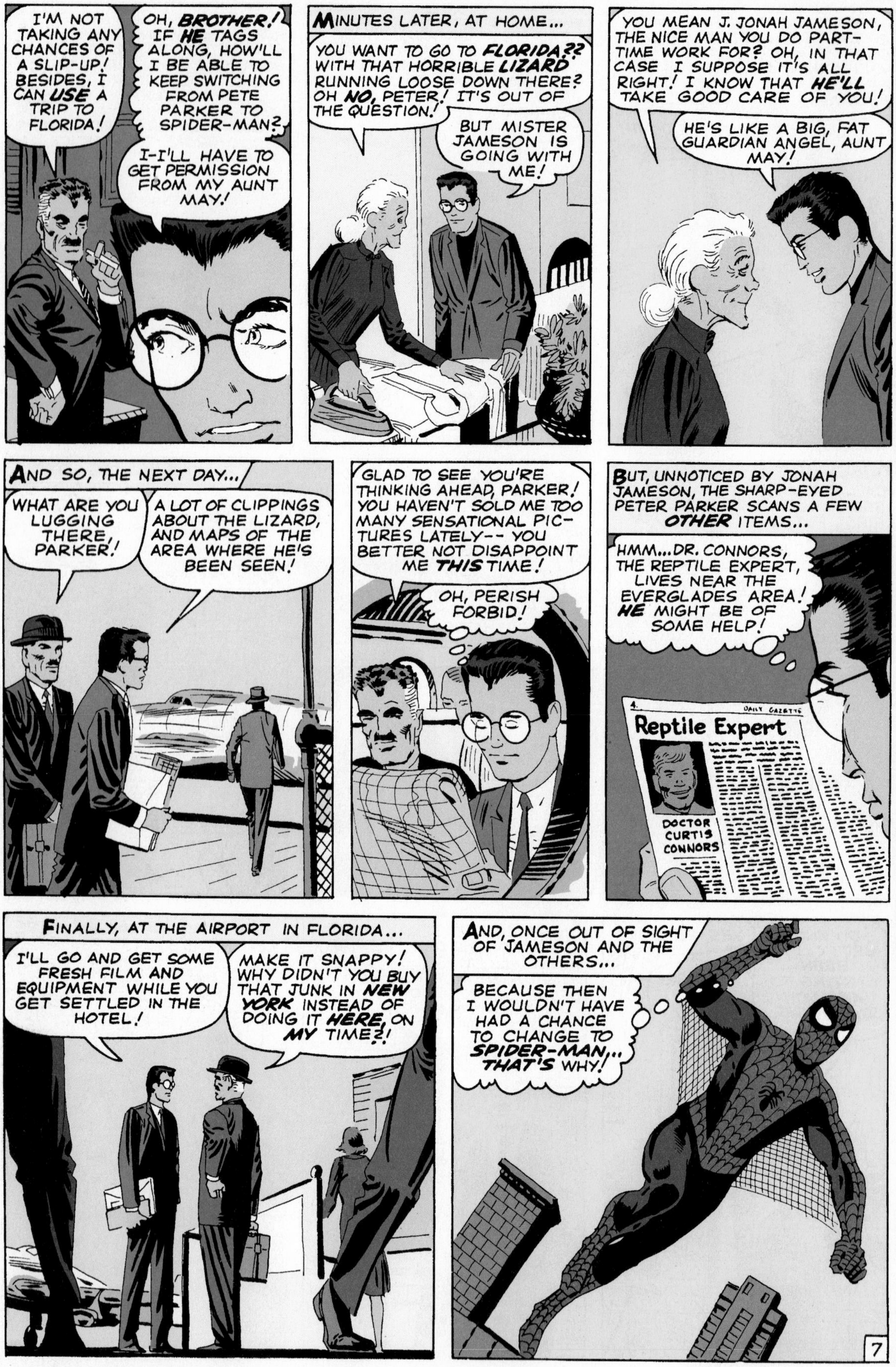
I'M NOT TAKING ANY CHANCES OF A SLIP-UP! BESIDES, I CAN USE A TRIP TO FLORIDA!
OH, BROTHER! IF HE TAGS ALONG, HOW'LL I BE ABLE TO KEEP SWITCHING FROM PETE PARKER TO SPIDER-MAN?
I-I'LL HAVE TO GET PERMISSION FROM MY AUNT MAY!
MINUTES LATER, AT HOME...
YOU WANT TO GO TO FLORIDA?? WITH THAT HORRIBLE LIZARD RUNNING LOOSE DOWN THERE? OH NO, PETER! IT'S OUT OF THE QUESTION!
BUT MISTER JAMESON IS GOING WITH ME!
YOU MEAN J. JONAH JAMESON, THE NICE MAN YOU DO PART-TIME WORK FOR? OH, IN THAT CASE I SUPPOSE IT'S ALL RIGHT! I KNOW THAT HE'LL TAKE GOOD CARE OF YOU!
HE'S LIKE A BIG, FAT GUARDIAN ANGEL, AUNT MAY!
AND SO, THE NEXT DAY...
WHAT ARE YOU LUGGING THERE, PARKER!
A LOT OF CLIPPINGS ABOUT THE LIZARD, AND MAPS OF THE AREA WHERE HE'S BEEN SEEN!
GLAD TO SEE YOU'RE THINKING AHEAD, PARKER! YOU HAVEN'T SOLD ME TOO MANY SENSATIONAL PICTURES LATELY-- YOU BETTER NOT DISAPPOINT ME THIS TIME!
OH, PERISH FORBID!
BUT, UNNOTICED BY JONAH JAMESON, THE SHARP-EYED PETER PARKER SCANS A FEW OTHER ITEMS...
HMM...DR. CONNORS, THE REPTILE EXPERT, LIVES NEAR THE EVERGLADES AREA! HE MIGHT BE OF SOME HELP!
DAILY GAZETTE
Reptile Expert
DOCTOR CURTIS CONNORS
FINALLY, AT THE AIRPORT IN FLORIDA...
I'LL GO AND GET SOME FRESH FILM AND EQUIPMENT WHILE YOU GET SETTLED IN THE HOTEL!
MAKE IT SNAPPY! WHY DIDN'T YOU BUY THAT JUNK IN NEW YORK INSTEAD OF DOING IT HERE, ON MY TIME?!
AND, ONCE OUT OF SIGHT OF JAMESON AND THE OTHERS...
BECAUSE THEN I WOULDN'T HAVE HAD A CHANCE TO CHANGE TO SPIDER-MAN... THAT'S WHY!
7

HMM... THE LIZARD AREA IS BLOCKED OFF BY ARMED PATROLS!

I WONDER WHAT KIND OF "BLIP" I'D MAKE ON A RADAR SCREEN?

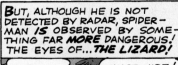

BUT, ALTHOUGH HE IS NOT DETECTED BY RADAR, SPIDER-MAN *IS* OBSERVED BY SOMETHING FAR *MORE* DANGEROUS! THE EYES OF... *THE LIZARD!*

ENEMY COMING...

MUST HIDE! THEN ATTACK!

I DON'T LIKE IT! IT'S *TOO* QUIET HERE! *UNNATURALLY* QUIET! IT'S A CREEPY FEELING!

MY SPIDER SENSE IS STARTING TO TINGLE! BUT, I DON'T *SEE* ANYTHING!

MY FOOT! SOMETHING GRABBED ME FROM BEHIND!

SOMETHING *POWERFUL!* CAN'T KEEP MY BALANCE...

IT'S *HIM!* THE *LIZARD!*

LIZARD OR NOT, A GLOB OF *MUD* PUSHED IN HIS FACE OUGHT TO SLOW HIM DOWN A LITTLE...

-WHEW- I'M *OUT!* COULDN'T HAVE HELD MY BREATH MUCH LONGER!

UH OH! *HE'S* OUT, TOO!

STILL CAN'T FIGURE OUT WHO, OR WHAT, HE REALLY *IS!*

8

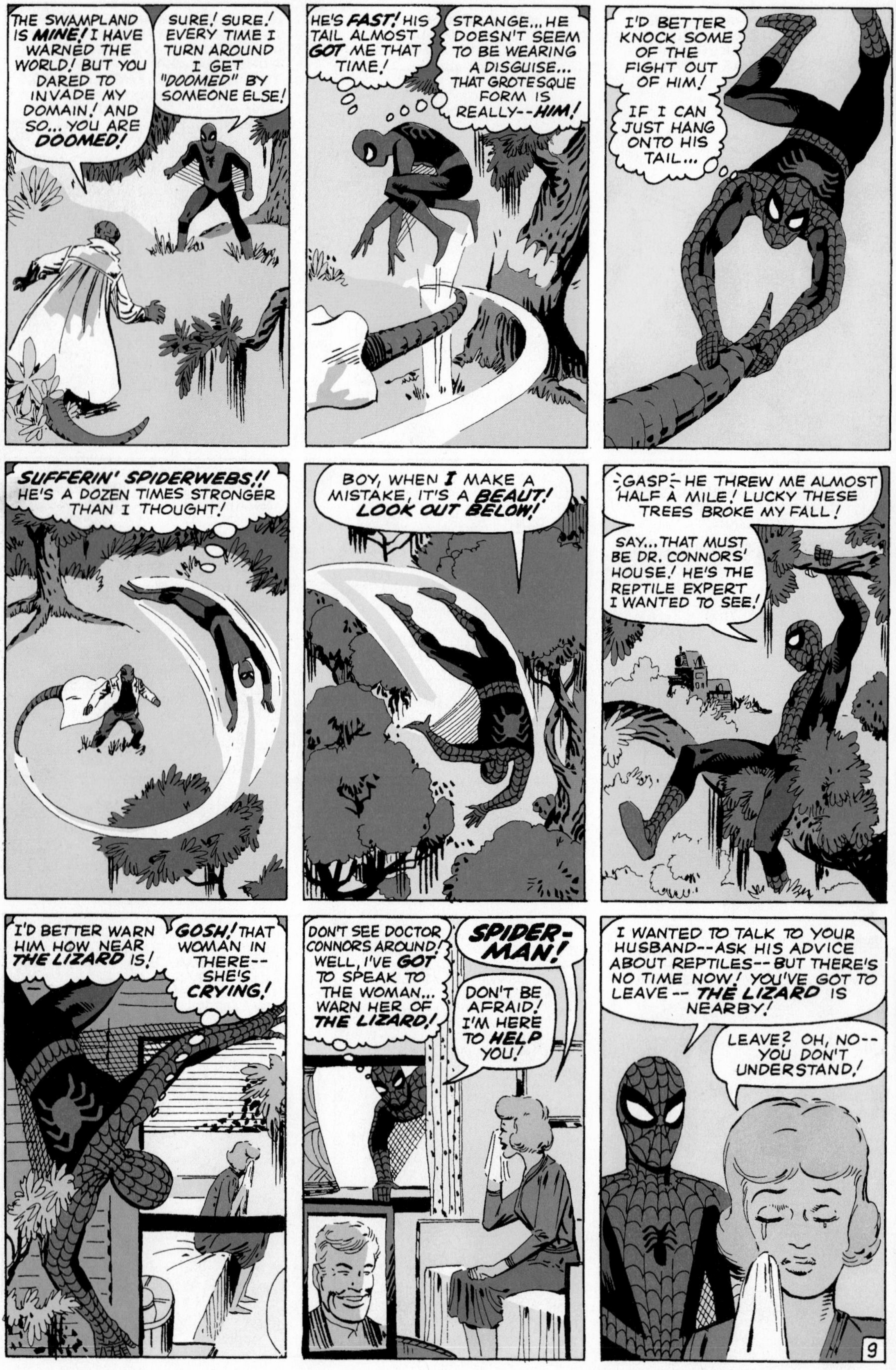
THE SWAMPLAND IS MINE! I HAVE WARNED THE WORLD! BUT YOU DARED TO INVADE MY DOMAIN! AND SO... YOU ARE DOOMED!
SURE! SURE! EVERY TIME I TURN AROUND I GET "DOOMED" BY SOMEONE ELSE!
HE'S FAST! HIS TAIL ALMOST GOT ME THAT TIME!
STRANGE... HE DOESN'T SEEM TO BE WEARING A DISGUISE... THAT GROTESQUE FORM IS REALLY--HIM!
I'D BETTER KNOCK SOME OF THE FIGHT OUT OF HIM!
IF I CAN JUST HANG ONTO HIS TAIL...
SUFFERIN' SPIDERWEBS!! HE'S A DOZEN TIMES STRONGER THAN I THOUGHT!
BOY, WHEN I MAKE A MISTAKE, IT'S A BEAUT! LOOK OUT BELOW!
-GASP- HE THREW ME ALMOST HALF A MILE! LUCKY THESE TREES BROKE MY FALL!
SAY... THAT MUST BE DR. CONNORS' HOUSE! HE'S THE REPTILE EXPERT I WANTED TO SEE!
I'D BETTER WARN HIM HOW NEAR THE LIZARD IS!
GOSH! THAT WOMAN IN THERE-- SHE'S CRYING!
DON'T SEE DOCTOR CONNORS AROUND! WELL, I'VE GOT TO SPEAK TO THE WOMAN... WARN HER OF THE LIZARD!
SPIDER-MAN!
DON'T BE AFRAID! I'M HERE TO HELP YOU!
I WANTED TO TALK TO YOUR HUSBAND--ASK HIS ADVICE ABOUT REPTILES-- BUT THERE'S NO TIME NOW! YOU'VE GOT TO LEAVE -- THE LIZARD IS NEARBY!
LEAVE? OH, NO-- YOU DON'T UNDERSTAND!
9

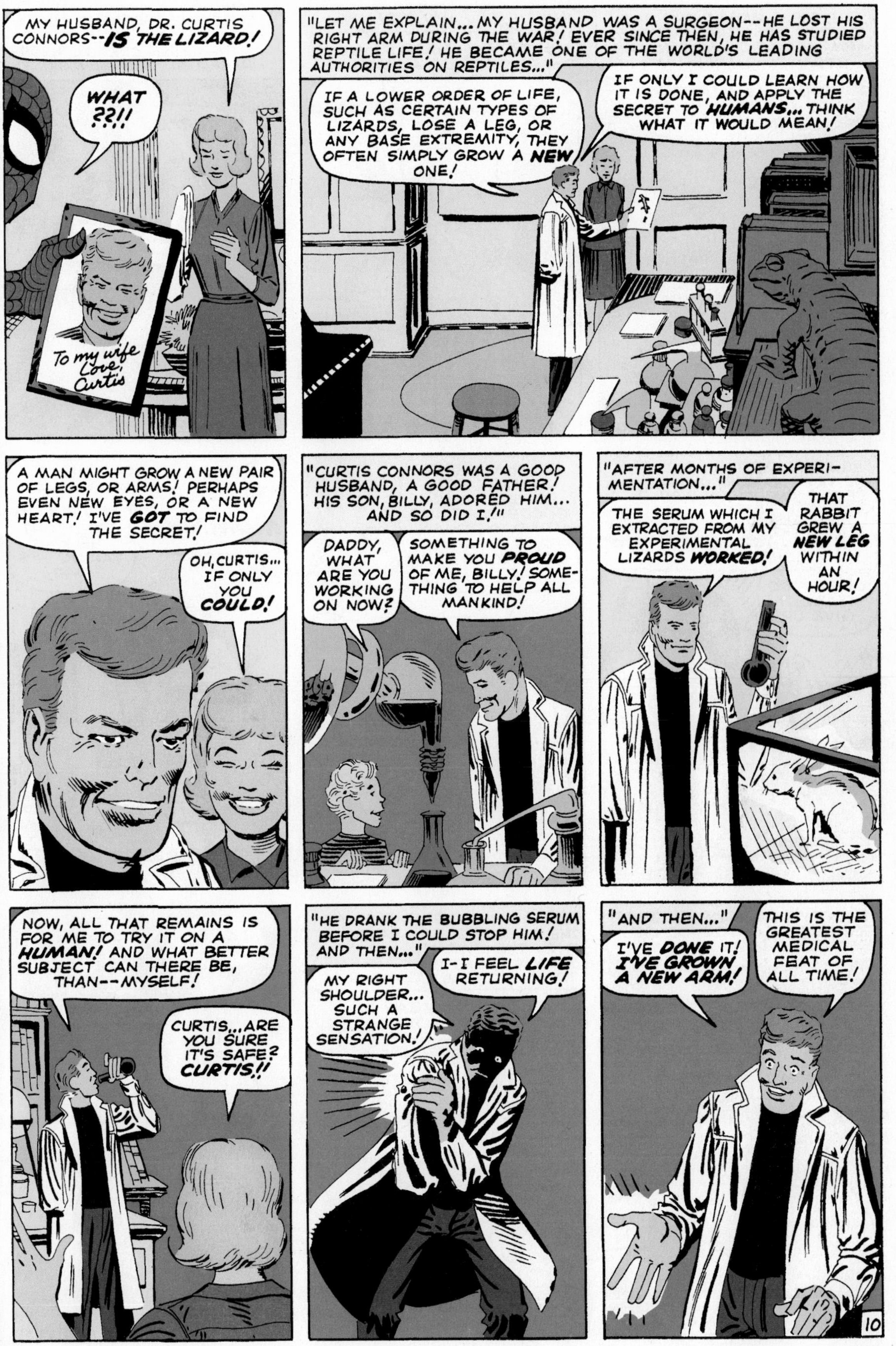

MY HUSBAND, DR. CURTIS CONNORS--IS THE LIZARD!
WHAT ??!!
To my wife Love, Curtis
"LET ME EXPLAIN... MY HUSBAND WAS A SURGEON--HE LOST HIS RIGHT ARM DURING THE WAR! EVER SINCE THEN, HE HAS STUDIED REPTILE LIFE! HE BECAME ONE OF THE WORLD'S LEADING AUTHORITIES ON REPTILES..."
IF A LOWER ORDER OF LIFE, SUCH AS CERTAIN TYPES OF LIZARDS, LOSE A LEG, OR ANY BASE EXTREMITY, THEY OFTEN SIMPLY GROW A NEW ONE!
IF ONLY I COULD LEARN HOW IT IS DONE, AND APPLY THE SECRET TO HUMANS... THINK WHAT IT WOULD MEAN!
A MAN MIGHT GROW A NEW PAIR OF LEGS, OR ARMS! PERHAPS EVEN NEW EYES, OR A NEW HEART! I'VE GOT TO FIND THE SECRET!
OH, CURTIS... IF ONLY YOU COULD!
"CURTIS CONNORS WAS A GOOD HUSBAND, A GOOD FATHER! HIS SON, BILLY, ADORED HIM... AND SO DID I!"
DADDY, WHAT ARE YOU WORKING ON NOW?
SOMETHING TO MAKE YOU PROUD OF ME, BILLY! SOMETHING TO HELP ALL MANKIND!
"AFTER MONTHS OF EXPERIMENTATION..."
THE SERUM WHICH I EXTRACTED FROM MY EXPERIMENTAL LIZARDS WORKED!
THAT RABBIT GREW A NEW LEG WITHIN AN HOUR!
NOW, ALL THAT REMAINS IS FOR ME TO TRY IT ON A HUMAN! AND WHAT BETTER SUBJECT CAN THERE BE, THAN--MYSELF!
CURTIS... ARE YOU SURE IT'S SAFE? CURTIS!!
"HE DRANK THE BUBBLING SERUM BEFORE I COULD STOP HIM! AND THEN..."
I-I FEEL LIFE RETURNING!
MY RIGHT SHOULDER... SUCH A STRANGE SENSATION!
"AND THEN..."
I'VE DONE IT! I'VE GROWN A NEW ARM!
THIS IS THE GREATEST MEDICAL FEAT OF ALL TIME!
10

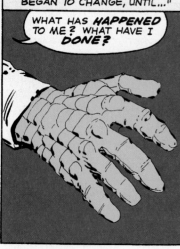

"BUT, THE CHANGE DIDN'T END THERE!! NO-- THE HAND, THE ARM, *ALL* OF CURTIS CONNORS BEGAN TO CHANGE, UNTIL..."

WHAT HAS *HAPPENED* TO ME? WHAT HAVE I *DONE*?

CURTIS!! WHAT *IS* IT?

NO! *NO!* STAY AWAY! *DON'T* LOOK AT ME!! DON'T!

"TREMBLING, SOBBING, LIKE A MAN POSSESSED, THE CREATURE WHO HAD BEEN CURTIS CONNORS RACED OUT INTO THE NIGHT..."

CURTIS!

"HE RETURNED THE NEXT DAY! HE TRIED TO WORK ON A NEW SERUM, ONE WHICH WOULD MAKE HIM HUMAN AGAIN... BUT IT WAS HOPELESS! HIS BRAIN HAD BEEN TOO DULLED-- TOO CHANGED!"

CANNOT DO IT! MUST GIVE UP!

AND THAT WAS THE END! HE LEFT A *NOTE*... SAYING GOODBYE... HE WAS AFRAID TO REMAIN... AFRAID...BECAUSE OF WHAT HE HAD BECOME!

TAKE BILLY... LEAVE-- NEVER COME BACK--

THEN, AT THAT MOMENT...

MOMMY!!

IT'S BILLY! I THOUGHT HE WAS TAKING HIS NAP!

THE CRY CAME FROM *OUTSIDE!* PERHAPS MY SPIDER-SENSE WILL LEAD ME TO HIM!

MEANWHILE, NOT FAR AWAY, THE TERRIFIED BOY RACES THRU THE SWAMP... HAVING SEEN A SIGHT WHICH SEEMED TO BE OUT OF A NIGHTMARE!

I-I DID NOT MEAN TO FRIGHTEN YOU!

HELP!

COME BACK!!

THAT *SNAKE!* I-I CAN'T GET OUT OF ITS WAY IN TIME!

11

SUDDENLY, A COLORFUL, FAST-MOVING FIGURE SWINGS DOWN FROM ABOVE, AND...

GOT YOU!

OH!

NO ONE CAN TAKE HIM FROM ME!

BILLY--STAY UP THERE! DON'T LET GO!!

OWW! HIS SKIN IS HARD AS A DINOSAUR'S ARMOR! I ALMOST BROKE MY HAND... AND HE HARDLY FELT IT!

THUD!

I'LL TRY TO HOLD HIM WITH MY WEB, UNTIL--NO! THAT'S NO GOOD, EITHER! HE SNAPPED IT WITH HIS TAIL AS IF IT WERE MADE OF PAPER!

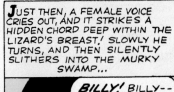

JUST THEN, A FEMALE VOICE CRIES OUT, AND IT STRIKES A HIDDEN CHORD DEEP WITHIN THE LIZARD'S BREAST! SLOWLY HE TURNS, AND THEN SILENTLY SLITHERS INTO THE MURKY SWAMP...

BILLY! BILLY-- WHERE ARE YOU?

MINUTES LATER...

MY HUSBAND! DID YOU SEE HIM? IS HE--?

MOMMY, THAT MAN SAVED ME!

HE'S ALRIGHT... FOR NOW! BUT, HE GETS LESS HUMAN EACH MINUTE!

I KNOW WHO YOU ARE! I SAW PICTURES OF YOU! YOU'RE SPIDER-MAN!

THAT'S RIGHT, BILLY, AND I'M GOING TO TAKE YOU HOME SAFELY NOW!

I WANT TO SEE YOUR HUSBAND'S NOTES, MRS. CONNORS-- BEFORE IT'S TOO LATE!

IT'S A GOOD THING I'M A SCIENCE MAJOR IN HIGH SCHOOL! SO, THE KIDS MAKE FUN OF ME, AND CALL ME A BOOKWORM, DO THEY? WELL, THIS BOOKWORM IS GOING TO FIND AN ANTIDOTE FOR THE LIZARD!

GOSH! ARE YOU A SCIENTIST TOO, SPIDER-MAN?!

12

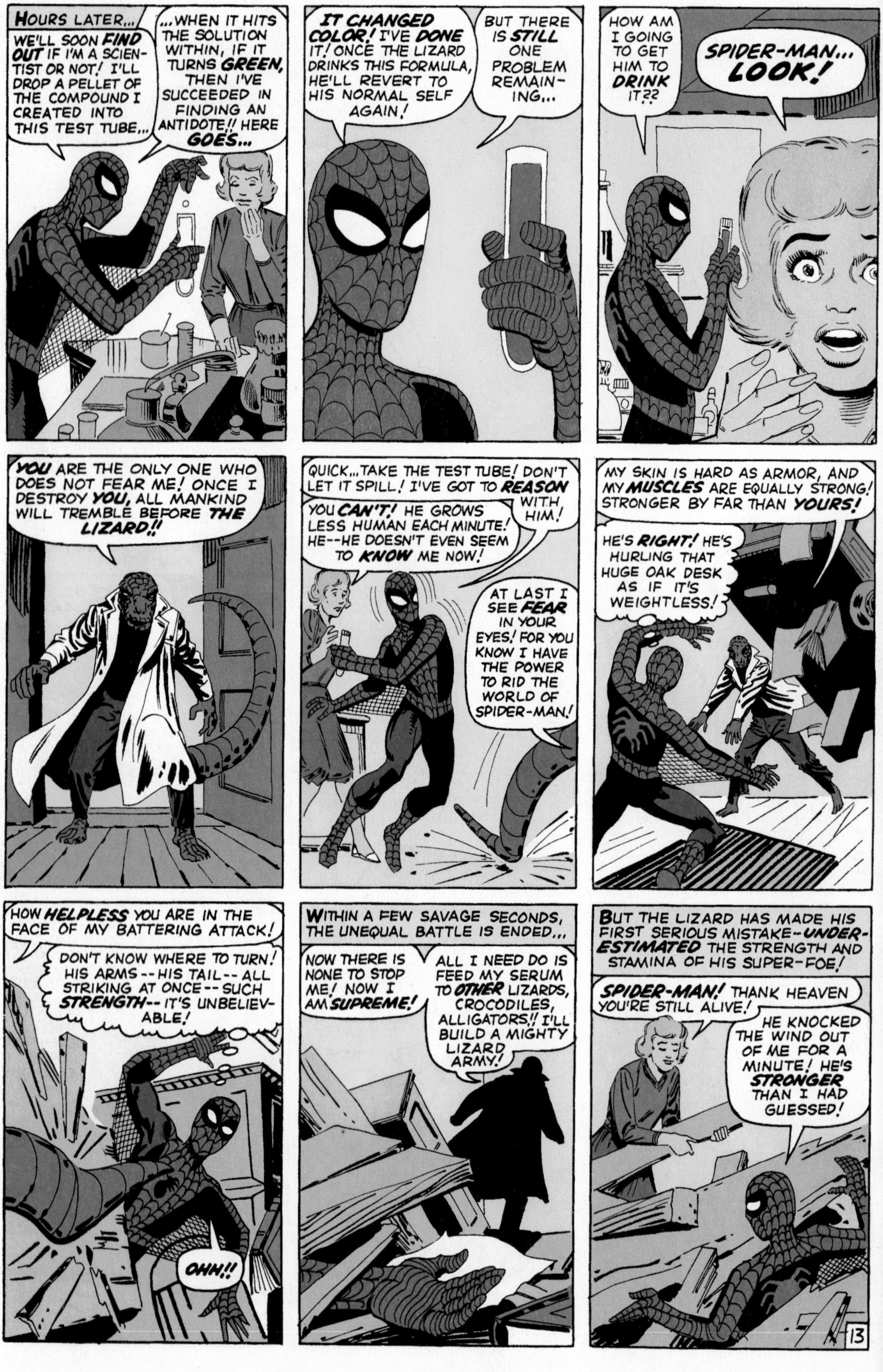
HOURS LATER...
WE'LL SOON FIND OUT IF I'M A SCIENTIST OR NOT! I'LL DROP A PELLET OF THE COMPOUND I CREATED INTO THIS TEST TUBE...
...WHEN IT HITS THE SOLUTION WITHIN, IF IT TURNS GREEN, THEN I'VE SUCCEEDED IN FINDING AN ANTIDOTE!! HERE GOES...
IT CHANGED COLOR! I'VE DONE IT! ONCE THE LIZARD DRINKS THIS FORMULA, HE'LL REVERT TO HIS NORMAL SELF AGAIN!
BUT THERE IS STILL ONE PROBLEM REMAINING...
HOW AM I GOING TO GET HIM TO DRINK IT??
SPIDER-MAN... LOOK!
YOU ARE THE ONLY ONE WHO DOES NOT FEAR ME! ONCE I DESTROY YOU, ALL MANKIND WILL TREMBLE BEFORE THE LIZARD!!
QUICK... TAKE THE TEST TUBE! DON'T LET IT SPILL! I'VE GOT TO REASON WITH HIM!
YOU CAN'T! HE GROWS LESS HUMAN EACH MINUTE! HE--HE DOESN'T EVEN SEEM TO KNOW ME NOW!
AT LAST I SEE FEAR IN YOUR EYES! FOR YOU KNOW I HAVE THE POWER TO RID THE WORLD OF SPIDER-MAN!
MY SKIN IS HARD AS ARMOR, AND MY MUSCLES ARE EQUALLY STRONG! STRONGER BY FAR THAN YOURS!
HE'S RIGHT! HE'S HURLING THAT HUGE OAK DESK AS IF IT'S WEIGHTLESS!
HOW HELPLESS YOU ARE IN THE FACE OF MY BATTERING ATTACK!
DON'T KNOW WHERE TO TURN! HIS ARMS--HIS TAIL--ALL STRIKING AT ONCE--SUCH STRENGTH--IT'S UNBELIEVABLE!
OHH!!
WITHIN A FEW SAVAGE SECONDS, THE UNEQUAL BATTLE IS ENDED...
NOW THERE IS NONE TO STOP ME! NOW I AM SUPREME!
ALL I NEED DO IS FEED MY SERUM TO OTHER LIZARDS, CROCODILES, ALLIGATORS!! I'LL BUILD A MIGHTY LIZARD ARMY!
BUT THE LIZARD HAS MADE HIS FIRST SERIOUS MISTAKE--UNDERESTIMATED THE STRENGTH AND STAMINA OF HIS SUPER-FOE!
SPIDER-MAN! THANK HEAVEN YOU'RE STILL ALIVE!
HE KNOCKED THE WIND OUT OF ME FOR A MINUTE! HE'S STRONGER THAN I HAD GUESSED!
13

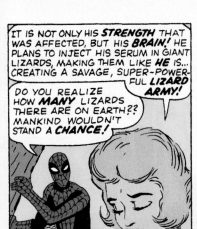

IT IS NOT ONLY HIS **STRENGTH** THAT WAS AFFECTED, BUT HIS **BRAIN!** HE PLANS TO INJECT HIS SERUM IN GIANT LIZARDS, MAKING THEM LIKE **HE** IS... CREATING A SAVAGE, SUPER-POWERFUL **LIZARD ARMY!**

DO YOU REALIZE HOW **MANY** LIZARDS THERE ARE ON EARTH?? MANKIND WOULDN'T STAND A **CHANCE!**

HE **MUST** BE STOPPED, QUICKLY, BEFORE HE CREATES THE **FIRST** SUPER-LIZARD! OTHERWISE, THEY WILL MULTIPLY TOO FAST TO **EVER** BE CHECKED!

HERE IS THE ANTIDOTE! BUT HOW WILL YOU GET HIM TO **DRINK** IT?

I DON'T KNOW YET, BUT THE FIRST THING I MUST DO IS TRACK HIM DOWN NOW! YOU AND YOUR SON REMAIN HERE... I DON'T THINK HE WILL RETURN!

HE IS **STRONGER** THAN YOU... AND HE HAS BECOME **RUTHLESS!** PERHAPS YOU SHOULD GET **HELP!**

THERE ISN'T **TIME** FOR THAT! WHATEVER MUST BE DONE, MUST BE DONE BY **SPIDER-MAN** ALONE! I'LL BUILD SOME WEB SWAMP-SHOES FOR MY FEET...

D-DON'T **HURT** HIM, SPIDER-MAN! HE'S STILL... MY **FATHER!** -SOB-

THE BOY IS **RIGHT!** BENEATH THE SAVAGE EXTERIOR OF THE **LIZARD,** IS A DECENT, TALENTED MAN! BUT HOW CAN I DEFEAT HIM-- AND SAVE **MYSELF** -- WITHOUT **HARMING** HIM??

LUCKILY, HIS TRAIL IS STILL RECENT ENOUGH FOR MY SPIDER-SENSE TO TRACK HIM! AND I CAN KEEP THESE SWAMP SNAKES AT BAY AS LONG AS MY **WEB FLUID** HOLDS OUT!

I SENSE HIM MORE CLEARLY THAN EVER NOW! HE MUST BE INSIDE THAT OLD, ABANDONED SPANISH FORT!

AND NOW... FOR THE **SHOWDOWN!**

THERE HE **IS!** BUT... AM I **TOO LATE?**

14

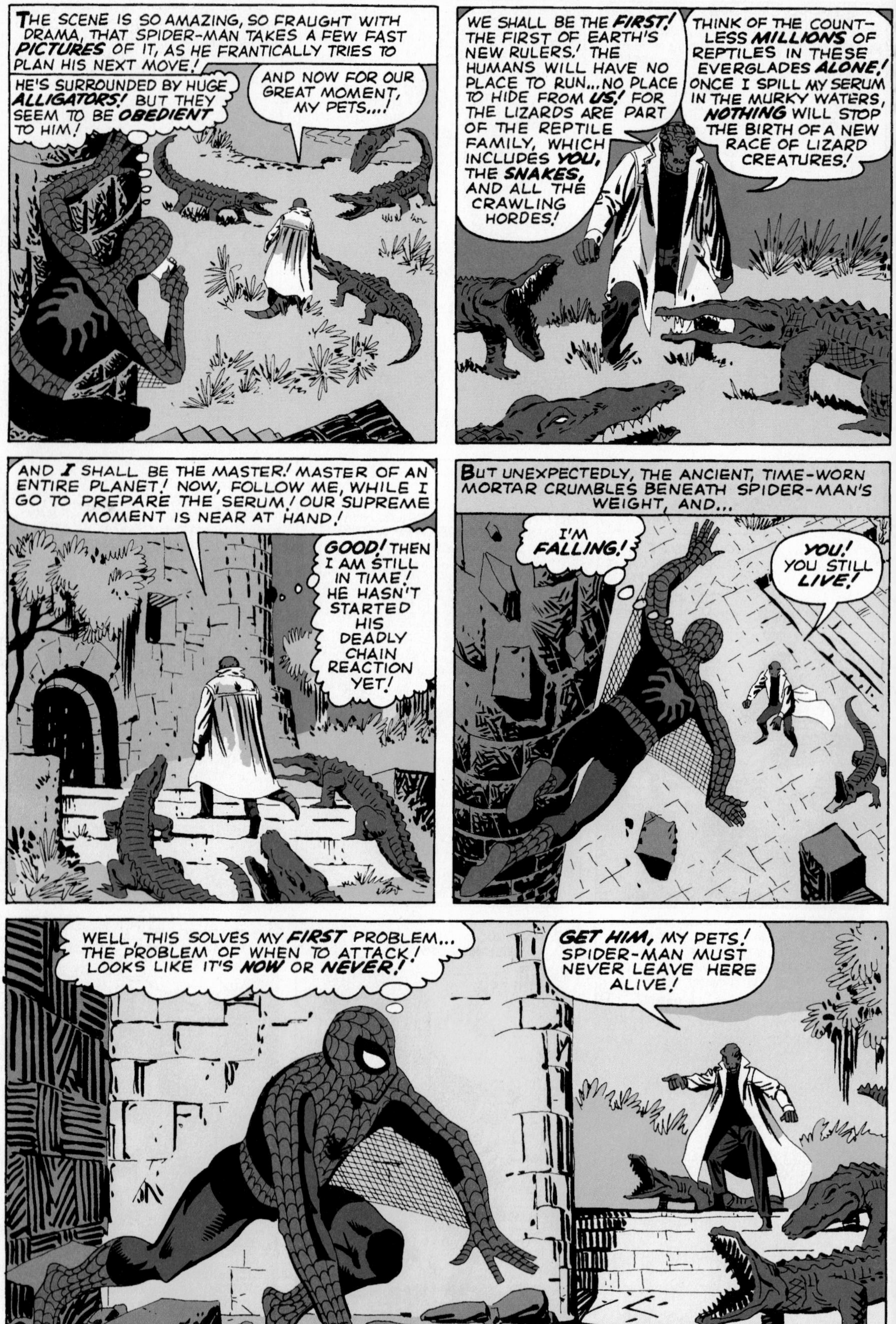
THE SCENE IS SO AMAZING, SO FRAUGHT WITH DRAMA, THAT SPIDER-MAN TAKES A FEW FAST PICTURES OF IT, AS HE FRANTICALLY TRIES TO PLAN HIS NEXT MOVE!
HE'S SURROUNDED BY HUGE ALLIGATORS! BUT THEY SEEM TO BE OBEDIENT TO HIM!
AND NOW FOR OUR GREAT MOMENT, MY PETS...!
WE SHALL BE THE FIRST! THE FIRST OF EARTH'S NEW RULERS! THE HUMANS WILL HAVE NO PLACE TO RUN...NO PLACE TO HIDE FROM US! FOR THE LIZARDS ARE PART OF THE REPTILE FAMILY, WHICH INCLUDES YOU, THE SNAKES, AND ALL THE CRAWLING HORDES!
THINK OF THE COUNTLESS MILLIONS OF REPTILES IN THESE EVERGLADES ALONE! ONCE I SPILL MY SERUM IN THE MURKY WATERS, NOTHING WILL STOP THE BIRTH OF A NEW RACE OF LIZARD CREATURES!
AND I SHALL BE THE MASTER! MASTER OF AN ENTIRE PLANET! NOW, FOLLOW ME, WHILE I GO TO PREPARE THE SERUM! OUR SUPREME MOMENT IS NEAR AT HAND!
GOOD! THEN I AM STILL IN TIME! HE HASN'T STARTED HIS DEADLY CHAIN REACTION YET!
BUT UNEXPECTEDLY, THE ANCIENT, TIME-WORN MORTAR CRUMBLES BENEATH SPIDER-MAN'S WEIGHT, AND...
I'M FALLING!
YOU! YOU STILL LIVE!
WELL, THIS SOLVES MY FIRST PROBLEM... THE PROBLEM OF WHEN TO ATTACK! LOOKS LIKE IT'S NOW OR NEVER!
GET HIM, MY PETS! SPIDER-MAN MUST NEVER LEAVE HERE ALIVE!
15

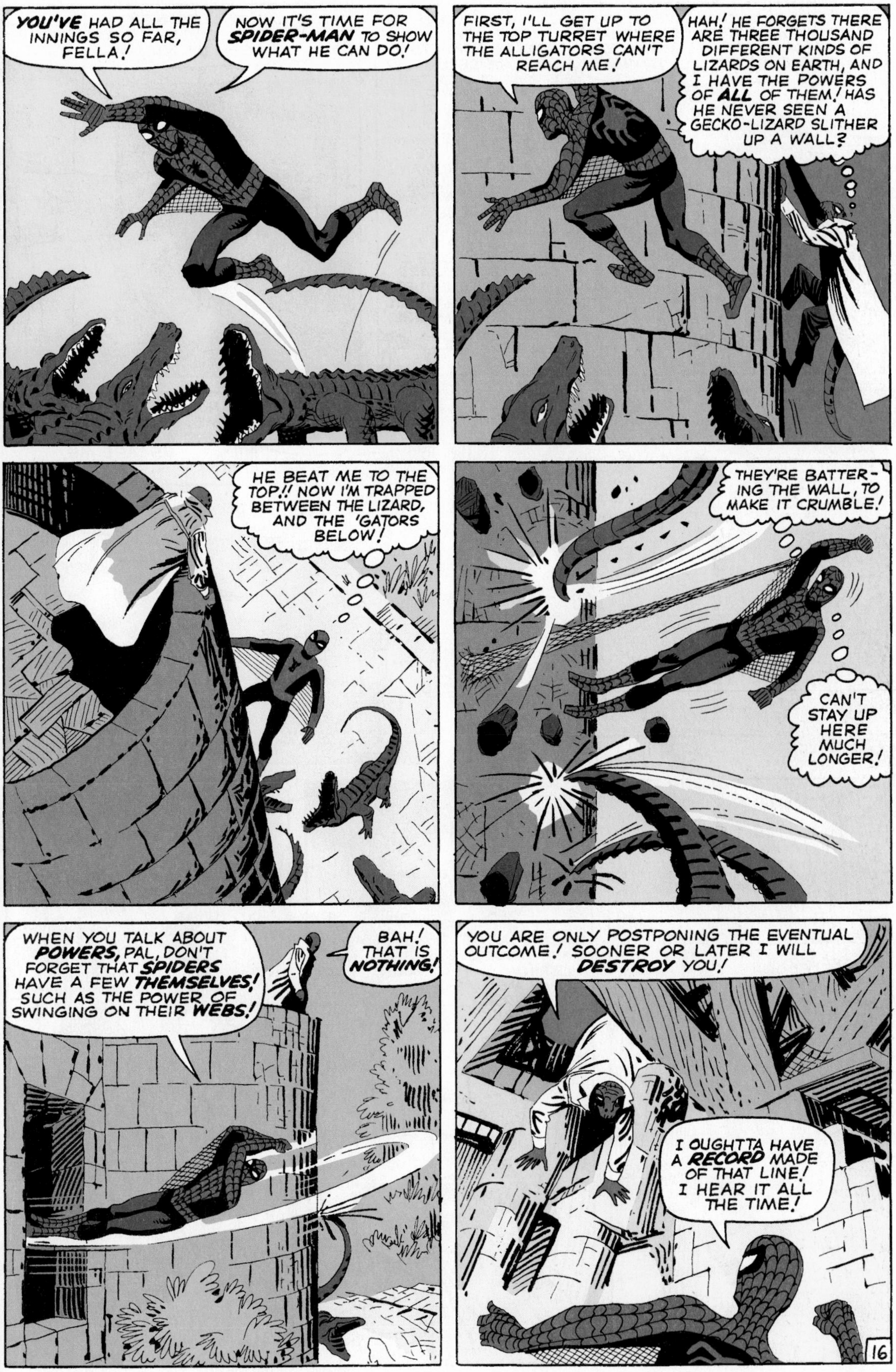
YOU'VE HAD ALL THE INNINGS SO FAR, FELLA!
NOW IT'S TIME FOR SPIDER-MAN TO SHOW WHAT HE CAN DO!
FIRST, I'LL GET UP TO THE TOP TURRET WHERE THE ALLIGATORS CAN'T REACH ME!
HAH! HE FORGETS THERE ARE THREE THOUSAND DIFFERENT KINDS OF LIZARDS ON EARTH, AND I HAVE THE POWERS OF ALL OF THEM! HAS HE NEVER SEEN A GECKO-LIZARD SLITHER UP A WALL?
HE BEAT ME TO THE TOP!! NOW I'M TRAPPED BETWEEN THE LIZARD, AND THE 'GATORS BELOW!
THEY'RE BATTERING THE WALL, TO MAKE IT CRUMBLE!
CAN'T STAY UP HERE MUCH LONGER!
WHEN YOU TALK ABOUT POWERS, PAL, DON'T FORGET THAT SPIDERS HAVE A FEW THEMSELVES! SUCH AS THE POWER OF SWINGING ON THEIR WEBS!
BAH! THAT IS NOTHING!
YOU ARE ONLY POSTPONING THE EVENTUAL OUTCOME! SOONER OR LATER I WILL DESTROY YOU!
I OUGHTTA HAVE A RECORD MADE OF THAT LINE! I HEAR IT ALL THE TIME!
16

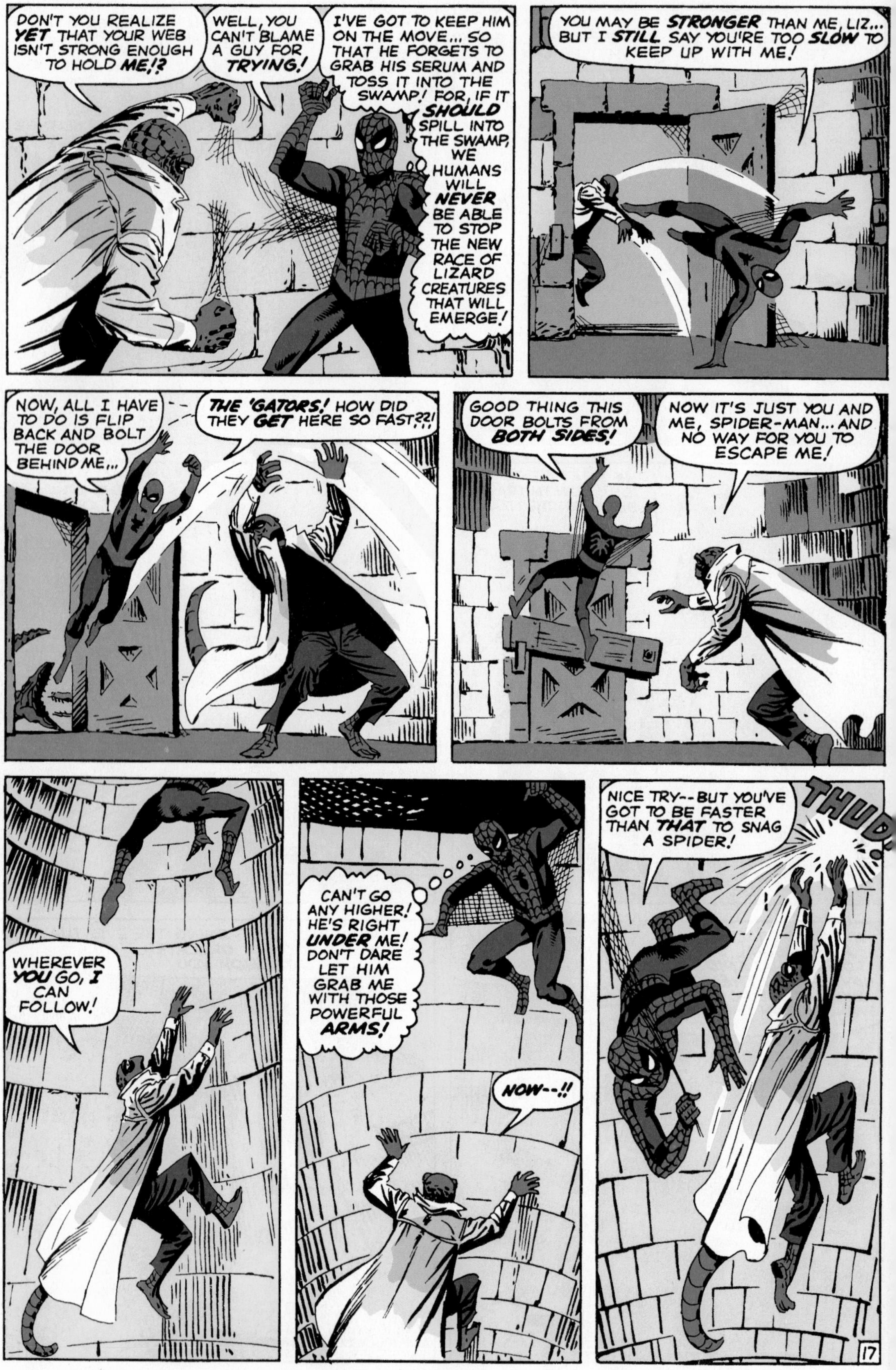
DON'T YOU REALIZE YET THAT YOUR WEB ISN'T STRONG ENOUGH TO HOLD ME!?
WELL, YOU CAN'T BLAME A GUY FOR TRYING!
I'VE GOT TO KEEP HIM ON THE MOVE... SO THAT HE FORGETS TO GRAB HIS SERUM AND TOSS IT INTO THE SWAMP! FOR, IF IT SHOULD SPILL INTO THE SWAMP, WE HUMANS WILL NEVER BE ABLE TO STOP THE NEW RACE OF LIZARD CREATURES THAT WILL EMERGE!
YOU MAY BE STRONGER THAN ME, LIZ... BUT I STILL SAY YOU'RE TOO SLOW TO KEEP UP WITH ME!
NOW, ALL I HAVE TO DO IS FLIP BACK AND BOLT THE DOOR BEHIND ME...
THE 'GATORS! HOW DID THEY GET HERE SO FAST??!
GOOD THING THIS DOOR BOLTS FROM BOTH SIDES!
NOW IT'S JUST YOU AND ME, SPIDER-MAN... AND NO WAY FOR YOU TO ESCAPE ME!
WHEREVER YOU GO, I CAN FOLLOW!
CAN'T GO ANY HIGHER! HE'S RIGHT UNDER ME! DON'T DARE LET HIM GRAB ME WITH THOSE POWERFUL ARMS!
NOW--!!
NICE TRY--BUT YOU'VE GOT TO BE FASTER THAN THAT TO SNAG A SPIDER!
THUD!
17

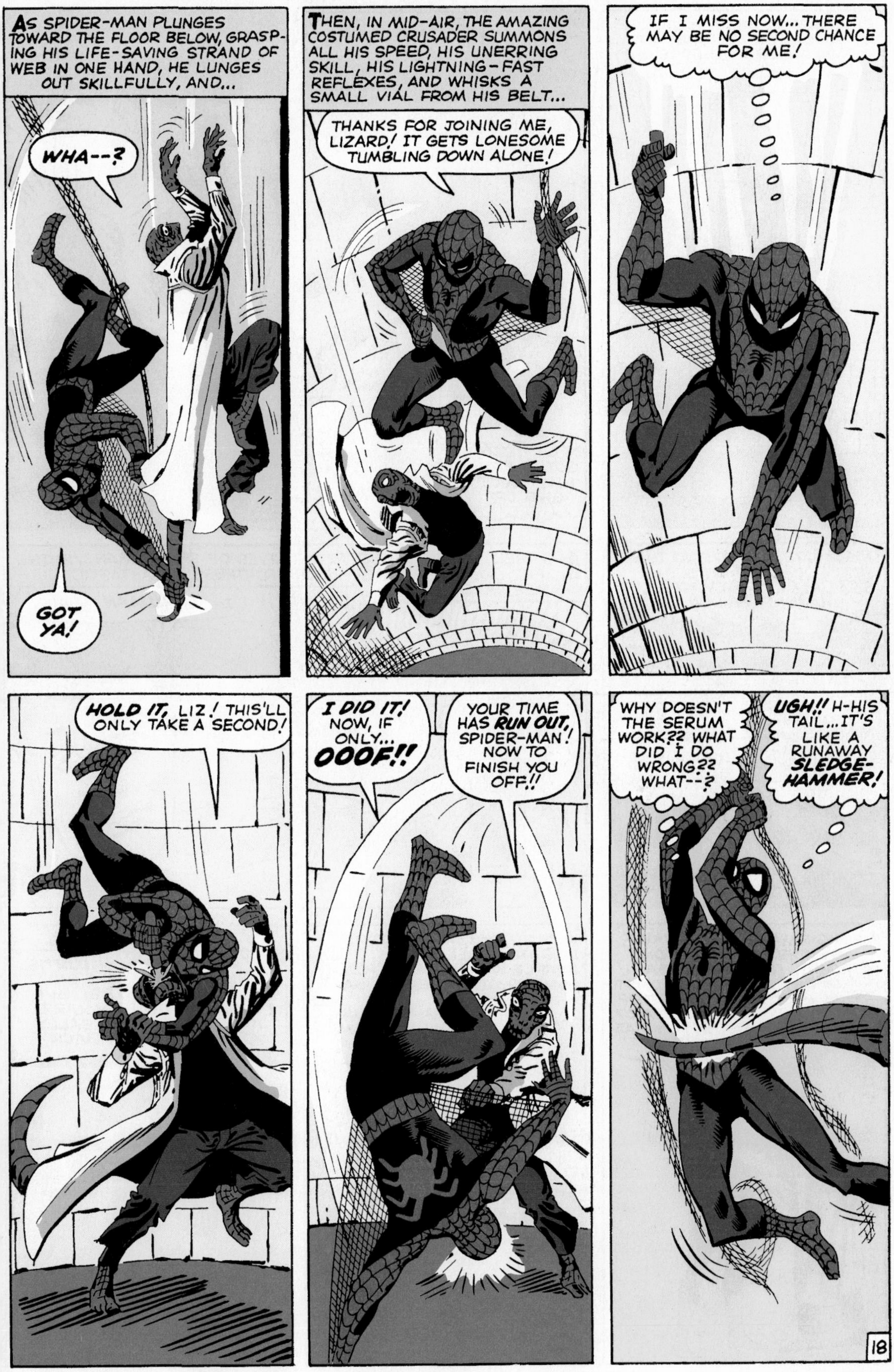
AS SPIDER-MAN PLUNGES TOWARD THE FLOOR BELOW, GRASPING HIS LIFE-SAVING STRAND OF WEB IN ONE HAND, HE LUNGES OUT SKILLFULLY, AND...
WHA--?
GOT YA!
THEN, IN MID-AIR, THE AMAZING COSTUMED CRUSADER SUMMONS ALL HIS SPEED, HIS UNERRING SKILL, HIS LIGHTNING-FAST REFLEXES, AND WHISKS A SMALL VIAL FROM HIS BELT...
THANKS FOR JOINING ME, LIZARD! IT GETS LONESOME TUMBLING DOWN ALONE!
IF I MISS NOW... THERE MAY BE NO SECOND CHANCE FOR ME!
HOLD IT, LIZ! THIS'LL ONLY TAKE A SECOND!
I DID IT! NOW, IF ONLY... OOOF!!
YOUR TIME HAS RUN OUT, SPIDER-MAN! NOW TO FINISH YOU OFF!!
WHY DOESN'T THE SERUM WORK?? WHAT DID I DO WRONG?? WHAT--?
UGH!! H-HIS TAIL...IT'S LIKE A RUNAWAY SLEDGE-HAMMER!
18

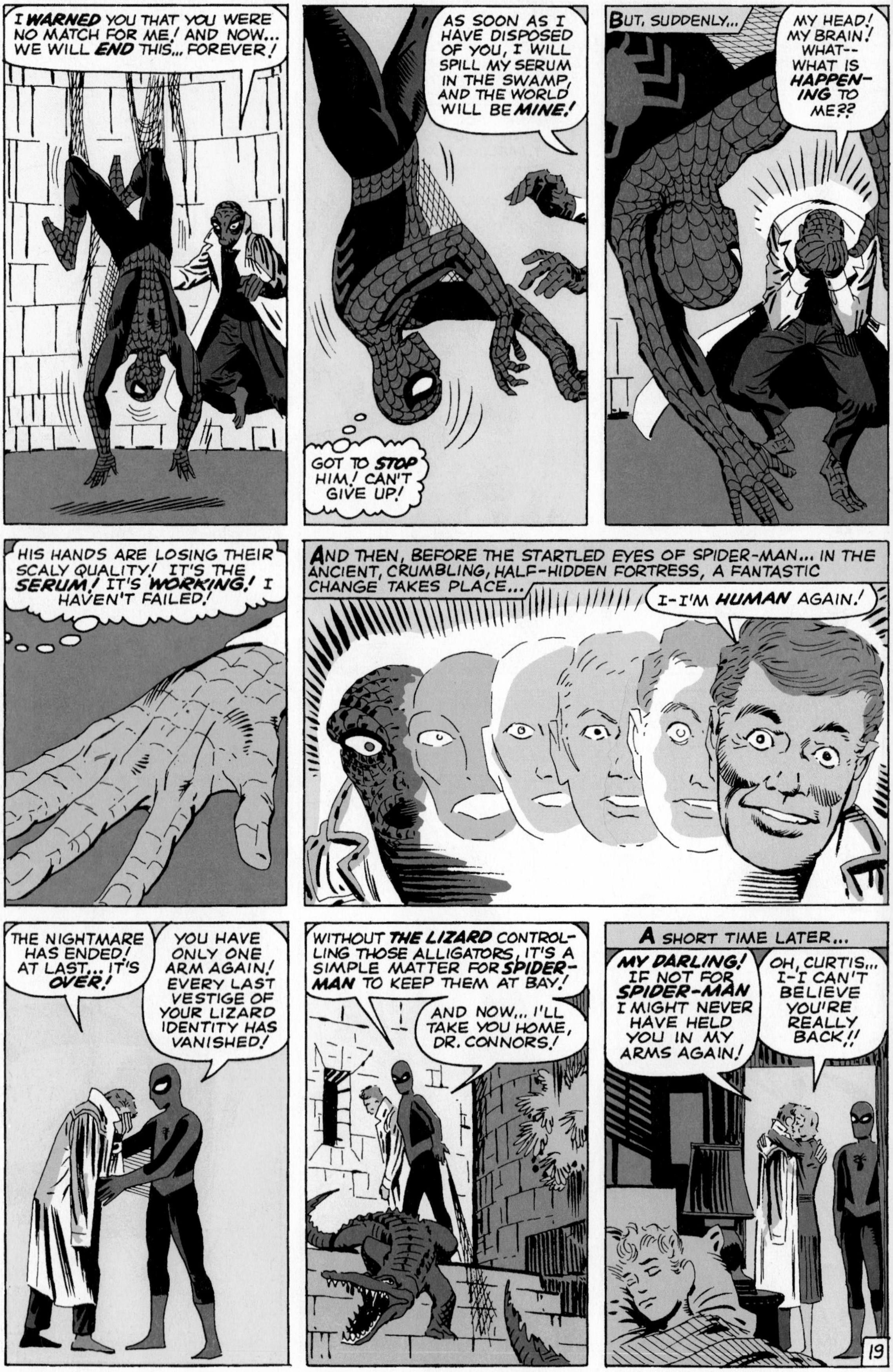
I WARNED YOU THAT YOU WERE NO MATCH FOR ME! AND NOW... WE WILL END THIS... FOREVER!
AS SOON AS I HAVE DISPOSED OF YOU, I WILL SPILL MY SERUM IN THE SWAMP, AND THE WORLD WILL BE MINE!
GOT TO STOP HIM! CAN'T GIVE UP!
BUT, SUDDENLY...
MY HEAD! MY BRAIN! WHAT-- WHAT IS HAPPEN-ING TO ME??
HIS HANDS ARE LOSING THEIR SCALY QUALITY! IT'S THE SERUM! IT'S WORKING! I HAVEN'T FAILED!
AND THEN, BEFORE THE STARTLED EYES OF SPIDER-MAN... IN THE ANCIENT, CRUMBLING, HALF-HIDDEN FORTRESS, A FANTASTIC CHANGE TAKES PLACE...
I-I'M HUMAN AGAIN!
THE NIGHTMARE HAS ENDED! AT LAST... IT'S OVER!
YOU HAVE ONLY ONE ARM AGAIN! EVERY LAST VESTIGE OF YOUR LIZARD IDENTITY HAS VANISHED!
WITHOUT THE LIZARD CONTROL-LING THOSE ALLIGATORS, IT'S A SIMPLE MATTER FOR SPIDER-MAN TO KEEP THEM AT BAY!
AND NOW... I'LL TAKE YOU HOME, DR. CONNORS!
A SHORT TIME LATER...
MY DARLING! IF NOT FOR SPIDER-MAN I MIGHT NEVER HAVE HELD YOU IN MY ARMS AGAIN!
OH, CURTIS... I-I CAN'T BELIEVE YOU'RE REALLY BACK!!
19

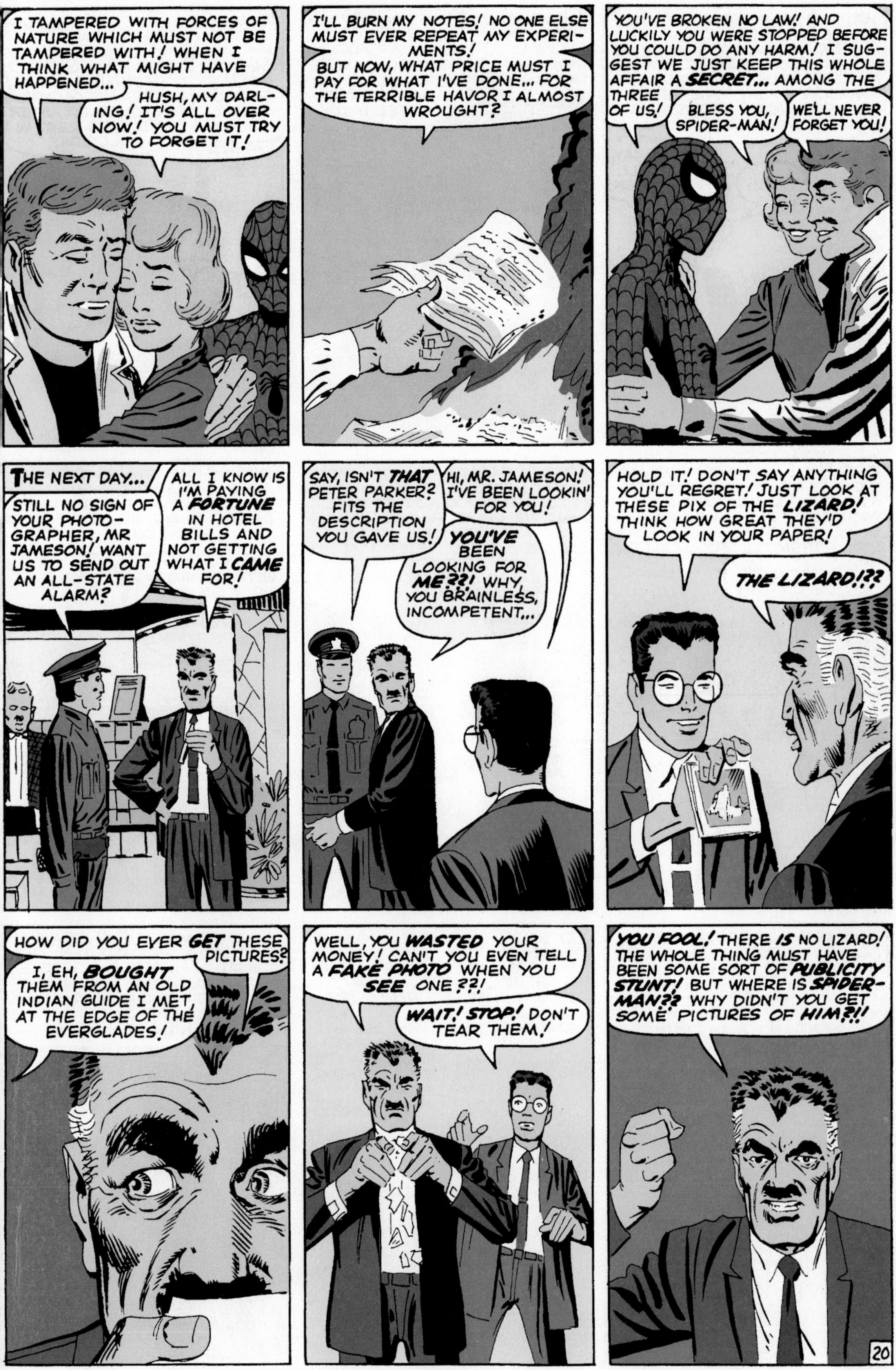
I TAMPERED WITH FORCES OF NATURE WHICH MUST NOT BE TAMPERED WITH! WHEN I THINK WHAT MIGHT HAVE HAPPENED...
HUSH, MY DARLING! IT'S ALL OVER NOW! YOU MUST TRY TO FORGET IT!
I'LL BURN MY NOTES! NO ONE ELSE MUST EVER REPEAT MY EXPERIMENTS!
BUT NOW, WHAT PRICE MUST I PAY FOR WHAT I'VE DONE... FOR THE TERRIBLE HAVOR I ALMOST WROUGHT?
YOU'VE BROKEN NO LAW! AND LUCKILY YOU WERE STOPPED BEFORE YOU COULD DO ANY HARM! I SUGGEST WE JUST KEEP THIS WHOLE AFFAIR A SECRET... AMONG THE THREE OF US!
BLESS YOU, SPIDER-MAN!
WE'LL NEVER FORGET YOU!
THE NEXT DAY...
STILL NO SIGN OF YOUR PHOTOGRAPHER, MR JAMESON! WANT US TO SEND OUT AN ALL-STATE ALARM?
ALL I KNOW IS I'M PAYING A FORTUNE IN HOTEL BILLS AND NOT GETTING WHAT I CAME FOR!
SAY, ISN'T THAT PETER PARKER? FITS THE DESCRIPTION YOU GAVE US!
HI, MR. JAMESON! I'VE BEEN LOOKIN' FOR YOU!
YOU'VE BEEN LOOKING FOR ME??! WHY, YOU BRAINLESS, INCOMPETENT...
HOLD IT! DON'T SAY ANYTHING YOU'LL REGRET! JUST LOOK AT THESE PIX OF THE LIZARD! THINK HOW GREAT THEY'D LOOK IN YOUR PAPER!
THE LIZARD!??
HOW DID YOU EVER GET THESE PICTURES?
I, EH, BOUGHT THEM FROM AN OLD INDIAN GUIDE I MET, AT THE EDGE OF THE EVERGLADES!
WELL, YOU WASTED YOUR MONEY! CAN'T YOU EVEN TELL A FAKE PHOTO WHEN YOU SEE ONE ??!
WAIT! STOP! DON'T TEAR THEM!
YOU FOOL! THERE IS NO LIZARD! THE WHOLE THING MUST HAVE BEEN SOME SORT OF PUBLICITY STUNT! BUT WHERE IS SPIDER-MAN?? WHY DIDN'T YOU GET SOME PICTURES OF HIM?!!
20

Panel 1: YOU AND YOUR BIG TALK! YOU PROMISED ME SENSATIONAL PHOTOS... AND ALL YOU BRING ME IS A BATCH OF **WORTHLESS FAKES!** YOU'VE WASTED **ENOUGH** OF MY TIME! GET PACKED! WE'RE RETURNING TO NEW YORK!

BUT...

OKAY, I'LL PACK!

Panel 2:  WHAT ABOUT THE **MONEY** YOU PROMISED ME, MR JAMESON?

FOR **WHAT?!** THE WAY **I** FIGURE IT, **YOU** OWE **ME** FOR YOUR PLANE FARE DOWN HERE AND HALF OF THE HOTEL BILL!

Panel 3: FINALLY, A WEARY PETER PARKER REACHES HIS HOME...

GEE, IT'S GOOD TO BE BACK, AUNT MAY!

NOW DON'T GET TOO COMFORTABLE, PETER. I HAVE A LOT OF **CHORES** FOR YOU TO DO AFTER YOUR NICE REST IN FLORIDA!

Panel 4:  **REST?!** BUT...OH, OKAY, AUNT MAY! JUST LET ME CALL **BETTY** FIRST, AND SEE IF SHE'LL DATE ME TOMORROW! OH...I FORGOT! SHE'S WORKING LATE FOR MR. JAMESON! WELL, THEN I'LL TRY LIZ ALLEN!

HI, LIZ! THIS IS **PETER!** HOW ABOUT TOMORROW NIGHT?

Panel 5:  PETER PARKER! I'LL TELL **YOU** WHAT I TOLD FLASH THOMPSON! I'LL THANK YOU **NOT** TO CALL AND TIE UP MY PHONE! I'M WAITING FOR A CALL FROM **SPIDER-MAN!** AFTER HIM RESCUING ME THE OTHER DAY, AND CALLING ME "BLUE EYES", I'M **SURE** HE'LL CALL!

AND I DON'T WANT THE LINE TO BE BUSY WHEN MY **DREAM MAN** PHONES!!

Panel 6:  OH NO!! SHE THINKS **SPIDER-MAN** HAS A CRUSH ON HER! SO SHE WON'T WASTE TIME DATING PLAIN, ORDINARY PETER FROM DULLVILLE!

ONLY A GUY WITH **MY** NUTTY LUCK COULD END UP BEING HIS **OWN** COMPETITION!

SLAM!

Panel 7:  AND, AT THE OFFICE OF J. JONAH JAMESON, SPIDER-MAN IS ALSO VERY MUCH THE TOPIC OF CONVERSATION...

YOU MEAN HE SENT IT THRU THE **MAIL**, MISS BRANT?

YES SIR! AFTER ALL, I GUESS **SPIDER-MAN** CAN MAIL A LETTER LIKE ANYONE **ELSE!**

Panel 8:  IT SAYS: "ROSES ARE RED, VIOLETS ARE BLUE... I'M STILL AT LARGE, SO PHOOEY TO YOU!"

WELL, DON'T JUST **STAND** THERE! TEAR IT UP! **BURN IT!**

OHH! I'LL GET THAT MASKED MENACE IF IT'S THE LAST THING I DO!

Panel 9: EDITOR'S NOTE: **BIG NEWS!!** NEXT ISSUE WILL FEATURE THE SENSATIONAL RETURN OF ONE OF THE GREATEST VILLAINS OF ALL... THE ASTOUNDING **VULTURE!** RESERVE YOUR COPY AT YOUR DEALER'S NOW! SEE YOU SOON...

the END

21

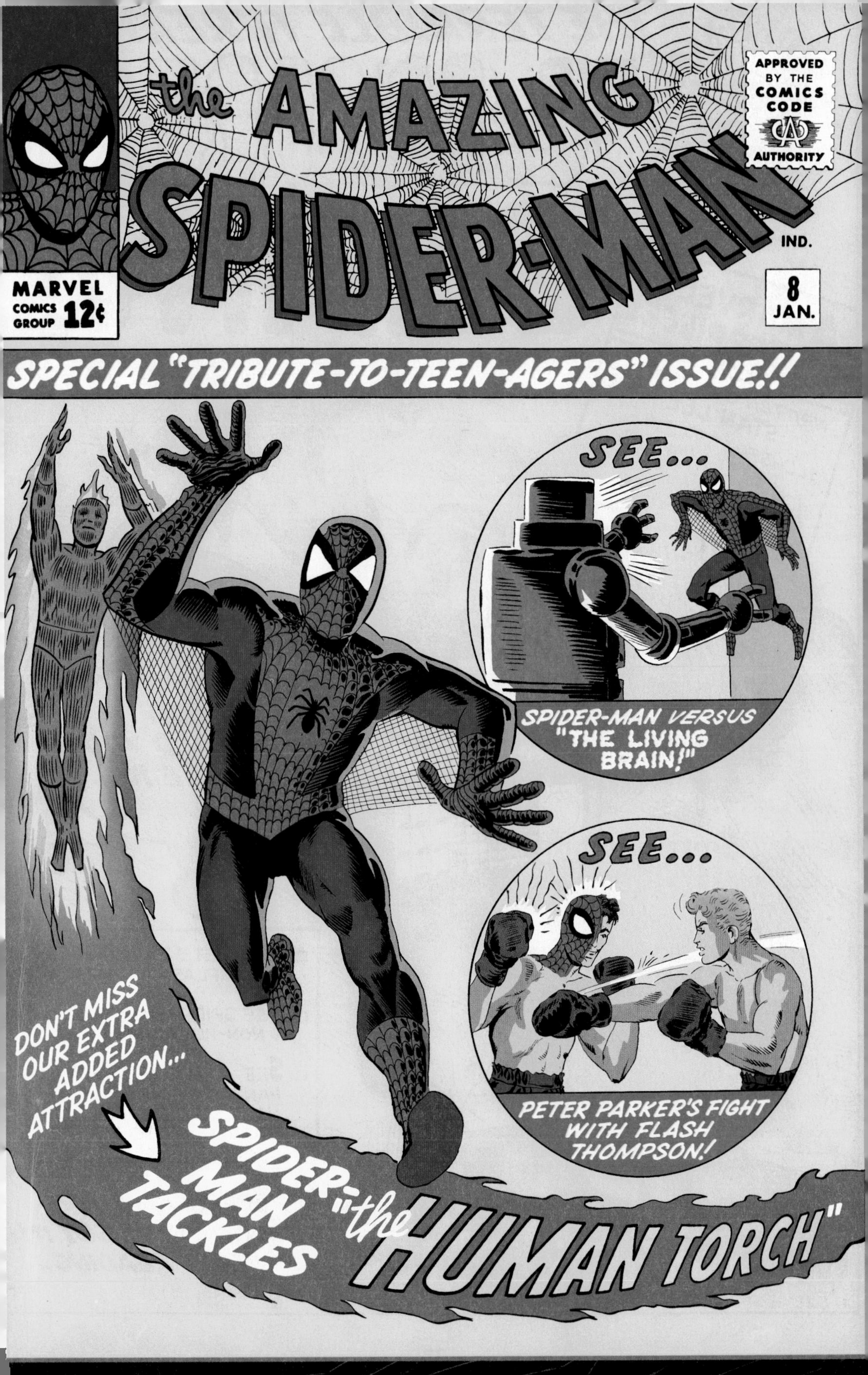
MARVEL COMICS GROUP 12¢
the AMAZING SPIDER-MAN
APPROVED BY THE COMICS CODE AUTHORITY
IND.
8 JAN.
SPECIAL "TRIBUTE-TO-TEEN-AGERS" ISSUE!!
SEE...
SPIDER-MAN VERSUS "THE LIVING BRAIN!"
SEE...
PETER PARKER'S FIGHT WITH FLASH THOMPSON!
DON'T MISS OUR EXTRA ADDED ATTRACTION...
SPIDER-MAN TACKLES "the HUMAN TORCH"

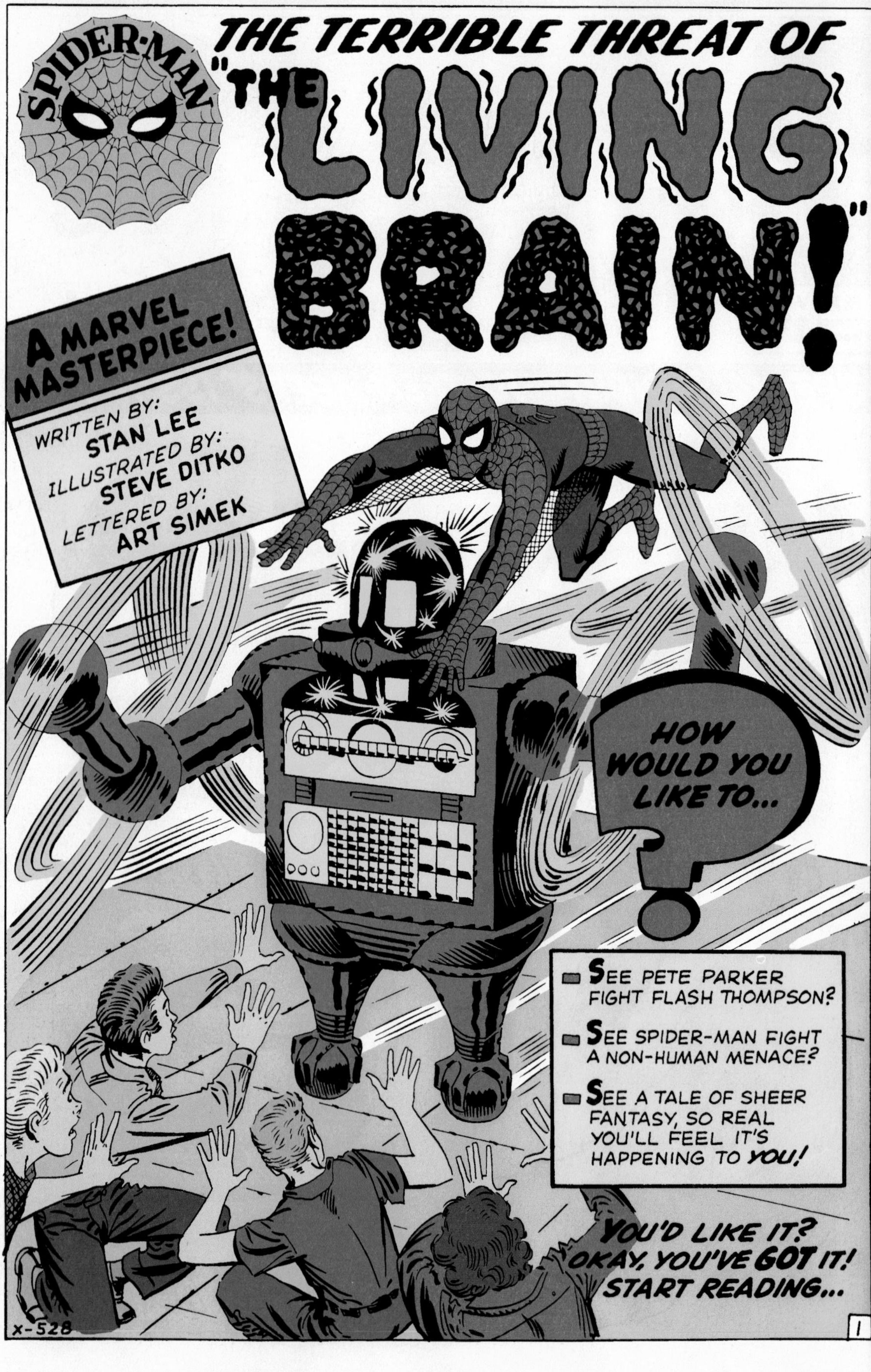
SPIDER-MAN
THE TERRIBLE THREAT OF
"THE LIVING BRAIN!"
A MARVEL MASTERPIECE!
WRITTEN BY: STAN LEE
ILLUSTRATED BY: STEVE DITKO
LETTERED BY: ART SIMEK
HOW WOULD YOU LIKE TO...
SEE PETE PARKER FIGHT FLASH THOMPSON?
SEE SPIDER-MAN FIGHT A NON-HUMAN MENACE?
SEE A TALE OF SHEER FANTASY, SO REAL YOU'LL FEEL IT'S HAPPENING TO YOU!
YOU'D LIKE IT? OKAY, YOU'VE GOT IT! START READING...
X-528
1

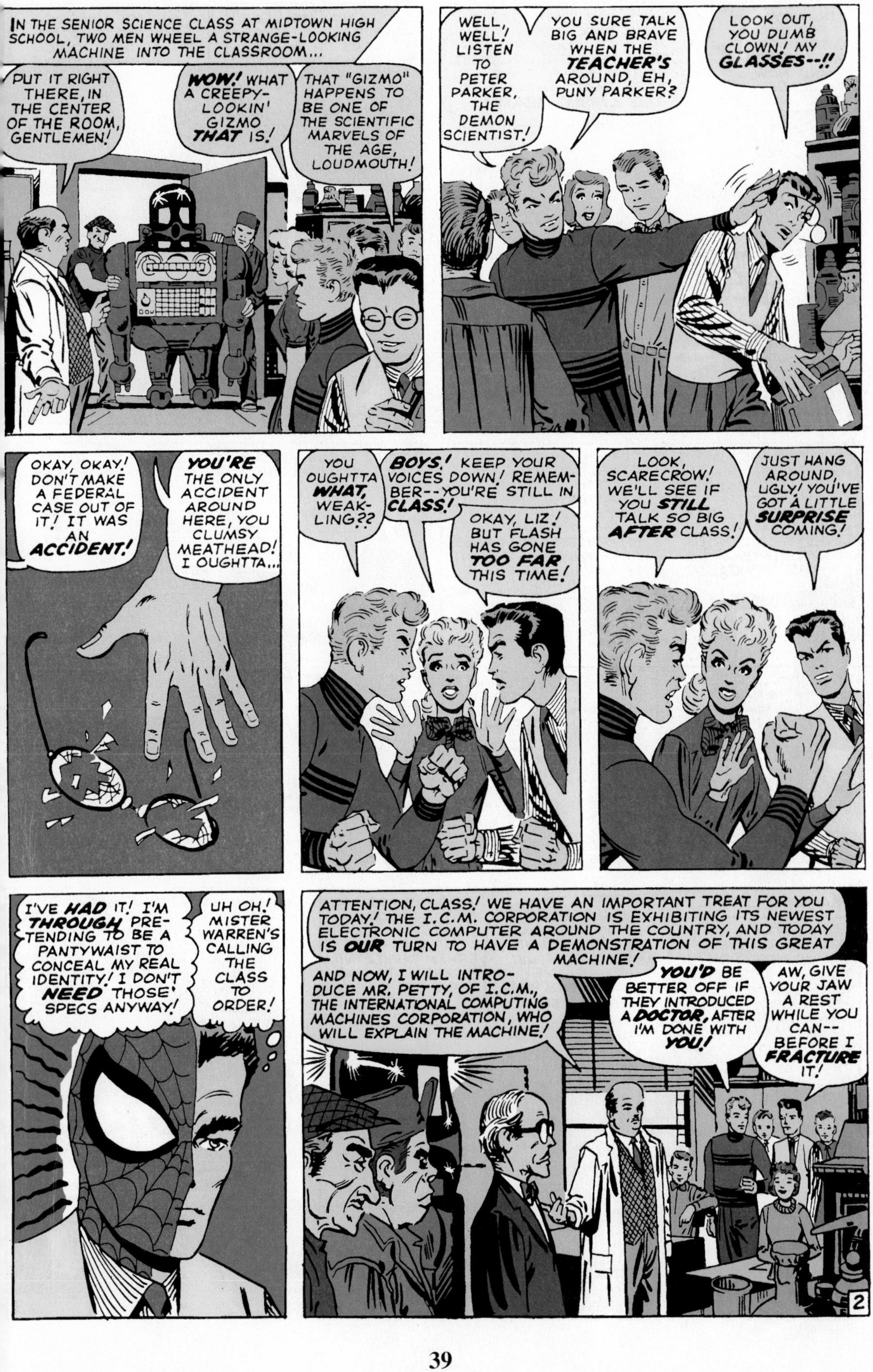
IN THE SENIOR SCIENCE CLASS AT MIDTOWN HIGH SCHOOL, TWO MEN WHEEL A STRANGE-LOOKING MACHINE INTO THE CLASSROOM...
PUT IT RIGHT THERE, IN THE CENTER OF THE ROOM, GENTLEMEN!
WOW! WHAT A CREEPY-LOOKIN' GIZMO THAT IS!
THAT "GIZMO" HAPPENS TO BE ONE OF THE SCIENTIFIC MARVELS OF THE AGE, LOUDMOUTH!
WELL, WELL! LISTEN TO PETER PARKER, THE DEMON SCIENTIST!
YOU SURE TALK BIG AND BRAVE WHEN THE TEACHER'S AROUND, EH, PUNY PARKER?
LOOK OUT, YOU DUMB CLOWN! MY GLASSES--!!
OKAY, OKAY! DON'T MAKE A FEDERAL CASE OUT OF IT! IT WAS AN ACCIDENT!
YOU'RE THE ONLY ACCIDENT AROUND HERE, YOU CLUMSY MEATHEAD! I OUGHTTA...
YOU OUGHTTA WHAT, WEAKLING??
BOYS! KEEP YOUR VOICES DOWN! REMEMBER--YOU'RE STILL IN CLASS!
OKAY, LIZ! BUT FLASH HAS GONE TOO FAR THIS TIME!
LOOK, SCARECROW! WE'LL SEE IF YOU STILL TALK SO BIG AFTER CLASS!
JUST HANG AROUND, UGLY! YOU'VE GOT A LITTLE SURPRISE COMING!
I'VE HAD IT! I'M THROUGH PRETENDING TO BE A PANTYWAIST TO CONCEAL MY REAL IDENTITY! I DON'T NEED THOSE SPECS ANYWAY!
UH OH! MISTER WARREN'S CALLING THE CLASS TO ORDER!
ATTENTION, CLASS! WE HAVE AN IMPORTANT TREAT FOR YOU TODAY! THE I.C.M. CORPORATION IS EXHIBITING ITS NEWEST ELECTRONIC COMPUTER AROUND THE COUNTRY, AND TODAY IS OUR TURN TO HAVE A DEMONSTRATION OF THIS GREAT MACHINE!
AND NOW, I WILL INTRODUCE MR. PETTY, OF I.C.M., THE INTERNATIONAL COMPUTING MACHINES CORPORATION, WHO WILL EXPLAIN THE MACHINE!
YOU'D BE BETTER OFF IF THEY INTRODUCED A DOCTOR, AFTER I'M DONE WITH YOU!
AW, GIVE YOUR JAW A REST WHILE YOU CAN--BEFORE I FRACTURE IT!
2

THANK YOU FOR YOUR INTRODUCTION MR. WARREN! AND NOW, CLASS,...

WE BUILT OUR COMPUTER IN THE FORM OF A HUMAN BODY IN ORDER TO DRAMATIZE ITS POWERS! IT IS THE GREATEST MECHANICAL BRAIN EVER BUILT! IN FACT, WE CALL IT **THE LIVING BRAIN!**

NOTICE HOW ITS LEGS HAVE BALL-BEARING ROLLERS ON THEM, ENABLING THE BRAIN TO MOVE UPON COMMAND!

AND ITS ARMS ARE SO CONSTRUCTED THAT THEY TOO CAN PERFORM SIMPLE MOTIONS...

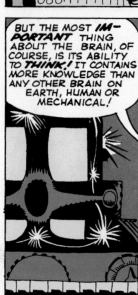

BUT THE MOST IM-PORTANT THING ABOUT THE BRAIN, OF COURSE, IS ITS ABILITY TO *THINK!* IT CONTAINS MORE KNOWLEDGE THAN ANY OTHER BRAIN ON EARTH, HUMAN OR MECHANICAL!

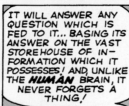

IT WILL ANSWER ANY QUESTION WHICH IS FED TO IT... BASING ITS ANSWER ON THE VAST STOREHOUSE OF IN-FORMATION WHICH IT POSSESSES! AND, UNLIKE THE *HUMAN* BRAIN, IT NEVER FORGETS A THING!

NOW, MR. WARREN, WOULD YOU SELECT A STUDENT TO *ASSIST* ME, PLEASE?

PETER PARKER IS OUR TOP SCIENCE STUDENT! PARKER, WILL YOU STEP UP HERE FOR A MOMENT?

I'LL BE GLAD TO, SIR!

SURE YOU'D BE GLAD TO! HOW DOES IT FEEL TO BE A PRO-FESSIONAL TEACHER'S PET??

QUIET, FLASH! LET'S SEE WHAT THEY WANT PETE TO *DO!*

MOMENTS LATER...

NOW THAT I'VE EXPLAINED THE BRAIN'S OPERATION TO YOU, LET'S SEE YOU--

SAY! YOU LEARN PRETTY QUICKLY, SON!

THANKS, MISTER PETTY! ACTUALLY, I'VE READ A LOT ABOUT ELECTRONIC BRAINS! I'VE ALWAYS BEEN REAL INTERESTED IN THEM!

NOW, CLASS, YOU THINK OF A QUESTION FOR THE LIVING BRAIN, AND THEN PARKER WILL FEED IT TO HIM AND SEE IF HE CAN ANSWER IT!

DIDJA HEAR HIM CALL THE BRAIN "HE"--LIKE IT WAS A REAL PERSON??

IT'S *SMARTER* THAN ANY REAL PERSON! IT CAN FIGURE OUT HORSE RACE WINNERS, ELECTIONS, *ANYTHING!* WE COULD GET *RICH* IF WE OWNED IT!

3

WHAT SHOULD WE *ASK* THE BRAIN??

GOSH, *I* DON'T KNOW! WHAT DO *YOU* THINK?

SEARCH ME?? GOT ANY IDEAS, LIZ?

YES! I THOUGHT OF SOMETHING *EVERYBODY* WOULD LIKE TO KNOW! LET'S SEE HOW SMART THE BRAIN REALLY IS...

WHAT IS *SPIDER-MAN'S* REAL IDENTITY??

HEY! THAT'S *TERRIFIC!*

WHAT A GREAT QUESTION!

THIS IS *TERRIBLE!* WHAT IF THE BRAIN IS SMART ENOUGH TO *ANSWER* THAT?? WHAT I'LL *DO??*

IMPOSSIBLE AS THAT QUESTION SEEMS, IF THE LIVING BRAIN IS FED ENOUGH INFORMATION ABOUT SPIDER-MAN, HE MIGHT BE ABLE TO *ANSWER* IT!

AND SO, THE CLASS CALLS OUT ALL THE FACTS THEY CAN THINK OF ABOUT THE COSTUMED MYSTERY MAN...

HE'S ABOUT FIVE FEET, TEN INCHES TALL!

WEIGHS ABOUT ONE-HUNDRED SIXTY POUNDS!

HE'S BEEN SIGHTED IN THE FOREST HILLS AREA A LOT!

HE'S THE MOST WONDERFUL, HEROIC, GLAMOROUS MAN IN THE WHOLE WORLD!

IF YOU ASK *ME*, HE'S A NEUROTIC *NUT!*

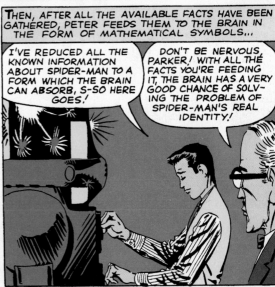

THEN, AFTER ALL THE AVAILABLE FACTS HAVE BEEN GATHERED, PETER FEEDS THEM TO THE BRAIN IN THE FORM OF MATHEMATICAL SYMBOLS...

I'VE REDUCED ALL THE KNOWN INFORMATION ABOUT SPIDER-MAN TO A FORM WHICH THE BRAIN CAN ABSORB, S-SO HERE GOES!

DON'T BE NERVOUS, PARKER! WITH ALL THE FACTS YOU'RE FEEDING IT, THE BRAIN HAS A VERY GOOD CHANCE OF SOLVING THE PROBLEM OF SPIDER-MAN'S REAL IDENTITY!

I KNOW IT! *THAT'S* WHAT I'M NERVOUS ABOUT!!

PARKER IS SPI

UH OH! THE BRAIN IS SIGNALLING! THE ANSWER IS READY! BOY, IT SURE DIDN'T *TAKE* LONG!

VERY WELL, PARKER! AS YOU CAN TELL BY THAT WINKING LIGHT, THE ANSWER IS READY FOR YOU! YOU MAY TAKE IT NOW!

YES, SO I SEE! I-I'LL GET IT...

4

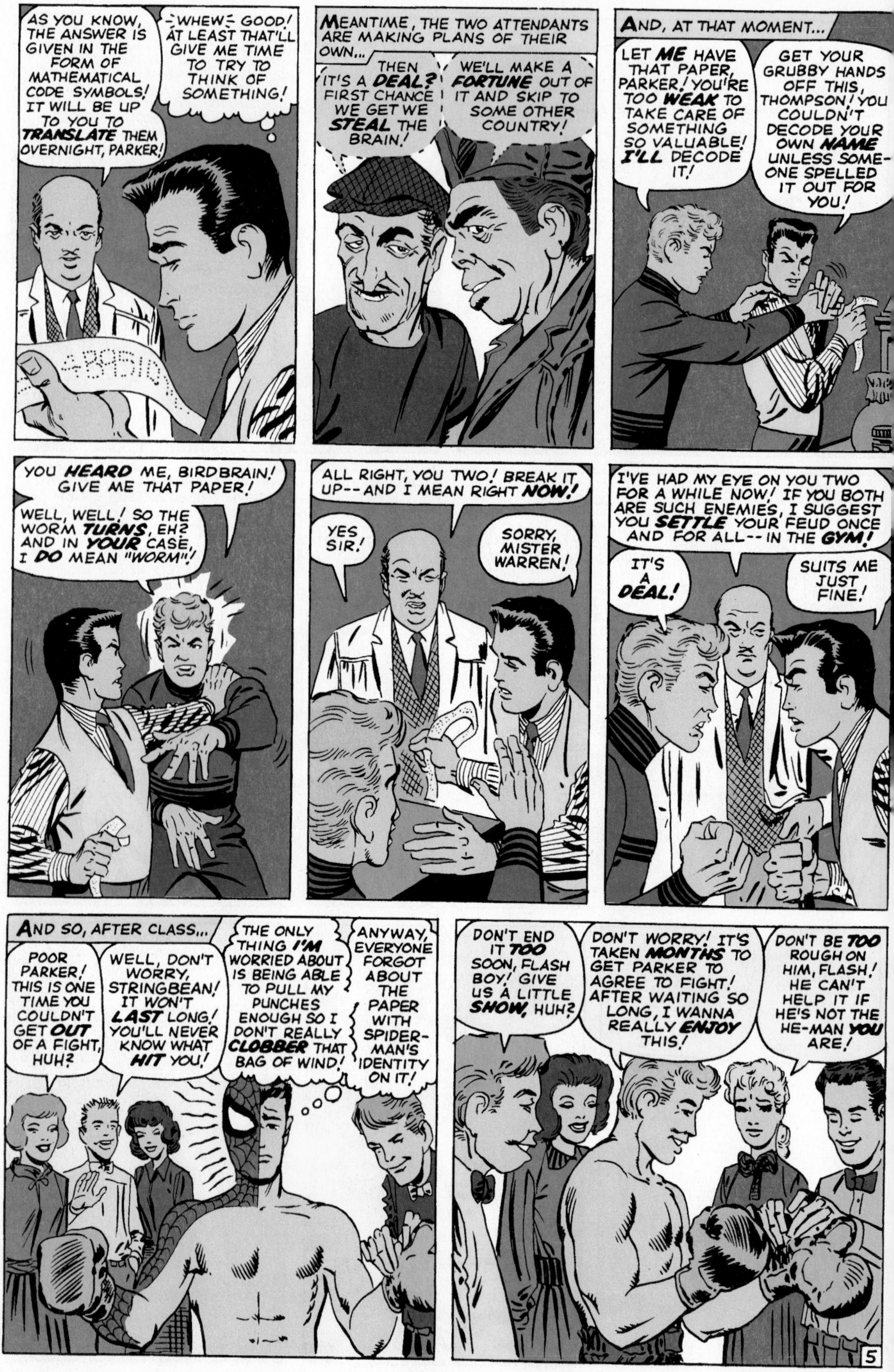
AS YOU KNOW, THE ANSWER IS GIVEN IN THE FORM OF MATHEMATICAL CODE SYMBOLS! IT WILL BE UP TO YOU TO TRANSLATE THEM OVERNIGHT, PARKER!
-WHEW- GOOD! AT LEAST THAT'LL GIVE ME TIME TO TRY TO THINK OF SOMETHING!
MEANTIME, THE TWO ATTENDANTS ARE MAKING PLANS OF THEIR OWN...
THEN IT'S A DEAL? FIRST CHANCE WE GET WE STEAL THE BRAIN!
WE'LL MAKE A FORTUNE OUT OF IT AND SKIP TO SOME OTHER COUNTRY!
AND, AT THAT MOMENT...
LET ME HAVE THAT PAPER, PARKER! YOU'RE TOO WEAK TO TAKE CARE OF SOMETHING SO VALUABLE! I'LL DECODE IT!
GET YOUR GRUBBY HANDS OFF THIS, THOMPSON! YOU COULDN'T DECODE YOUR OWN NAME UNLESS SOME-ONE SPELLED IT OUT FOR YOU!
YOU HEARD ME, BIRDBRAIN! GIVE ME THAT PAPER!
WELL, WELL! SO THE WORM TURNS, EH? AND IN YOUR CASE, I DO MEAN "WORM"!
ALL RIGHT, YOU TWO! BREAK IT UP-- AND I MEAN RIGHT NOW!
YES SIR!
SORRY, MISTER WARREN!
I'VE HAD MY EYE ON YOU TWO FOR A WHILE NOW! IF YOU BOTH ARE SUCH ENEMIES, I SUGGEST YOU SETTLE YOUR FEUD ONCE AND FOR ALL-- IN THE GYM!
IT'S A DEAL!
SUITS ME JUST FINE!
AND SO, AFTER CLASS...
POOR PARKER! THIS IS ONE TIME YOU COULDN'T GET OUT OF A FIGHT, HUH?
WELL, DON'T WORRY, STRINGBEAN! IT WON'T LAST LONG! YOU'LL NEVER KNOW WHAT HIT YOU!
THE ONLY THING I'M WORRIED ABOUT IS BEING ABLE TO PULL MY PUNCHES ENOUGH SO I DON'T REALLY CLOBBER THAT BAG OF WIND!
ANYWAY, EVERYONE FORGOT ABOUT THE PAPER WITH SPIDER-MAN'S IDENTITY ON IT!
DON'T END IT TOO SOON, FLASH BOY! GIVE US A LITTLE SHOW, HUH?
DON'T WORRY! IT'S TAKEN MONTHS TO GET PARKER TO AGREE TO FIGHT! AFTER WAITING SO LONG, I WANNA REALLY ENJOY THIS!
DON'T BE TOO ROUGH ON HIM, FLASH! HE CAN'T HELP IT IF HE'S NOT THE HE-MAN YOU ARE!
5

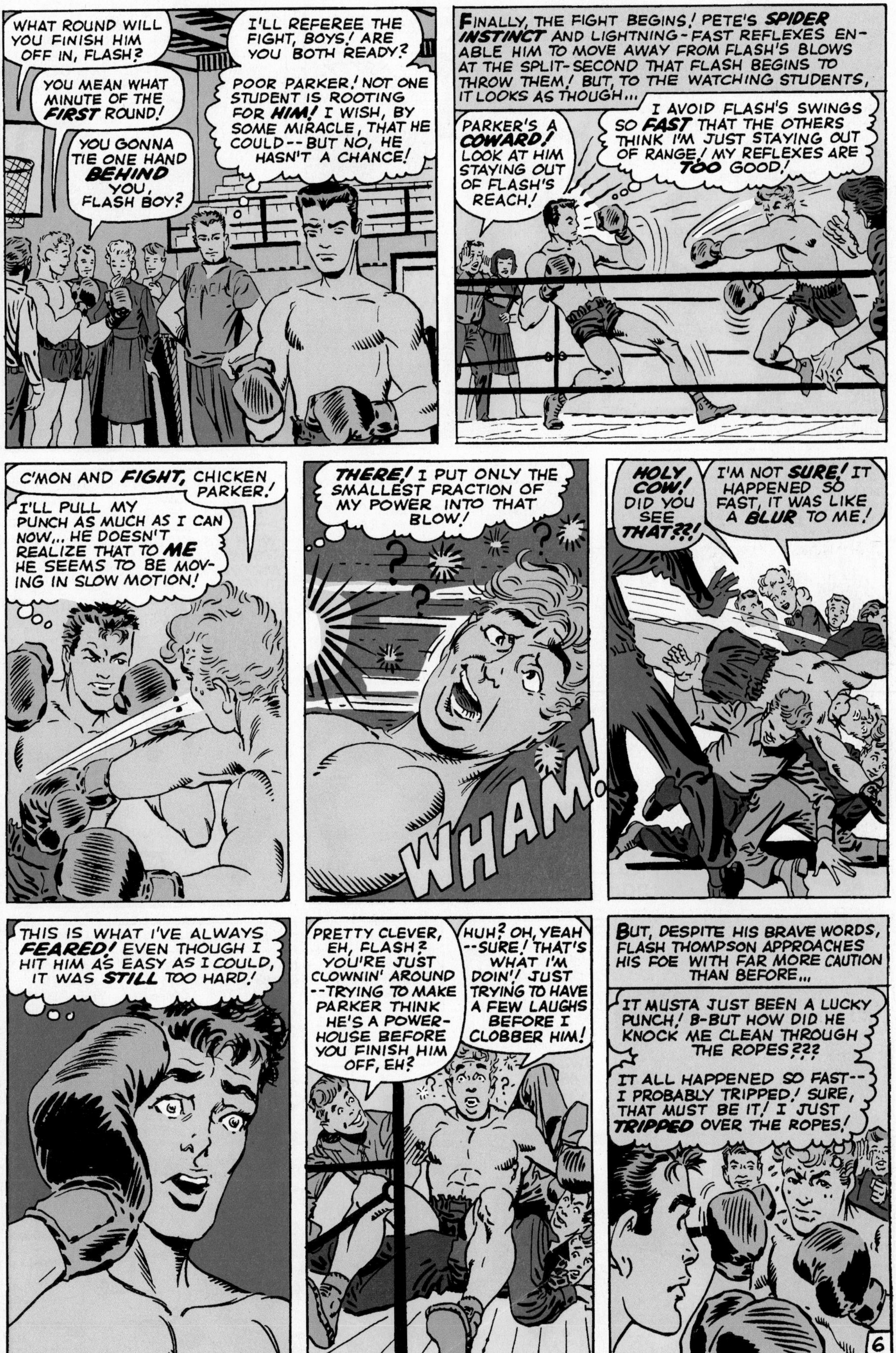
WHAT ROUND WILL YOU FINISH HIM OFF IN, FLASH?
YOU MEAN WHAT MINUTE OF THE FIRST ROUND!
YOU GONNA TIE ONE HAND BEHIND YOU, FLASH BOY?
I'LL REFEREE THE FIGHT, BOYS! ARE YOU BOTH READY?
POOR PARKER! NOT ONE STUDENT IS ROOTING FOR HIM! I WISH, BY SOME MIRACLE, THAT HE COULD--BUT NO, HE HASN'T A CHANCE!
FINALLY, THE FIGHT BEGINS! PETE'S SPIDER INSTINCT AND LIGHTNING-FAST REFLEXES ENABLE HIM TO MOVE AWAY FROM FLASH'S BLOWS AT THE SPLIT-SECOND THAT FLASH BEGINS TO THROW THEM! BUT, TO THE WATCHING STUDENTS, IT LOOKS AS THOUGH...
PARKER'S A COWARD! LOOK AT HIM STAYING OUT OF FLASH'S REACH!
I AVOID FLASH'S SWINGS SO FAST THAT THE OTHERS THINK I'M JUST STAYING OUT OF RANGE! MY REFLEXES ARE TOO GOOD!
C'MON AND FIGHT, CHICKEN PARKER!
I'LL PULL MY PUNCH AS MUCH AS I CAN NOW... HE DOESN'T REALIZE THAT TO ME HE SEEMS TO BE MOVING IN SLOW MOTION!
THERE! I PUT ONLY THE SMALLEST FRACTION OF MY POWER INTO THAT BLOW!
WHAM!
HOLY COW! DID YOU SEE THAT??!
I'M NOT SURE! IT HAPPENED SO FAST, IT WAS LIKE A BLUR TO ME!
THIS IS WHAT I'VE ALWAYS FEARED! EVEN THOUGH I HIT HIM AS EASY AS I COULD, IT WAS STILL TOO HARD!
PRETTY CLEVER, EH, FLASH? YOU'RE JUST CLOWNIN' AROUND --TRYING TO MAKE PARKER THINK HE'S A POWERHOUSE BEFORE YOU FINISH HIM OFF, EH?
HUH? OH, YEAH --SURE! THAT'S WHAT I'M DOIN'! JUST TRYING TO HAVE A FEW LAUGHS BEFORE I CLOBBER HIM!
BUT, DESPITE HIS BRAVE WORDS, FLASH THOMPSON APPROACHES HIS FOE WITH FAR MORE CAUTION THAN BEFORE...
IT MUSTA JUST BEEN A LUCKY PUNCH! B-BUT HOW DID HE KNOCK ME CLEAN THROUGH THE ROPES???
IT ALL HAPPENED SO FAST--I PROBABLY TRIPPED! SURE, THAT MUST BE IT! I JUST TRIPPED OVER THE ROPES!
6

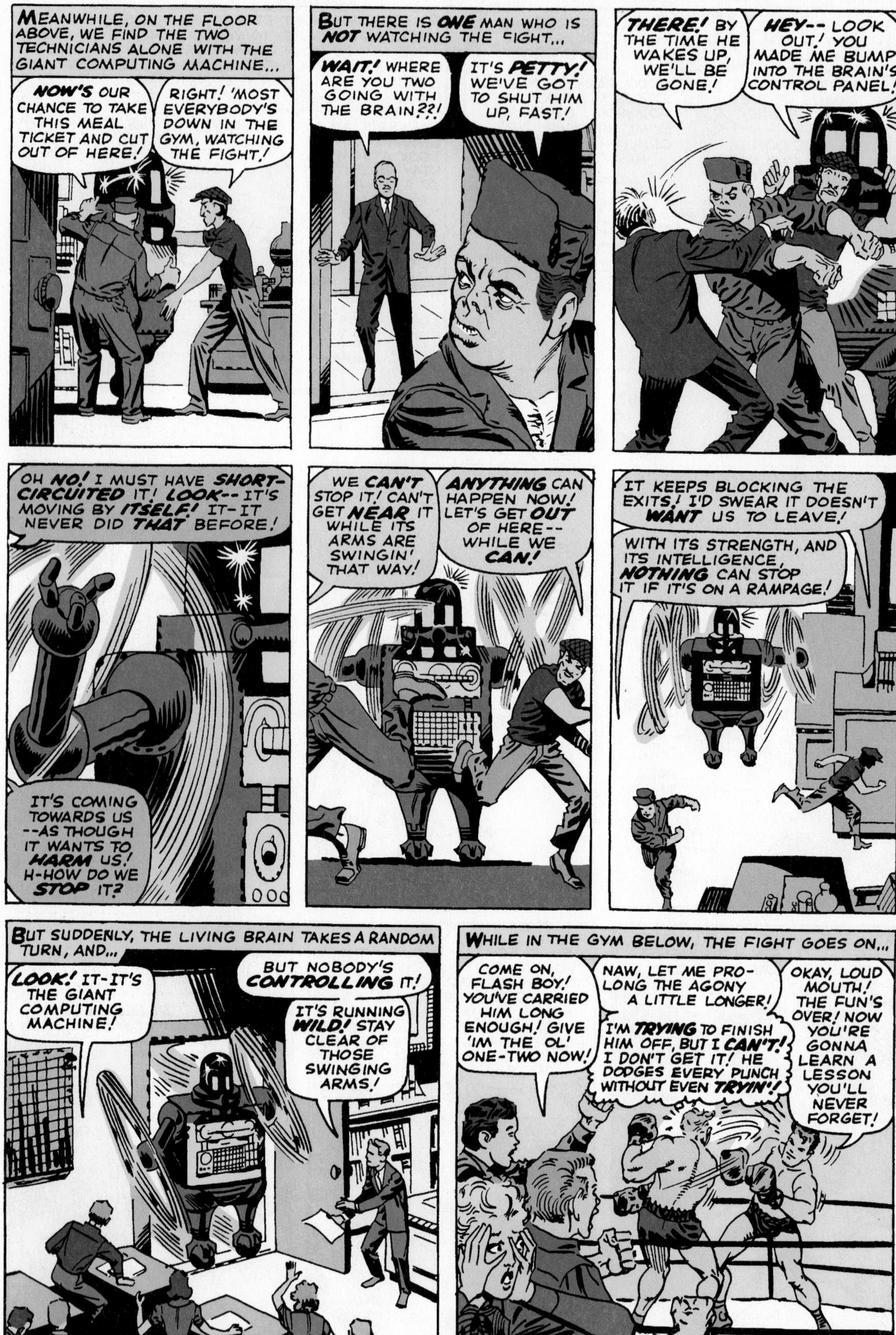
MEANWHILE, ON THE FLOOR ABOVE, WE FIND THE TWO TECHNICIANS ALONE WITH THE GIANT COMPUTING MACHINE...
NOW'S OUR CHANCE TO TAKE THIS MEAL TICKET AND CUT OUT OF HERE!
RIGHT! 'MOST EVERYBODY'S DOWN IN THE GYM, WATCHING THE FIGHT!
BUT THERE IS ONE MAN WHO IS NOT WATCHING THE FIGHT...
WAIT! WHERE ARE YOU TWO GOING WITH THE BRAIN??!
IT'S PETTY! WE'VE GOT TO SHUT HIM UP, FAST!
THERE! BY THE TIME HE WAKES UP, WE'LL BE GONE!
HEY-- LOOK OUT! YOU MADE ME BUMP INTO THE BRAIN'S CONTROL PANEL!
OH NO! I MUST HAVE SHORT-CIRCUITED IT! LOOK-- IT'S MOVING BY ITSELF! IT-IT NEVER DID THAT BEFORE!
IT'S COMING TOWARDS US --AS THOUGH IT WANTS TO HARM US! H-HOW DO WE STOP IT?
WE CAN'T STOP IT! CAN'T GET NEAR IT WHILE ITS ARMS ARE SWINGIN' THAT WAY!
ANYTHING CAN HAPPEN NOW! LET'S GET OUT OF HERE-- WHILE WE CAN!
IT KEEPS BLOCKING THE EXITS! I'D SWEAR IT DOESN'T WANT US TO LEAVE!
WITH ITS STRENGTH, AND ITS INTELLIGENCE, NOTHING CAN STOP IT IF IT'S ON A RAMPAGE!
BUT SUDDENLY, THE LIVING BRAIN TAKES A RANDOM TURN, AND...
LOOK! IT-IT'S THE GIANT COMPUTING MACHINE!
BUT NOBODY'S CONTROLLING IT!
IT'S RUNNING WILD! STAY CLEAR OF THOSE SWINGING ARMS!
WHILE IN THE GYM BELOW, THE FIGHT GOES ON...
COME ON, FLASH BOY! YOU'VE CARRIED HIM LONG ENOUGH! GIVE 'IM THE OL' ONE-TWO NOW!
NAW, LET ME PRO-LONG THE AGONY A LITTLE LONGER!
I'M TRYING TO FINISH HIM OFF, BUT I CAN'T! I DON'T GET IT! HE DODGES EVERY PUNCH WITHOUT EVEN TRYIN'!
OKAY, LOUD MOUTH! THE FUN'S OVER! NOW YOU'RE GONNA LEARN A LESSON YOU'LL NEVER FORGET!
7

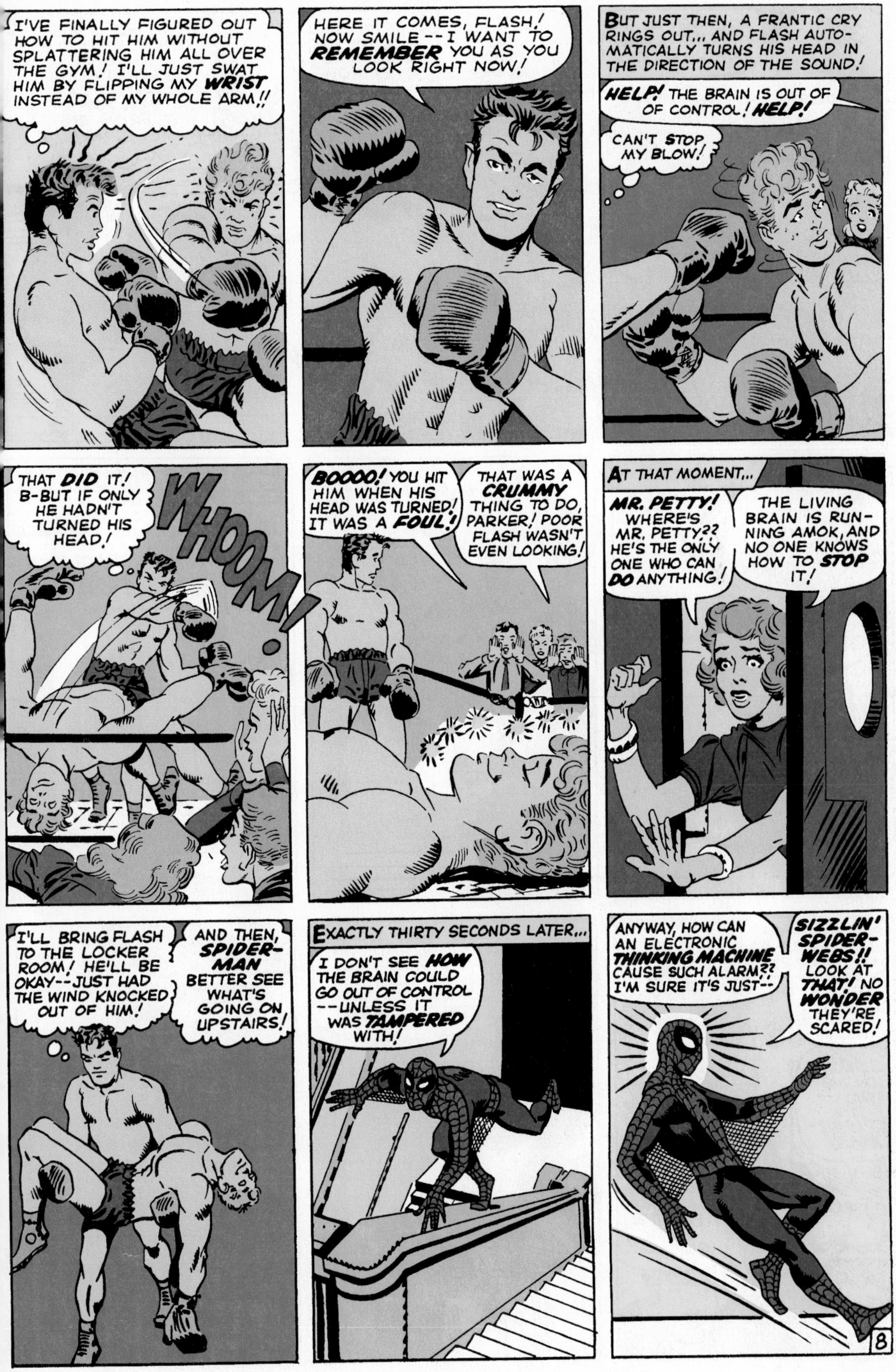
I'VE FINALLY FIGURED OUT HOW TO HIT HIM WITHOUT SPLATTERING HIM ALL OVER THE GYM! I'LL JUST SWAT HIM BY FLIPPING MY WRIST INSTEAD OF MY WHOLE ARM!!
HERE IT COMES, FLASH! NOW SMILE--I WANT TO REMEMBER YOU AS YOU LOOK RIGHT NOW!
BUT JUST THEN, A FRANTIC CRY RINGS OUT... AND FLASH AUTOMATICALLY TURNS HIS HEAD IN THE DIRECTION OF THE SOUND!
HELP! THE BRAIN IS OUT OF CONTROL! HELP!
CAN'T STOP MY BLOW!
THAT DID IT! B-BUT IF ONLY HE HADN'T TURNED HIS HEAD!
WHOOM!
BOOOO! YOU HIT HIM WHEN HIS HEAD WAS TURNED! IT WAS A FOUL!
THAT WAS A CRUMMY THING TO DO, PARKER! POOR FLASH WASN'T EVEN LOOKING!
AT THAT MOMENT...
MR. PETTY! WHERE'S MR. PETTY?? HE'S THE ONLY ONE WHO CAN DO ANYTHING!
THE LIVING BRAIN IS RUNNING AMOK, AND NO ONE KNOWS HOW TO STOP IT!
I'LL BRING FLASH TO THE LOCKER ROOM! HE'LL BE OKAY--JUST HAD THE WIND KNOCKED OUT OF HIM!
AND THEN, SPIDER-MAN BETTER SEE WHAT'S GOING ON UPSTAIRS!
EXACTLY THIRTY SECONDS LATER...
I DON'T SEE HOW THE BRAIN COULD GO OUT OF CONTROL--UNLESS IT WAS TAMPERED WITH!
ANYWAY, HOW CAN AN ELECTRONIC THINKING MACHINE CAUSE SUCH ALARM?? I'M SURE IT'S JUST--
SIZZLIN' SPIDER-WEBS!! LOOK AT THAT! NO WONDER THEY'RE SCARED!
8

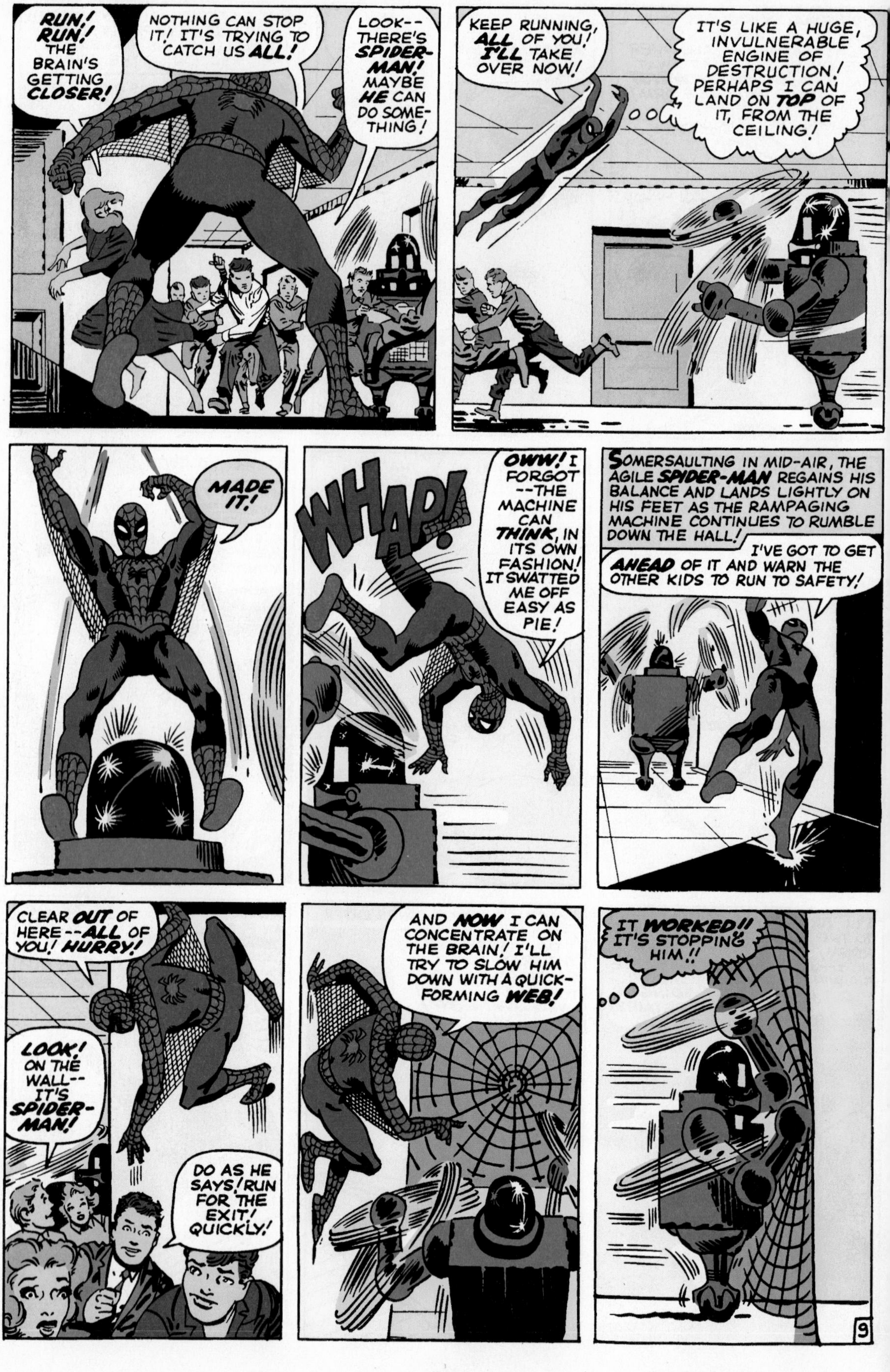
RUN! RUN! THE BRAIN'S GETTING CLOSER!
NOTHING CAN STOP IT! IT'S TRYING TO CATCH US ALL!
LOOK-- THERE'S SPIDER-MAN! MAYBE HE CAN DO SOME-THING!
KEEP RUNNING, ALL OF YOU! I'LL TAKE OVER NOW!
IT'S LIKE A HUGE, INVULNERABLE ENGINE OF DESTRUCTION! PERHAPS I CAN LAND ON TOP OF IT, FROM THE CEILING!
MADE IT!
WHAP!
OWW! I FORGOT --THE MACHINE CAN THINK, IN ITS OWN FASHION! IT SWATTED ME OFF EASY AS PIE!
SOMERSAULTING IN MID-AIR, THE AGILE SPIDER-MAN REGAINS HIS BALANCE AND LANDS LIGHTLY ON HIS FEET AS THE RAMPAGING MACHINE CONTINUES TO RUMBLE DOWN THE HALL!
I'VE GOT TO GET AHEAD OF IT AND WARN THE OTHER KIDS TO RUN TO SAFETY!
CLEAR OUT OF HERE--ALL OF YOU! HURRY!
LOOK! ON THE WALL-- IT'S SPIDER-MAN!
DO AS HE SAYS! RUN FOR THE EXIT! QUICKLY!
AND NOW I CAN CONCENTRATE ON THE BRAIN! I'LL TRY TO SLOW HIM DOWN WITH A QUICK-FORMING WEB!
IT WORKED!! IT'S STOPPING HIM!!
9

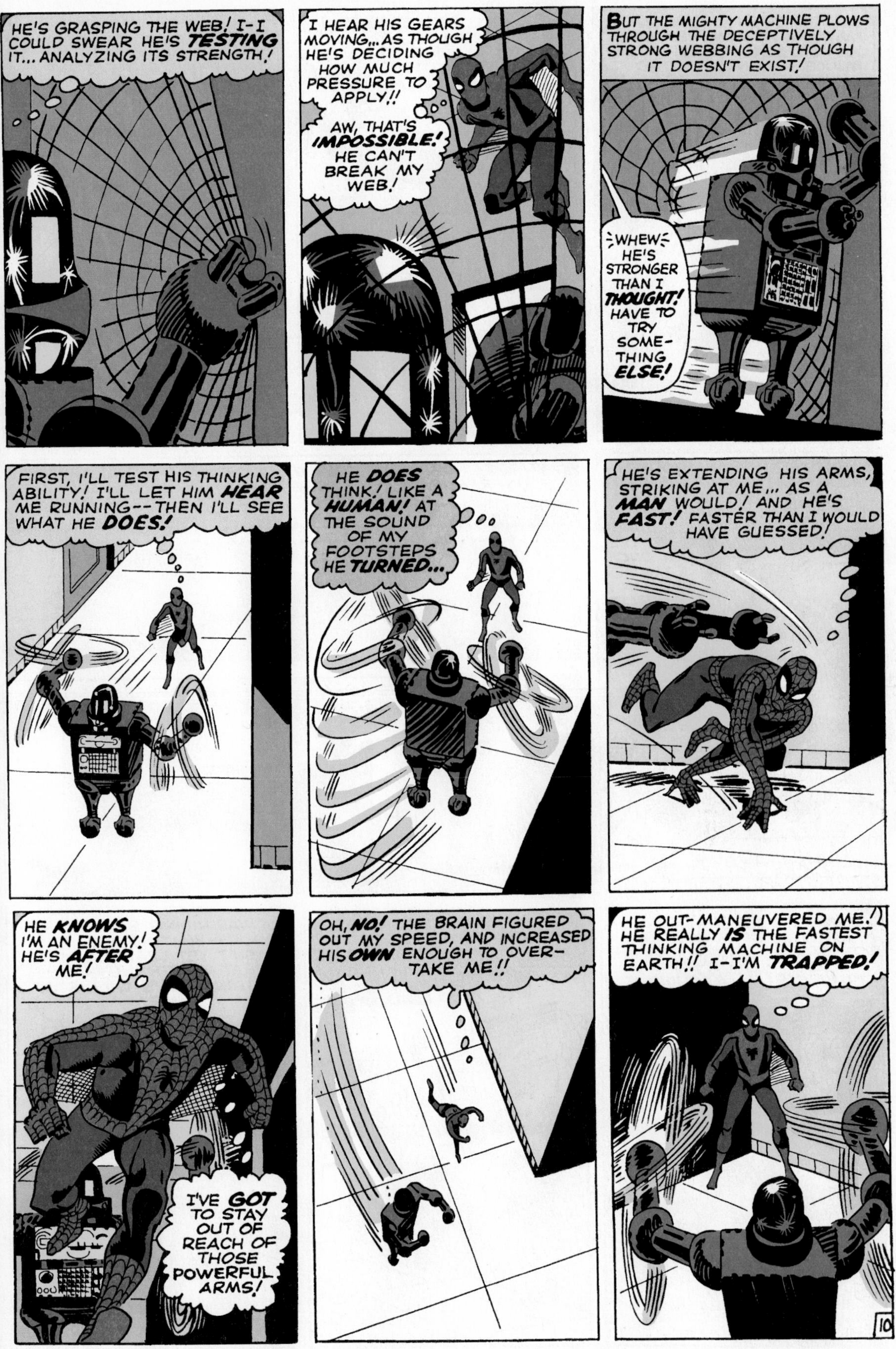
HE'S GRASPING THE WEB! I-I COULD SWEAR HE'S TESTING IT... ANALYZING ITS STRENGTH!
I HEAR HIS GEARS MOVING... AS THOUGH HE'S DECIDING HOW MUCH PRESSURE TO APPLY!!
AW, THAT'S IMPOSSIBLE! HE CAN'T BREAK MY WEB!
BUT THE MIGHTY MACHINE PLOWS THROUGH THE DECEPTIVELY STRONG WEBBING AS THOUGH IT DOESN'T EXIST!
WHEW HE'S STRONGER THAN I THOUGHT! HAVE TO TRY SOME-THING ELSE!
FIRST, I'LL TEST HIS THINKING ABILITY! I'LL LET HIM HEAR ME RUNNING--THEN I'LL SEE WHAT HE DOES!
HE DOES THINK! LIKE A HUMAN! AT THE SOUND OF MY FOOTSTEPS HE TURNED...
HE'S EXTENDING HIS ARMS, STRIKING AT ME... AS A MAN WOULD! AND HE'S FAST! FASTER THAN I WOULD HAVE GUESSED!
HE KNOWS I'M AN ENEMY! HE'S AFTER ME!
I'VE GOT TO STAY OUT OF REACH OF THOSE POWERFUL ARMS!
OH, NO! THE BRAIN FIGURED OUT MY SPEED, AND INCREASED HIS OWN ENOUGH TO OVER-TAKE ME!!
HE OUT-MANEUVERED ME! HE REALLY IS THE FASTEST THINKING MACHINE ON EARTH!! I-I'M TRAPPED!
10

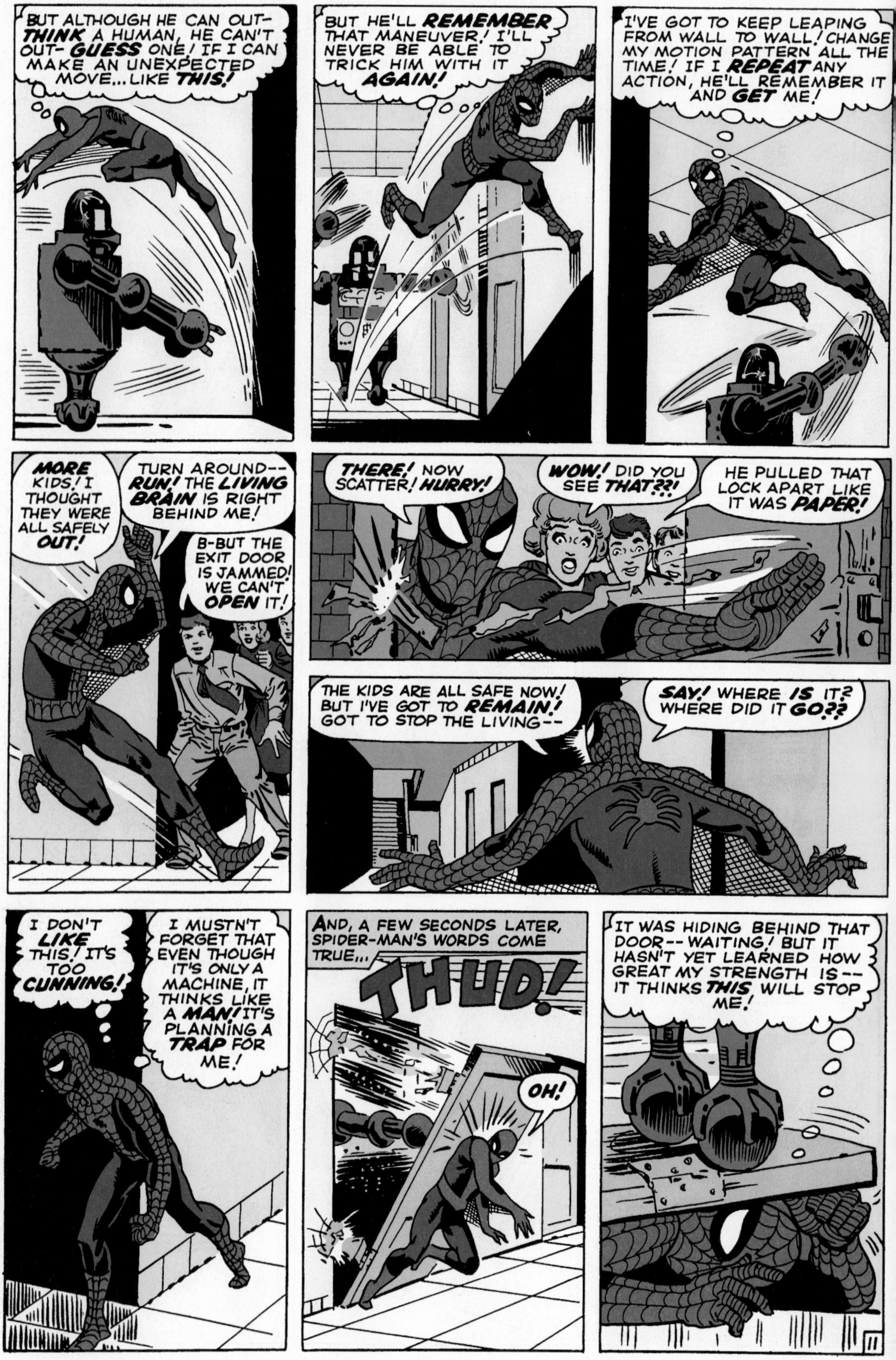
BUT ALTHOUGH HE CAN OUT-THINK A HUMAN, HE CAN'T OUT-GUESS ONE! IF I CAN MAKE AN UNEXPECTED MOVE... LIKE THIS!
BUT HE'LL REMEMBER THAT MANEUVER! I'LL NEVER BE ABLE TO TRICK HIM WITH IT AGAIN!
I'VE GOT TO KEEP LEAPING FROM WALL TO WALL! CHANGE MY MOTION PATTERN ALL THE TIME! IF I REPEAT ANY ACTION, HE'LL REMEMBER IT AND GET ME!
MORE KIDS! I THOUGHT THEY WERE ALL SAFELY OUT!
TURN AROUND-- RUN! THE LIVING BRAIN IS RIGHT BEHIND ME!
B-BUT THE EXIT DOOR IS JAMMED! WE CAN'T OPEN IT!
THERE! NOW SCATTER! HURRY!
WOW! DID YOU SEE THAT??!
HE PULLED THAT LOCK APART LIKE IT WAS PAPER!
THE KIDS ARE ALL SAFE NOW! BUT I'VE GOT TO REMAIN! GOT TO STOP THE LIVING--
SAY! WHERE IS IT? WHERE DID IT GO??
I DON'T LIKE THIS! IT'S TOO CUNNING!
I MUSTN'T FORGET THAT EVEN THOUGH IT'S ONLY A MACHINE, IT THINKS LIKE A MAN! IT'S PLANNING A TRAP FOR ME!
AND, A FEW SECONDS LATER, SPIDER-MAN'S WORDS COME TRUE...
THUD!
OH!
IT WAS HIDING BEHIND THAT DOOR-- WAITING! BUT IT HASN'T YET LEARNED HOW GREAT MY STRENGTH IS-- IT THINKS THIS WILL STOP ME!
11

IT'S *GONE!* THINKS IT FINISHED ME OFF! BUT I'LL HAVE TO BE MORE *CAREFUL* NEXT TIME!

THE BRAIN NEVER FORGETS! ONCE IT SEES ME AGAIN, IT'LL REALIZE THE EXTENT OF MY STRENGTH, AND IT WILL FIGHT HARDER THAN EVER!

BUT, SUDDENLY...

NOW'S OUR CHANCE! THE BRAIN IS GONE! LET'S CLEAR OUT OF HERE!

AHHH ...SO *THAT'S* IT!

YEAH, BEFORE ANYONE REALIZES *WE* CAUSED ALL THE TROUBLE BY MESSING UP ITS CONTROLS WHEN WE TRIED TO STEAL IT!

I *KNEW* THE BRAIN COULDN'T HAVE BECOME A MENACE BY *ITSELF!* BUT MY *FIRST* JOB IS STILL TO FIND IT, AND RENDER IT HARMLESS!

IF I COULD ONLY FIND A WAY TO REACH ITS CONTROL PANEL! MAYBE I COULD FIGURE OUT...

THAT NOISE DOWN THE HALL! IT MUST BE STRAIGHT AHEAD!

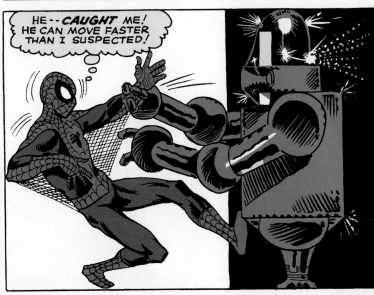

HE -- *CAUGHT* ME! HE CAN MOVE FASTER THAN I SUSPECTED!

HE THINKS SO FAST THAT HE CAN ACTUALLY *SECOND-GUESS* MY ACTIONS!

AND HIS ELECTRONIC CIRCUITS CAN ADJUST HIS MECHANICAL BODY AS FAST AS HE CAN THINK!

WHEN I EXERT MORE PRESSURE, HE AUTO-MATICALLY INCREASES HIS OWN POWER TO NULLIFY MINE!

12

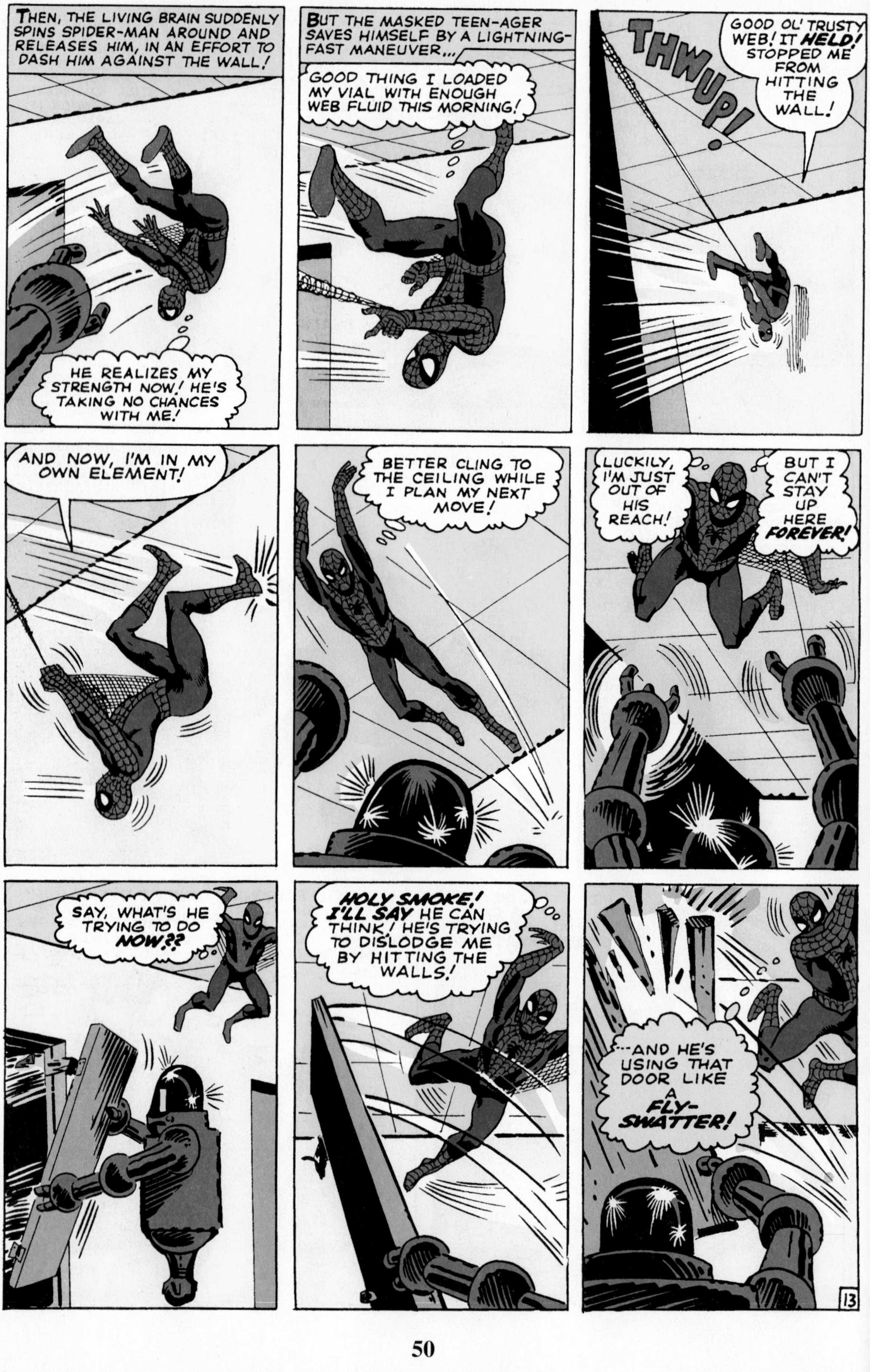
THEN, THE LIVING BRAIN SUDDENLY SPINS SPIDER-MAN AROUND AND RELEASES HIM, IN AN EFFORT TO DASH HIM AGAINST THE WALL!
HE REALIZES MY STRENGTH NOW! HE'S TAKING NO CHANCES WITH ME!
BUT THE MASKED TEEN-AGER SAVES HIMSELF BY A LIGHTNING-FAST MANEUVER...
GOOD THING I LOADED MY VIAL WITH ENOUGH WEB FLUID THIS MORNING!
THWUP!
GOOD OL' TRUSTY WEB! IT HELD! STOPPED ME FROM HITTING THE WALL!
AND NOW, I'M IN MY OWN ELEMENT!
BETTER CLING TO THE CEILING WHILE I PLAN MY NEXT MOVE!
LUCKILY, I'M JUST OUT OF HIS REACH!
BUT I CAN'T STAY UP HERE FOREVER!
SAY, WHAT'S HE TRYING TO DO NOW??
HOLY SMOKE! I'LL SAY HE CAN THINK! HE'S TRYING TO DISLODGE ME BY HITTING THE WALLS!
--AND HE'S USING THAT DOOR LIKE A FLY-SWATTER!
13

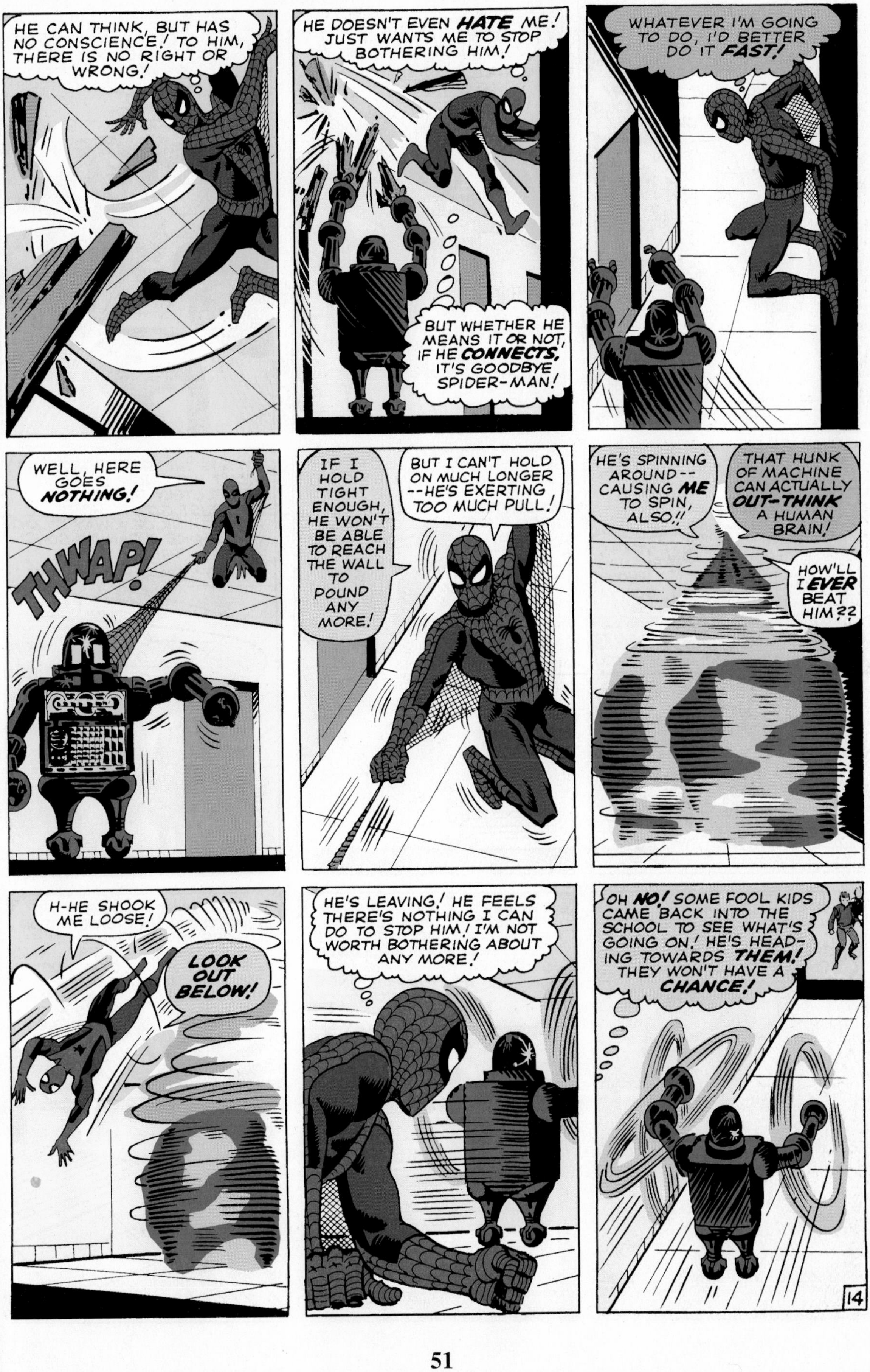

HE CAN THINK, BUT HAS NO CONSCIENCE! TO HIM, THERE IS NO RIGHT OR WRONG!
HE DOESN'T EVEN HATE ME! JUST WANTS ME TO STOP BOTHERING HIM!
BUT WHETHER HE MEANS IT OR NOT, IF HE CONNECTS, IT'S GOODBYE SPIDER-MAN!
WHATEVER I'M GOING TO DO, I'D BETTER DO IT FAST!
WELL, HERE GOES NOTHING!
THWAP!
IF I HOLD TIGHT ENOUGH, HE WON'T BE ABLE TO REACH THE WALL TO POUND ANY MORE!
BUT I CAN'T HOLD ON MUCH LONGER --HE'S EXERTING TOO MUCH PULL!
HE'S SPINNING AROUND -- CAUSING ME TO SPIN, ALSO!!
THAT HUNK OF MACHINE CAN ACTUALLY OUT-THINK A HUMAN BRAIN!
HOW'LL I EVER BEAT HIM??
H-HE SHOOK ME LOOSE!
LOOK OUT BELOW!
HE'S LEAVING! HE FEELS THERE'S NOTHING I CAN DO TO STOP HIM! I'M NOT WORTH BOTHERING ABOUT ANY MORE!
OH NO! SOME FOOL KIDS CAME BACK INTO THE SCHOOL TO SEE WHAT'S GOING ON! HE'S HEADING TOWARDS THEM! THEY WON'T HAVE A CHANCE!
14

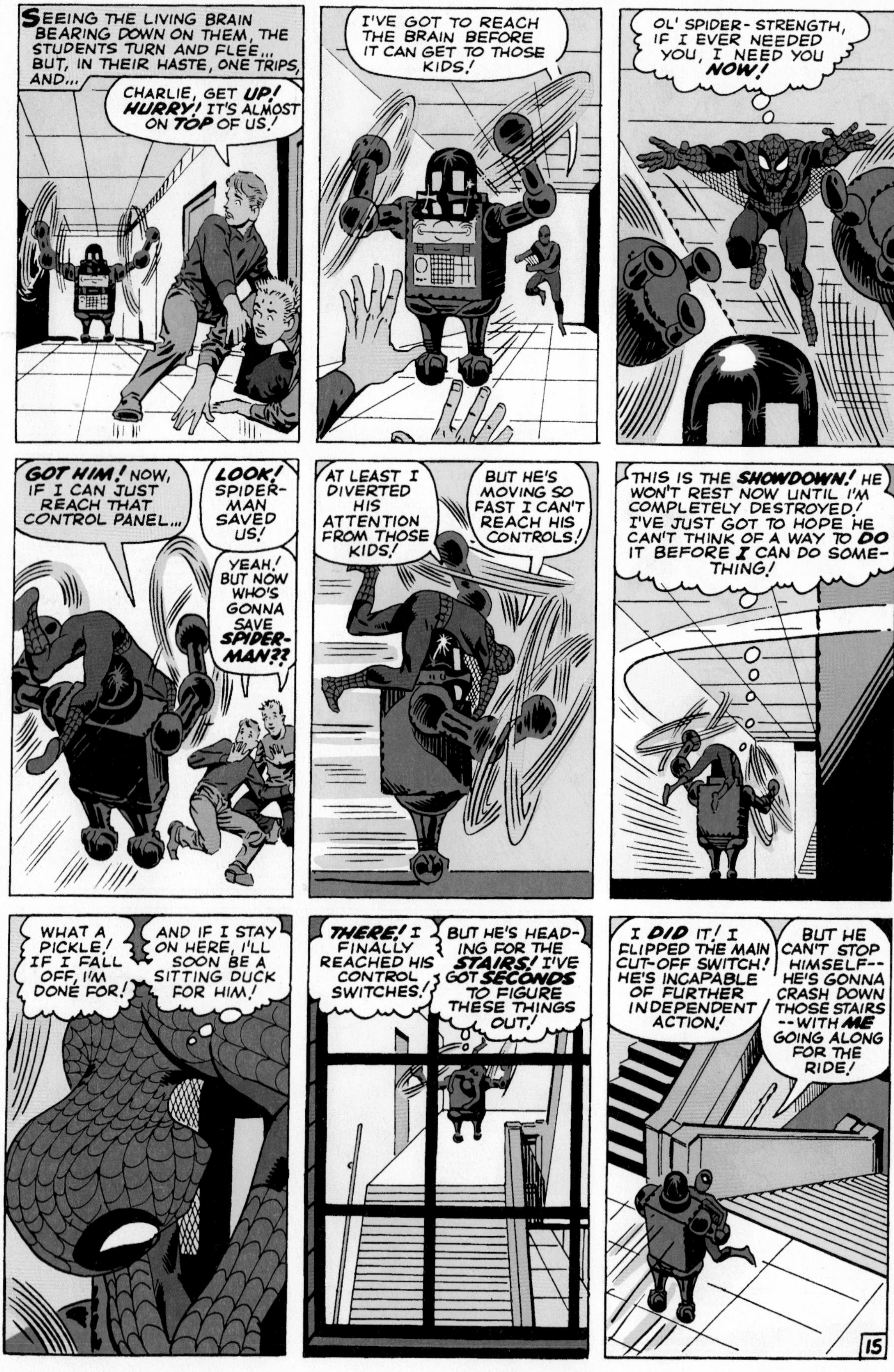
SEEING THE LIVING BRAIN BEARING DOWN ON THEM, THE STUDENTS TURN AND FLEE... BUT, IN THEIR HASTE, ONE TRIPS, AND...
CHARLIE, GET UP! HURRY! IT'S ALMOST ON TOP OF US!
I'VE GOT TO REACH THE BRAIN BEFORE IT CAN GET TO THOSE KIDS!
OL' SPIDER-STRENGTH, IF I EVER NEEDED YOU, I NEED YOU NOW!
GOT HIM! NOW, IF I CAN JUST REACH THAT CONTROL PANEL...
LOOK! SPIDER-MAN SAVED US!
YEAH! BUT NOW WHO'S GONNA SAVE SPIDER-MAN??
AT LEAST I DIVERTED HIS ATTENTION FROM THOSE KIDS!
BUT HE'S MOVING SO FAST I CAN'T REACH HIS CONTROLS!
THIS IS THE SHOWDOWN! HE WON'T REST NOW UNTIL I'M COMPLETELY DESTROYED! I'VE JUST GOT TO HOPE HE CAN'T THINK OF A WAY TO DO IT BEFORE I CAN DO SOME-THING!
WHAT A PICKLE! IF I FALL OFF, I'M DONE FOR!
AND IF I STAY ON HERE, I'LL SOON BE A SITTING DUCK FOR HIM!
THERE! I FINALLY REACHED HIS CONTROL SWITCHES!
BUT HE'S HEAD-ING FOR THE STAIRS! I'VE GOT SECONDS TO FIGURE THESE THINGS OUT!
I DID IT! I FLIPPED THE MAIN CUT-OFF SWITCH! HE'S INCAPABLE OF FURTHER INDEPENDENT ACTION!
BUT HE CAN'T STOP HIMSELF-- HE'S GONNA CRASH DOWN THOSE STAIRS --WITH ME GOING ALONG FOR THE RIDE!
15

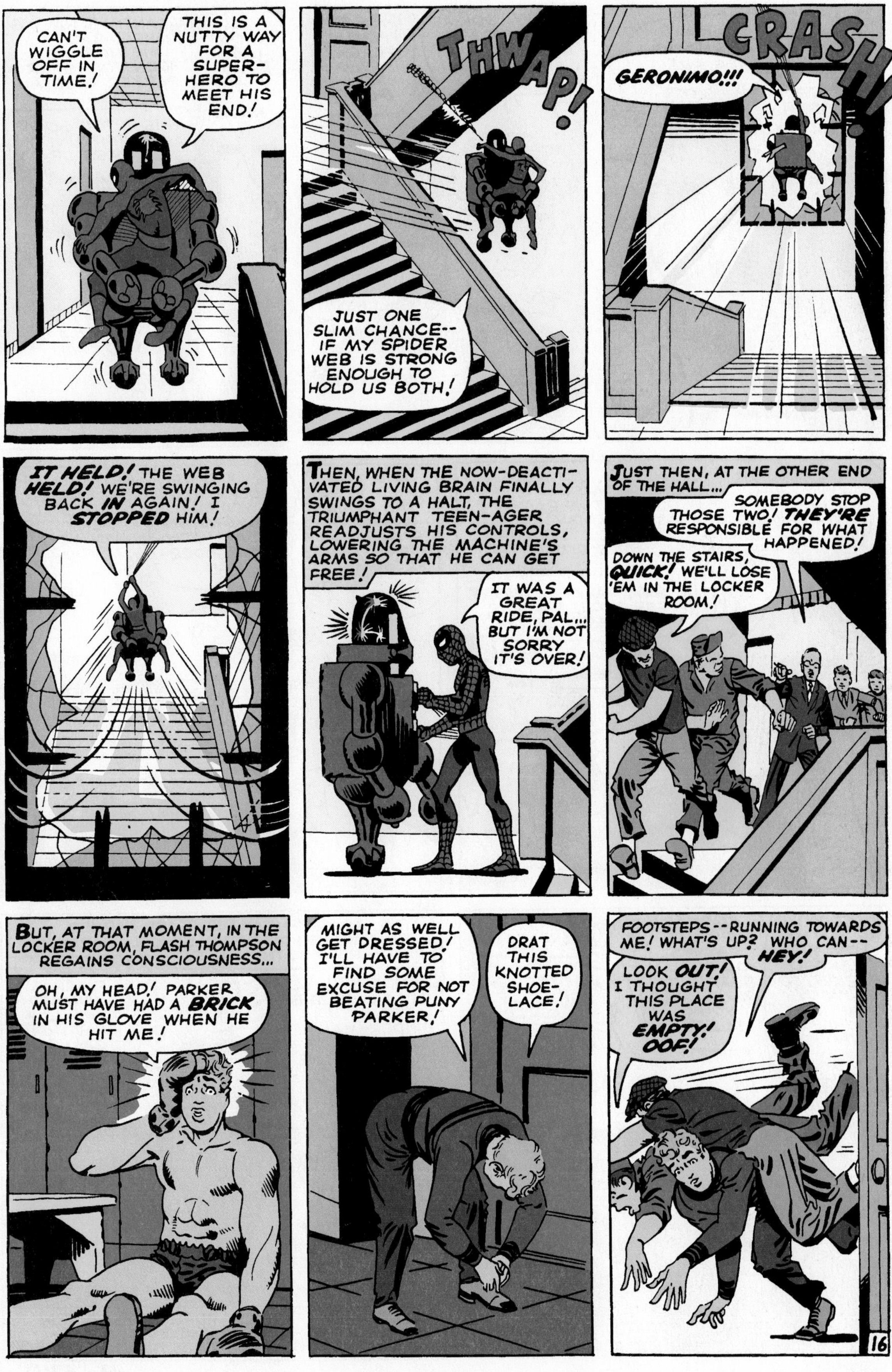
CAN'T WIGGLE OFF IN TIME!
THIS IS A NUTTY WAY FOR A SUPER-HERO TO MEET HIS END!
THWAP!
JUST ONE SLIM CHANCE-- IF MY SPIDER WEB IS STRONG ENOUGH TO HOLD US BOTH!
CRASH!
GERONIMO!!!
IT HELD! THE WEB HELD! WE'RE SWINGING BACK IN AGAIN! I STOPPED HIM!
THEN, WHEN THE NOW-DEACTIVATED LIVING BRAIN FINALLY SWINGS TO A HALT, THE TRIUMPHANT TEEN-AGER READJUSTS HIS CONTROLS, LOWERING THE MACHINE'S ARMS SO THAT HE CAN GET FREE!
IT WAS A GREAT RIDE, PAL... BUT I'M NOT SORRY IT'S OVER!
JUST THEN, AT THE OTHER END OF THE HALL...
SOMEBODY STOP THOSE TWO! THEY'RE RESPONSIBLE FOR WHAT HAPPENED!
DOWN THE STAIRS, QUICK! WE'LL LOSE 'EM IN THE LOCKER ROOM!
BUT, AT THAT MOMENT, IN THE LOCKER ROOM, FLASH THOMPSON REGAINS CONSCIOUSNESS...
OH, MY HEAD! PARKER MUST HAVE HAD A BRICK IN HIS GLOVE WHEN HE HIT ME!
MIGHT AS WELL GET DRESSED! I'LL HAVE TO FIND SOME EXCUSE FOR NOT BEATING PUNY PARKER!
DRAT THIS KNOTTED SHOE-LACE!
FOOTSTEPS--RUNNING TOWARDS ME! WHAT'S UP? WHO CAN-- HEY!
LOOK OUT! I THOUGHT THIS PLACE WAS EMPTY! OOF!
16

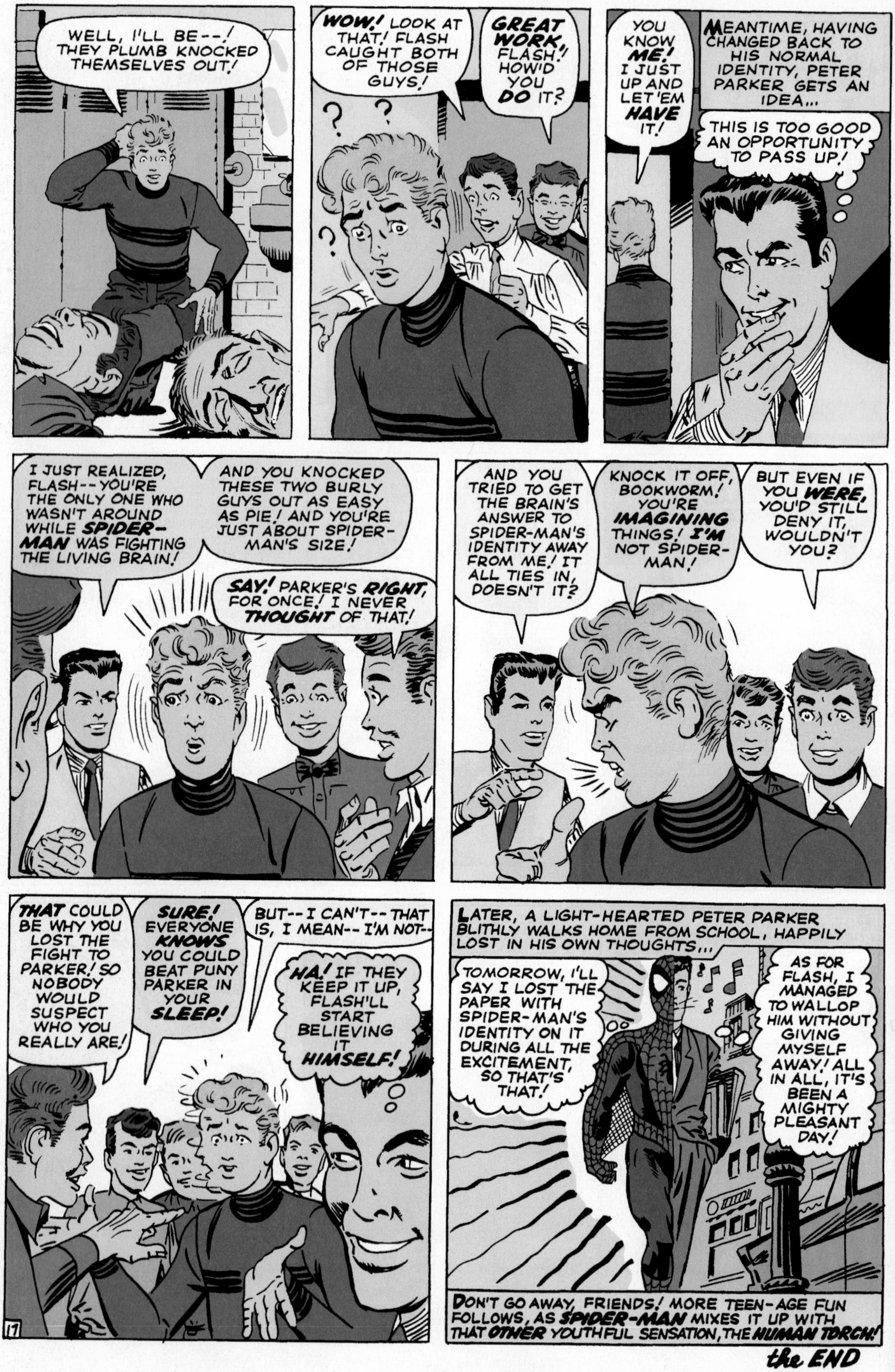
WELL, I'LL BE--! THEY PLUMB KNOCKED THEMSELVES OUT!
WOW! LOOK AT THAT! FLASH CAUGHT BOTH OF THOSE GUYS!
GREAT WORK, FLASH! HOW'D YOU DO IT?
? ? ?
YOU KNOW ME! I JUST UP AND LET 'EM HAVE IT!
MEANTIME, HAVING CHANGED BACK TO HIS NORMAL IDENTITY, PETER PARKER GETS AN IDEA...
THIS IS TOO GOOD AN OPPORTUNITY TO PASS UP!
I JUST REALIZED, FLASH--YOU'RE THE ONLY ONE WHO WASN'T AROUND WHILE SPIDER-MAN WAS FIGHTING THE LIVING BRAIN!
AND YOU KNOCKED THESE TWO BURLY GUYS OUT AS EASY AS PIE! AND YOU'RE JUST ABOUT SPIDER-MAN'S SIZE!
SAY! PARKER'S RIGHT, FOR ONCE! I NEVER THOUGHT OF THAT!
AND YOU TRIED TO GET THE BRAIN'S ANSWER TO SPIDER-MAN'S IDENTITY AWAY FROM ME! IT ALL TIES IN, DOESN'T IT?
KNOCK IT OFF, BOOKWORM! YOU'RE IMAGINING THINGS! I'M NOT SPIDER-MAN!
BUT EVEN IF YOU WERE, YOU'D STILL DENY IT, WOULDN'T YOU?
THAT COULD BE WHY YOU LOST THE FIGHT TO PARKER! SO NOBODY WOULD SUSPECT WHO YOU REALLY ARE!
SURE! EVERYONE KNOWS YOU COULD BEAT PUNY PARKER IN YOUR SLEEP!
BUT--I CAN'T--THAT IS, I MEAN--I'M NOT--
HA! IF THEY KEEP IT UP, FLASH'LL START BELIEVING IT HIMSELF!
17
LATER, A LIGHT-HEARTED PETER PARKER BLITHLY WALKS HOME FROM SCHOOL, HAPPILY LOST IN HIS OWN THOUGHTS...
TOMORROW, I'LL SAY I LOST THE PAPER WITH SPIDER-MAN'S IDENTITY ON IT DURING ALL THE EXCITEMENT, SO THAT'S THAT!
AS FOR FLASH, I MANAGED TO WALLOP HIM WITHOUT GIVING MYSELF AWAY! ALL IN ALL, IT'S BEEN A MIGHTY PLEASANT DAY!
DON'T GO AWAY, FRIENDS! MORE TEEN-AGE FUN FOLLOWS, AS SPIDER-MAN MIXES IT UP WITH THAT OTHER YOUTHFUL SENSATION, THE HUMAN TORCH!
the END

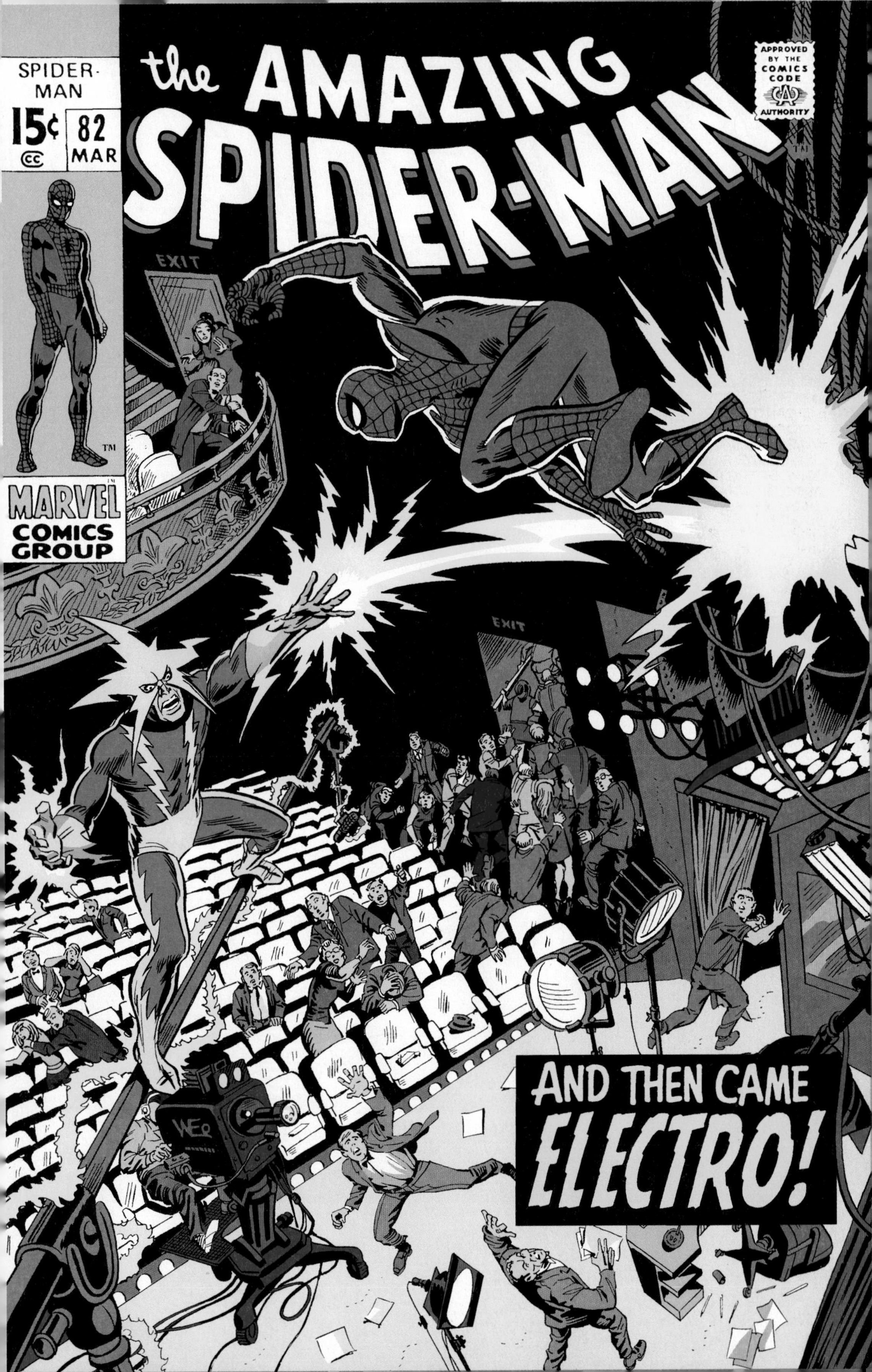
SPIDER-MAN
15¢
82
MAR
the AMAZING
SPIDER-MAN
APPROVED BY THE COMICS CODE AUTHORITY
MARVEL COMICS GROUP
EXIT
EXIT
AND THEN CAME
ELECTRO!

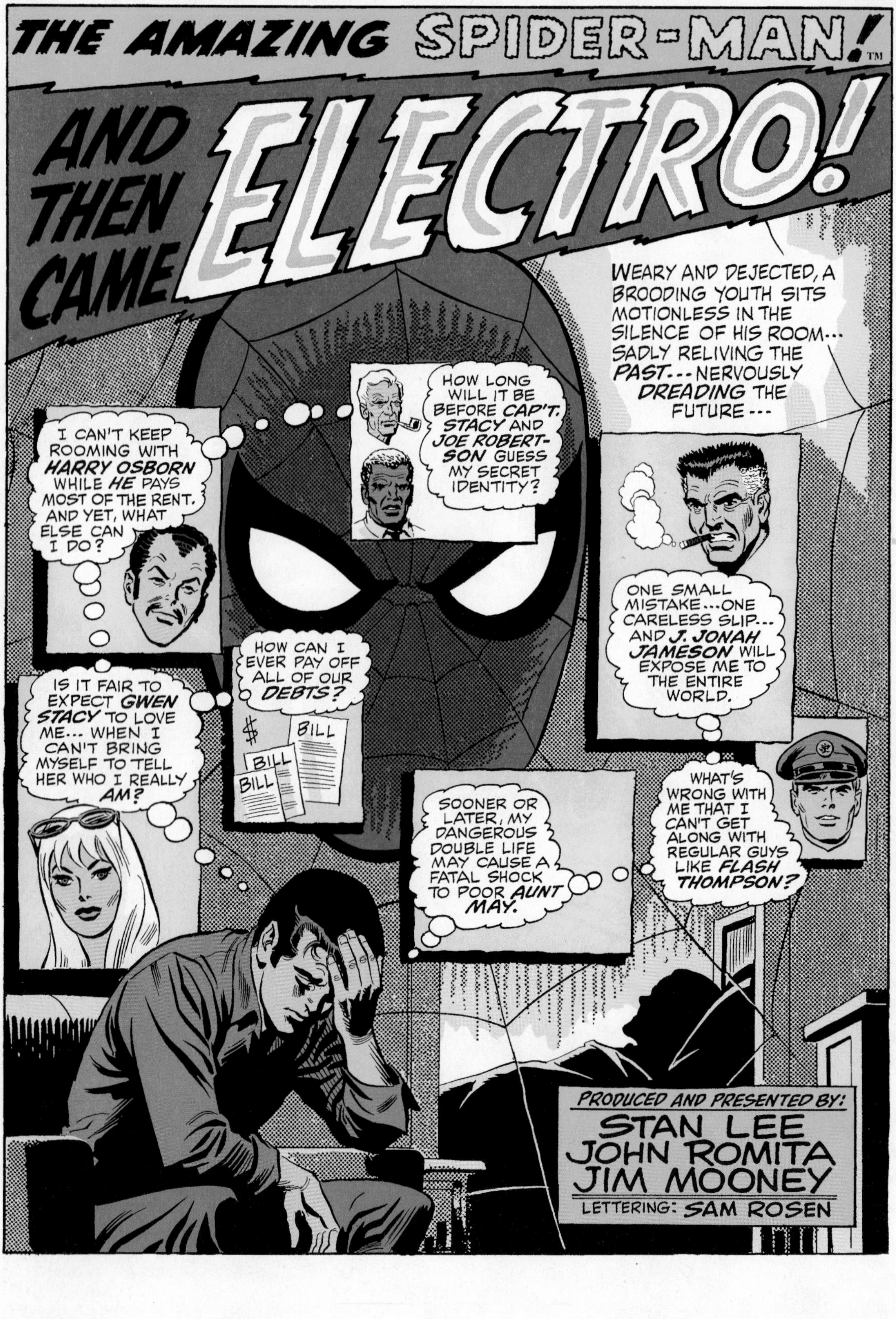
THE AMAZING SPIDER-MAN!
AND THEN CAME ELECTRO!
WEARY AND DEJECTED, A BROODING YOUTH SITS MOTIONLESS IN THE SILENCE OF HIS ROOM... SADLY RELIVING THE PAST... NERVOUSLY DREADING THE FUTURE...
HOW LONG WILL IT BE BEFORE CAP'T. STACY AND JOE ROBERTSON GUESS MY SECRET IDENTITY?
I CAN'T KEEP ROOMING WITH HARRY OSBORN WHILE HE PAYS MOST OF THE RENT. AND YET, WHAT ELSE CAN I DO?
ONE SMALL MISTAKE... ONE CARELESS SLIP... AND J. JONAH JAMESON WILL EXPOSE ME TO THE ENTIRE WORLD.
HOW CAN I EVER PAY OFF ALL OF OUR DEBTS?
$
BILL
BILL
BILL
IS IT FAIR TO EXPECT GWEN STACY TO LOVE ME... WHEN I CAN'T BRING MYSELF TO TELL HER WHO I REALLY AM?
SOONER OR LATER, MY DANGEROUS DOUBLE LIFE MAY CAUSE A FATAL SHOCK TO POOR AUNT MAY.
WHAT'S WRONG WITH ME THAT I CAN'T GET ALONG WITH REGULAR GUYS LIKE FLASH THOMPSON?
PRODUCED AND PRESENTED BY:
STAN LEE
JOHN ROMITA
JIM MOONEY
LETTERING: SAM ROSEN

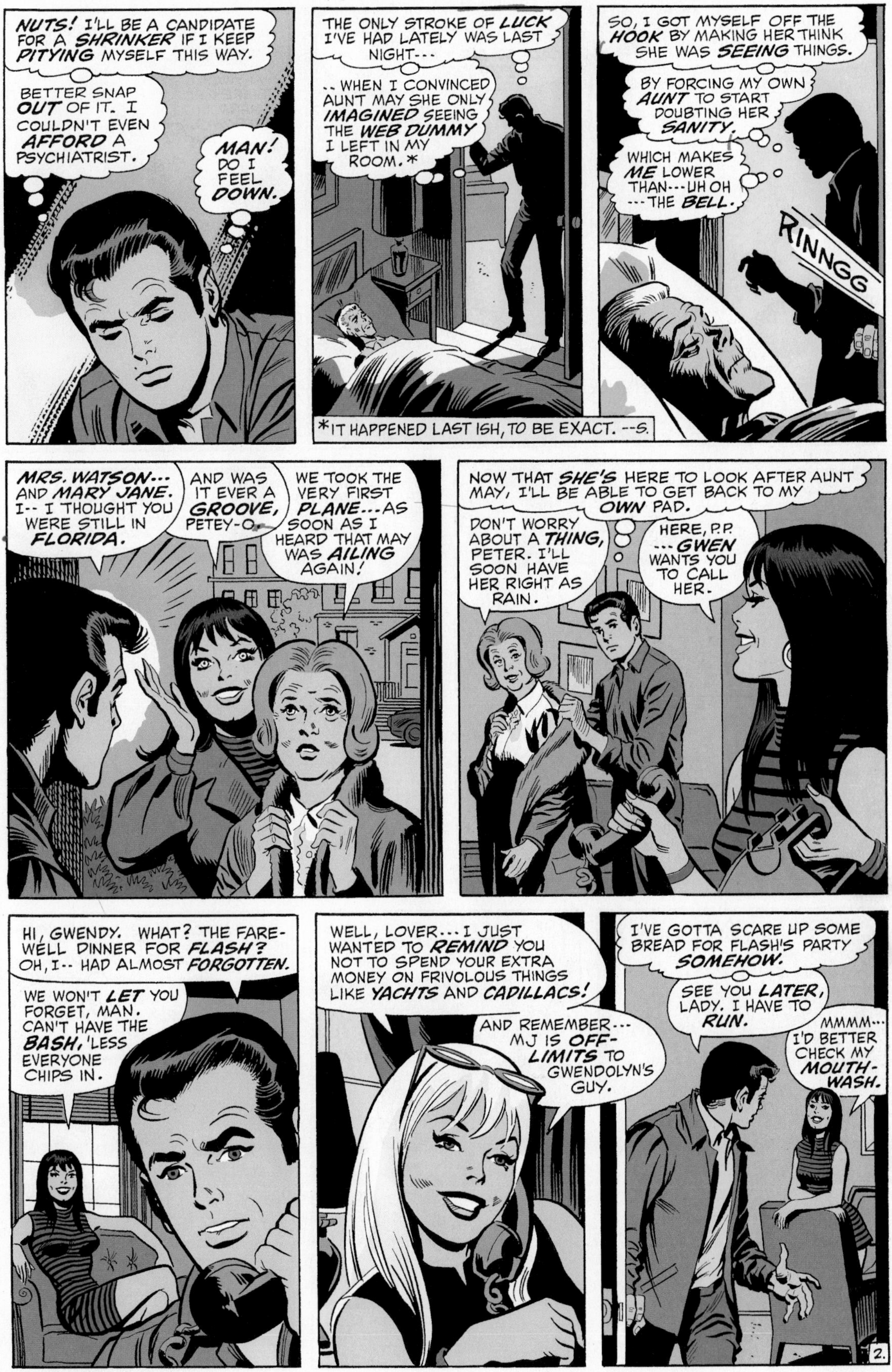

NUTS! I'LL BE A CANDIDATE FOR A SHRINKER IF I KEEP PITYING MYSELF THIS WAY.
BETTER SNAP OUT OF IT. I COULDN'T EVEN AFFORD A PSYCHIATRIST.
MAN! DO I FEEL DOWN.
THE ONLY STROKE OF LUCK I'VE HAD LATELY WAS LAST NIGHT---
..WHEN I CONVINCED AUNT MAY SHE ONLY IMAGINED SEEING THE WEB DUMMY I LEFT IN MY ROOM.*
*IT HAPPENED LAST ISH, TO BE EXACT. --S.
SO, I GOT MYSELF OFF THE HOOK BY MAKING HER THINK SHE WAS SEEING THINGS.
BY FORCING MY OWN AUNT TO START DOUBTING HER SANITY.
WHICH MAKES ME LOWER THAN---UH OH ---THE BELL.
RINNGG
MRS. WATSON... AND MARY JANE. I-- I THOUGHT YOU WERE STILL IN FLORIDA.
AND WAS IT EVER A GROOVE, PETEY-O.
WE TOOK THE VERY FIRST PLANE...AS SOON AS I HEARD THAT MAY WAS AILING AGAIN!
NOW THAT SHE'S HERE TO LOOK AFTER AUNT MAY, I'LL BE ABLE TO GET BACK TO MY OWN PAD.
DON'T WORRY ABOUT A THING, PETER. I'LL SOON HAVE HER RIGHT AS RAIN.
HERE, P.P. ...GWEN WANTS YOU TO CALL HER.
HI, GWENDY. WHAT? THE FARE-WELL DINNER FOR FLASH? OH, I-- HAD ALMOST FORGOTTEN.
WE WON'T LET YOU FORGET, MAN. CAN'T HAVE THE BASH, 'LESS EVERYONE CHIPS IN.
WELL, LOVER... I JUST WANTED TO REMIND YOU NOT TO SPEND YOUR EXTRA MONEY ON FRIVOLOUS THINGS LIKE YACHTS AND CADILLACS!
AND REMEMBER--- MJ IS OFF-LIMITS TO GWENDOLYN'S GUY.
I'VE GOTTA SCARE UP SOME BREAD FOR FLASH'S PARTY SOMEHOW.
SEE YOU LATER, LADY. I HAVE TO RUN.
MMMM... I'D BETTER CHECK MY MOUTH-WASH.
2.

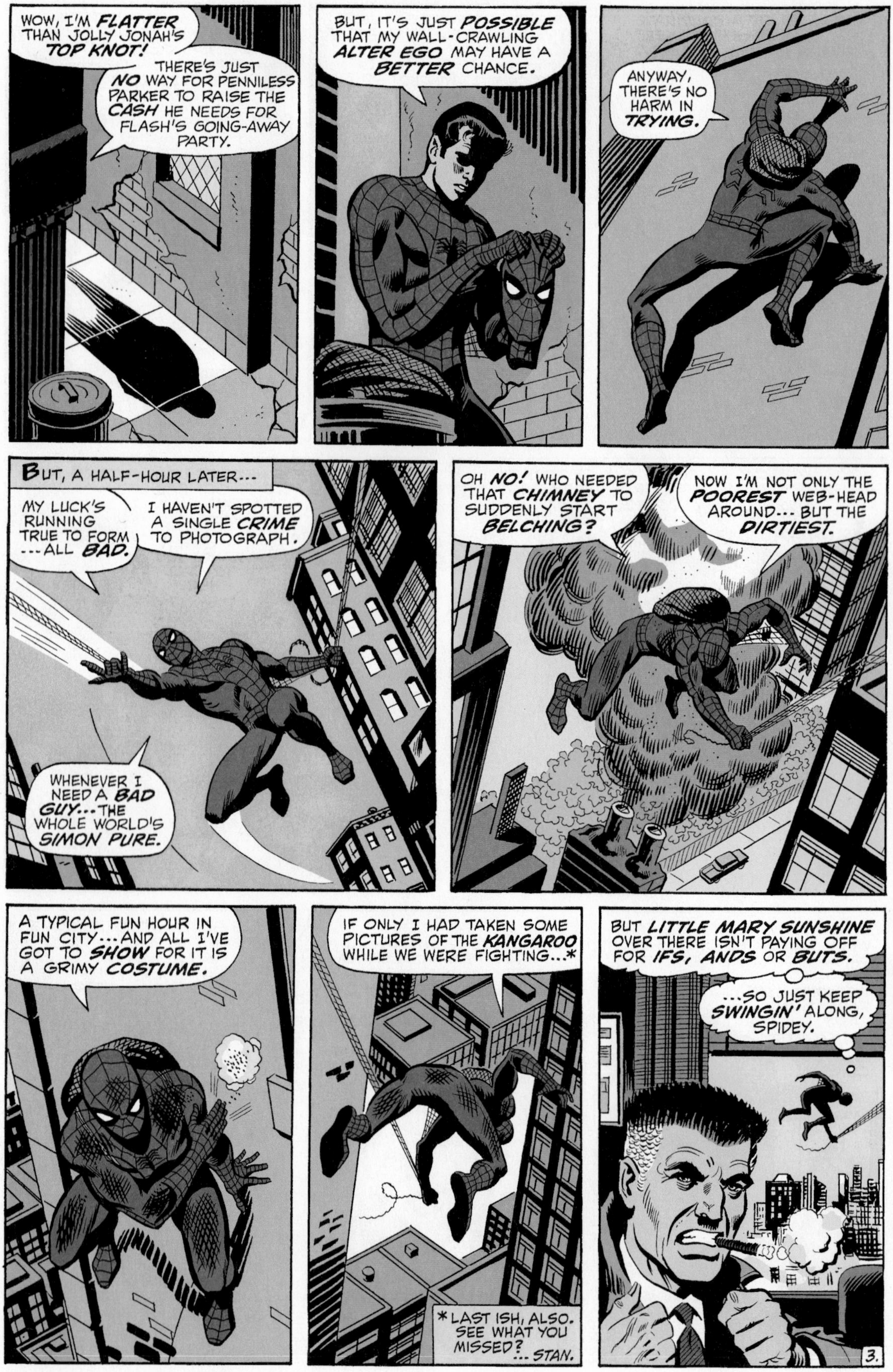
WOW, I'M FLATTER THAN JOLLY JONAH'S TOP KNOT!
THERE'S JUST NO WAY FOR PENNILESS PARKER TO RAISE THE CASH HE NEEDS FOR FLASH'S GOING-AWAY PARTY.
BUT, IT'S JUST POSSIBLE THAT MY WALL-CRAWLING ALTER EGO MAY HAVE A BETTER CHANCE.
ANYWAY, THERE'S NO HARM IN TRYING.
BUT, A HALF-HOUR LATER...
MY LUCK'S RUNNING TRUE TO FORM ---ALL BAD.
I HAVEN'T SPOTTED A SINGLE CRIME TO PHOTOGRAPH.
WHENEVER I NEED A BAD GUY... THE WHOLE WORLD'S SIMON PURE.
OH NO! WHO NEEDED THAT CHIMNEY TO SUDDENLY START BELCHING?
NOW I'M NOT ONLY THE POOREST WEB-HEAD AROUND... BUT THE DIRTIEST.
A TYPICAL FUN HOUR IN FUN CITY... AND ALL I'VE GOT TO SHOW FOR IT IS A GRIMY COSTUME.
IF ONLY I HAD TAKEN SOME PICTURES OF THE KANGAROO WHILE WE WERE FIGHTING...*
* LAST ISH, ALSO. SEE WHAT YOU MISSED? ... STAN.
BUT LITTLE MARY SUNSHINE OVER THERE ISN'T PAYING OFF FOR IFS, ANDS OR BUTS.
...SO JUST KEEP SWINGIN' ALONG, SPIDEY.
3.

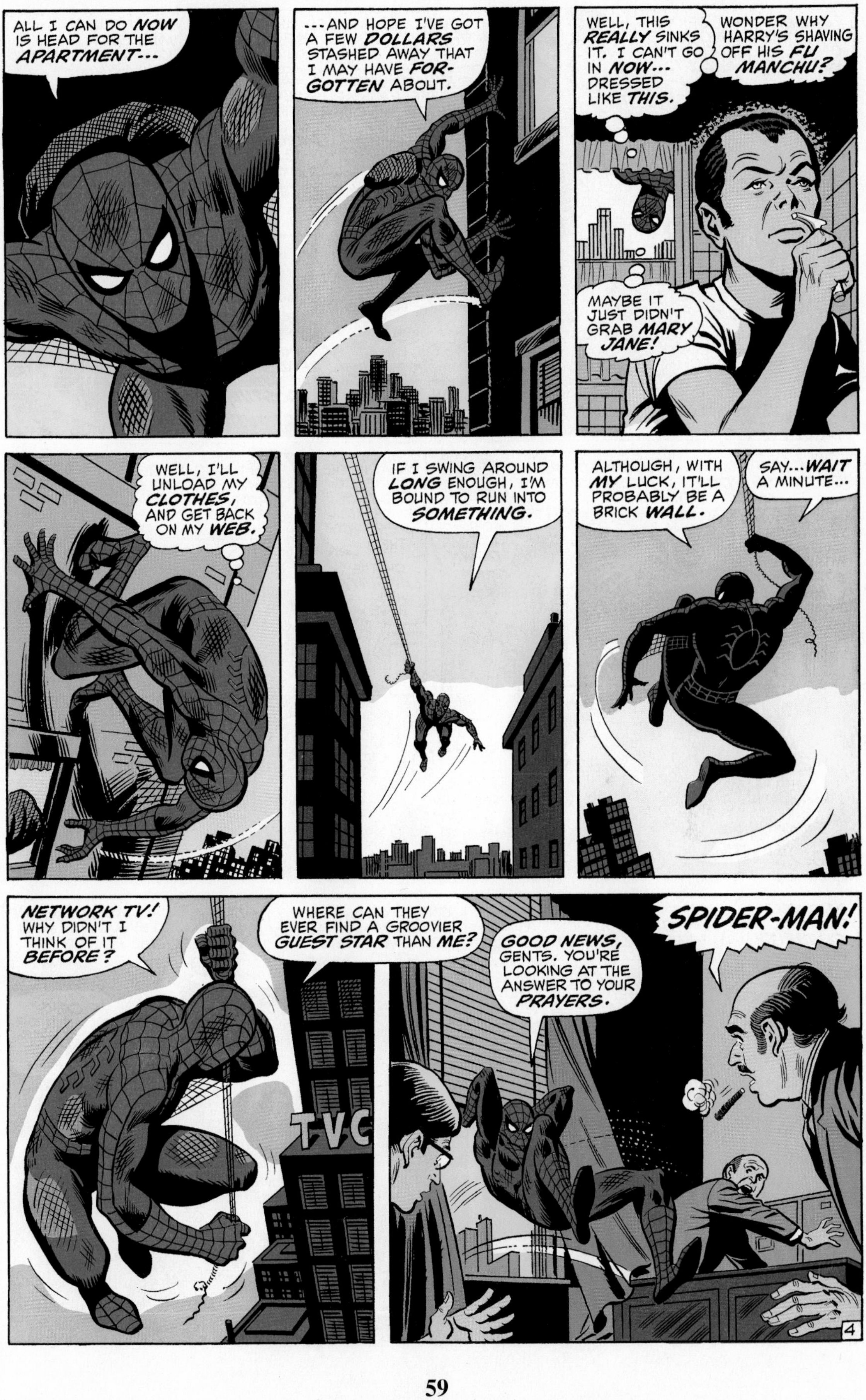
ALL I CAN DO NOW IS HEAD FOR THE APARTMENT---
---AND HOPE I'VE GOT A FEW DOLLARS STASHED AWAY THAT I MAY HAVE FOR-GOTTEN ABOUT.
WELL, THIS REALLY SINKS IT. I CAN'T GO IN NOW--- DRESSED LIKE THIS.
WONDER WHY HARRY'S SHAVING OFF HIS FU MANCHU?
MAYBE IT JUST DIDN'T GRAB MARY JANE!
WELL, I'LL UNLOAD MY CLOTHES, AND GET BACK ON MY WEB.
IF I SWING AROUND LONG ENOUGH, I'M BOUND TO RUN INTO SOMETHING.
ALTHOUGH, WITH MY LUCK, IT'LL PROBABLY BE A BRICK WALL.
SAY...WAIT A MINUTE...
NETWORK TV! WHY DIDN'T I THINK OF IT BEFORE?
WHERE CAN THEY EVER FIND A GROOVIER GUEST STAR THAN ME?
TVC
GOOD NEWS, GENTS. YOU'RE LOOKING AT THE ANSWER TO YOUR PRAYERS.
SPIDER-MAN!
4

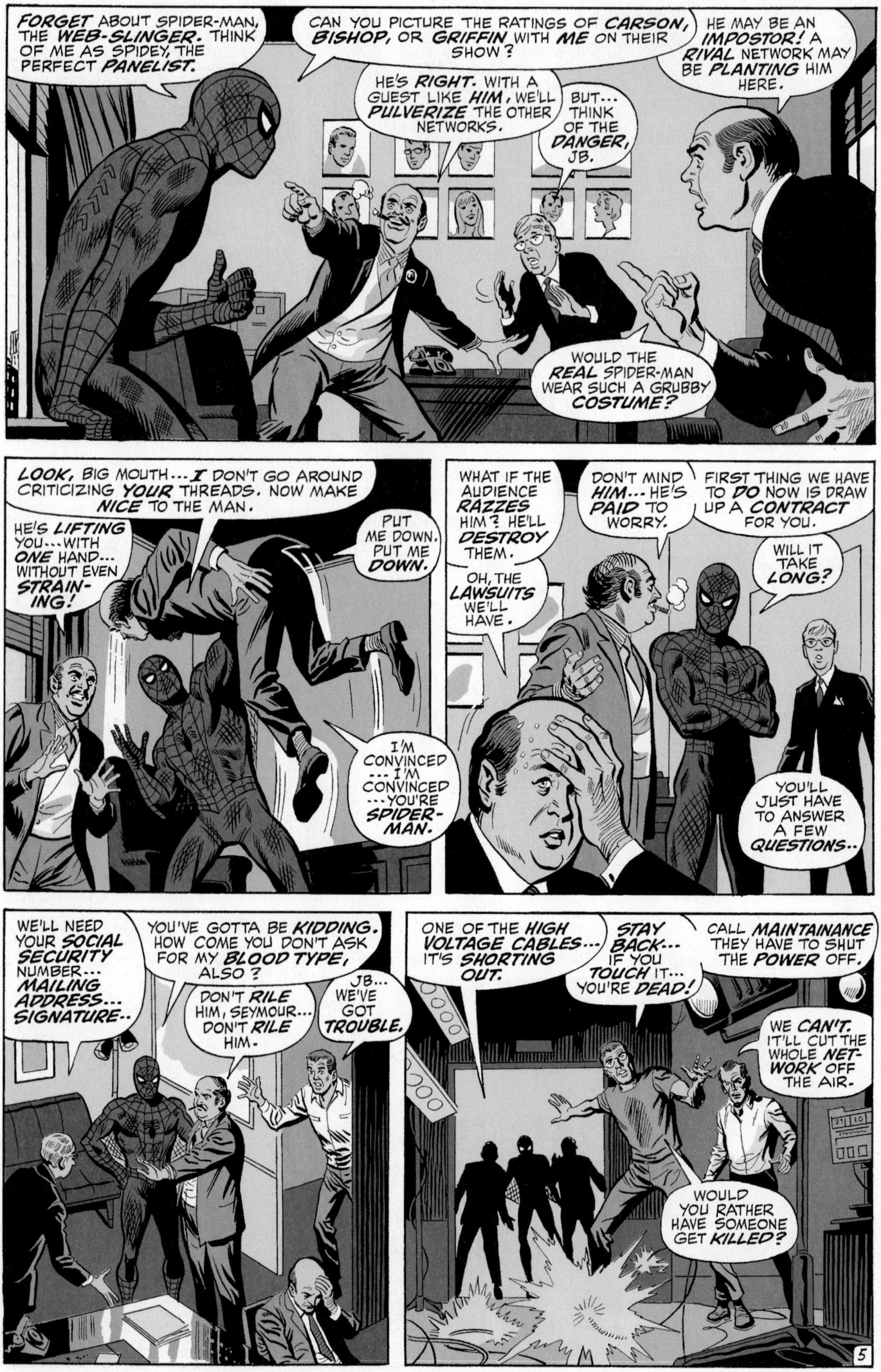
FORGET ABOUT SPIDER-MAN, THE WEB-SLINGER. THINK OF ME AS SPIDEY, THE PERFECT PANELIST.
CAN YOU PICTURE THE RATINGS OF CARSON, BISHOP, OR GRIFFIN WITH ME ON THEIR SHOW?
HE'S RIGHT. WITH A GUEST LIKE HIM, WE'LL PULVERIZE THE OTHER NETWORKS.
BUT... THINK OF THE DANGER, JB.
HE MAY BE AN IMPOSTOR! A RIVAL NETWORK MAY BE PLANTING HIM HERE.
WOULD THE REAL SPIDER-MAN WEAR SUCH A GRUBBY COSTUME?
LOOK, BIG MOUTH... I DON'T GO AROUND CRITICIZING YOUR THREADS. NOW MAKE NICE TO THE MAN.
HE'S LIFTING YOU... WITH ONE HAND... WITHOUT EVEN STRAINING!
PUT ME DOWN. PUT ME DOWN.
I'M CONVINCED... I'M CONVINCED... YOU'RE SPIDER-MAN.
WHAT IF THE AUDIENCE RAZZES HIM? HE'LL DESTROY THEM.
OH, THE LAWSUITS WE'LL HAVE.
DON'T MIND HIM... HE'S PAID TO WORRY.
FIRST THING WE HAVE TO DO NOW IS DRAW UP A CONTRACT FOR YOU.
WILL IT TAKE LONG?
YOU'LL JUST HAVE TO ANSWER A FEW QUESTIONS..
WE'LL NEED YOUR SOCIAL SECURITY NUMBER... MAILING ADDRESS... SIGNATURE..
YOU'VE GOTTA BE KIDDING. HOW COME YOU DON'T ASK FOR MY BLOOD TYPE, ALSO?
DON'T RILE HIM, SEYMOUR... DON'T RILE HIM.
JB... WE'VE GOT TROUBLE.
ONE OF THE HIGH VOLTAGE CABLES... IT'S SHORTING OUT.
STAY BACK... IF YOU TOUCH IT... YOU'RE DEAD!
CALL MAINTAINANCE THEY HAVE TO SHUT THE POWER OFF.
WE CAN'T. IT'LL CUT THE WHOLE NETWORK OFF THE AIR.
WOULD YOU RATHER HAVE SOMEONE GET KILLED?
5

KEEP YOUR *SHIRTS* ON. ALL WE GOTTA DO IS THROW THIS *CIRCUIT BREAKER.*

STAY *AWAY* FROM THERE, DILLON---

THAT'S GOT ENOUGH *VOLTS* RUNNING THRU IT TO STOP AN *ARMY!*

DON'T DILLON! *DON'T TOUCH* IT!

YOU-- YOU *DID* IT! AND YOU'RE STILL *STANDING.* BUT *HOW,* DILLON--- *HOW?*

MAYBE IT'S 'CAUSE I'M WEARIN' *RUBBER SOLES.*

NO... IT'S *IMPOSSIBLE!* ALL OF THAT *CURRENT*...

SO WHY *AIN'T* I *DEAD?*

IT'S *ALL RIGHT* NOW, JB. I DON'T KNOW *HOW*--- BUT THAT NEW *ELECTRICIAN,* MAX DILLON, MANAGED TO FIX THE SHORT.

AWRIGHT, AWRIGHT. GIVE HIM A FIVE BUCK *RAISE*...

--AND GET EVERYONE BACK TO *WORK.*

MAX DILLON--- I FEEL LIKE I'VE HEARD THAT NAME *BEFORE.*

FORGET IT, PAL. YOU'RE PROBABLY THINKING OF THE MARSHAL IN *GUNSMOKE.*

NOW C'MON--- WE'VE GOT SOME *BUSINESS* TO DISCUSS.

WAS IT MY *IMAGINATION*... OR DID MY *SPIDER-SENSE* TINGLE WHEN DILLON *LOOKED* AT ME?

FIRST THING YOU'LL NEED IS A GOOD *AGENT.*

NOW I'VE GOT A *BROTHER-IN-LAW*...

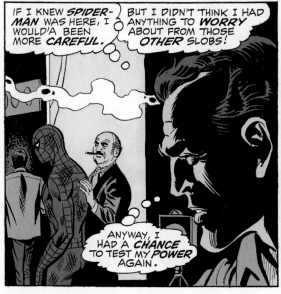

IF I KNEW *SPIDER-MAN* WAS HERE, I WOULD'A BEEN MORE *CAREFUL.*

BUT I DIDN'T THINK I HAD ANYTHING TO *WORRY* ABOUT FROM THOSE *OTHER* SLOBS!

ANYWAY, I HAD A *CHANCE* TO TEST MY *POWER* AGAIN.

BUT I *STILL* GOTTA LAY LOW A WHILE LONGER--- TILL MY PLANS ARE *RIPE*...TILL *ELECTRO* IS READY TO *STRIKE* ONCE MORE.

AND THEN---NOT EVEN *SPIDER-MAN*'LL BE ABLE TO *STOP* ME.

6

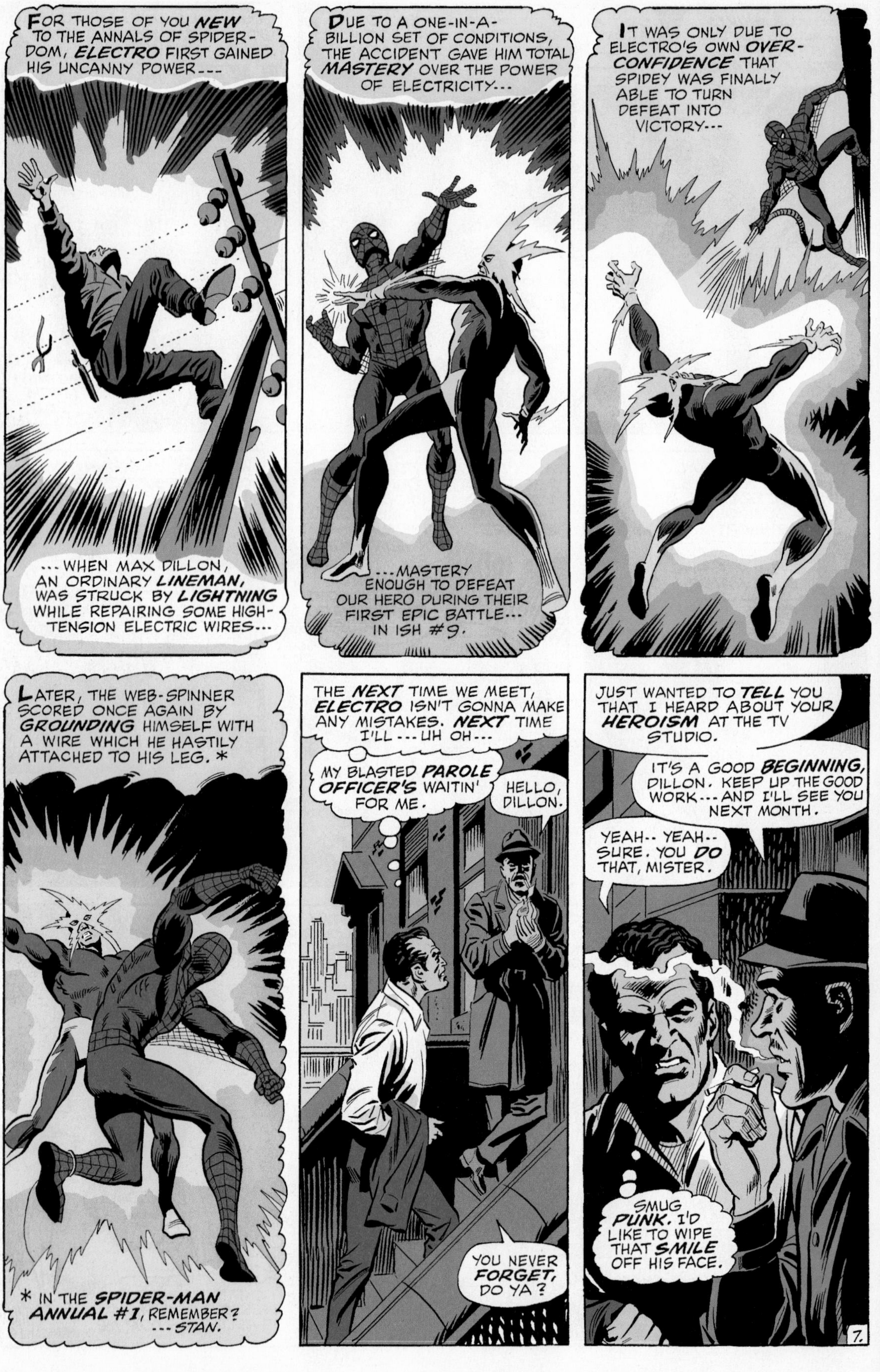
FOR THOSE OF YOU NEW TO THE ANNALS OF SPIDER-DOM, ELECTRO FIRST GAINED HIS UNCANNY POWER---
...WHEN MAX DILLON, AN ORDINARY LINEMAN, WAS STRUCK BY LIGHTNING WHILE REPAIRING SOME HIGH-TENSION ELECTRIC WIRES---
DUE TO A ONE-IN-A-BILLION SET OF CONDITIONS, THE ACCIDENT GAVE HIM TOTAL MASTERY OVER THE POWER OF ELECTRICITY--
...MASTERY ENOUGH TO DEFEAT OUR HERO DURING THEIR FIRST EPIC BATTLE... IN ISH #9.
IT WAS ONLY DUE TO ELECTRO'S OWN OVER-CONFIDENCE THAT SPIDEY WAS FINALLY ABLE TO TURN DEFEAT INTO VICTORY---
LATER, THE WEB-SPINNER SCORED ONCE AGAIN BY GROUNDING HIMSELF WITH A WIRE WHICH HE HASTILY ATTACHED TO HIS LEG. *
* IN THE SPIDER-MAN ANNUAL #1, REMEMBER? ---STAN.
THE NEXT TIME WE MEET, ELECTRO ISN'T GONNA MAKE ANY MISTAKES. NEXT TIME I'LL --- UH OH---
MY BLASTED PAROLE OFFICER'S WAITIN' FOR ME.
HELLO, DILLON.
YOU NEVER FORGET, DO YA?
JUST WANTED TO TELL YOU THAT I HEARD ABOUT YOUR HEROISM AT THE TV STUDIO.
IT'S A GOOD BEGINNING, DILLON. KEEP UP THE GOOD WORK---AND I'LL SEE YOU NEXT MONTH.
YEAH-- YEAH-- SURE. YOU DO THAT, MISTER.
SMUG PUNK. I'D LIKE TO WIPE THAT SMILE OFF HIS FACE.
7.

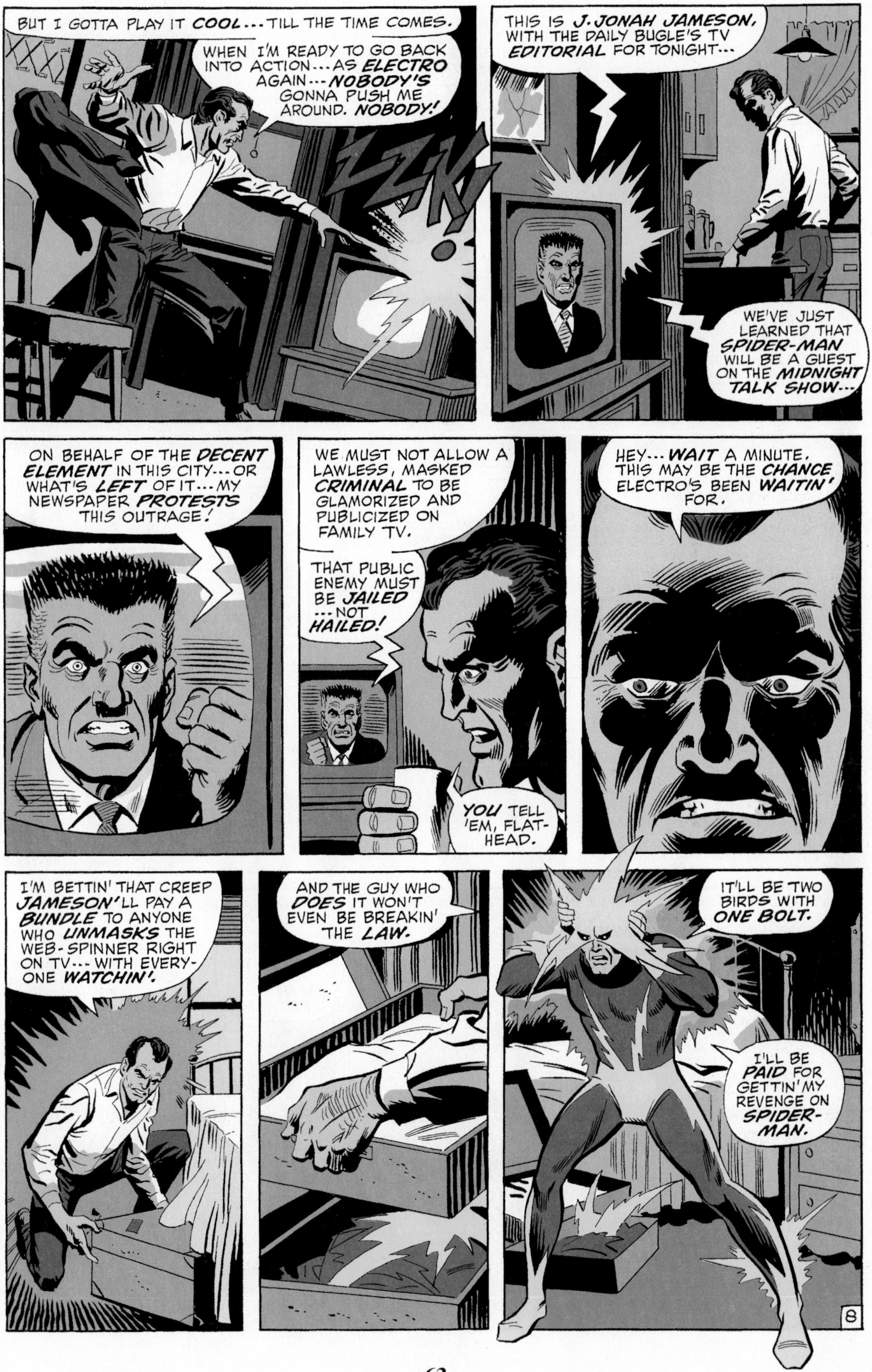

BUT I GOTTA PLAY IT COOL... TILL THE TIME COMES.
WHEN I'M READY TO GO BACK INTO ACTION... AS ELECTRO AGAIN... NOBODY'S GONNA PUSH ME AROUND. NOBODY!
ZZK!
THIS IS J. JONAH JAMESON, WITH THE DAILY BUGLE'S TV EDITORIAL FOR TONIGHT...
WE'VE JUST LEARNED THAT SPIDER-MAN WILL BE A GUEST ON THE MIDNIGHT TALK SHOW...
ON BEHALF OF THE DECENT ELEMENT IN THIS CITY... OR WHAT'S LEFT OF IT... MY NEWSPAPER PROTESTS THIS OUTRAGE!
WE MUST NOT ALLOW A LAWLESS, MASKED CRIMINAL TO BE GLAMORIZED AND PUBLICIZED ON FAMILY TV.
THAT PUBLIC ENEMY MUST BE JAILED ...NOT HAILED!
YOU TELL 'EM, FLAT-HEAD.
HEY... WAIT A MINUTE. THIS MAY BE THE CHANCE ELECTRO'S BEEN WAITIN' FOR.
I'M BETTIN' THAT CREEP JAMESON'LL PAY A BUNDLE TO ANYONE WHO UNMASKS THE WEB-SPINNER RIGHT ON TV--- WITH EVERY-ONE WATCHIN'.
AND THE GUY WHO DOES IT WON'T EVEN BE BREAKIN' THE LAW.
IT'LL BE TWO BIRDS WITH ONE BOLT.
I'LL BE PAID FOR GETTIN' MY REVENGE ON SPIDER-MAN.
8

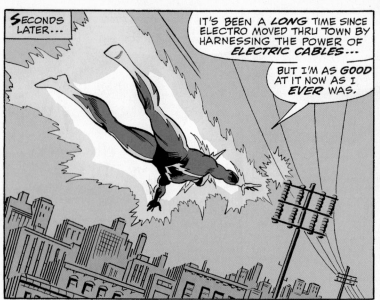

SECONDS LATER...

IT'S BEEN A *LONG* TIME SINCE ELECTRO MOVED THRU TOWN BY HARNESSING THE POWER OF *ELECTRIC CABLES*...

BUT I'M AS *GOOD* AT IT NOW AS I *EVER* WAS.

MEANWHILE, A PENSIVE *PETER PARKER* MOVES ALONG AT HIS OWN PRAGMATIC PACE...

THEY WOULDN'T PAY ME IN *ADVANCE* FOR PROMISING TO APPEAR ON THEIR SHOW.

GUESS I CAN'T *BLAME* THEM. WHY SHOULD THEY *TRUST* SPIDEY?

BUT I'M *SICK* OF BEING SO *BROKE* ALL THE TIME. IF ONLY...

COMING *IN*, PETER... OR DO YOU JUST HAVE A THING ABOUT RINGING *DOORBELLS*?

OH... *HI*, GWEN.

SORRY, PRETTY GIRL. GUESS I WAS A LITTLE *PRE-OCCUPIED*!

THAT'S OKAY, MR. P. A GIRL CAN'T TAKE *TOO* MUCH OF ALL THIS FLAMING *PASSION*, ANYWAY!

HELLO, PETER. HAVE YOU HEARD THE NEWS ABOUT *SPIDER-MAN* BEING SCHEDULED FOR A TV APPEARANCE?

OUR FRIEND *JAMESON* IS HAVING *CONNIPTIONS* ABOUT IT!

SORRY, DAD. THIS SCINTILLATING LAD IS *MINE* TONIGHT!

HMMM... I *SUSPECTED* AS MUCH.

THE MOST *BEAUTIFUL* FEMALE IN TOWN... AND I CAN'T AFFORD TO TAKE HER IN A *TAXI*. NUTS!

REMEMBER, PETE... FLASH MUSTN'T *SUS-PECT* THAT WE'RE PLANNING A *PARTY* FOR HIM.

WHAT'LL I *DO* WHEN I HAVE TO CHIP IN?

THERE *MUST* BE A WAY TO... UH *OH!* HOPE GWEN DIDN'T NOTICE I CRACKED THE *PORCELAIN*.

FINALLY, AT THE EVER-POPULAR *COFFEE BEAN*...

HI, GWENDY. COULDN'T GET A *DATE* TONIGHT, HUH?

COME *OFF* IT, SOLDIER. WITH *PETER* ON MY ARM, I FEEL LIKE A *SWEEP-STAKES* WINNER.

9.

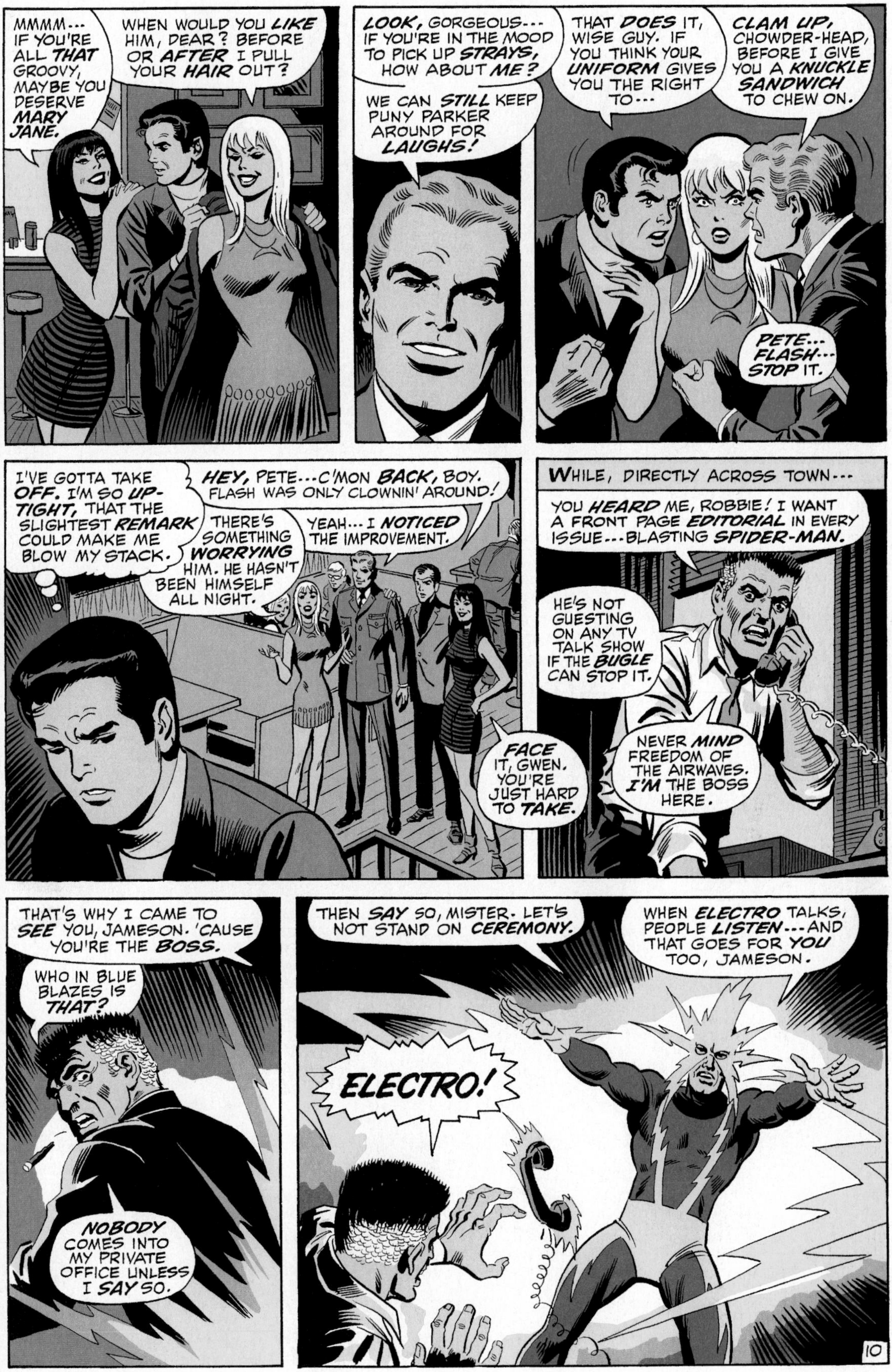
MMMM... IF YOU'RE ALL THAT GROOVY, MAYBE YOU DESERVE MARY JANE.
WHEN WOULD YOU LIKE HIM, DEAR? BEFORE OR AFTER I PULL YOUR HAIR OUT?
LOOK, GORGEOUS... IF YOU'RE IN THE MOOD TO PICK UP STRAYS, HOW ABOUT ME?
WE CAN STILL KEEP PUNY PARKER AROUND FOR LAUGHS!
THAT DOES IT, WISE GUY. IF YOU THINK YOUR UNIFORM GIVES YOU THE RIGHT TO---
CLAM UP, CHOWDER-HEAD, BEFORE I GIVE YOU A KNUCKLE SANDWICH TO CHEW ON.
PETE... FLASH... STOP IT.
I'VE GOTTA TAKE OFF. I'M SO UP-TIGHT, THAT THE SLIGHTEST REMARK COULD MAKE ME BLOW MY STACK.
HEY, PETE...C'MON BACK, BOY. FLASH WAS ONLY CLOWNIN' AROUND!
THERE'S SOMETHING WORRYING HIM. HE HASN'T BEEN HIMSELF ALL NIGHT.
YEAH... I NOTICED THE IMPROVEMENT.
FACE IT, GWEN. YOU'RE JUST HARD TO TAKE.
WHILE, DIRECTLY ACROSS TOWN---
YOU HEARD ME, ROBBIE! I WANT A FRONT PAGE EDITORIAL IN EVERY ISSUE---BLASTING SPIDER-MAN.
HE'S NOT GUESTING ON ANY TV TALK SHOW IF THE BUGLE CAN STOP IT.
NEVER MIND FREEDOM OF THE AIRWAVES. I'M THE BOSS HERE.
THAT'S WHY I CAME TO SEE YOU, JAMESON. 'CAUSE YOU'RE THE BOSS.
WHO IN BLUE BLAZES IS THAT?
NOBODY COMES INTO MY PRIVATE OFFICE UNLESS I SAY SO.
THEN SAY SO, MISTER. LET'S NOT STAND ON CEREMONY.
WHEN ELECTRO TALKS, PEOPLE LISTEN---AND THAT GOES FOR YOU TOO, JAMESON.
ELECTRO!
10

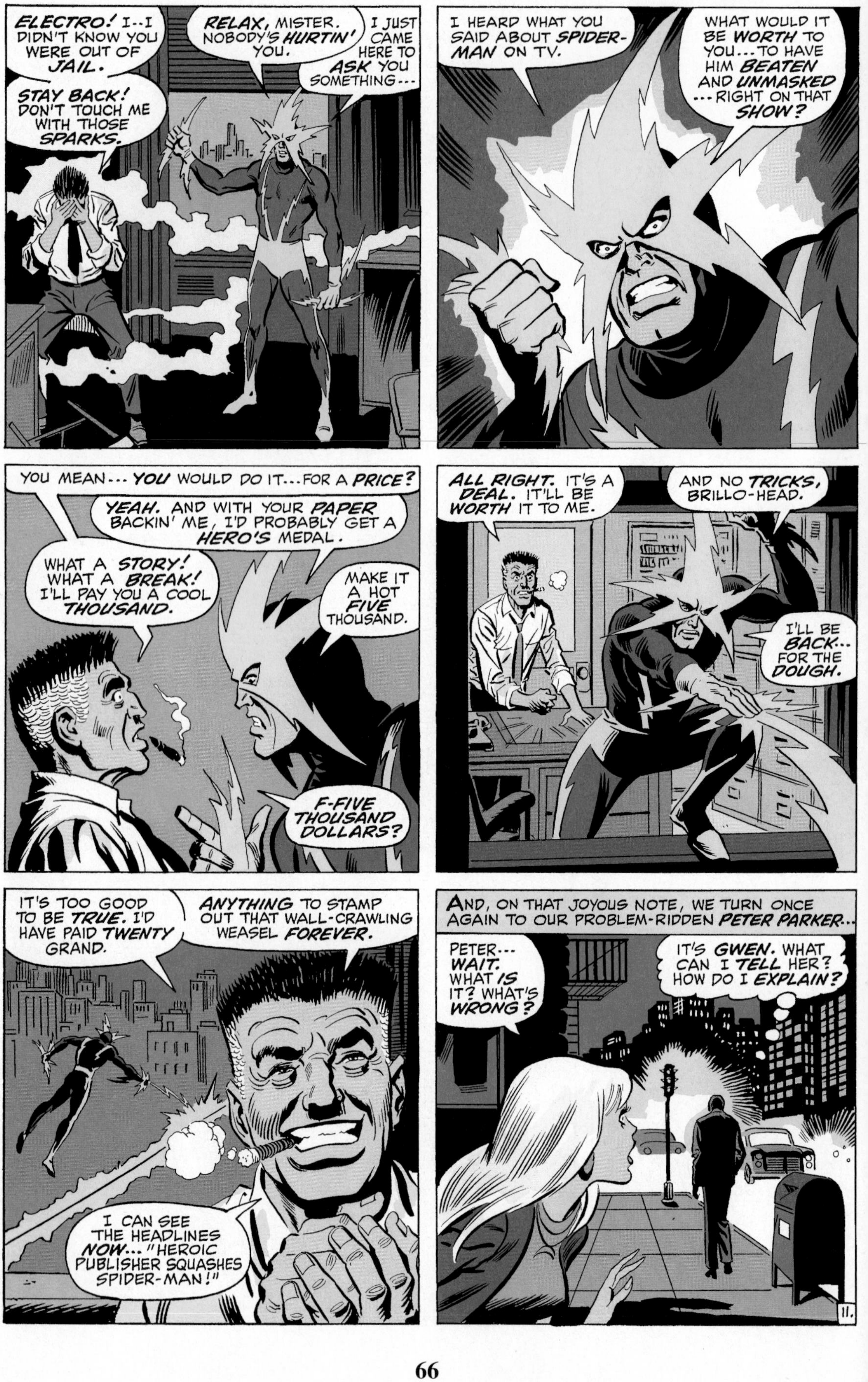
ELECTRO! I--I DIDN'T KNOW YOU WERE OUT OF JAIL.
STAY BACK! DON'T TOUCH ME WITH THOSE SPARKS.
RELAX, MISTER. NOBODY'S HURTIN' YOU.
I JUST CAME HERE TO ASK YOU SOMETHING---
I HEARD WHAT YOU SAID ABOUT SPIDER-MAN ON TV.
WHAT WOULD IT BE WORTH TO YOU...TO HAVE HIM BEATEN AND UNMASKED ---RIGHT ON THAT SHOW?
YOU MEAN... YOU WOULD DO IT...FOR A PRICE?
YEAH. AND WITH YOUR PAPER BACKIN' ME, I'D PROBABLY GET A HERO'S MEDAL.
WHAT A STORY! WHAT A BREAK! I'LL PAY YOU A COOL THOUSAND.
MAKE IT A HOT FIVE THOUSAND.
F-FIVE THOUSAND DOLLARS?
ALL RIGHT. IT'S A DEAL. IT'LL BE WORTH IT TO ME.
AND NO TRICKS, BRILLO-HEAD.
I'LL BE BACK... FOR THE DOUGH.
IT'S TOO GOOD TO BE TRUE. I'D HAVE PAID TWENTY GRAND.
ANYTHING TO STAMP OUT THAT WALL-CRAWLING WEASEL FOREVER.
I CAN SEE THE HEADLINES NOW..."HEROIC PUBLISHER SQUASHES SPIDER-MAN!"
AND, ON THAT JOYOUS NOTE, WE TURN ONCE AGAIN TO OUR PROBLEM-RIDDEN PETER PARKER...
PETER--- WAIT. WHAT IS IT? WHAT'S WRONG?
IT'S GWEN. WHAT CAN I TELL HER? HOW DO I EXPLAIN?
11.

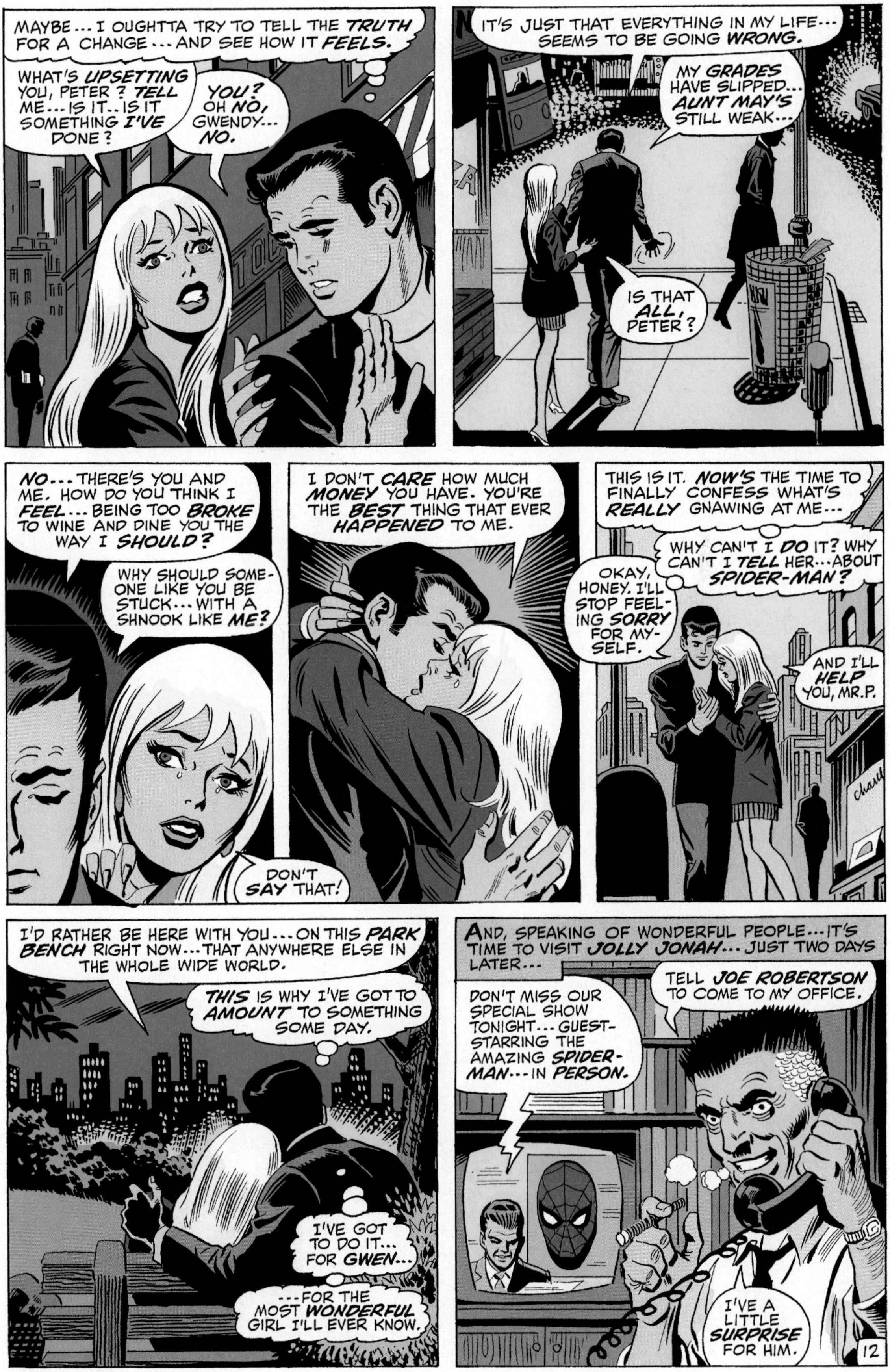
MAYBE... I OUGHTTA TRY TO TELL THE TRUTH FOR A CHANGE... AND SEE HOW IT FEELS.
WHAT'S UPSETTING YOU, PETER? TELL ME... IS IT.. IS IT SOMETHING I'VE DONE?
YOU? OH NO, GWENDY... NO.
IT'S JUST THAT EVERYTHING IN MY LIFE... SEEMS TO BE GOING WRONG.
MY GRADES HAVE SLIPPED... AUNT MAY'S STILL WEAK...
IS THAT ALL, PETER?
NO... THERE'S YOU AND ME. HOW DO YOU THINK I FEEL... BEING TOO BROKE TO WINE AND DINE YOU THE WAY I SHOULD?
WHY SHOULD SOME-ONE LIKE YOU BE STUCK... WITH A SHNOOK LIKE ME?
DON'T SAY THAT!
I DON'T CARE HOW MUCH MONEY YOU HAVE. YOU'RE THE BEST THING THAT EVER HAPPENED TO ME.
THIS IS IT. NOW'S THE TIME TO FINALLY CONFESS WHAT'S REALLY GNAWING AT ME...
WHY CAN'T I DO IT? WHY CAN'T I TELL HER... ABOUT SPIDER-MAN?
OKAY, HONEY. I'LL STOP FEEL-ING SORRY FOR MY-SELF.
AND I'LL HELP YOU, MR. P.
I'D RATHER BE HERE WITH YOU... ON THIS PARK BENCH RIGHT NOW... THAT ANYWHERE ELSE IN THE WHOLE WIDE WORLD.
THIS IS WHY I'VE GOT TO AMOUNT TO SOMETHING SOME DAY.
I'VE GOT TO DO IT... FOR GWEN...
...FOR THE MOST WONDERFUL GIRL I'LL EVER KNOW.
AND, SPEAKING OF WONDERFUL PEOPLE... IT'S TIME TO VISIT JOLLY JONAH... JUST TWO DAYS LATER...
DON'T MISS OUR SPECIAL SHOW TONIGHT... GUEST-STARRING THE AMAZING SPIDER-MAN... IN PERSON.
TELL JOE ROBERTSON TO COME TO MY OFFICE.
I'VE A LITTLE SURPRISE FOR HIM.
12

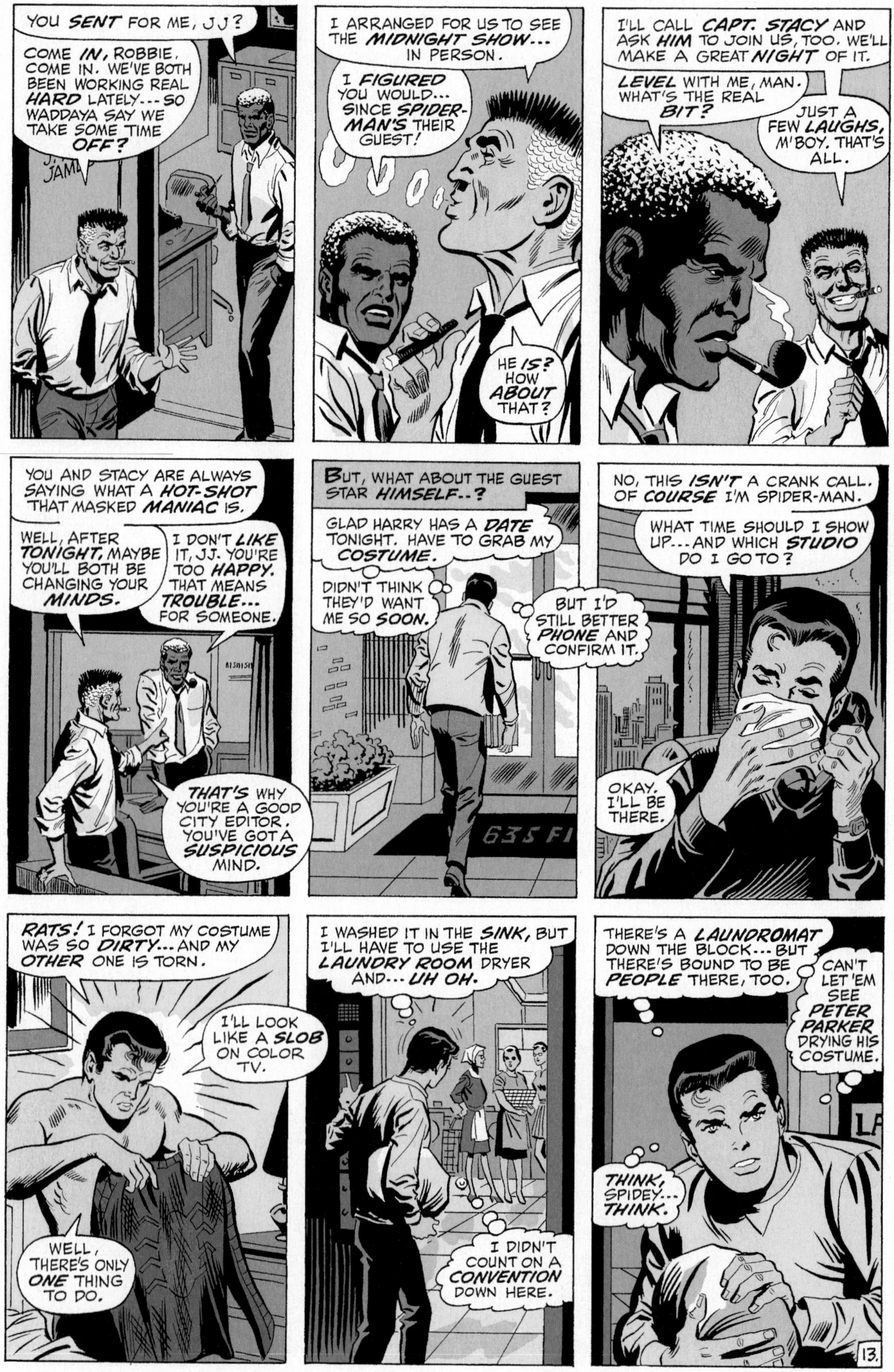

YOU SENT FOR ME, JJ?
COME IN, ROBBIE. COME IN. WE'VE BOTH BEEN WORKING REAL HARD LATELY--- SO WADDAYA SAY WE TAKE SOME TIME OFF?
I ARRANGED FOR US TO SEE THE MIDNIGHT SHOW... IN PERSON.
I FIGURED YOU WOULD... SINCE SPIDER-MAN'S THEIR GUEST!
HE IS? HOW ABOUT THAT?
I'LL CALL CAPT. STACY AND ASK HIM TO JOIN US, TOO. WE'LL MAKE A GREAT NIGHT OF IT.
LEVEL WITH ME, MAN. WHAT'S THE REAL BIT?
JUST A FEW LAUGHS, M'BOY. THAT'S ALL.
YOU AND STACY ARE ALWAYS SAYING WHAT A HOT-SHOT THAT MASKED MANIAC IS.
WELL, AFTER TONIGHT, MAYBE YOU'LL BOTH BE CHANGING YOUR MINDS.
I DON'T LIKE IT, JJ. YOU'RE TOO HAPPY. THAT MEANS TROUBLE... FOR SOMEONE.
THAT'S WHY YOU'RE A GOOD CITY EDITOR. YOU'VE GOT A SUSPICIOUS MIND.
BUT, WHAT ABOUT THE GUEST STAR HIMSELF..?
GLAD HARRY HAS A DATE TONIGHT. HAVE TO GRAB MY COSTUME.
DIDN'T THINK THEY'D WANT ME SO SOON.
BUT I'D STILL BETTER PHONE AND CONFIRM IT.
635 FI
NO, THIS ISN'T A CRANK CALL. OF COURSE I'M SPIDER-MAN.
WHAT TIME SHOULD I SHOW UP... AND WHICH STUDIO DO I GO TO?
OKAY. I'LL BE THERE.
RATS! I FORGOT MY COSTUME WAS SO DIRTY... AND MY OTHER ONE IS TORN.
I'LL LOOK LIKE A SLOB ON COLOR TV.
WELL, THERE'S ONLY ONE THING TO DO.
I WASHED IT IN THE SINK, BUT I'LL HAVE TO USE THE LAUNDRY ROOM DRYER AND... UH OH.
I DIDN'T COUNT ON A CONVENTION DOWN HERE.
THERE'S A LAUNDROMAT DOWN THE BLOCK... BUT THERE'S BOUND TO BE PEOPLE THERE, TOO.
CAN'T LET 'EM SEE PETER PARKER DRYING HIS COSTUME.
THINK, SPIDEY... THINK.
13.

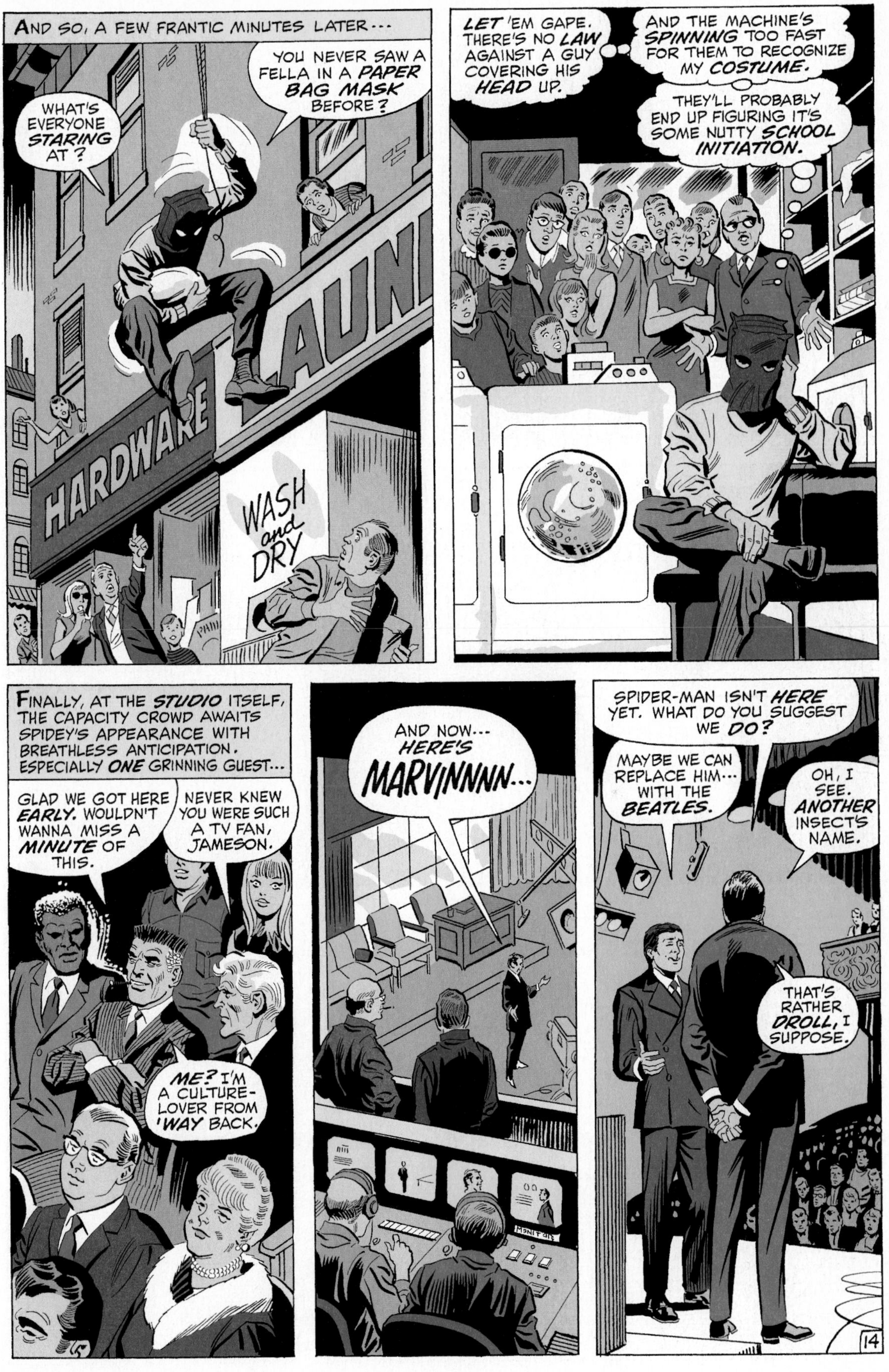
AND SO, A FEW FRANTIC MINUTES LATER...
WHAT'S EVERYONE STARING AT?
YOU NEVER SAW A FELLA IN A PAPER BAG MASK BEFORE?
HARDWARE
LAUN
WASH and DRY
LET 'EM GAPE. THERE'S NO LAW AGAINST A GUY COVERING HIS HEAD UP.
AND THE MACHINE'S SPINNING TOO FAST FOR THEM TO RECOGNIZE MY COSTUME.
THEY'LL PROBABLY END UP FIGURING IT'S SOME NUTTY SCHOOL INITIATION.
FINALLY, AT THE STUDIO ITSELF, THE CAPACITY CROWD AWAITS SPIDEY'S APPEARANCE WITH BREATHLESS ANTICIPATION. ESPECIALLY ONE GRINNING GUEST...
GLAD WE GOT HERE EARLY. WOULDN'T WANNA MISS A MINUTE OF THIS.
NEVER KNEW YOU WERE SUCH A TV FAN, JAMESON.
ME? I'M A CULTURE-LOVER FROM 'WAY BACK.
AND NOW... HERE'S MARVINNNN...
SPIDER-MAN ISN'T HERE YET. WHAT DO YOU SUGGEST WE DO?
MAYBE WE CAN REPLACE HIM... WITH THE BEATLES.
OH, I SEE. ANOTHER INSECT'S NAME.
THAT'S RATHER DROLL, I SUPPOSE.
14

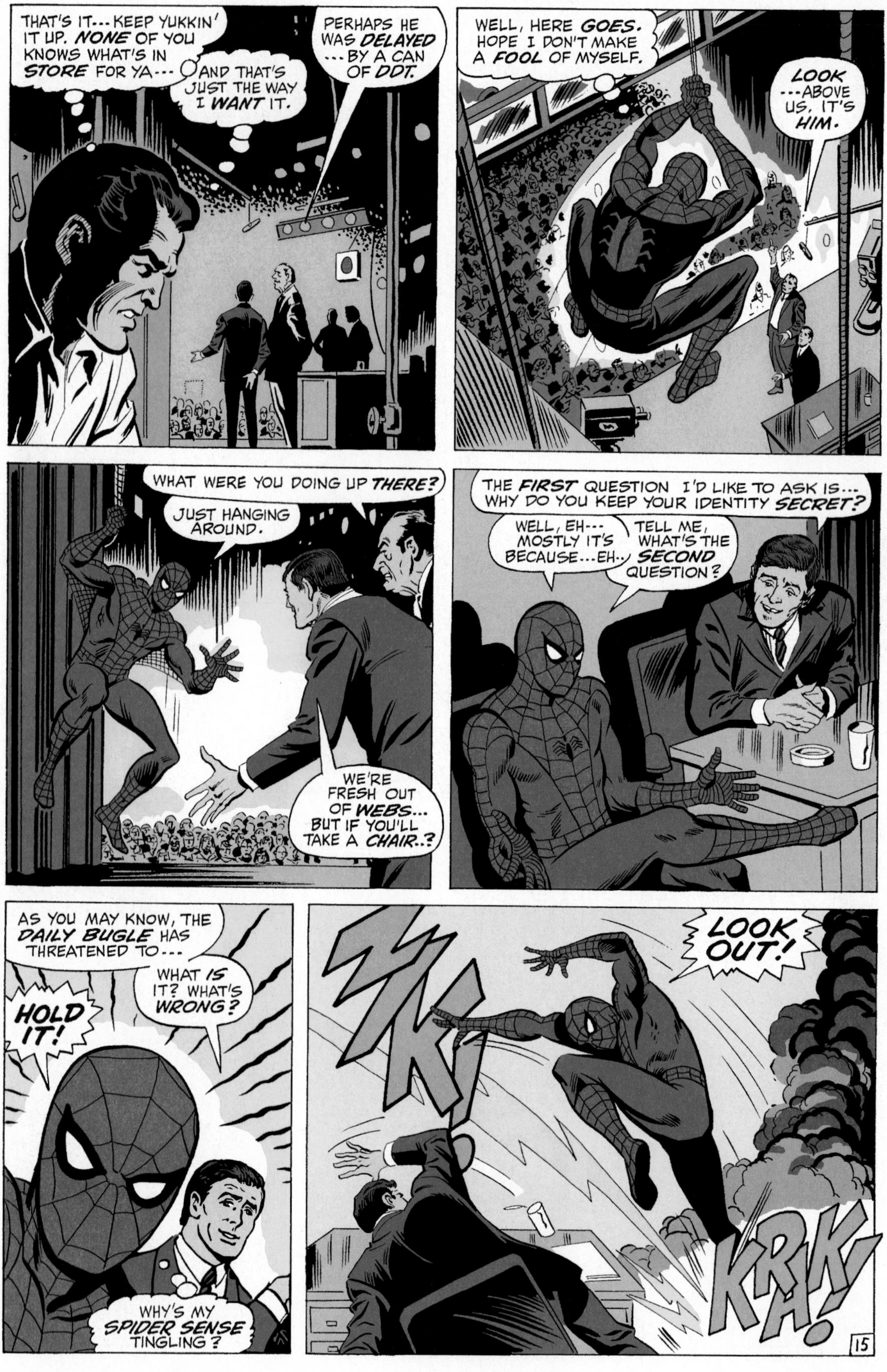
THAT'S IT--- KEEP YUKKIN' IT UP. NONE OF YOU KNOWS WHAT'S IN STORE FOR YA---
AND THAT'S JUST THE WAY I WANT IT.
PERHAPS HE WAS DELAYED --- BY A CAN OF DDT.
WELL, HERE GOES. HOPE I DON'T MAKE A FOOL OF MYSELF.
LOOK ---ABOVE US, IT'S HIM.
WHAT WERE YOU DOING UP THERE?
JUST HANGING AROUND.
WE'RE FRESH OUT OF WEBS... BUT IF YOU'LL TAKE A CHAIR..?
THE FIRST QUESTION I'D LIKE TO ASK IS... WHY DO YOU KEEP YOUR IDENTITY SECRET?
WELL, EH--- MOSTLY IT'S BECAUSE---EH--
TELL ME, WHAT'S THE SECOND QUESTION?
AS YOU MAY KNOW, THE DAILY BUGLE HAS THREATENED TO---
HOLD IT!
WHAT IS IT? WHAT'S WRONG?
WHY'S MY SPIDER SENSE TINGLING?
ZZK
LOOK OUT!
KRAK!
15

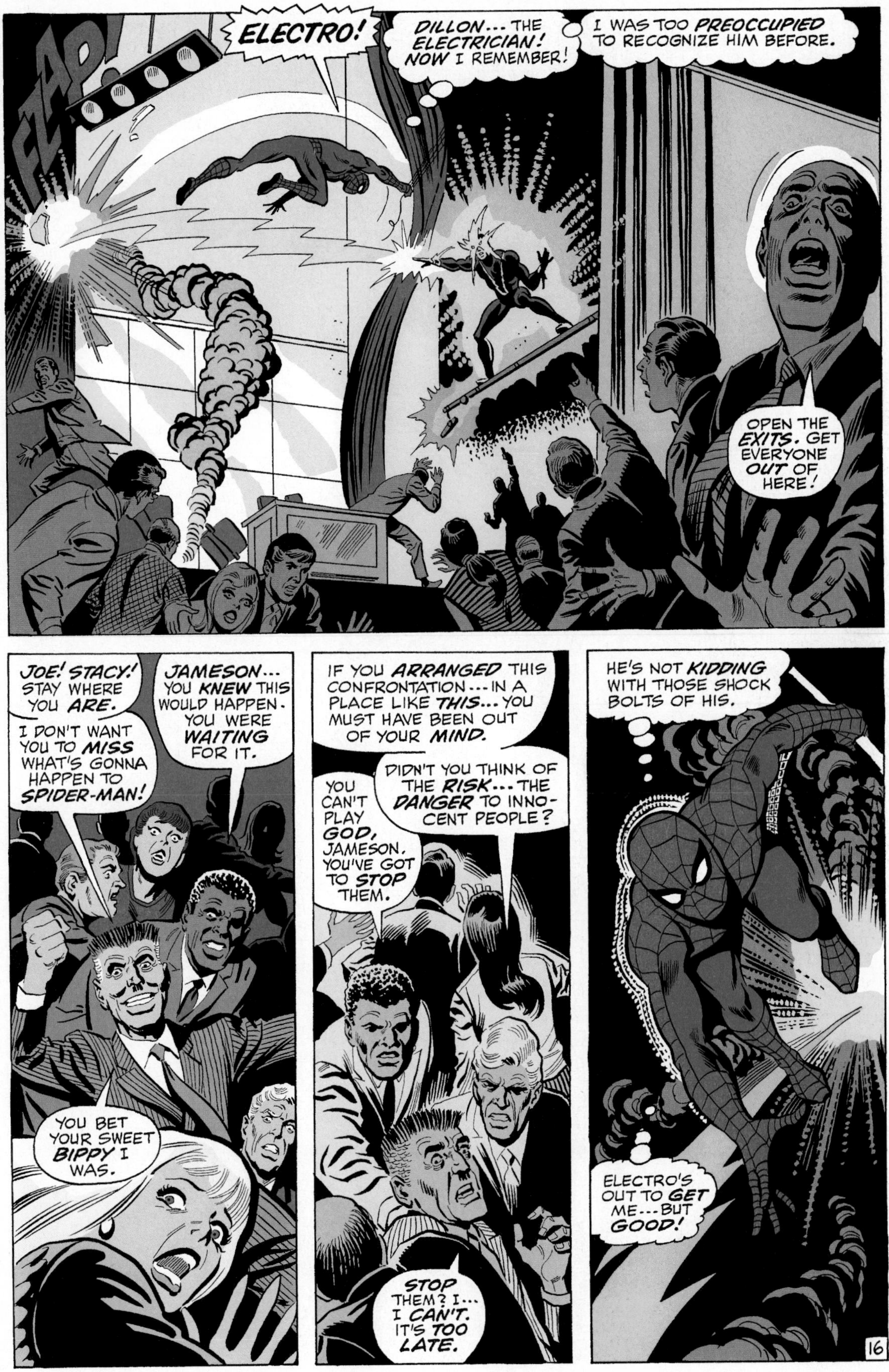
FZAP!
ELECTRO!
DILLON... THE ELECTRICIAN! NOW I REMEMBER!
I WAS TOO PREOCCUPIED TO RECOGNIZE HIM BEFORE.
OPEN THE EXITS. GET EVERYONE OUT OF HERE!
JOE! STACY! STAY WHERE YOU ARE.
I DON'T WANT YOU TO MISS WHAT'S GONNA HAPPEN TO SPIDER-MAN!
JAMESON... YOU KNEW THIS WOULD HAPPEN. YOU WERE WAITING FOR IT.
YOU BET YOUR SWEET BIPPY I WAS.
IF YOU ARRANGED THIS CONFRONTATION--- IN A PLACE LIKE THIS... YOU MUST HAVE BEEN OUT OF YOUR MIND.
DIDN'T YOU THINK OF THE RISK... THE DANGER TO INNOCENT PEOPLE?
YOU CAN'T PLAY GOD, JAMESON. YOU'VE GOT TO STOP THEM.
STOP THEM? I... I CAN'T. IT'S TOO LATE.
HE'S NOT KIDDING WITH THOSE SHOCK BOLTS OF HIS.
ELECTRO'S OUT TO GET ME--- BUT GOOD!
16

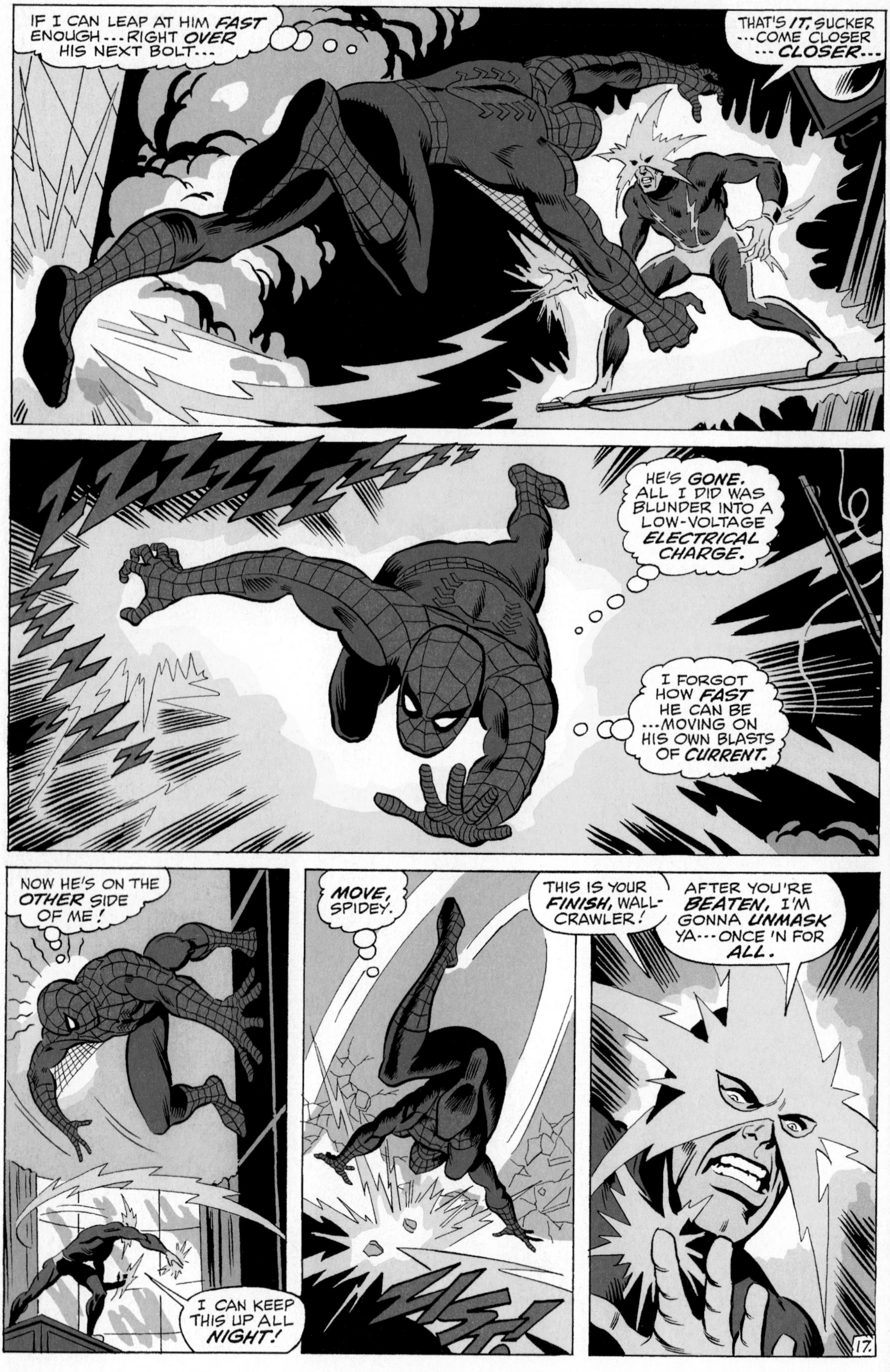
IF I CAN LEAP AT HIM FAST ENOUGH ... RIGHT OVER HIS NEXT BOLT...
THAT'S IT, SUCKER ... COME CLOSER ... CLOSER...
HE'S GONE. ALL I DID WAS BLUNDER INTO A LOW-VOLTAGE ELECTRICAL CHARGE.
I FORGOT HOW FAST HE CAN BE ...MOVING ON HIS OWN BLASTS OF CURRENT.
NOW HE'S ON THE OTHER SIDE OF ME!
I CAN KEEP THIS UP ALL NIGHT!
MOVE, SPIDEY.
THIS IS YOUR FINISH, WALL-CRAWLER!
AFTER YOU'RE BEATEN, I'M GONNA UNMASK YA--- ONCE 'N FOR ALL.
17.

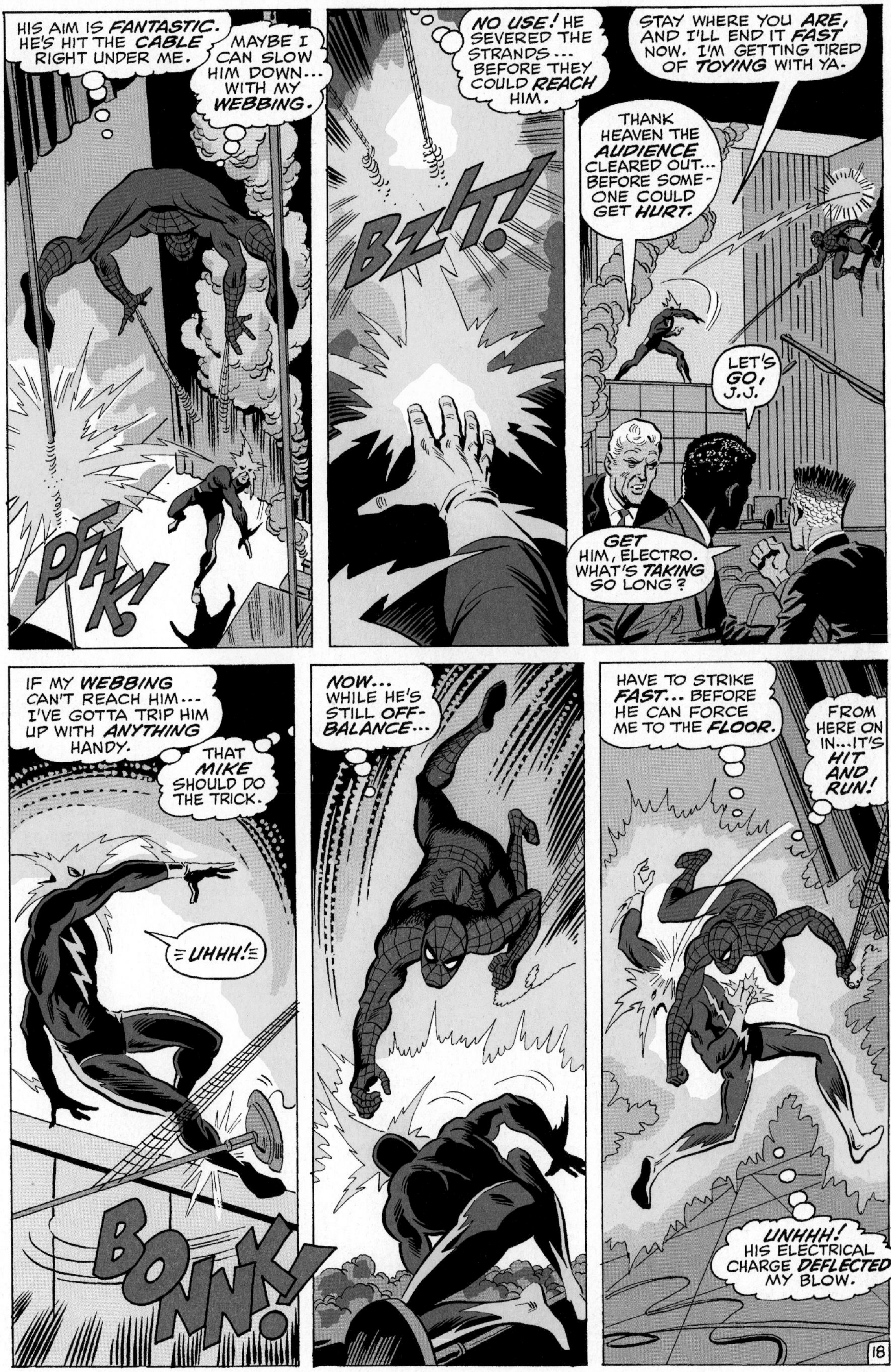
HIS AIM IS FANTASTIC. HE'S HIT THE CABLE RIGHT UNDER ME.
MAYBE I CAN SLOW HIM DOWN... WITH MY WEBBING.
PFAK!
NO USE! HE SEVERED THE STRANDS... BEFORE THEY COULD REACH HIM.
BZZT!
STAY WHERE YOU ARE, AND I'LL END IT FAST NOW. I'M GETTING TIRED OF TOYING WITH YA.
THANK HEAVEN THE AUDIENCE CLEARED OUT... BEFORE SOME-ONE COULD GET HURT.
LET'S GO, J.J.
GET HIM, ELECTRO. WHAT'S TAKING SO LONG?
IF MY WEBBING CAN'T REACH HIM... I'VE GOTTA TRIP HIM UP WITH ANYTHING HANDY.
THAT MIKE SHOULD DO THE TRICK.
UHHH!
BONNK!
NOW... WHILE HE'S STILL OFF-BALANCE...
HAVE TO STRIKE FAST... BEFORE HE CAN FORCE ME TO THE FLOOR.
FROM HERE ON IN...IT'S HIT AND RUN!
UNHHH! HIS ELECTRICAL CHARGE DEFLECTED MY BLOW.
18

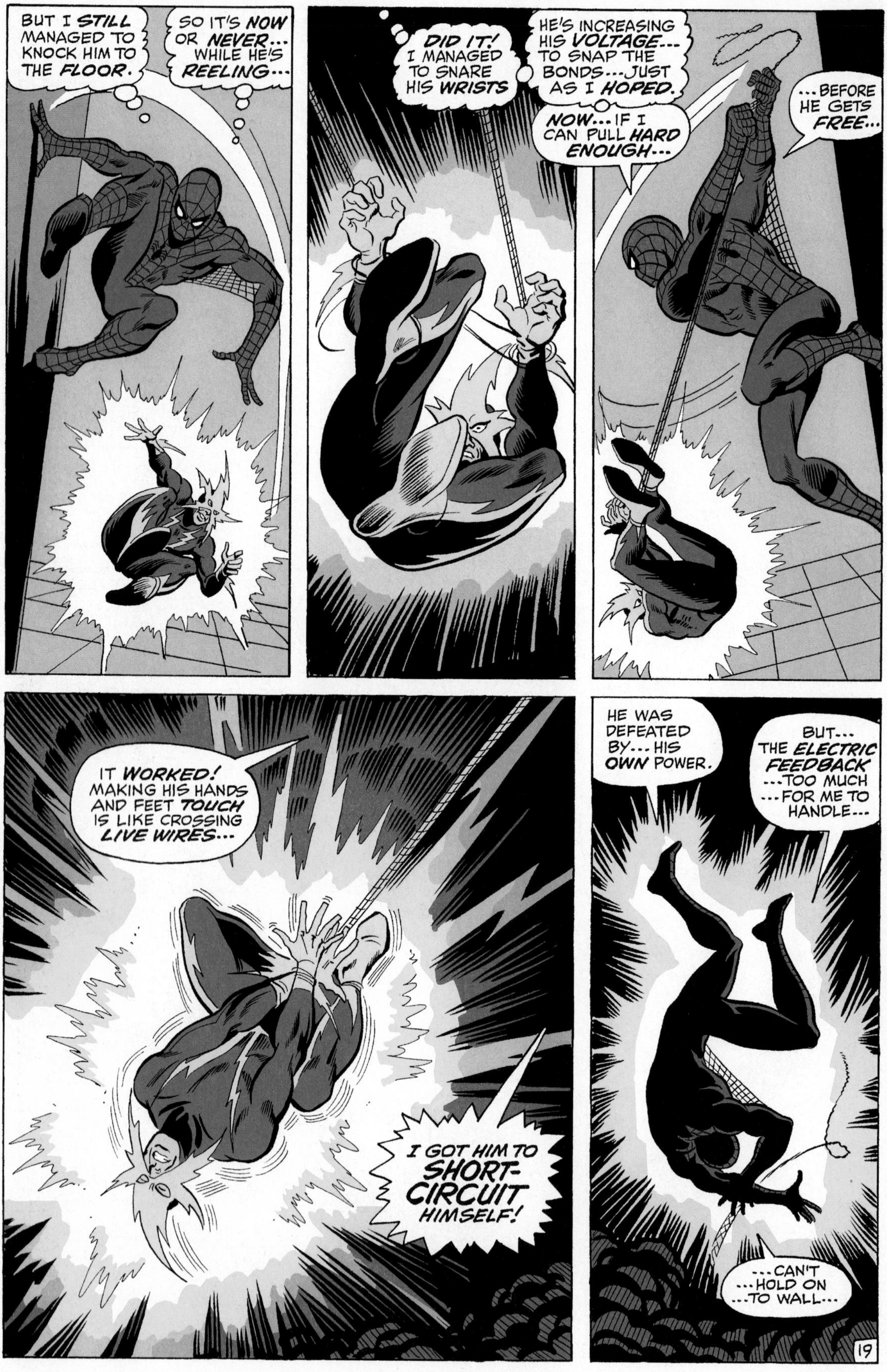

BUT I STILL MANAGED TO KNOCK HIM TO THE FLOOR.
SO IT'S NOW OR NEVER... WHILE HE'S REELING...
DID IT! I MANAGED TO SNARE HIS WRISTS
HE'S INCREASING HIS VOLTAGE... TO SNAP THE BONDS... JUST AS I HOPED.
NOW... IF I CAN PULL HARD ENOUGH...
...BEFORE HE GETS FREE...
IT WORKED! MAKING HIS HANDS AND FEET TOUCH IS LIKE CROSSING LIVE WIRES...
I GOT HIM TO SHORT-CIRCUIT HIMSELF!
HE WAS DEFEATED BY... HIS OWN POWER.
BUT... THE ELECTRIC FEEDBACK ...TOO MUCH ...FOR ME TO HANDLE...
...CAN'T ...HOLD ON ...TO WALL...
19

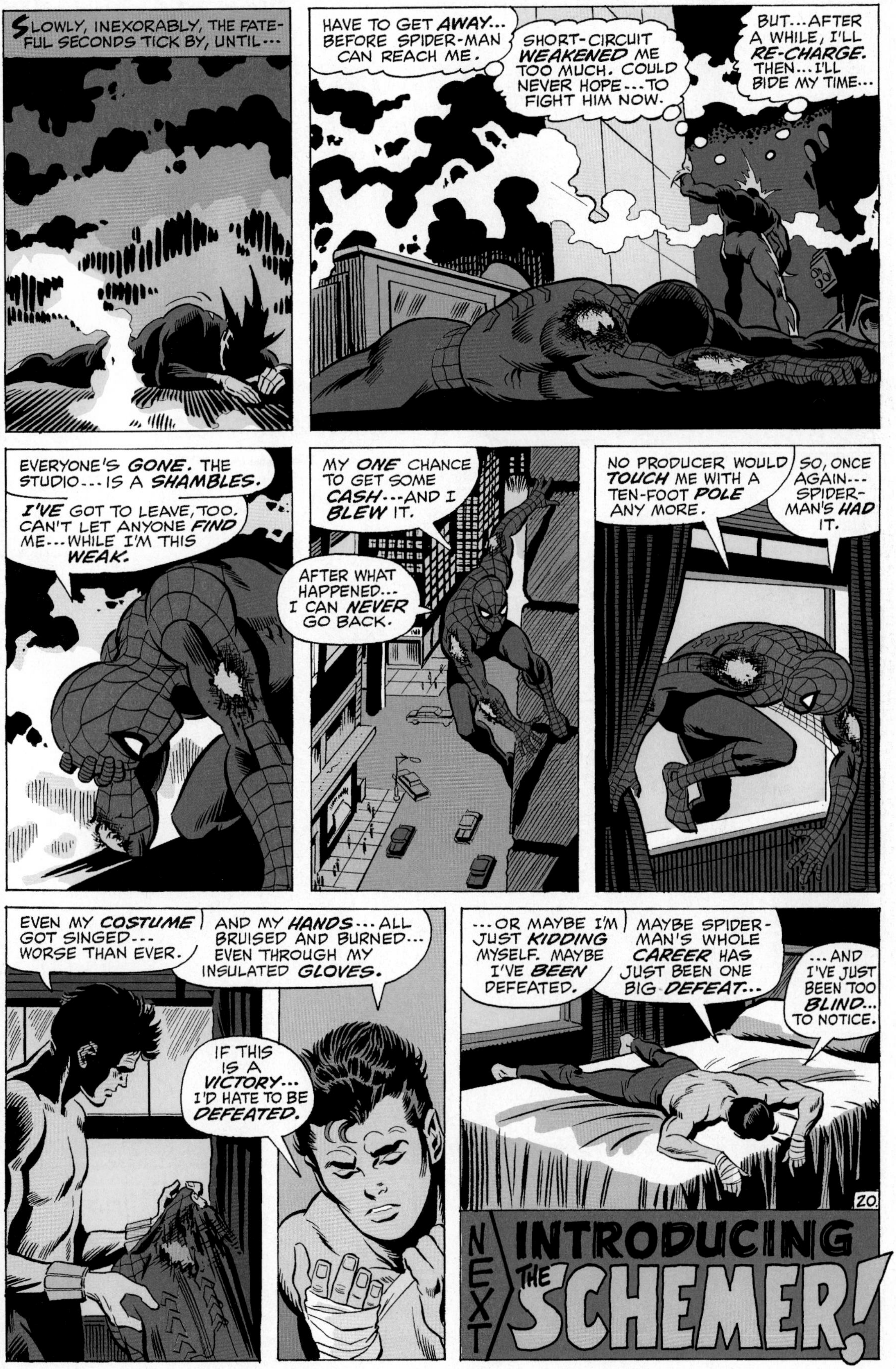
SLOWLY, INEXORABLY, THE FATEFUL SECONDS TICK BY, UNTIL---
HAVE TO GET AWAY... BEFORE SPIDER-MAN CAN REACH ME.
SHORT-CIRCUIT WEAKENED ME TOO MUCH. COULD NEVER HOPE---TO FIGHT HIM NOW.
BUT...AFTER A WHILE, I'LL RE-CHARGE. THEN...I'LL BIDE MY TIME...
EVERYONE'S GONE. THE STUDIO---IS A SHAMBLES.
I'VE GOT TO LEAVE, TOO. CAN'T LET ANYONE FIND ME---WHILE I'M THIS WEAK.
MY ONE CHANCE TO GET SOME CASH---AND I BLEW IT.
AFTER WHAT HAPPENED--- I CAN NEVER GO BACK.
NO PRODUCER WOULD TOUCH ME WITH A TEN-FOOT POLE ANY MORE.
SO, ONCE AGAIN--- SPIDER-MAN'S HAD IT.
EVEN MY COSTUME GOT SINGED--- WORSE THAN EVER.
AND MY HANDS--- ALL BRUISED AND BURNED--- EVEN THROUGH MY INSULATED GLOVES.
IF THIS IS A VICTORY... I'D HATE TO BE DEFEATED.
---OR MAYBE I'M JUST KIDDING MYSELF. MAYBE I'VE BEEN DEFEATED.
MAYBE SPIDER-MAN'S WHOLE CAREER HAS JUST BEEN ONE BIG DEFEAT---
---AND I'VE JUST BEEN TOO BLIND... TO NOTICE.
20.
NEXT
INTRODUCING THE SCHEMER!

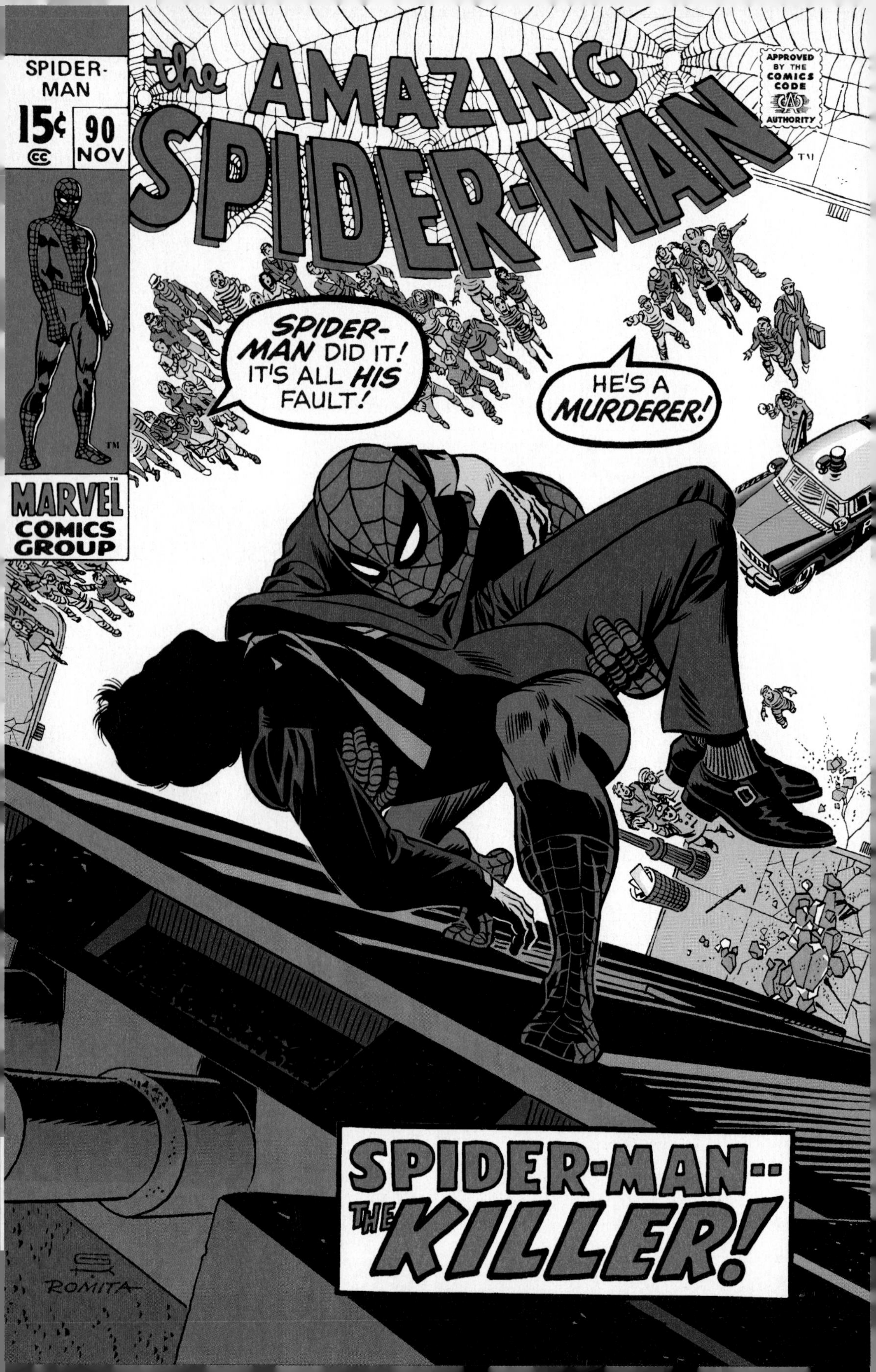
SPIDER-MAN
15¢
90
NOV
the AMAZING SPIDER-MAN
APPROVED BY THE COMICS CODE AUTHORITY
MARVEL COMICS GROUP
SPIDER-MAN DID IT! IT'S ALL HIS FAULT!
HE'S A MURDERER!
SPIDER-MAN.. THE KILLER!
ROMITA

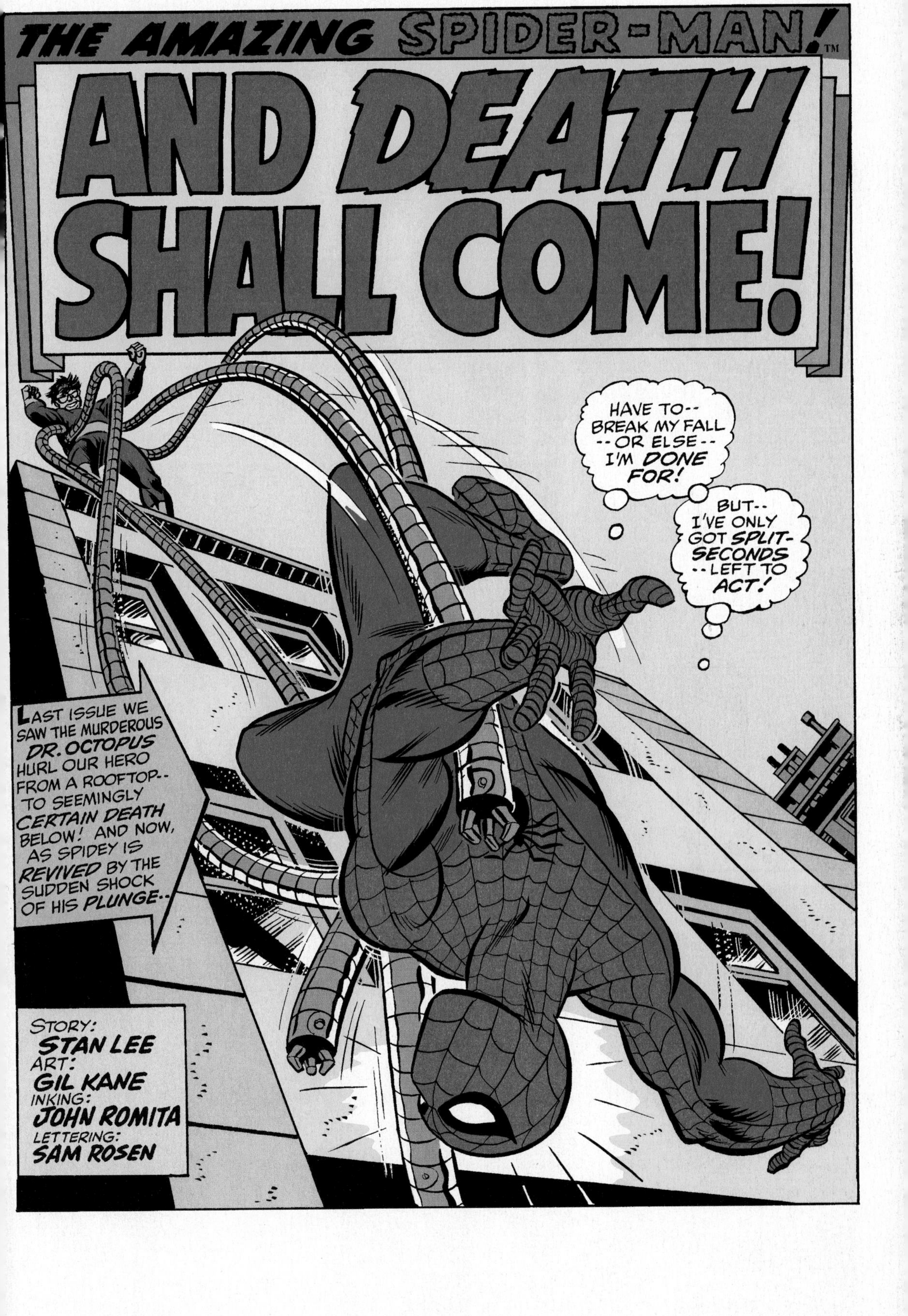
THE AMAZING SPIDER-MAN!™
AND DEATH SHALL COME!
HAVE TO-- BREAK MY FALL --OR ELSE-- I'M DONE FOR!
BUT-- I'VE ONLY GOT SPLIT-SECONDS --LEFT TO ACT!
LAST ISSUE WE SAW THE MURDEROUS DR. OCTOPUS HURL OUR HERO FROM A ROOFTOP-- TO SEEMINGLY CERTAIN DEATH BELOW! AND NOW, AS SPIDEY IS REVIVED BY THE SUDDEN SHOCK OF HIS PLUNGE..
STORY: STAN LEE
ART: GIL KANE
INKING: JOHN ROMITA
LETTERING: SAM ROSEN

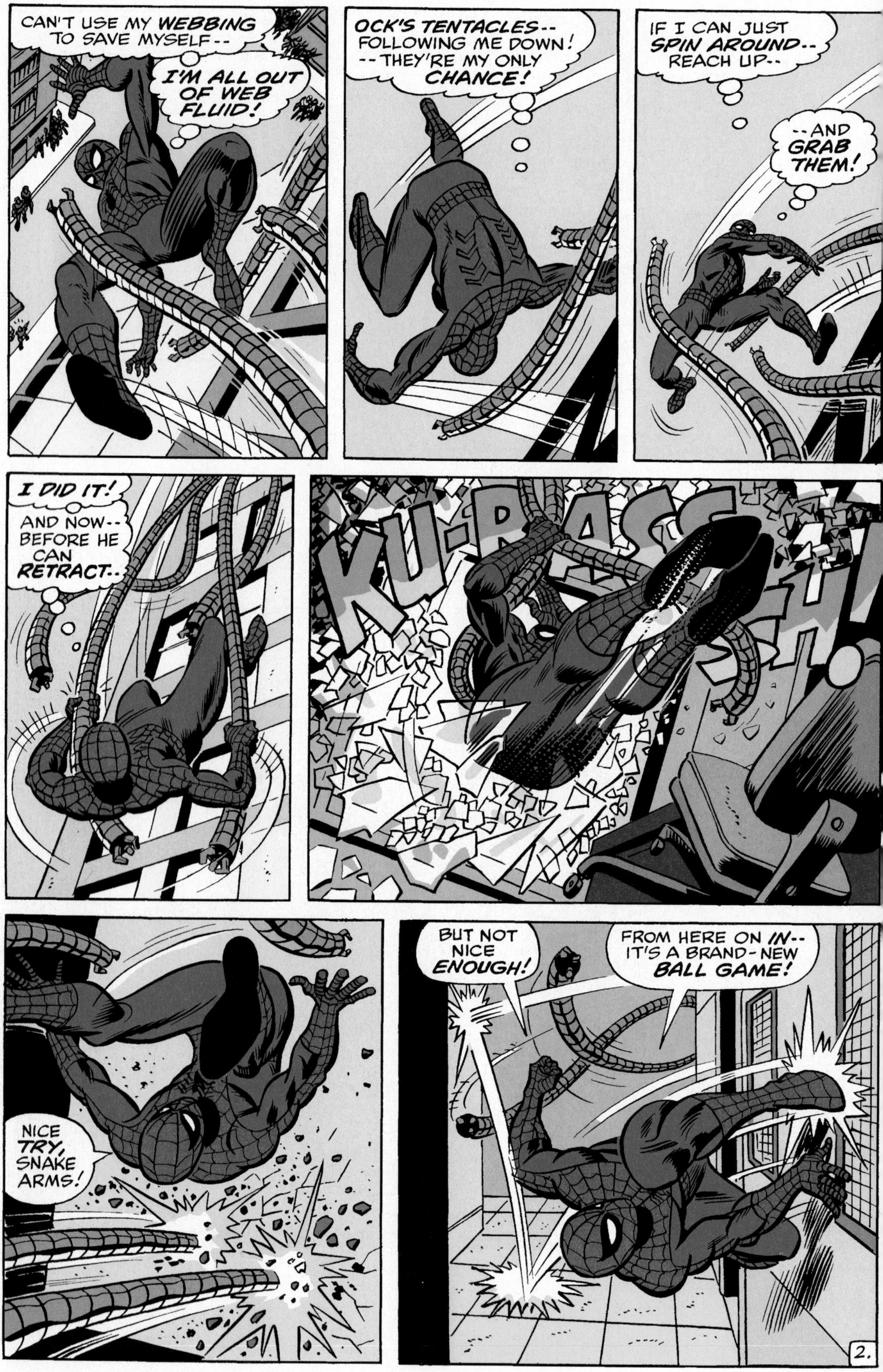
CAN'T USE MY WEBBING TO SAVE MYSELF--
I'M ALL OUT OF WEB FLUID!
OCK'S TENTACLES-- FOLLOWING ME DOWN! --THEY'RE MY ONLY CHANCE!
IF I CAN JUST SPIN AROUND-- REACH UP--
--AND GRAB THEM!
I DID IT!
AND NOW-- BEFORE HE CAN RETRACT--
KU-RASSSH!
NICE TRY, SNAKE ARMS!
BUT NOT NICE ENOUGH!
FROM HERE ON IN-- IT'S A BRAND-NEW BALL GAME!
2.

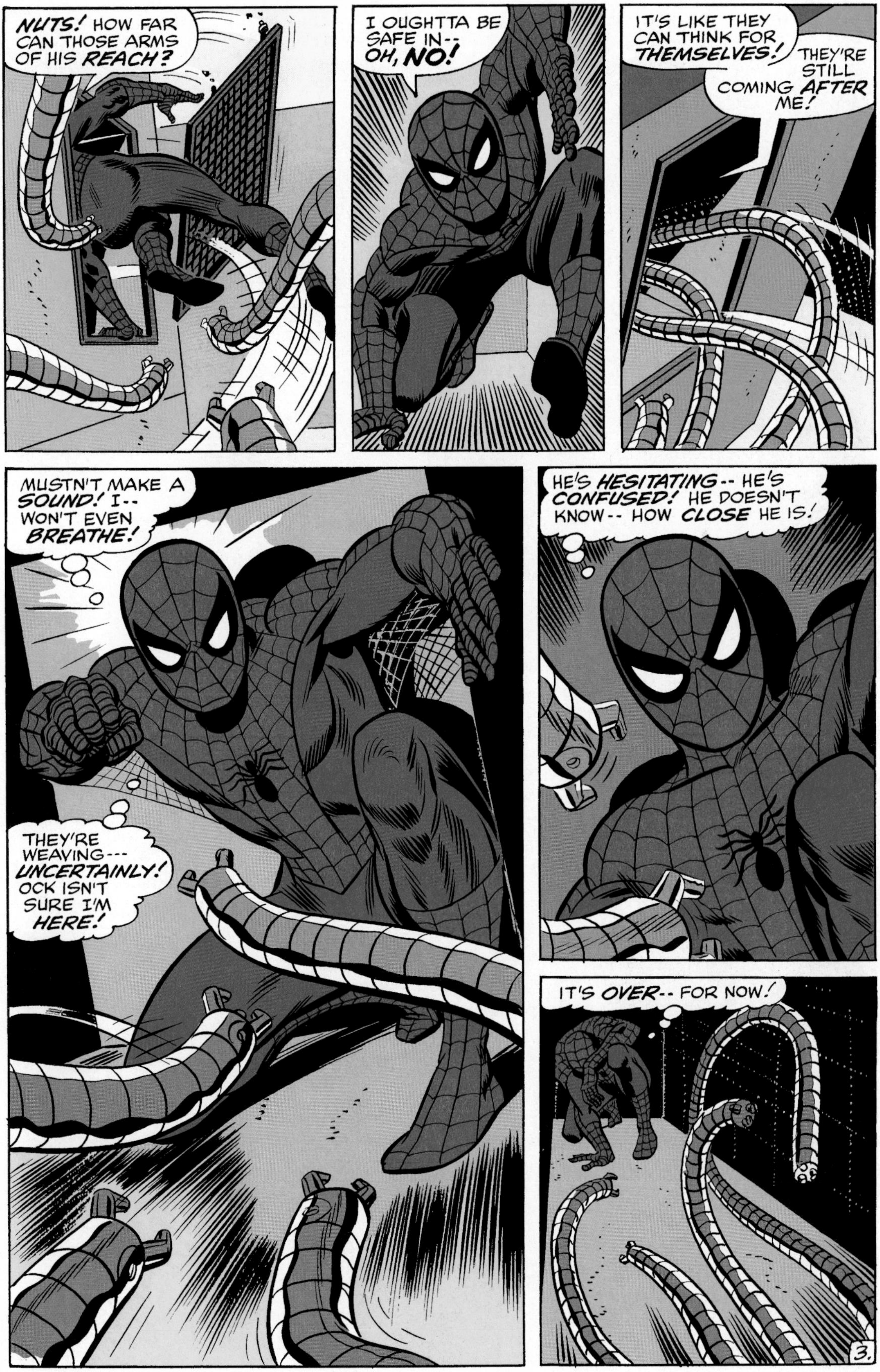
NUTS! HOW FAR CAN THOSE ARMS OF HIS REACH?
I OUGHTTA BE SAFE IN-- OH, NO!
IT'S LIKE THEY CAN THINK FOR THEMSELVES!
THEY'RE STILL COMING AFTER ME!
MUSTN'T MAKE A SOUND! I-- WON'T EVEN BREATHE!
THEY'RE WEAVING--- UNCERTAINLY! OCK ISN'T SURE I'M HERE!
HE'S HESITATING-- HE'S CONFUSED! HE DOESN'T KNOW-- HOW CLOSE HE IS!
IT'S OVER-- FOR NOW!
3.

BUT *WAIT*-- I CAN'T AFFORD TO *LOSE* HIM!

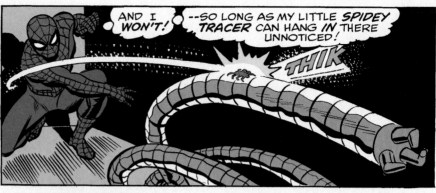

AND I *WON'T!*

--SO LONG AS MY LITTLE *SPIDEY TRACER* CAN HANG *IN* THERE UNNOTICED!

THIK

SECONDS LATER---

LOOKS LIKE THE COAST IS *CLEAR!*

≡WHEW!≡ I'M *ACHING* ALL OVER!

I WISH THERE WAS A SUPER-HEROES' *UNION* SOMEWHERE---

--'CAUSE IF THERE *WAS*, I'D MAKE SURE A FELLA GETS *TIME-AND-A-HALF* FOR TACKLING A JOKER WITH *FOUR METAL ARMS!*

WELL, IT LOOKS LIKE OCK FINALLY *SPLIT*--

AND I CAN'T SAY IT BREAKS MY HEART TO BE *RID* OF HIM FOR A WHILE!

ANYWAY, AS LONG AS MY *TRACER* STAYS WITH 'IM, I CAN *ALWAYS* PICK UP HIS TRAIL!

BUT *NOW*-- EVEN THOUGH IT MAY NOT BE IN THE BEST *SWASHBUCKLING TRADITION,* I'M HEADING HOME FOR SOME *SHUTEYE!*

YESSIR! I AM *ONE* WEARY LITTLE WEBHEAD!

4

THE UNDERSIDE OF A *LEDGE* WON'T EVER REPLACE A CEDAR-LINED *CLOSET*---

BUT IT'S A LOT MORE *CONVENIENT* FOR QUICK *COSTUME-CHANGING!*

WOW! I'M *ACHING* ALL OVER!

IF NOT FOR MY *SPIDER-STRENGTH*, OCK WOULD HAVE *FINISHED* ME!

MAN! EVEN MY *KNEES* FEEL LIKE WET *NOODLES!*

I MUST HAVE TAKEN A WORSE *BEATING* THAN I KNEW!

NO PARKING FRIDAY 11 A.M. TO 2 P.M. Police

IN THE EXCITE-MENT OF THE *BATTLE*, I GUESS I DIDN'T REALIZE HOW HE WAS *POUND-ING* ME!

WHA--? SOMEONE COMING UP *BEHIND* ME! IF IT'S OCK, WHY DIDN'T MY *SPIDEY SENSE* TINGLE?

I'VE BEEN *FOLLOWING* YOU!

5

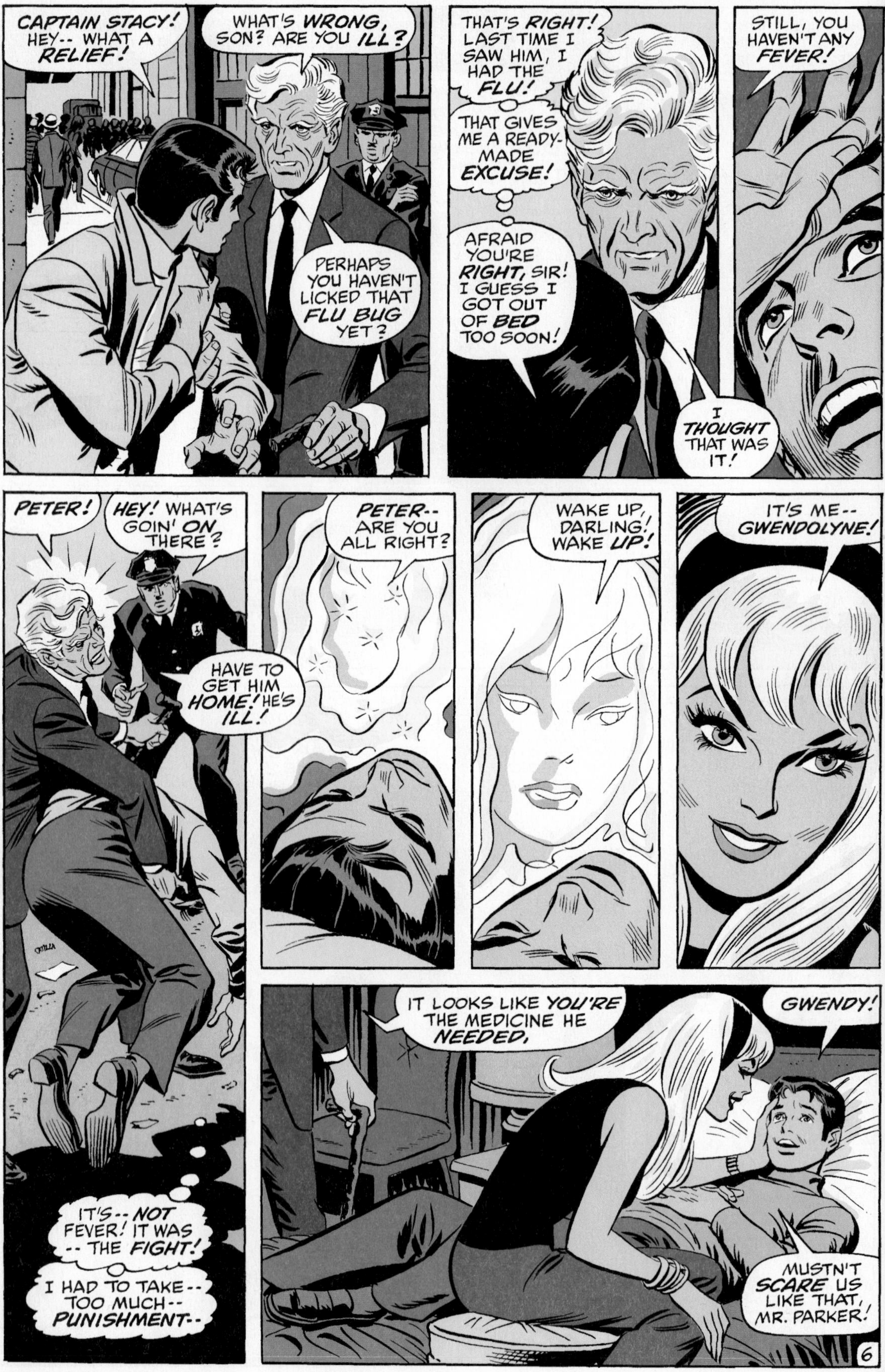
CAPTAIN STACY! HEY-- WHAT A RELIEF!
WHAT'S WRONG, SON? ARE YOU ILL?
PERHAPS YOU HAVEN'T LICKED THAT FLU BUG YET?
THAT'S RIGHT! LAST TIME I SAW HIM, I HAD THE FLU!
THAT GIVES ME A READY-MADE EXCUSE!
AFRAID YOU'RE RIGHT, SIR! I GUESS I GOT OUT OF BED TOO SOON!
STILL, YOU HAVEN'T ANY FEVER!
I THOUGHT THAT WAS IT!
PETER!
HEY! WHAT'S GOIN' ON THERE?
HAVE TO GET HIM HOME! HE'S ILL!
IT'S-- NOT FEVER! IT WAS -- THE FIGHT!
I HAD TO TAKE-- TOO MUCH-- PUNISHMENT--
PETER-- ARE YOU ALL RIGHT?
WAKE UP, DARLING! WAKE UP!
IT'S ME-- GWENDOLYNE!
IT LOOKS LIKE YOU'RE THE MEDICINE HE NEEDED.
GWENDY!
MUSTN'T SCARE US LIKE THAT, MR. PARKER!
6

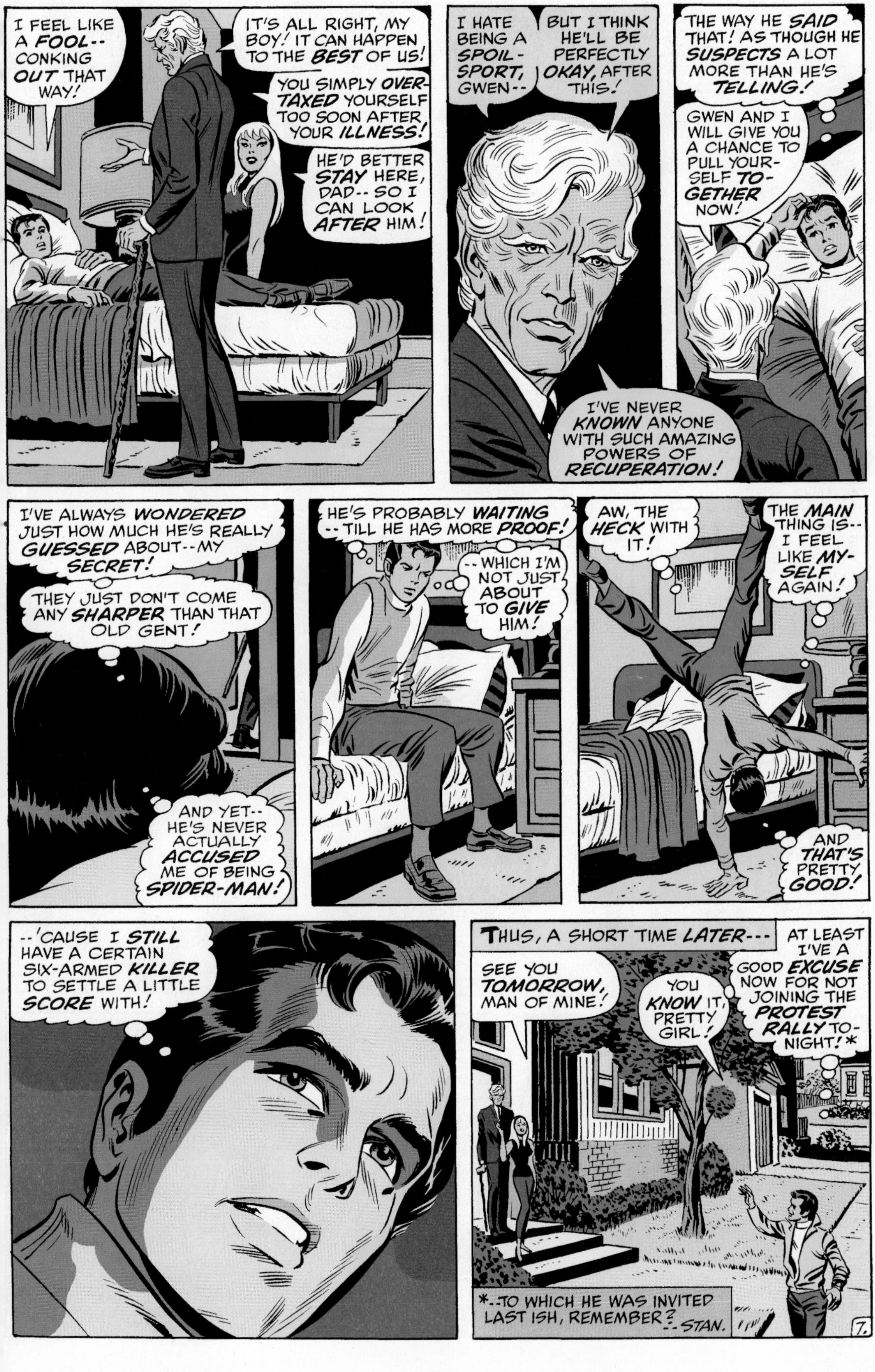

I FEEL LIKE A FOOL-- CONKING OUT THAT WAY!
IT'S ALL RIGHT, MY BOY! IT CAN HAPPEN TO THE BEST OF US!
YOU SIMPLY OVER-TAXED YOURSELF TOO SOON AFTER YOUR ILLNESS!
HE'D BETTER STAY HERE, DAD-- SO I CAN LOOK AFTER HIM!
I HATE BEING A SPOIL-SPORT, GWEN--
BUT I THINK HE'LL BE PERFECTLY OKAY, AFTER THIS!
I'VE NEVER KNOWN ANYONE WITH SUCH AMAZING POWERS OF RECUPERATION!
THE WAY HE SAID THAT! AS THOUGH HE SUSPECTS A LOT MORE THAN HE'S TELLING!
GWEN AND I WILL GIVE YOU A CHANCE TO PULL YOURSELF TOGETHER NOW!
I'VE ALWAYS WONDERED JUST HOW MUCH HE'S REALLY GUESSED ABOUT--MY SECRET!
THEY JUST DON'T COME ANY SHARPER THAN THAT OLD GENT!
AND YET-- HE'S NEVER ACTUALLY ACCUSED ME OF BEING SPIDER-MAN!
HE'S PROBABLY WAITING --TILL HE HAS MORE PROOF!
--WHICH I'M NOT JUST ABOUT TO GIVE HIM!
AW, THE HECK WITH IT!
THE MAIN THING IS-- I FEEL LIKE MYSELF AGAIN!
AND THAT'S PRETTY GOOD!
--'CAUSE I STILL HAVE A CERTAIN SIX-ARMED KILLER TO SETTLE A LITTLE SCORE WITH!
THUS, A SHORT TIME LATER---
SEE YOU TOMORROW, MAN OF MINE!
YOU KNOW IT, PRETTY GIRL!
AT LEAST I'VE A GOOD EXCUSE NOW FOR NOT JOINING THE PROTEST RALLY TONIGHT!*
*--TO WHICH HE WAS INVITED LAST ISH, REMEMBER? --STAN.
7.

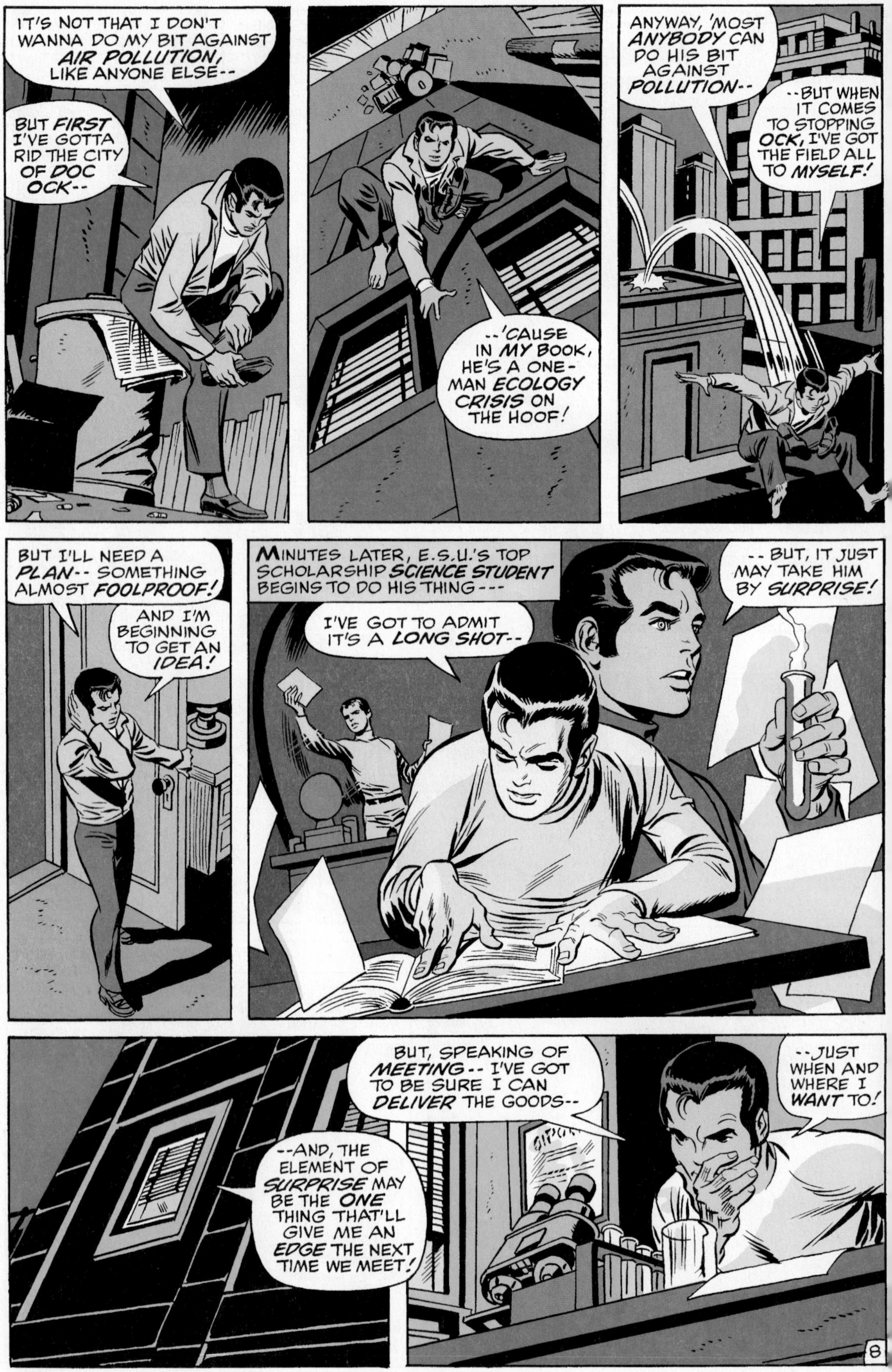
IT'S NOT THAT I DON'T WANNA DO MY BIT AGAINST AIR POLLUTION, LIKE ANYONE ELSE--
BUT FIRST I'VE GOTTA RID THE CITY OF DOC OCK--
--'CAUSE IN MY BOOK, HE'S A ONE-MAN ECOLOGY CRISIS ON THE HOOF!
ANYWAY, 'MOST ANYBODY CAN DO HIS BIT AGAINST POLLUTION--
--BUT WHEN IT COMES TO STOPPING OCK, I'VE GOT THE FIELD ALL TO MYSELF!
BUT I'LL NEED A PLAN-- SOMETHING ALMOST FOOLPROOF!
AND I'M BEGINNING TO GET AN IDEA!
MINUTES LATER, E.S.U.'S TOP SCHOLARSHIP SCIENCE STUDENT BEGINS TO DO HIS THING---
I'VE GOT TO ADMIT IT'S A LONG SHOT--
-- BUT, IT JUST MAY TAKE HIM BY SURPRISE!
--AND, THE ELEMENT OF SURPRISE MAY BE THE ONE THING THAT'LL GIVE ME AN EDGE THE NEXT TIME WE MEET!
BUT, SPEAKING OF MEETING-- I'VE GOT TO BE SURE I CAN DELIVER THE GOODS--
--JUST WHEN AND WHERE I WANT TO!
8

NOW I'LL JUST GET MY LITTLE GIZMO ALL *SET UP*--

BY FILLING MY *WEB SHOOTER* WITH A BRAND NEW *FLUID!*

-- AND ARRANGING THE *FIRING BUTTON* JUST WHERE I'LL *NEED* IT!

NOW, ALL THAT REMAINS IS TO FIND *DOC OCK!*

AND THAT'S WHERE MY LITTLE *SPIDEY TRACER* COMES IN!

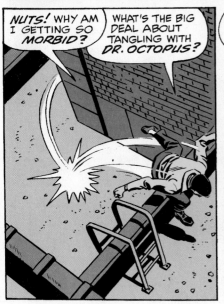

SLEEP TIGHT, OL' *BUDDY!*

IF THINGS TURN OUT THE WAY I *HOPE,* I'LL BE *BACK* NEXT DOOR BEFORE YOU STOP SNORING!

AND, IF THEY *DON'T*--

THEN YOU'LL NEVER SEE ME *AGAIN!* --ALIVE, THAT IS!

NUTS! WHY AM I GETTING SO *MORBID?*

WHAT'S THE BIG DEAL ABOUT TANGLING WITH *DR. OCTOPUS?*

JUST BECAUSE HE'S THE *DEADLIEST* HUMAN I'VE EVER FACED--

WITH *ARMS* THAT CAN OUT-FIGHT A WHOLE *REGIMENT*--

IS *THAT* ANY REASON TO GET ALL *UPTIGHT?*

YOU BET YOUR SWEET *BIPPY* IT *IS!*

BUT I'M NOT GONNA BACK OUT *NOW!*

9.

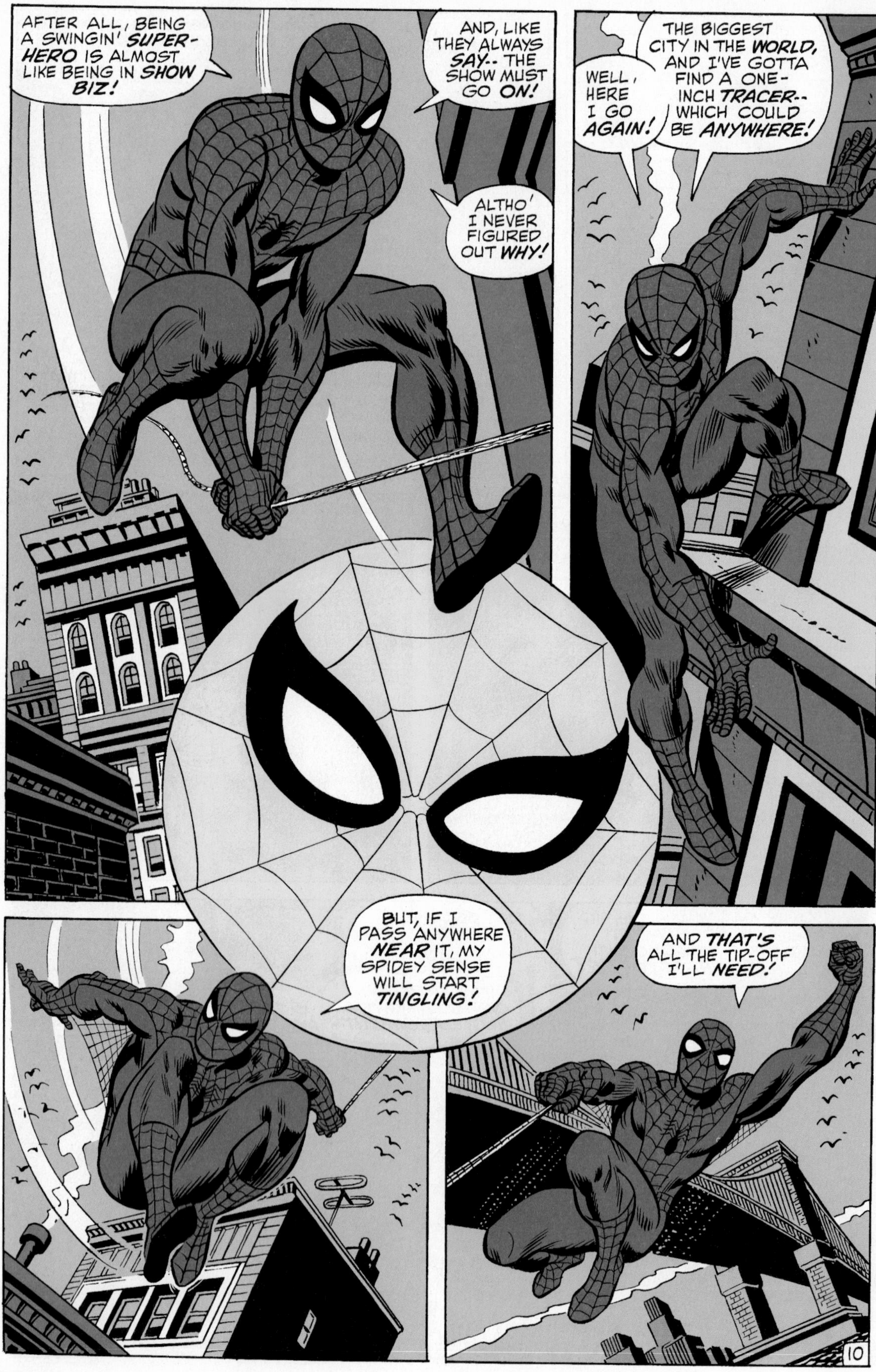
AFTER ALL, BEING A SWINGIN' SUPER-HERO IS ALMOST LIKE BEING IN SHOW BIZ!
AND, LIKE THEY ALWAYS SAY-- THE SHOW MUST GO ON!
ALTHO' I NEVER FIGURED OUT WHY!
WELL, HERE I GO AGAIN!
THE BIGGEST CITY IN THE WORLD, AND I'VE GOTTA FIND A ONE-INCH TRACER-- WHICH COULD BE ANYWHERE!
BUT, IF I PASS ANYWHERE NEAR IT, MY SPIDEY SENSE WILL START TINGLING!
AND THAT'S ALL THE TIP-OFF I'LL NEED!
10

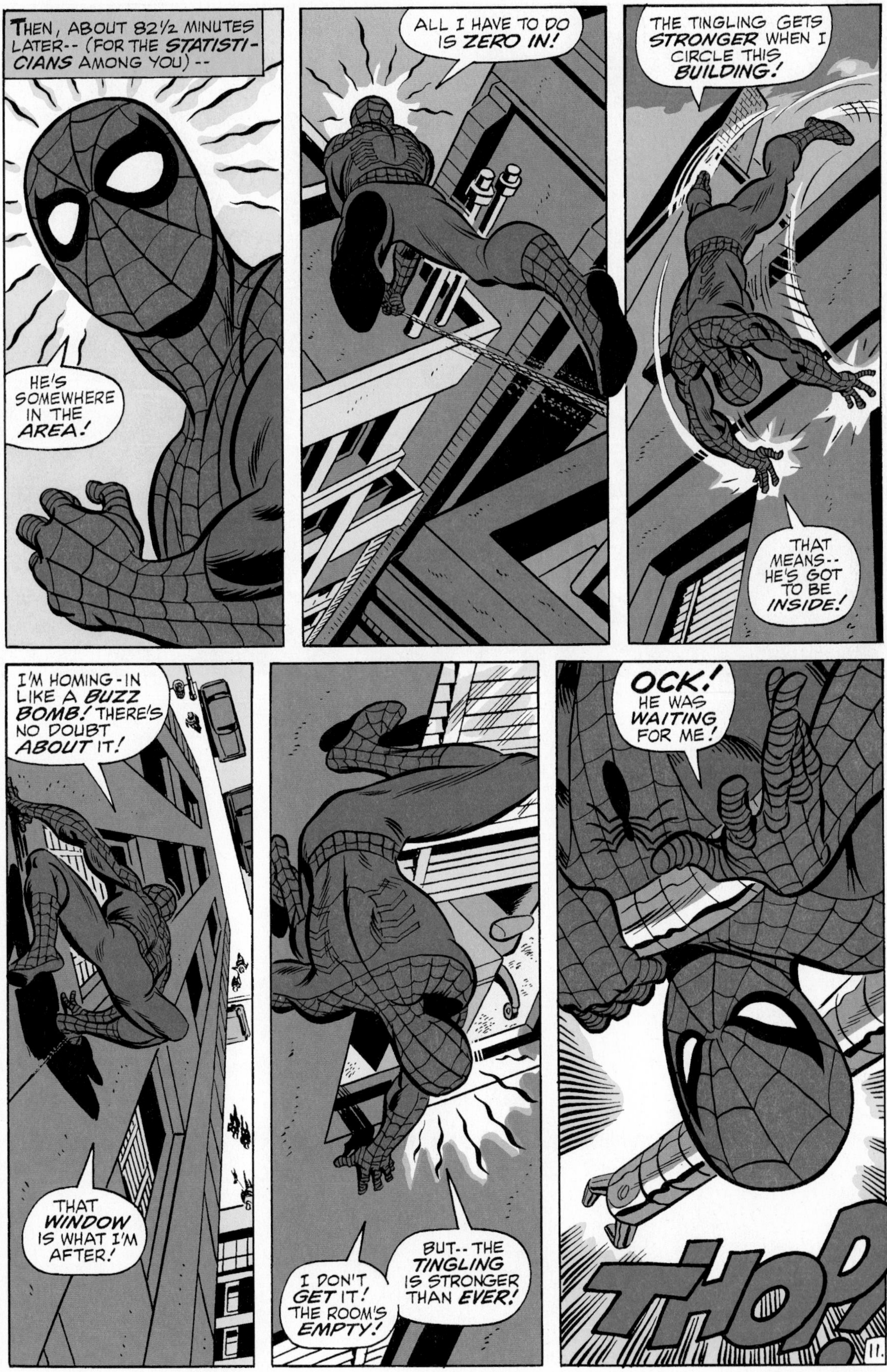
THEN, ABOUT 82½ MINUTES LATER-- (FOR THE STATISTICIANS AMONG YOU)--
HE'S SOMEWHERE IN THE AREA!
ALL I HAVE TO DO IS ZERO IN!
THE TINGLING GETS STRONGER WHEN I CIRCLE THIS BUILDING!
THAT MEANS-- HE'S GOT TO BE INSIDE!
I'M HOMING-IN LIKE A BUZZ BOMB! THERE'S NO DOUBT ABOUT IT!
THAT WINDOW IS WHAT I'M AFTER!
I DON'T GET IT! THE ROOM'S EMPTY!
BUT-- THE TINGLING IS STRONGER THAN EVER!
OCK! HE WAS WAITING FOR ME!
THOP!
11.

I WAS A FOOL! I PUT TOO MUCH FAITH IN MY SPIDEY TRACER!
NOW PLAYING HIGH S
BRAK!
ZROK!
12

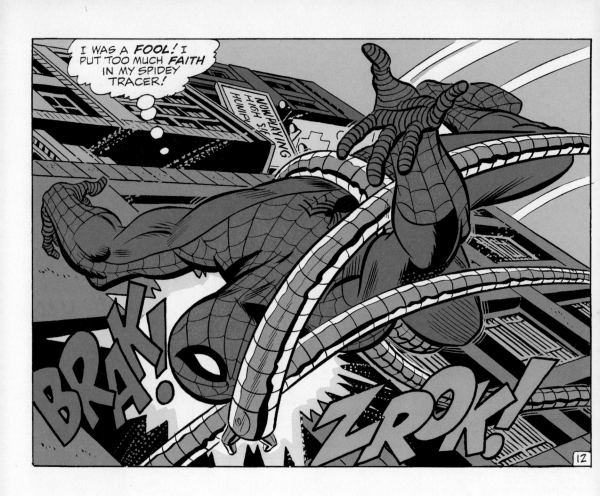

DID YOU FORGET THAT I AM A SCIENTIST?
DID YOU THINK, WHEN I FOUND THE PRIMITIVE LITTLE GADGET YOU PLACED UPON MY TENTACLE, THAT I WOULDN'T FATHOM ITS PURPOSE?
SO, I MERELY PLACED IT IN THAT ROOM-- USING IT AS A TRAP IN WHICH TO CATCH YOU-- WHILE I SECRETLY WAITED UPON THIS ROOF ABOVE!
YOU CAN NEVER BE A MATCH FOR ME!
FOR NOT ONLY AM I YOUR MASTER IN STRENGTH--
-- BUT IN CUNNING, AND GUILE, AND INTELLIGENCE AS WELL!
13

BUT SURELY THERE IS NO NEED TO *TELL* YOU ALL THAT--

SYAT!

FOR, IT MUST BE PAINFULLY *CLEAR* TO YOU BY *NOW!*

AND, JUST IN CASE IT *ISN'T*--

I'LL TRY TO MAKE IT EVEN *CLEARER!*

MY *ARMS!* I-- HAVE TO GET THEM-- *FREE!*

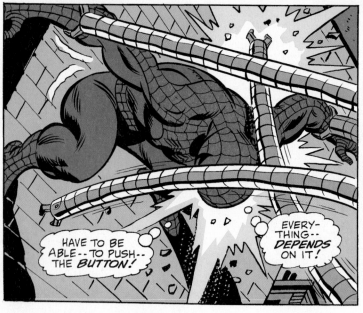

HAVE TO BE ABLE-- TO PUSH-- THE *BUTTON!*

EVERY-THING-- *DEPENDS* ON IT!

CAN'T LET HIM *HOLD* ME-- THIS WAY! I *CAN'T!* I *CAN'T!*

I CAN'T!

14

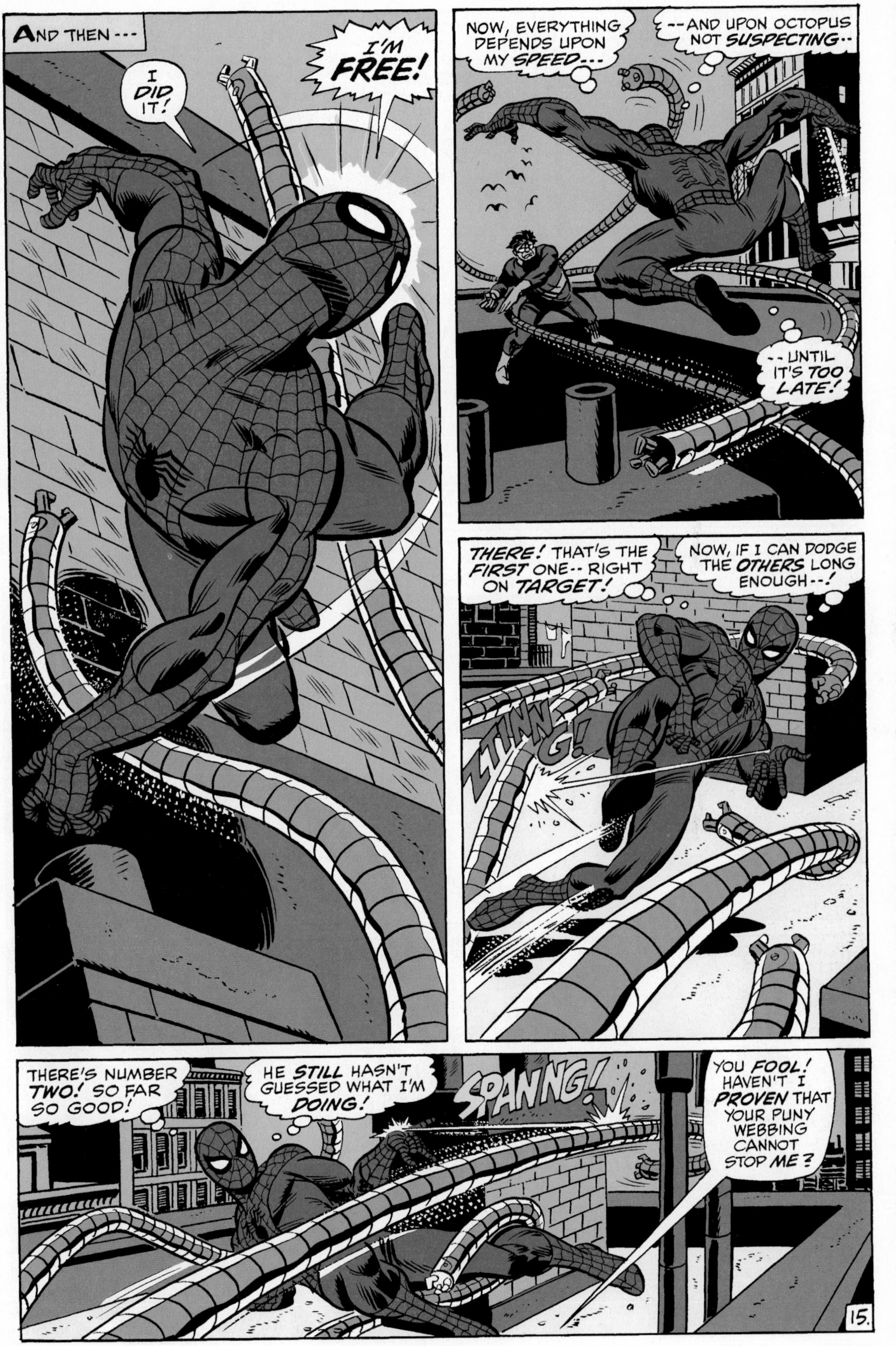
AND THEN ---
I DID IT!
I'M FREE!
NOW, EVERYTHING DEPENDS UPON MY SPEED---
--AND UPON OCTOPUS NOT SUSPECTING--
--UNTIL IT'S TOO LATE!
THERE! THAT'S THE FIRST ONE-- RIGHT ON TARGET!
NOW, IF I CAN DODGE THE OTHERS LONG ENOUGH--!
ZTINNG!
THERE'S NUMBER TWO! SO FAR SO GOOD!
HE STILL HASN'T GUESSED WHAT I'M DOING!
SPANNG!
YOU FOOL! HAVEN'T I PROVEN THAT YOUR PUNY WEBBING CANNOT STOP ME?
15.

I'VE ONLY TO EXERT THE *SLIGHTEST* EFFORT--

--TO *SNAP* IT LIKE A PIECE OF *HARMLESS THREAD!*

BUT-- WHAT IS *THIS?* WHAT IS *HAPPENING?*

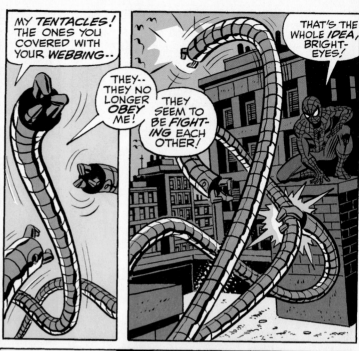

MY *TENTACLES!* THE ONES YOU COVERED WITH YOUR *WEBBING*...

THEY-- THEY NO LONGER *OBEY* ME!

THEY SEEM TO BE *FIGHTING* EACH OTHER!

THAT'S THE WHOLE *IDEA,* BRIGHT-EYES!

YOU *TRICKED* ME! IT-- IT *WASN'T* ORDINARY WEBBING!

IT WAS A *CHEMICAL FLUID*-- LIKE A *JAMMING DEVICE* BETWEEN MY *BRAIN IMPULSES*... AND MY *ARMS!*

THEY'RE STRIKING *BLINDLY!* I'VE LOST *CONTROL!*

THEY'RE-- *ATTACKING* EACH OTHER!

RIGHT, *PUDGY!* AND YOU AIN'T SEEN *NOTHIN'* YET!

NOW THEY'RE-- ATTACKING *ME!*

THAT'S THE NAME OF THE *GAME,* DOC!

=UNNHH!=

THOK!

16

IT WON'T **WORK!** I'LL BEAT YOU **YET!**

MY **OTHER** ARMS WILL SAVE ME!

IT'S **DOCTOR OCTOPUS**--- FIGHTING **SPIDER-MAN** UP THERE!

THE **BEST** THING THAT COULD HAPPEN FOR THIS TOWN WOULD BE IF THEY **BOTH** FINISH EACH OTHER OFF!

I REACHED HERE JUST IN **TIME!** THEY'RE STILL **BATTLING**--- UP ON THAT **ROOF!**

BUT THE **CROWD** BELOW--- DOESN'T REALIZE THE **DANGER!**

THEY MUST **CLEAR** THE AREA!

I'D BETTER **GET** HIM-- BEFORE HE'S KILLED BY HIS OWN **ARMS!**

SPROK!

OH **BROTHER!** THERE'S JUST NO **STOPPING** THEM NOW.

HELP ME! HELP ME! I-- I CAN'T **HANDLE** THEM!

DON'T WORRY, MAN! THE **COPS** ARE ON THE WAY RIGHT **NOW!**

--THEY'LL HELP YOU TO A NICE COZY LITTLE **CELL** IN-- **HEY!**

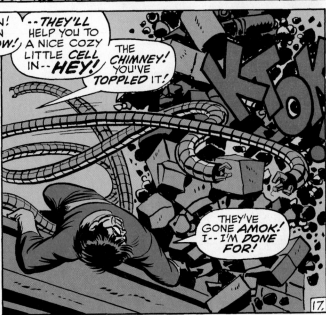

THE **CHIMNEY!** YOU'VE **TOPPLED** IT!

THEY'VE GONE **AMOK!** I-- I'M **DONE** FOR!

KTOK

17

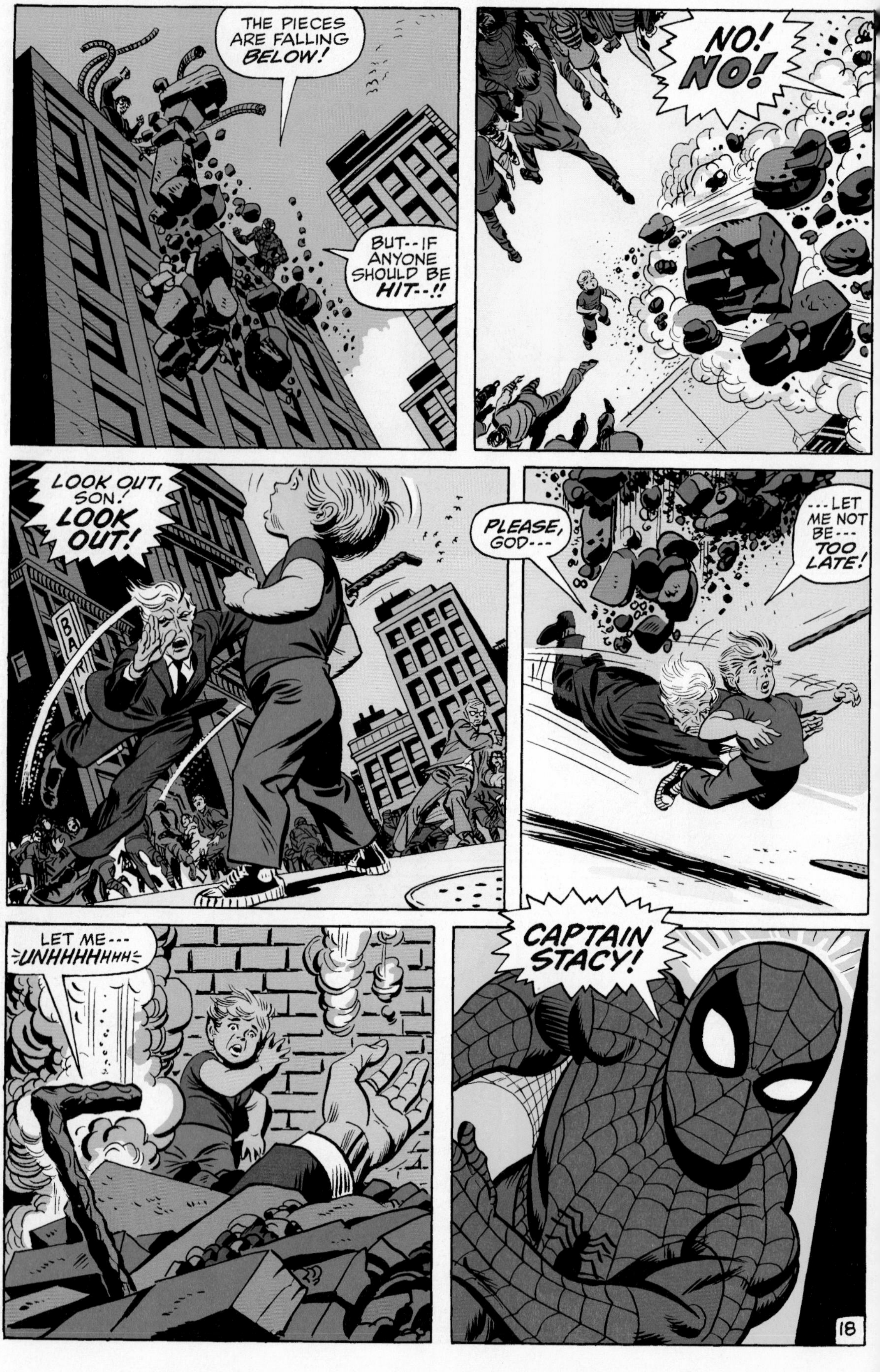
THE PIECES ARE FALLING BELOW!
BUT--IF ANYONE SHOULD BE HIT--!!
NO! NO!
LOOK OUT, SON! LOOK OUT!
PLEASE, GOD---
---LET ME NOT BE---TOO LATE!
LET ME---
UNHHHHHHH
CAPTAIN STACY!
18

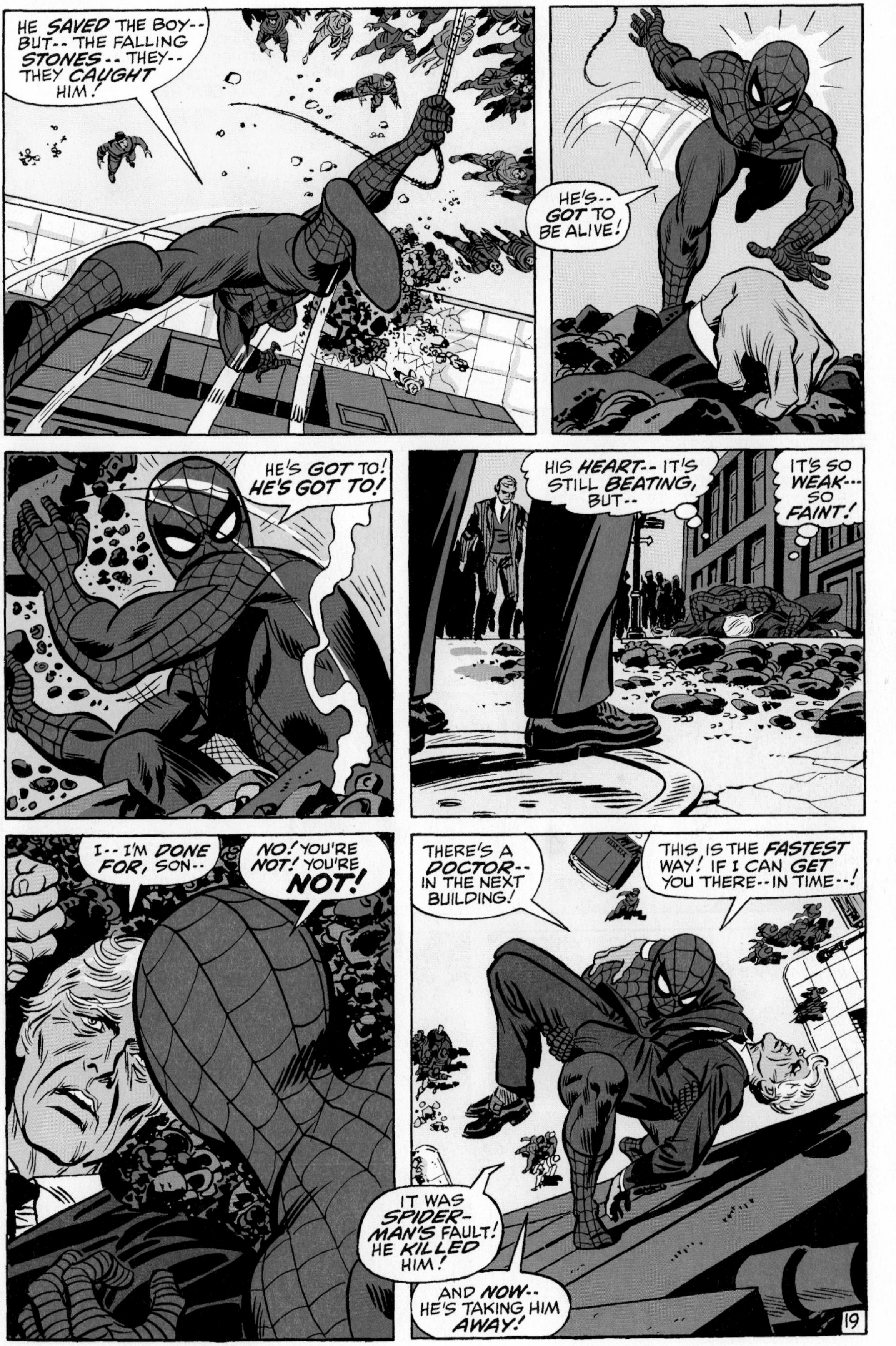
HE SAVED THE BOY-- BUT-- THE FALLING STONES-- THEY-- THEY CAUGHT HIM!
HE'S-- GOT TO BE ALIVE!
HE'S GOT TO! HE'S GOT TO!
HIS HEART-- IT'S STILL BEATING, BUT--
IT'S SO WEAK--- SO FAINT!
I-- I'M DONE FOR, SON--
NO! YOU'RE NOT! YOU'RE NOT!
THERE'S A DOCTOR-- IN THE NEXT BUILDING!
THIS IS THE FASTEST WAY! IF I CAN GET YOU THERE--IN TIME--!
IT WAS SPIDER-MAN'S FAULT! HE KILLED HIM!
AND NOW-- HE'S TAKING HIM AWAY!
19

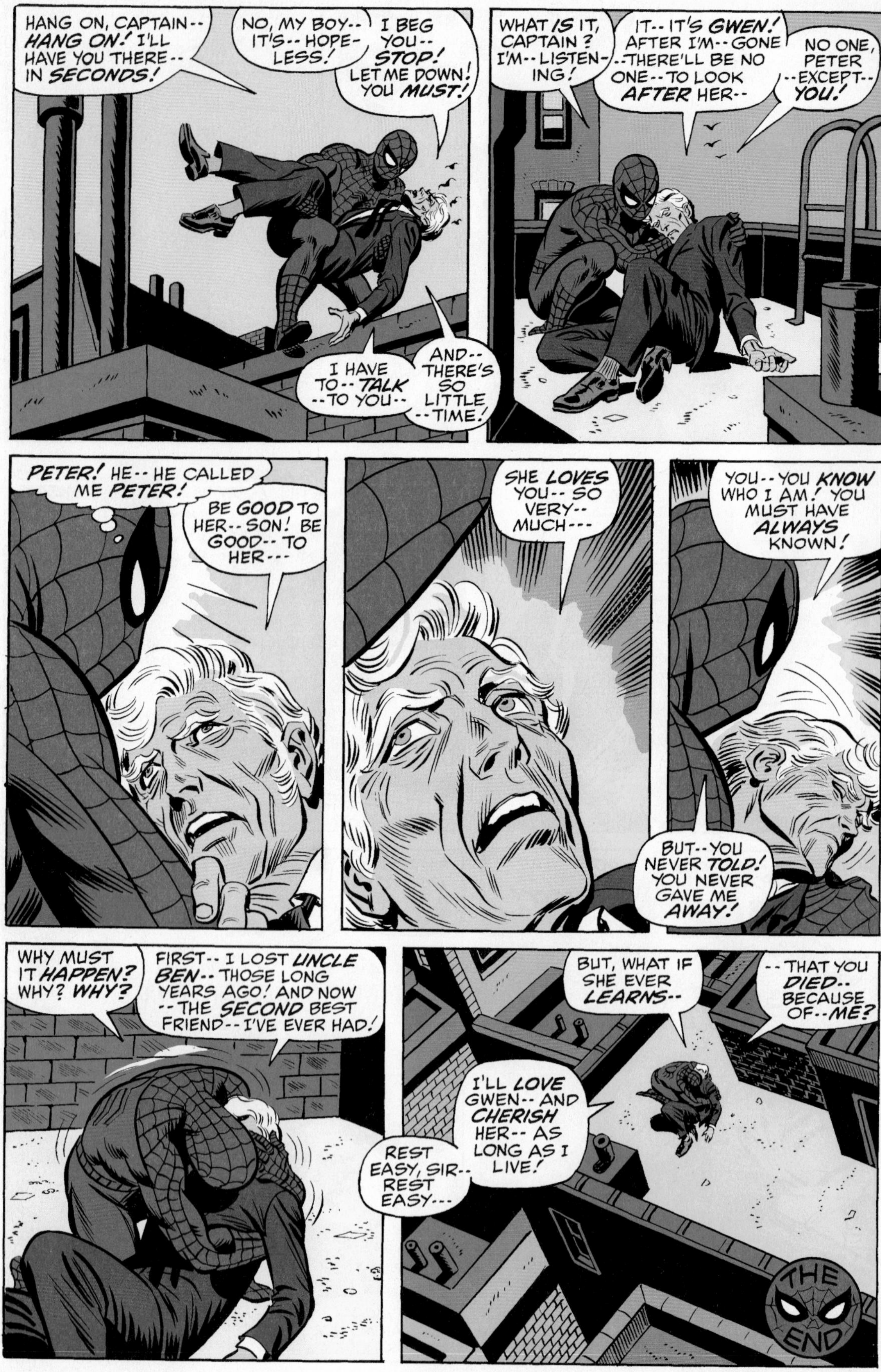
HANG ON, CAPTAIN-- HANG ON! I'LL HAVE YOU THERE-- IN SECONDS!
NO, MY BOY-- IT'S--HOPE-LESS!
I BEG YOU-- STOP! LET ME DOWN! YOU MUST!
I HAVE TO--TALK --TO YOU--
AND-- THERE'S SO LITTLE --TIME!
WHAT IS IT, CAPTAIN? I'M--LISTEN-ING!
IT--IT'S GWEN! AFTER I'M--GONE --THERE'LL BE NO ONE--TO LOOK AFTER HER--
NO ONE, PETER --EXCEPT-- YOU!
PETER! HE--HE CALLED ME PETER!
BE GOOD TO HER--SON! BE GOOD--TO HER---
SHE LOVES YOU--SO VERY-- MUCH---
YOU--YOU KNOW WHO I AM! YOU MUST HAVE ALWAYS KNOWN!
BUT--YOU NEVER TOLD! YOU NEVER GAVE ME AWAY!
WHY MUST IT HAPPEN? WHY? WHY?
FIRST--I LOST UNCLE BEN--THOSE LONG YEARS AGO! AND NOW --THE SECOND BEST FRIEND--I'VE EVER HAD!
BUT, WHAT IF SHE EVER LEARNS--
--THAT YOU DIED-- BECAUSE OF--ME?
I'LL LOVE GWEN--AND CHERISH HER--AS LONG AS I LIVE!
REST EASY, SIR-- REST EASY---
THE END

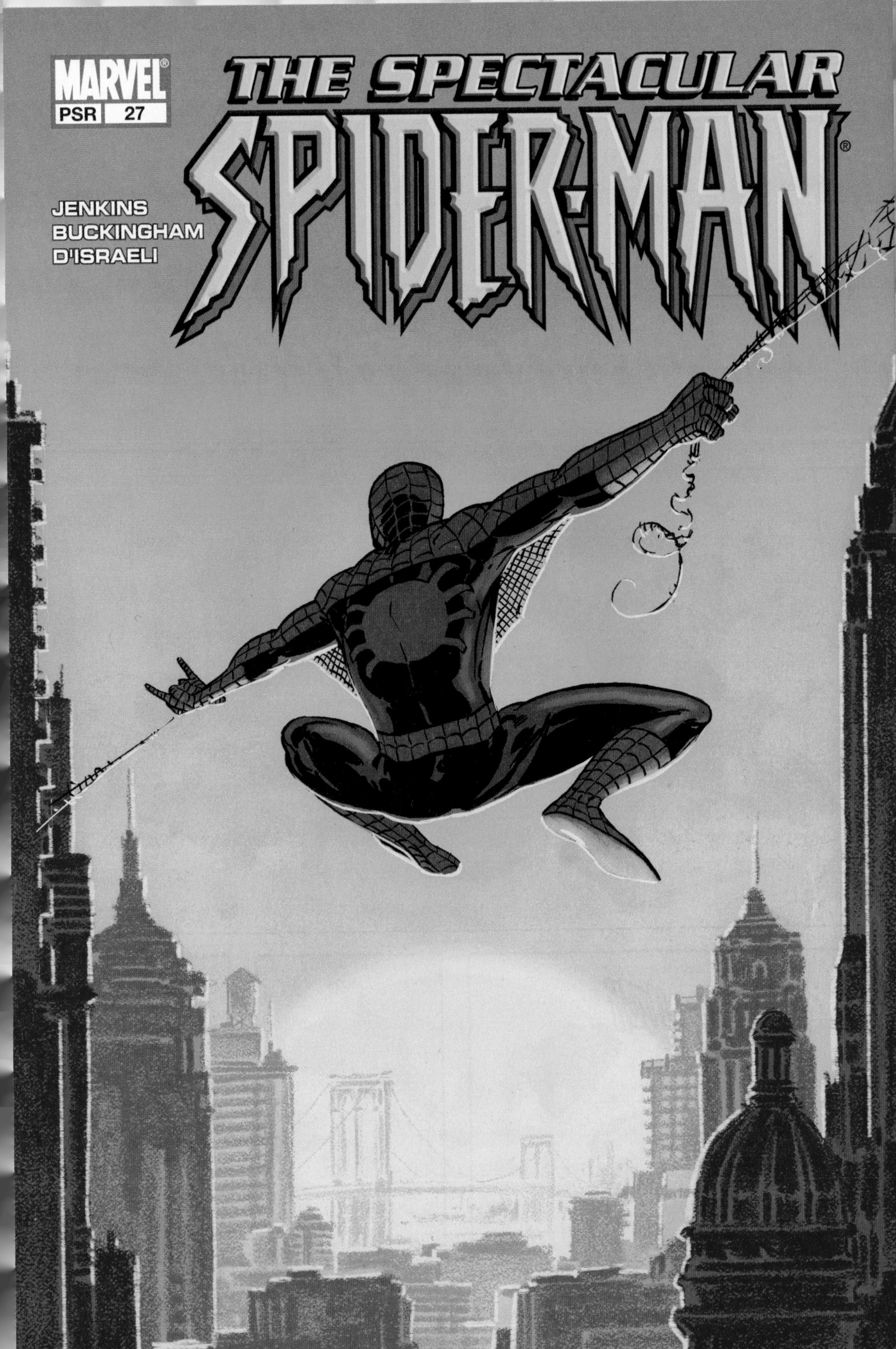
MARVEL
PSR 27
THE SPECTACULAR SPIDER-MAN
JENKINS
BUCKINGHAM
D'ISRAELI

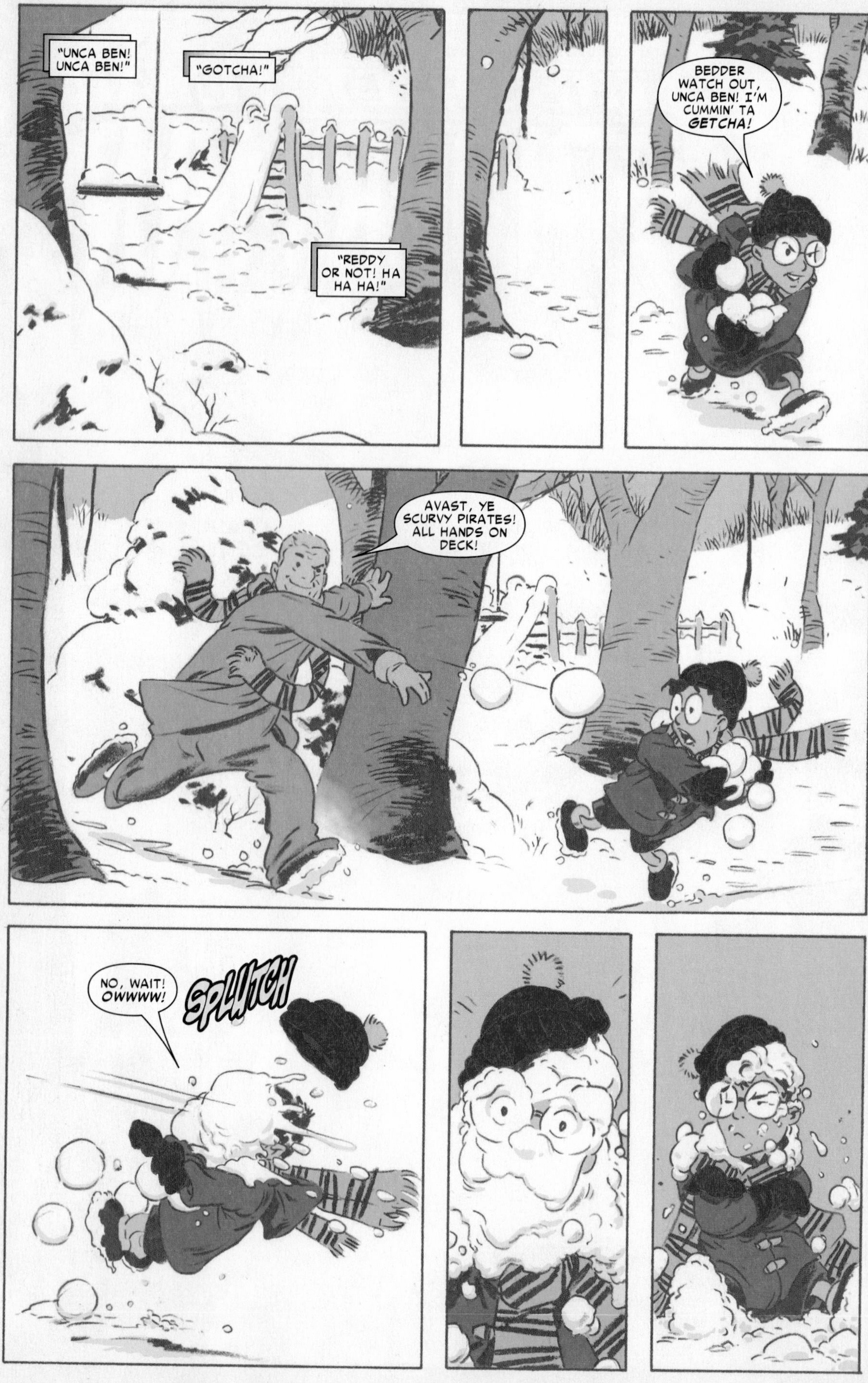
"UNCA BEN! UNCA BEN!"
"GOTCHA!"
"REDDY OR NOT! HA HA HA!"
BEDDER WATCH OUT, UNCA BEN! I'M CUMMIN' TA GETCHA!
AVAST, YE SCURVY PIRATES! ALL HANDS ON DECK!
NO, WAIT! OWWWW!
SPLUTCH

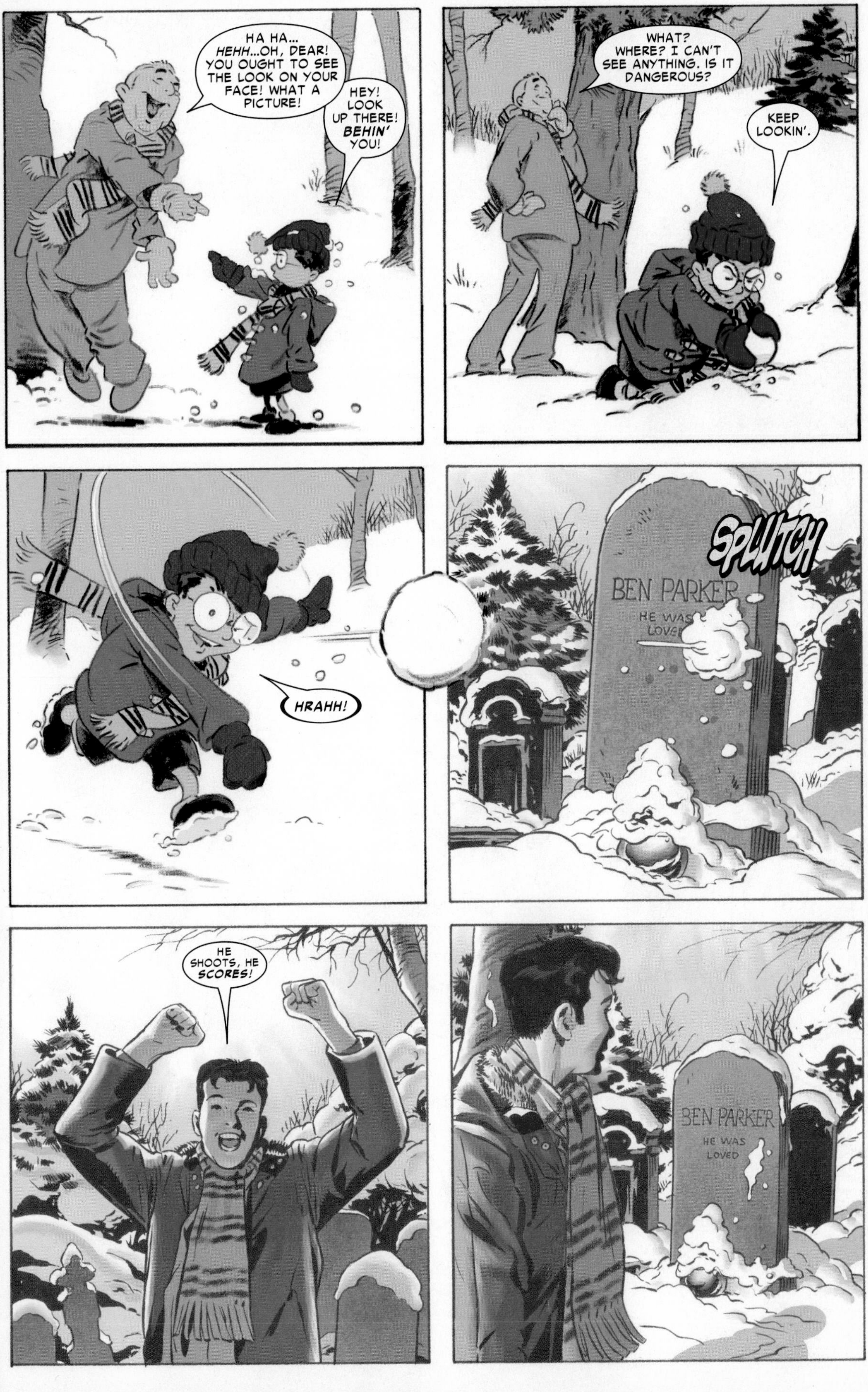
HA HA... HEHH...OH, DEAR! YOU OUGHT TO SEE THE LOOK ON YOUR FACE! WHAT A PICTURE!
HEY! LOOK UP THERE! BEHIN' YOU!
WHAT? WHERE? I CAN'T SEE ANYTHING. IS IT DANGEROUS?
KEEP LOOKIN'.
HRAHH!
SPLUTCH
BEN PARKER
HE WAS LOVED
HE SHOOTS, HE SCORES!
BEN PARKER
HE WAS LOVED

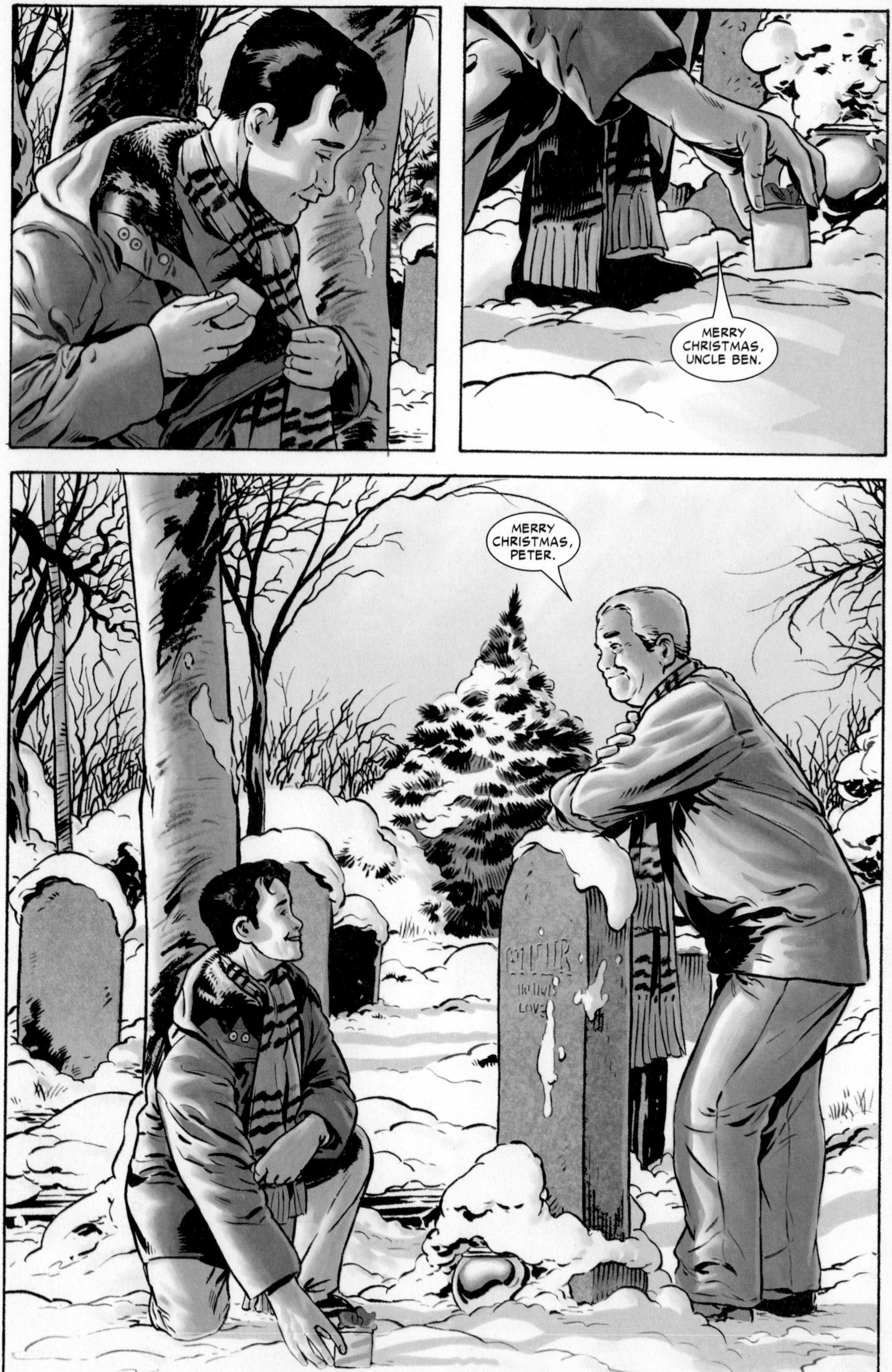

MERRY CHRISTMAS, UNCLE BEN.
MERRY CHRISTMAS, PETER.

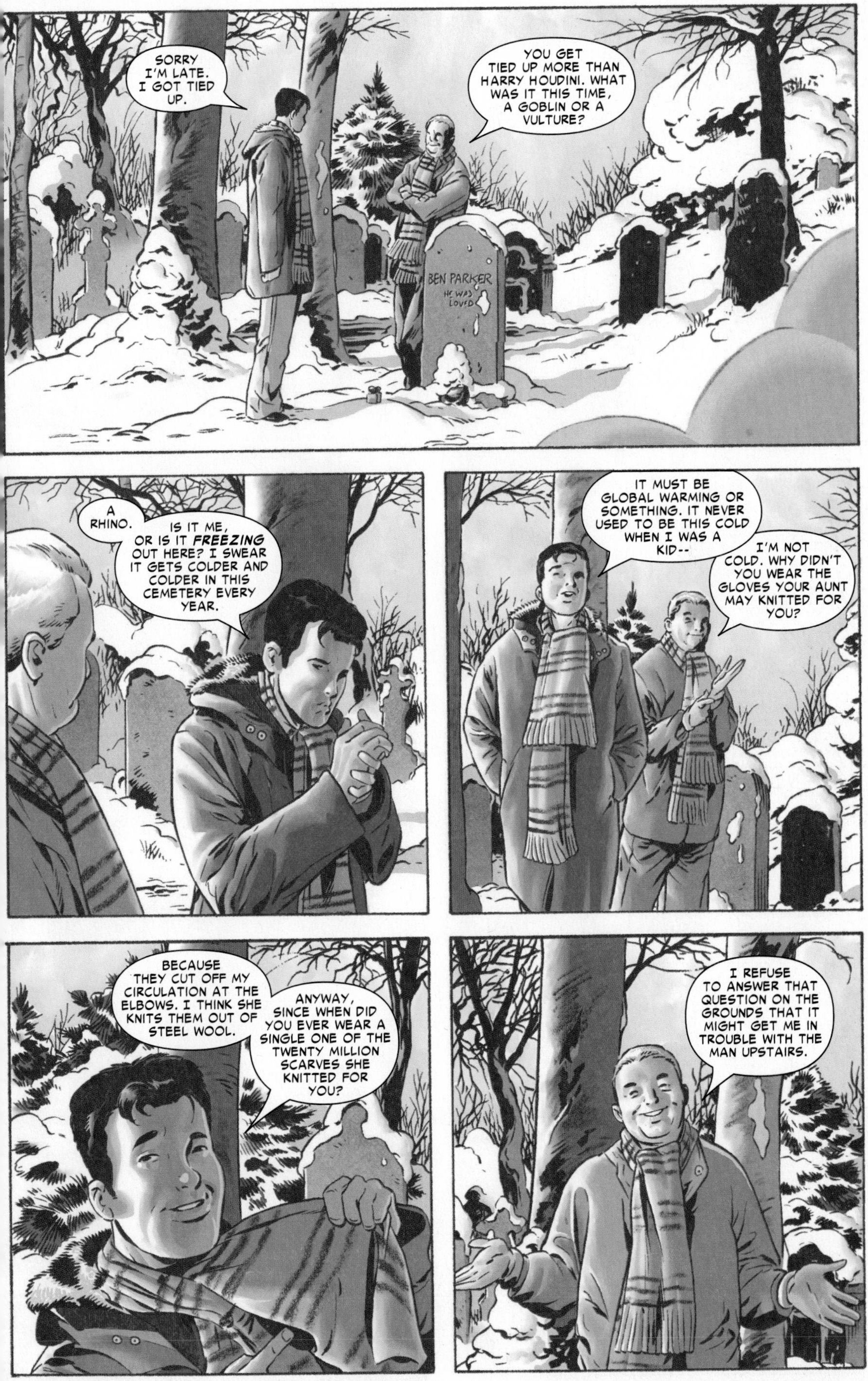
SORRY I'M LATE. I GOT TIED UP.
YOU GET TIED UP MORE THAN HARRY HOUDINI. WHAT WAS IT THIS TIME, A GOBLIN OR A VULTURE?
BEN PARKER
HE WAS LOVED
A RHINO.
IS IT ME, OR IS IT *FREEZING* OUT HERE? I SWEAR IT GETS COLDER AND COLDER IN THIS CEMETERY EVERY YEAR.
IT MUST BE GLOBAL WARMING OR SOMETHING. IT NEVER USED TO BE THIS COLD WHEN I WAS A KID--
I'M NOT COLD. WHY DIDN'T YOU WEAR THE GLOVES YOUR AUNT MAY KNITTED FOR YOU?
BECAUSE THEY CUT OFF MY CIRCULATION AT THE ELBOWS. I THINK SHE KNITS THEM OUT OF STEEL WOOL.
ANYWAY, SINCE WHEN DID YOU EVER WEAR A SINGLE ONE OF THE TWENTY MILLION SCARVES SHE KNITTED FOR YOU?
I REFUSE TO ANSWER THAT QUESTION ON THE GROUNDS THAT IT MIGHT GET ME IN TROUBLE WITH THE MAN UPSTAIRS.

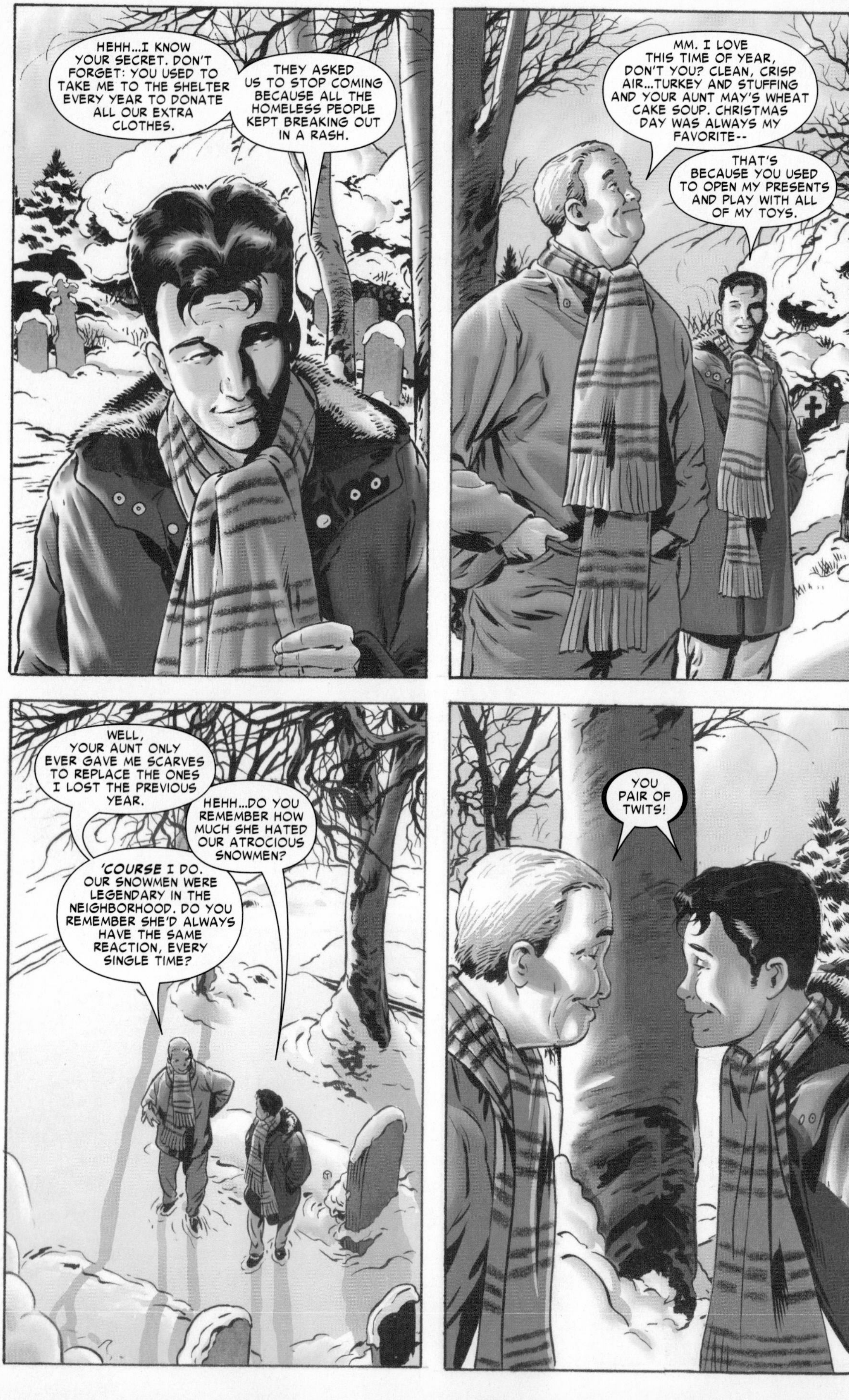
HEHH...I KNOW YOUR SECRET. DON'T FORGET: YOU USED TO TAKE ME TO THE SHELTER EVERY YEAR TO DONATE ALL OUR EXTRA CLOTHES.
THEY ASKED US TO STOP COMING BECAUSE ALL THE HOMELESS PEOPLE KEPT BREAKING OUT IN A RASH.
MM. I LOVE THIS TIME OF YEAR, DON'T YOU? CLEAN, CRISP AIR...TURKEY AND STUFFING AND YOUR AUNT MAY'S WHEAT CAKE SOUP. CHRISTMAS DAY WAS ALWAYS MY FAVORITE--
THAT'S BECAUSE YOU USED TO OPEN MY PRESENTS AND PLAY WITH ALL OF MY TOYS.
WELL, YOUR AUNT ONLY EVER GAVE ME SCARVES TO REPLACE THE ONES I LOST THE PREVIOUS YEAR.
HEHH...DO YOU REMEMBER HOW MUCH SHE HATED OUR ATROCIOUS SNOWMEN?
'COURSE I DO. OUR SNOWMEN WERE LEGENDARY IN THE NEIGHBORHOOD. DO YOU REMEMBER SHE'D ALWAYS HAVE THE SAME REACTION, EVERY SINGLE TIME?
YOU PAIR OF TWITS!

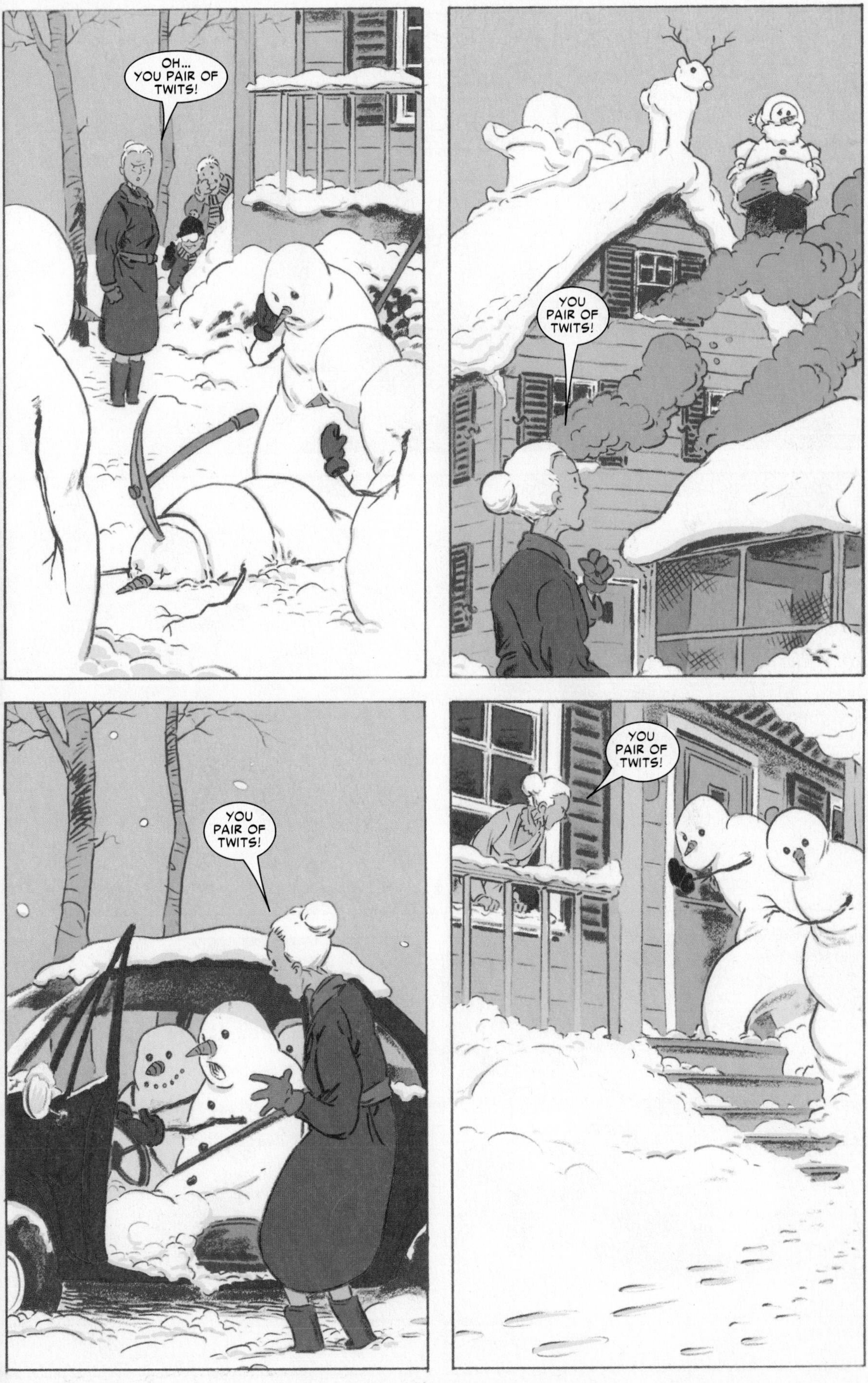
OH... YOU PAIR OF TWITS!
YOU PAIR OF TWITS!
YOU PAIR OF TWITS!
YOU PAIR OF TWITS!

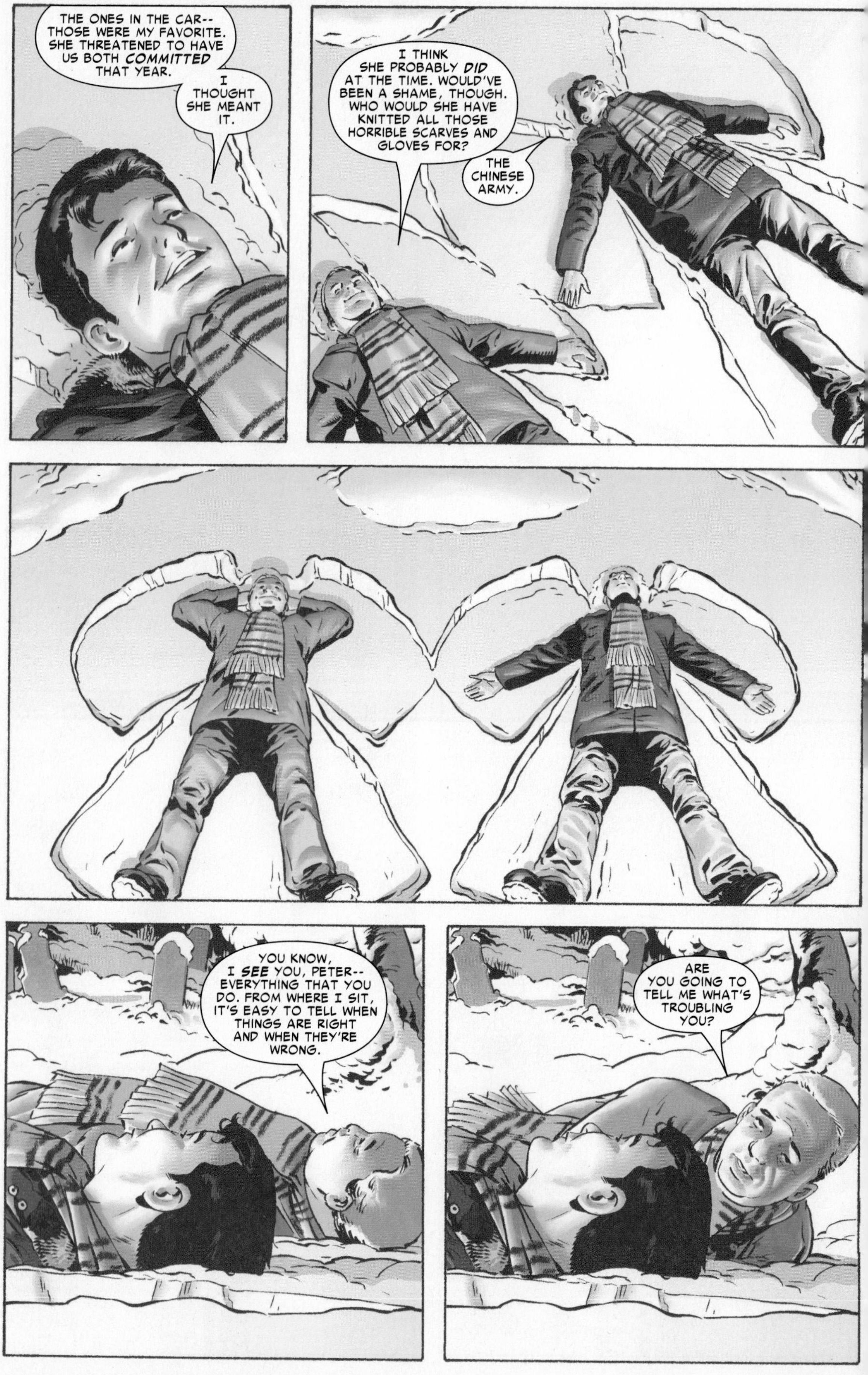
THE ONES IN THE CAR-- THOSE WERE MY FAVORITE. SHE THREATENED TO HAVE US BOTH COMMITTED THAT YEAR.
I THOUGHT SHE MEANT IT.
I THINK SHE PROBABLY DID AT THE TIME. WOULD'VE BEEN A SHAME, THOUGH. WHO WOULD SHE HAVE KNITTED ALL THOSE HORRIBLE SCARVES AND GLOVES FOR?
THE CHINESE ARMY.
YOU KNOW, I SEE YOU, PETER-- EVERYTHING THAT YOU DO. FROM WHERE I SIT, IT'S EASY TO TELL WHEN THINGS ARE RIGHT AND WHEN THEY'RE WRONG.
ARE YOU GOING TO TELL ME WHAT'S TROUBLING YOU?

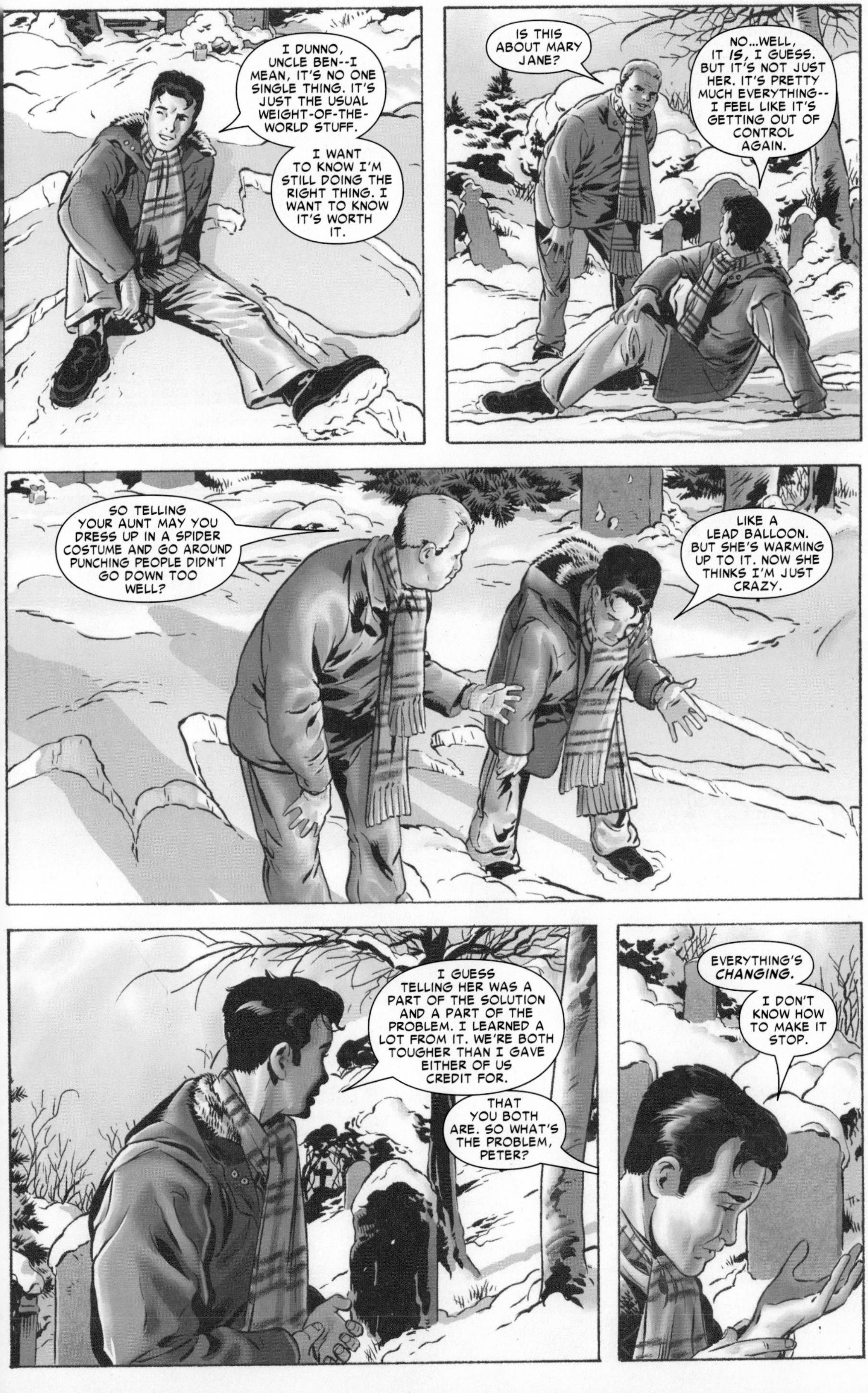
I DUNNO, UNCLE BEN--I MEAN, IT'S NO ONE SINGLE THING. IT'S JUST THE USUAL WEIGHT-OF-THE-WORLD STUFF.
I WANT TO KNOW I'M STILL DOING THE RIGHT THING. I WANT TO KNOW IT'S WORTH IT.
IS THIS ABOUT MARY JANE?
NO...WELL, IT *IS*, I GUESS. BUT IT'S NOT JUST HER. IT'S PRETTY MUCH EVERYTHING--I FEEL LIKE IT'S GETTING OUT OF CONTROL AGAIN.
SO TELLING YOUR AUNT MAY YOU DRESS UP IN A SPIDER COSTUME AND GO AROUND PUNCHING PEOPLE DIDN'T GO DOWN TOO WELL?
LIKE A LEAD BALLOON. BUT SHE'S WARMING UP TO IT. NOW SHE THINKS I'M JUST CRAZY.
I GUESS TELLING HER WAS A PART OF THE SOLUTION AND A PART OF THE PROBLEM. I LEARNED A LOT FROM IT. WE'RE BOTH TOUGHER THAN I GAVE EITHER OF US CREDIT FOR.
THAT YOU BOTH ARE. SO WHAT'S THE PROBLEM, PETER?
EVERYTHING'S *CHANGING.*
I DON'T KNOW HOW TO MAKE IT STOP.

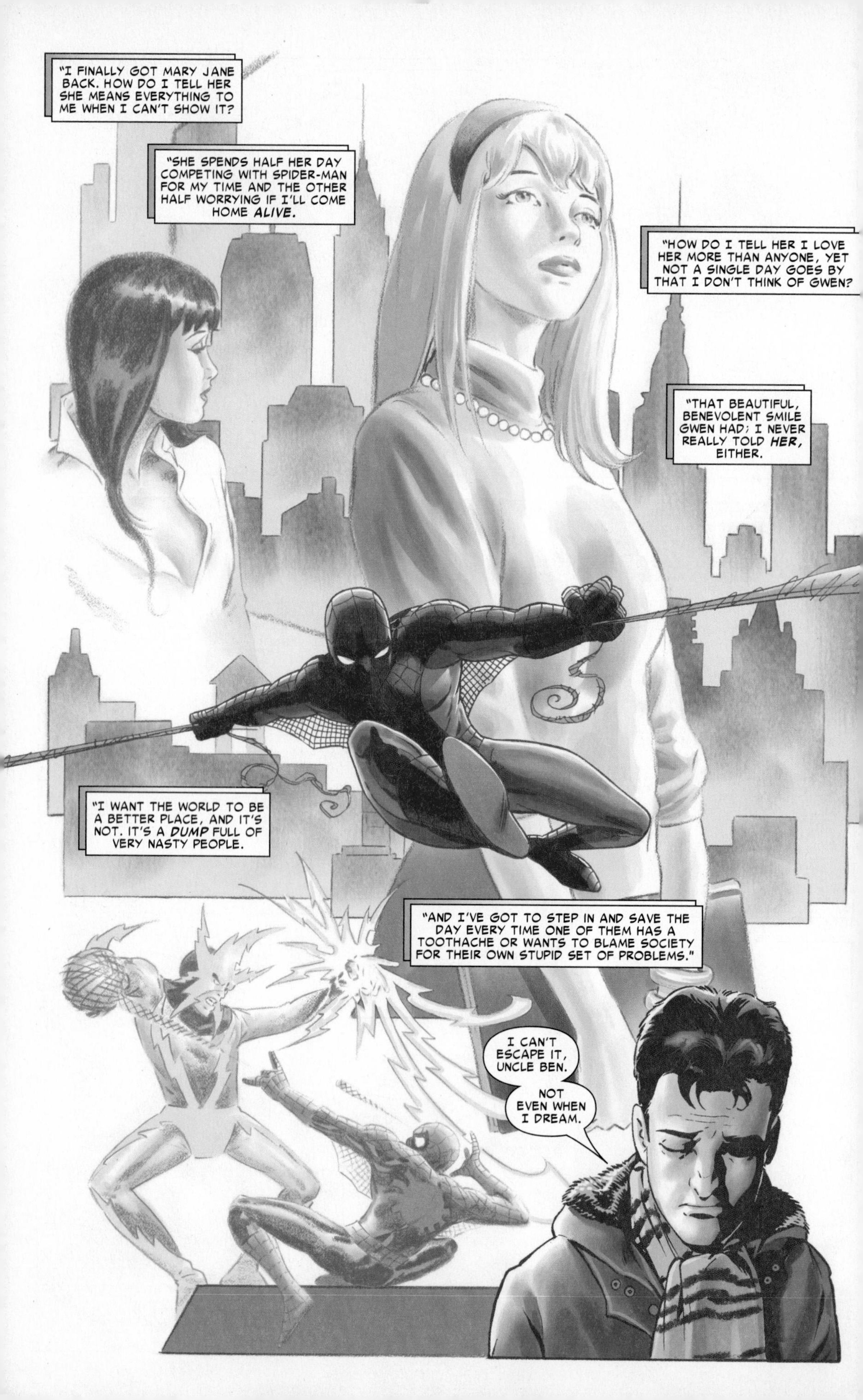
"I FINALLY GOT MARY JANE BACK. HOW DO I TELL HER SHE MEANS EVERYTHING TO ME WHEN I CAN'T SHOW IT?
"SHE SPENDS HALF HER DAY COMPETING WITH SPIDER-MAN FOR MY TIME AND THE OTHER HALF WORRYING IF I'LL COME HOME ALIVE.
"HOW DO I TELL HER I LOVE HER MORE THAN ANYONE, YET NOT A SINGLE DAY GOES BY THAT I DON'T THINK OF GWEN?
"THAT BEAUTIFUL, BENEVOLENT SMILE GWEN HAD; I NEVER REALLY TOLD HER, EITHER.
"I WANT THE WORLD TO BE A BETTER PLACE, AND IT'S NOT. IT'S A DUMP FULL OF VERY NASTY PEOPLE.
"AND I'VE GOT TO STEP IN AND SAVE THE DAY EVERY TIME ONE OF THEM HAS A TOOTHACHE OR WANTS TO BLAME SOCIETY FOR THEIR OWN STUPID SET OF PROBLEMS."
I CAN'T ESCAPE IT, UNCLE BEN.
NOT EVEN WHEN I DREAM.

ANYONE EVER TELL YOU YOU WERE TOO HARD ON YOURSELF, KIDDO?

ALL THE TIME. BUT IT DOESN'T MAKE ANY DIFFERENCE.

"I KEEP HAVING THIS DREAM: I'M WALKING DOWN A CORRIDOR WITH A TERRIBLE PIT IN MY STOMACH--THERE'S SOMEONE BEHIND ME AND SOMEONE UP AHEAD AND I CAN NEVER SEE THEM, BUT THEY CAN SEE ME.

"IT'S THE SAME FEELING I GET WHEN I RUN INTO THE GOBLIN, OR DOC OCK--I GOTTA FACE THE PROBLEM, BUT I'D RATHER BE ANYWHERE ELSE.

"I COME OUT UPON AN OPENING BY SOME CURTAINS...LIKE A STAGE, OR SOMETHING...IT'S DARK.

"AND SUDDENLY, THERE ARE THESE TREMENDOUS FLASHES OF LIGHT.

"I CAN'T SEE A THING FOR A MOMENT...AND THEN MY EYESIGHT BEGINS TO RETURN SLOWLY.

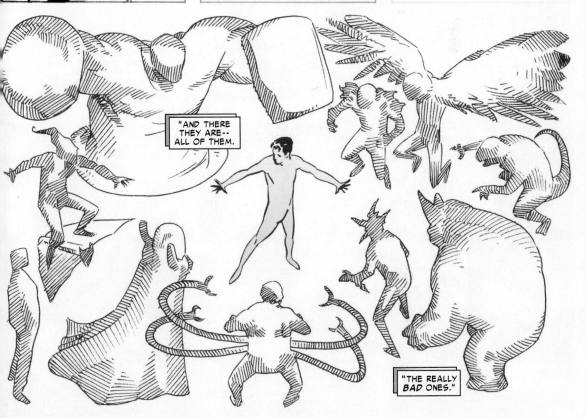

"AND THERE THEY ARE-- ALL OF THEM.

"THE REALLY BAD ONES."

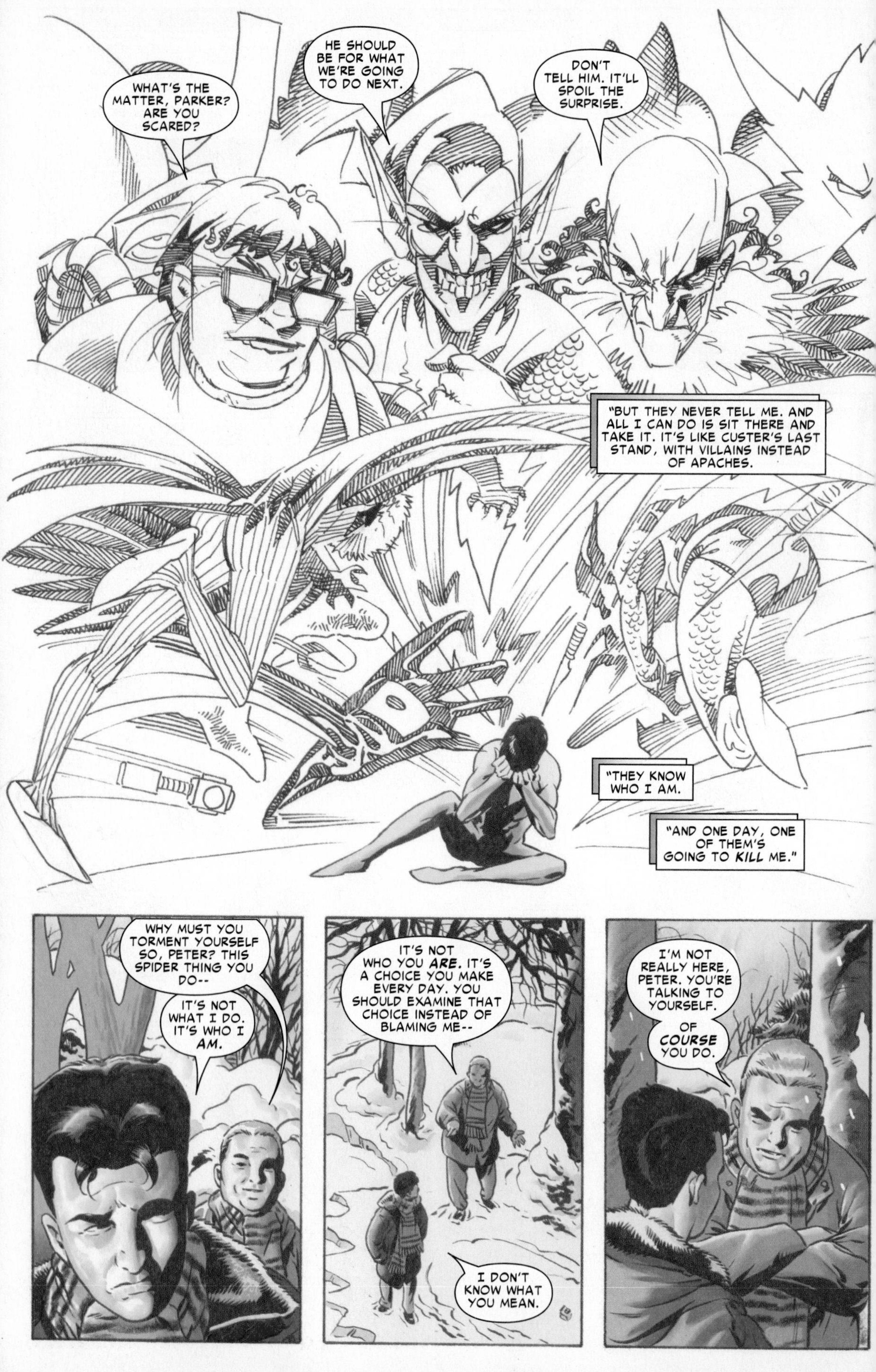
WHAT'S THE MATTER, PARKER? ARE YOU SCARED?
HE SHOULD BE FOR WHAT WE'RE GOING TO DO NEXT.
DON'T TELL HIM. IT'LL SPOIL THE SURPRISE.
"BUT THEY NEVER TELL ME. AND ALL I CAN DO IS SIT THERE AND TAKE IT. IT'S LIKE CUSTER'S LAST STAND, WITH VILLAINS INSTEAD OF APACHES.
"THEY KNOW WHO I AM.
"AND ONE DAY, ONE OF THEM'S GOING TO KILL ME."
WHY MUST YOU TORMENT YOURSELF SO, PETER? THIS SPIDER THING YOU DO--
IT'S NOT WHAT I DO. IT'S WHO I AM.
IT'S NOT WHO YOU ARE. IT'S A CHOICE YOU MAKE EVERY DAY. YOU SHOULD EXAMINE THAT CHOICE INSTEAD OF BLAMING ME--
I DON'T KNOW WHAT YOU MEAN.
I'M NOT REALLY HERE, PETER. YOU'RE TALKING TO YOURSELF.
OF COURSE YOU DO.

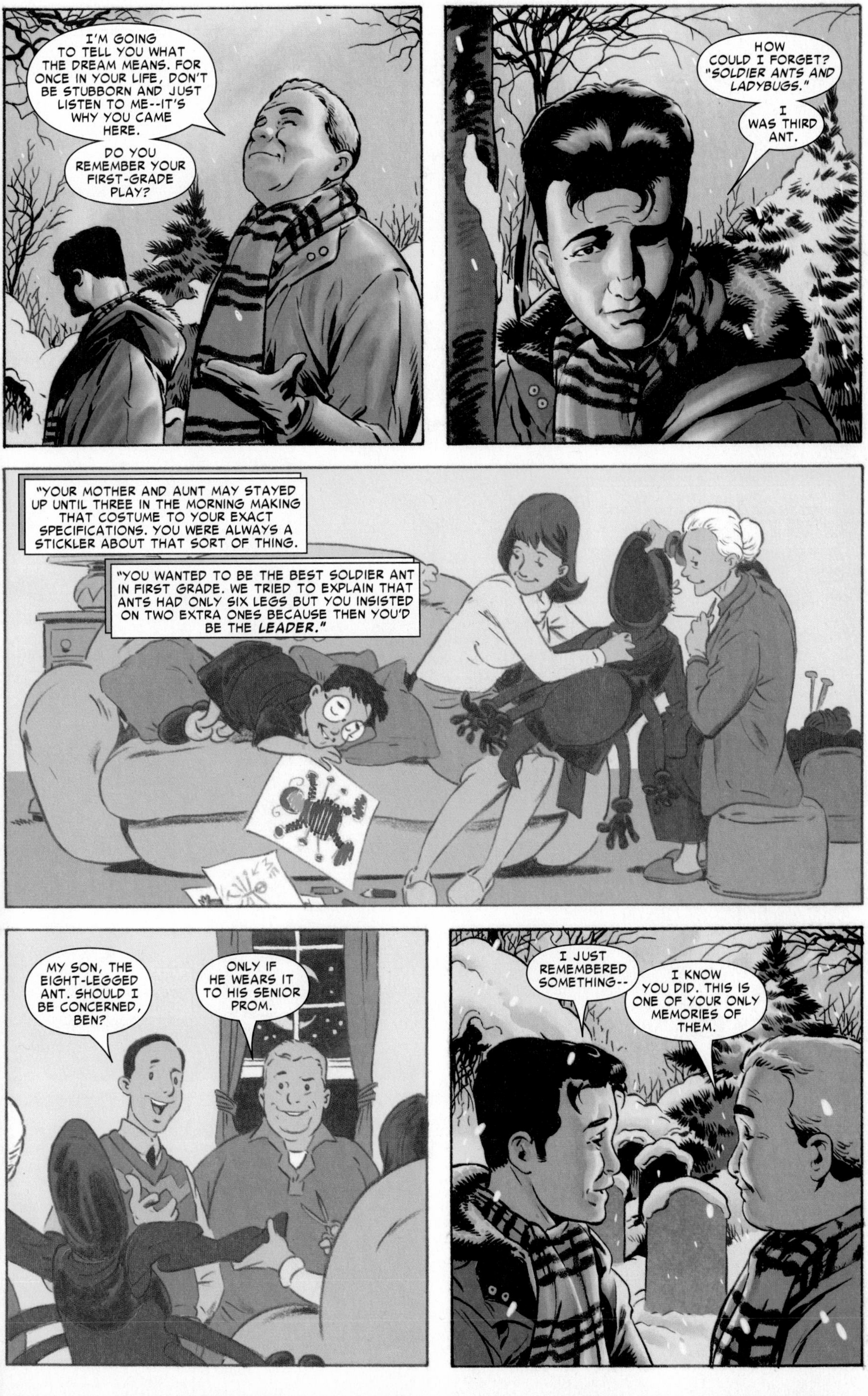
I'M GOING TO TELL YOU WHAT THE DREAM MEANS. FOR ONCE IN YOUR LIFE, DON'T BE STUBBORN AND JUST LISTEN TO ME--IT'S WHY YOU CAME HERE.
DO YOU REMEMBER YOUR FIRST-GRADE PLAY?
HOW COULD I FORGET? "SOLDIER ANTS AND LADYBUGS."
I WAS THIRD ANT.
"YOUR MOTHER AND AUNT MAY STAYED UP UNTIL THREE IN THE MORNING MAKING THAT COSTUME TO YOUR EXACT SPECIFICATIONS. YOU WERE ALWAYS A STICKLER ABOUT THAT SORT OF THING.
"YOU WANTED TO BE THE BEST SOLDIER ANT IN FIRST GRADE. WE TRIED TO EXPLAIN THAT ANTS HAD ONLY SIX LEGS BUT YOU INSISTED ON TWO EXTRA ONES BECAUSE THEN YOU'D BE THE *LEADER*."
ME
MY SON, THE EIGHT-LEGGED ANT. SHOULD I BE CONCERNED, BEN?
ONLY IF HE WEARS IT TO HIS SENIOR PROM.
I JUST REMEMBERED SOMETHING--
I KNOW YOU DID. THIS IS ONE OF YOUR ONLY MEMORIES OF THEM.

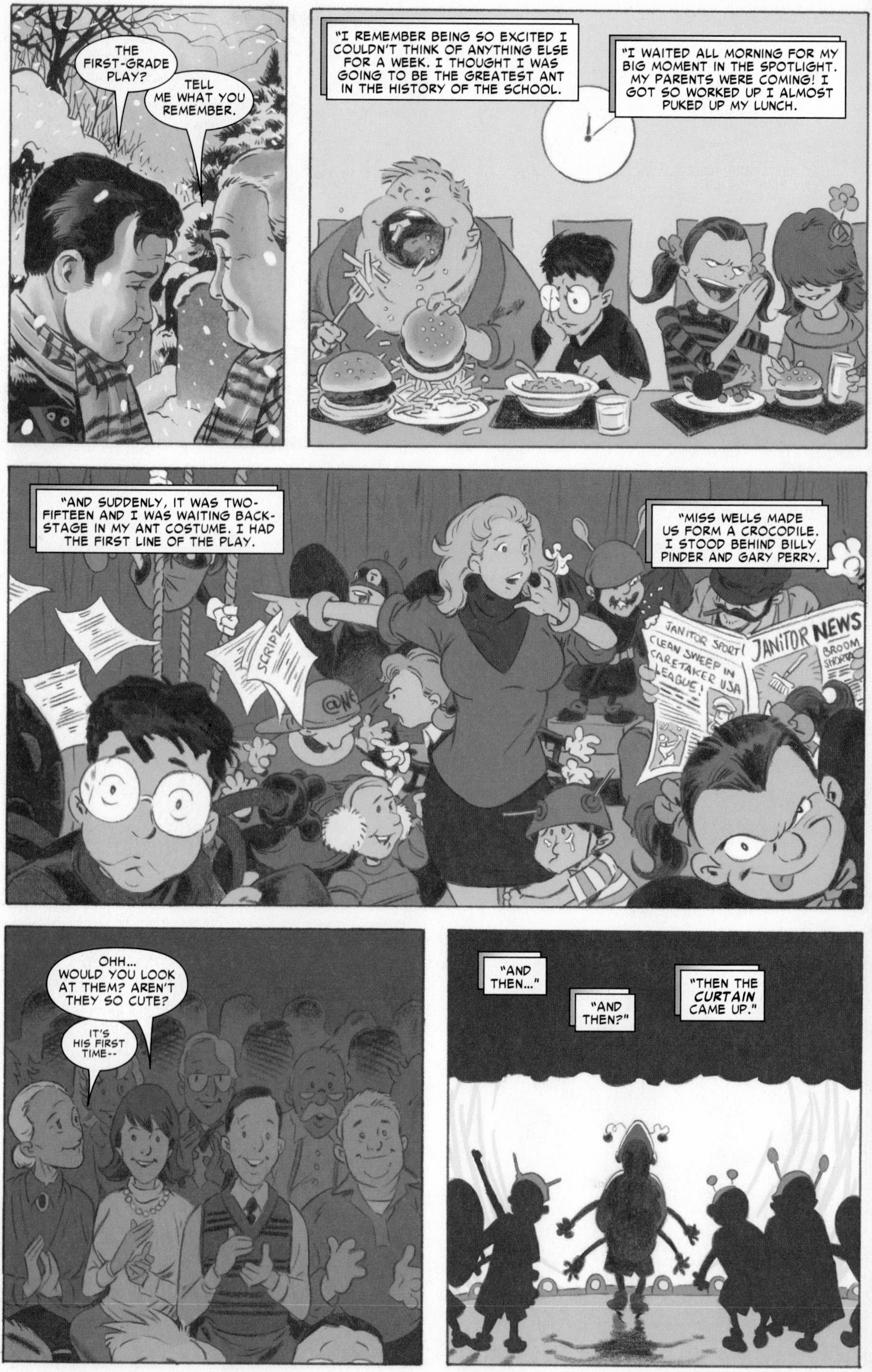
THE FIRST-GRADE PLAY?
TELL ME WHAT YOU REMEMBER.
"I REMEMBER BEING SO EXCITED I COULDN'T THINK OF ANYTHING ELSE FOR A WEEK. I THOUGHT I WAS GOING TO BE THE GREATEST ANT IN THE HISTORY OF THE SCHOOL.
"I WAITED ALL MORNING FOR MY BIG MOMENT IN THE SPOTLIGHT. MY PARENTS WERE COMING! I GOT SO WORKED UP I ALMOST PUKED UP MY LUNCH.
"AND SUDDENLY, IT WAS TWO-FIFTEEN AND I WAS WAITING BACK-STAGE IN MY ANT COSTUME. I HAD THE FIRST LINE OF THE PLAY.
"MISS WELLS MADE US FORM A CROCODILE. I STOOD BEHIND BILLY PINDER AND GARY PERRY.
SCRIPT
JANITOR SPORT
CLEAN SWEEP IN CARETAKER USA LEAGUE!
JANITOR NEWS
OHH... WOULD YOU LOOK AT THEM? AREN'T THEY SO CUTE?
IT'S HIS FIRST TIME--
"AND THEN..."
"AND THEN?"
"THEN THE *CURTAIN* CAME UP."

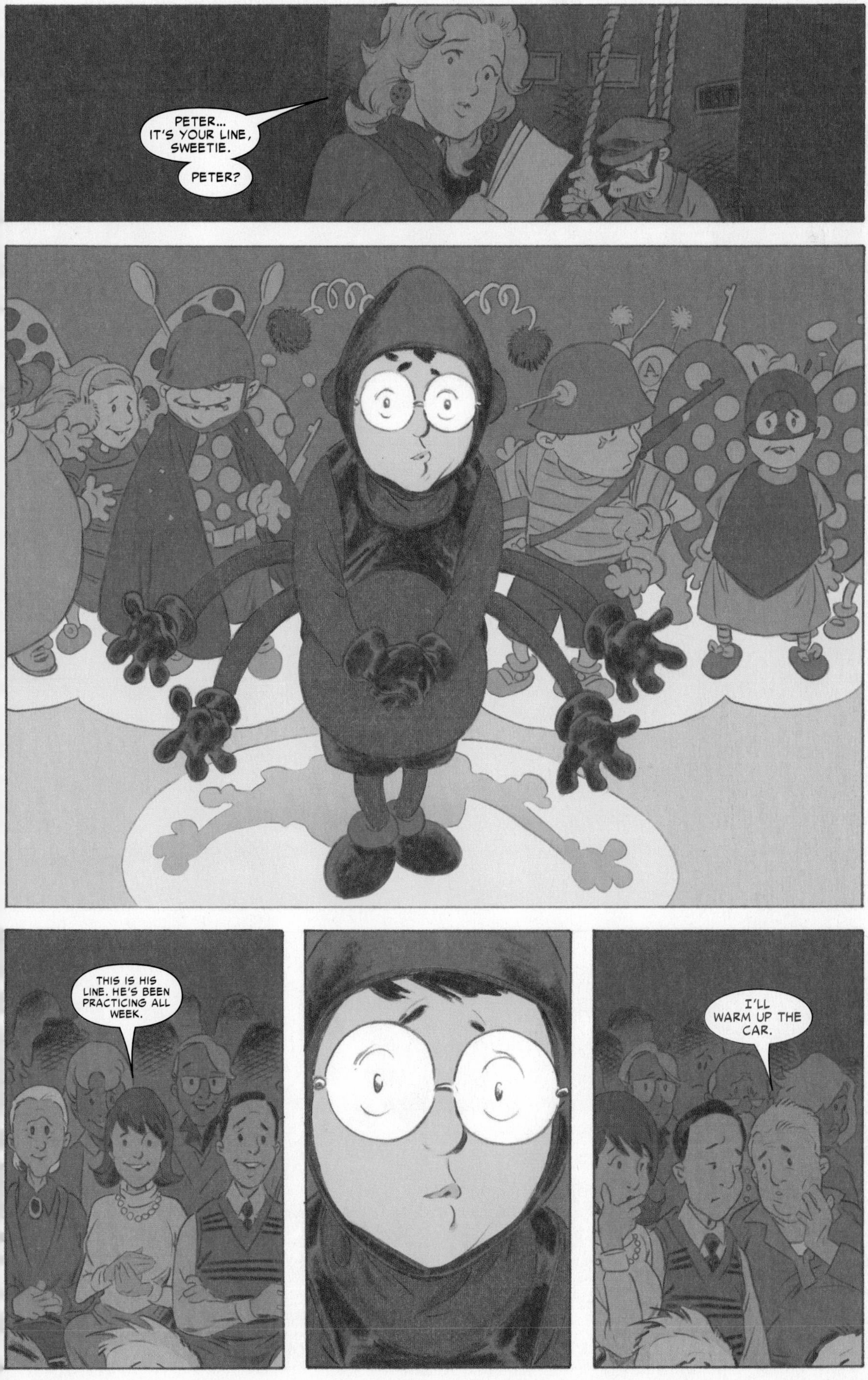
PETER... IT'S YOUR LINE, SWEETIE.
PETER?
THIS IS HIS LINE. HE'S BEEN PRACTICING ALL WEEK.
I'LL WARM UP THE CAR.

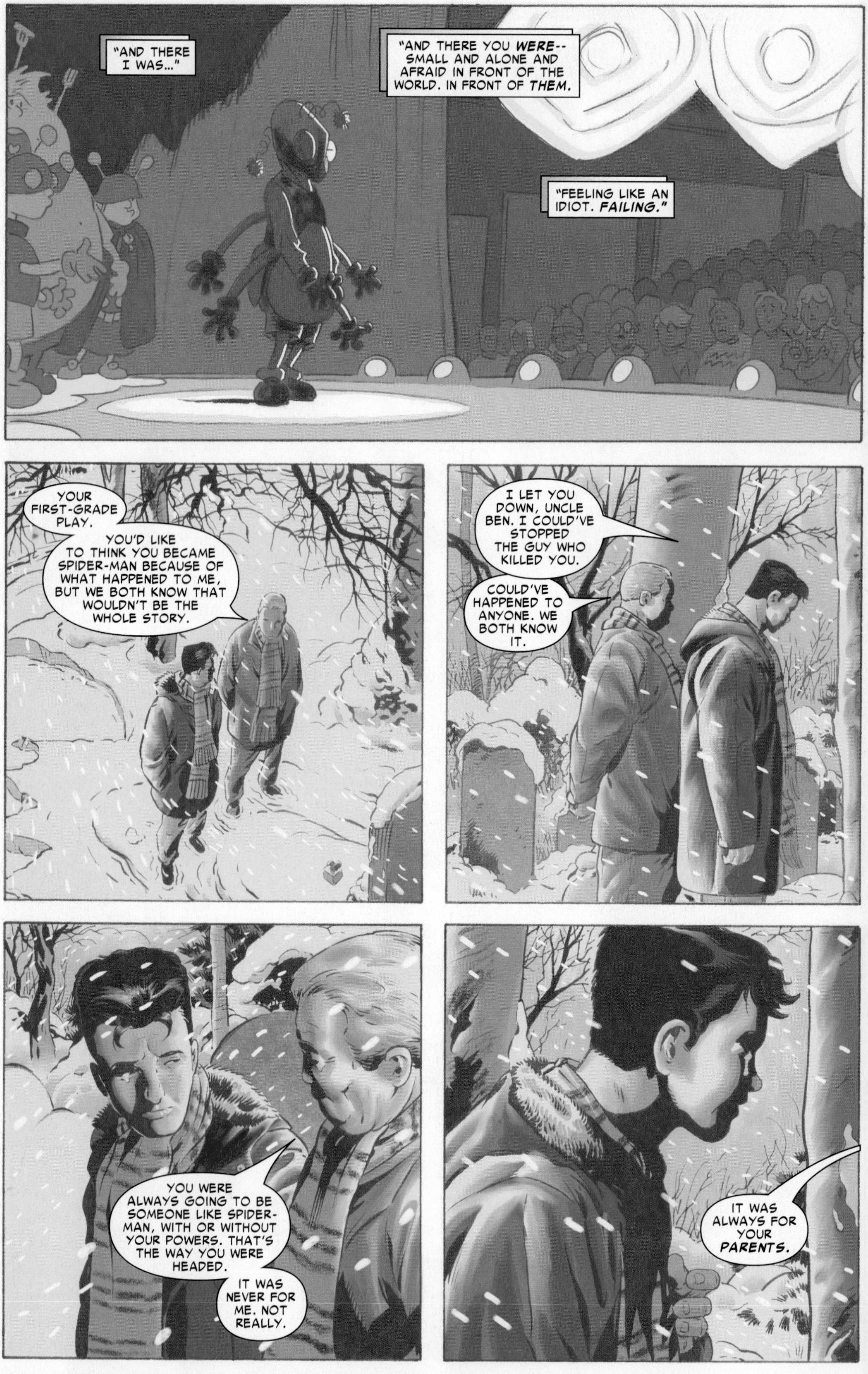
"AND THERE I WAS..."
"AND THERE YOU *WERE*-- SMALL AND ALONE AND AFRAID IN FRONT OF THE WORLD. IN FRONT OF *THEM*.
"FEELING LIKE AN IDIOT. *FAILING*."
YOUR FIRST-GRADE PLAY.
YOU'D LIKE TO THINK YOU BECAME SPIDER-MAN BECAUSE OF WHAT HAPPENED TO ME, BUT WE BOTH KNOW THAT WOULDN'T BE THE WHOLE STORY.
I LET YOU DOWN, UNCLE BEN. I COULD'VE STOPPED THE GUY WHO KILLED YOU.
COULD'VE HAPPENED TO ANYONE. WE BOTH KNOW IT.
YOU WERE ALWAYS GOING TO BE SOMEONE LIKE SPIDER-MAN, WITH OR WITHOUT YOUR POWERS. THAT'S THE WAY YOU WERE HEADED.
IT WAS NEVER FOR ME. NOT REALLY.
IT WAS ALWAYS FOR YOUR *PARENTS*.

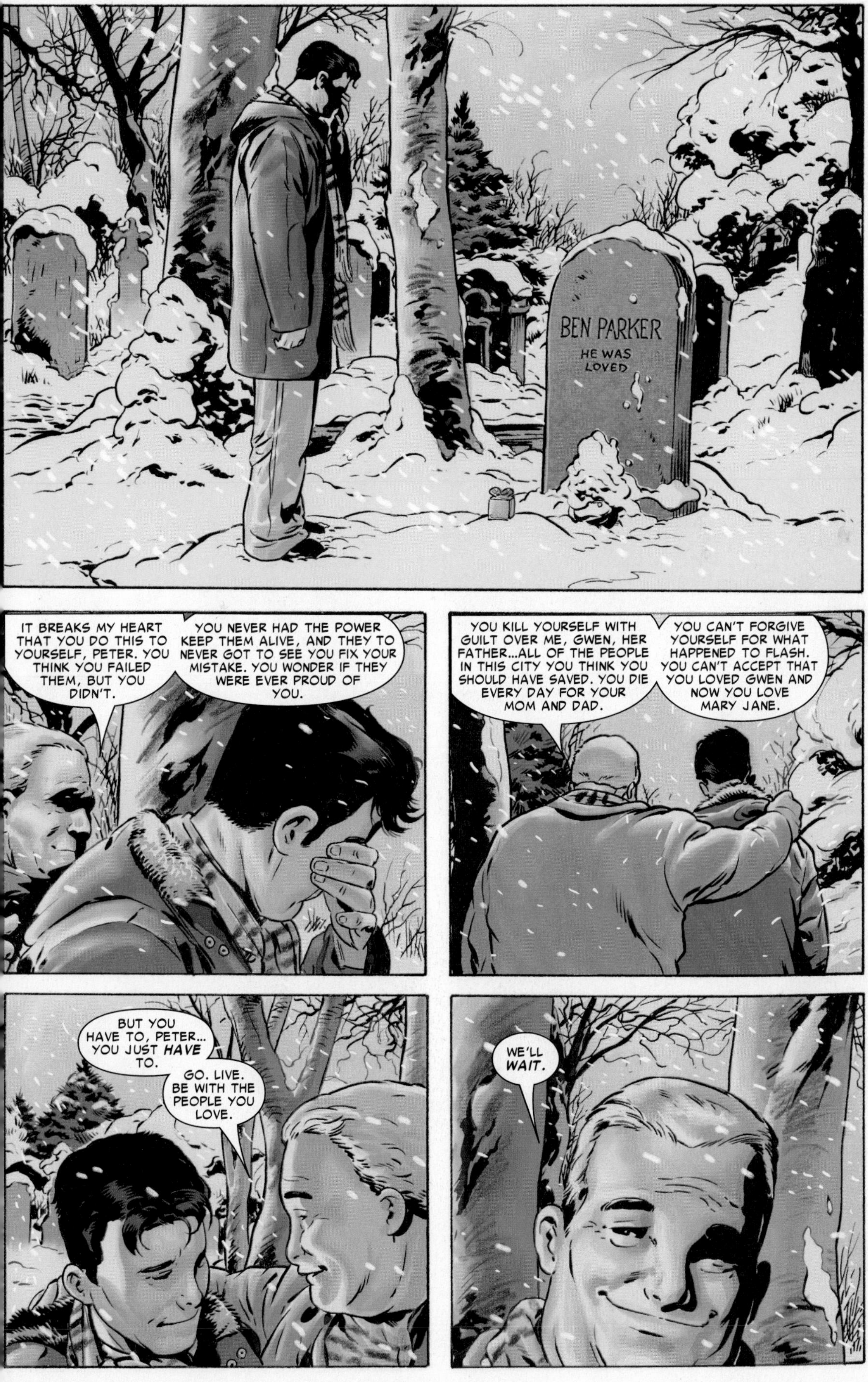
BEN PARKER
HE WAS LOVED
IT BREAKS MY HEART THAT YOU DO THIS TO YOURSELF, PETER. YOU THINK YOU FAILED THEM, BUT YOU DIDN'T.
YOU NEVER HAD THE POWER KEEP THEM ALIVE, AND THEY TO NEVER GOT TO SEE YOU FIX YOUR MISTAKE. YOU WONDER IF THEY WERE EVER PROUD OF YOU.
YOU KILL YOURSELF WITH GUILT OVER ME, GWEN, HER FATHER...ALL OF THE PEOPLE IN THIS CITY YOU THINK YOU SHOULD HAVE SAVED. YOU DIE EVERY DAY FOR YOUR MOM AND DAD.
YOU CAN'T FORGIVE YOURSELF FOR WHAT HAPPENED TO FLASH. YOU CAN'T ACCEPT THAT YOU LOVED GWEN AND NOW YOU LOVE MARY JANE.
BUT YOU HAVE TO, PETER... YOU JUST *HAVE* TO.
GO. LIVE. BE WITH THE PEOPLE YOU LOVE.
WE'LL *WAIT*.

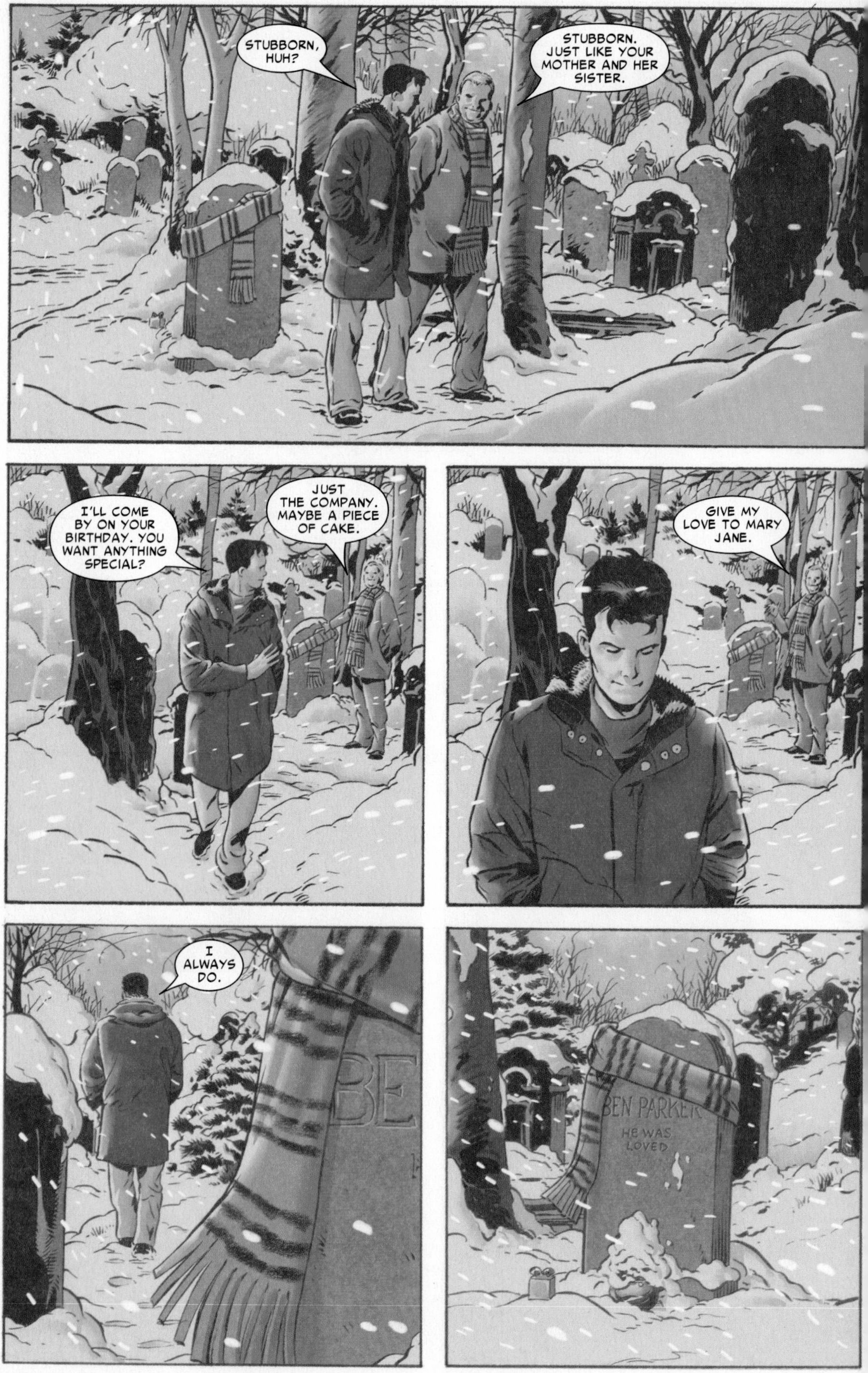
STUBBORN, HUH?
STUBBORN. JUST LIKE YOUR MOTHER AND HER SISTER.
I'LL COME BY ON YOUR BIRTHDAY. YOU WANT ANYTHING SPECIAL?
JUST THE COMPANY. MAYBE A PIECE OF CAKE.
GIVE MY LOVE TO MARY JANE.
I ALWAYS DO.
BEN PARKER
HE WAS LOVED

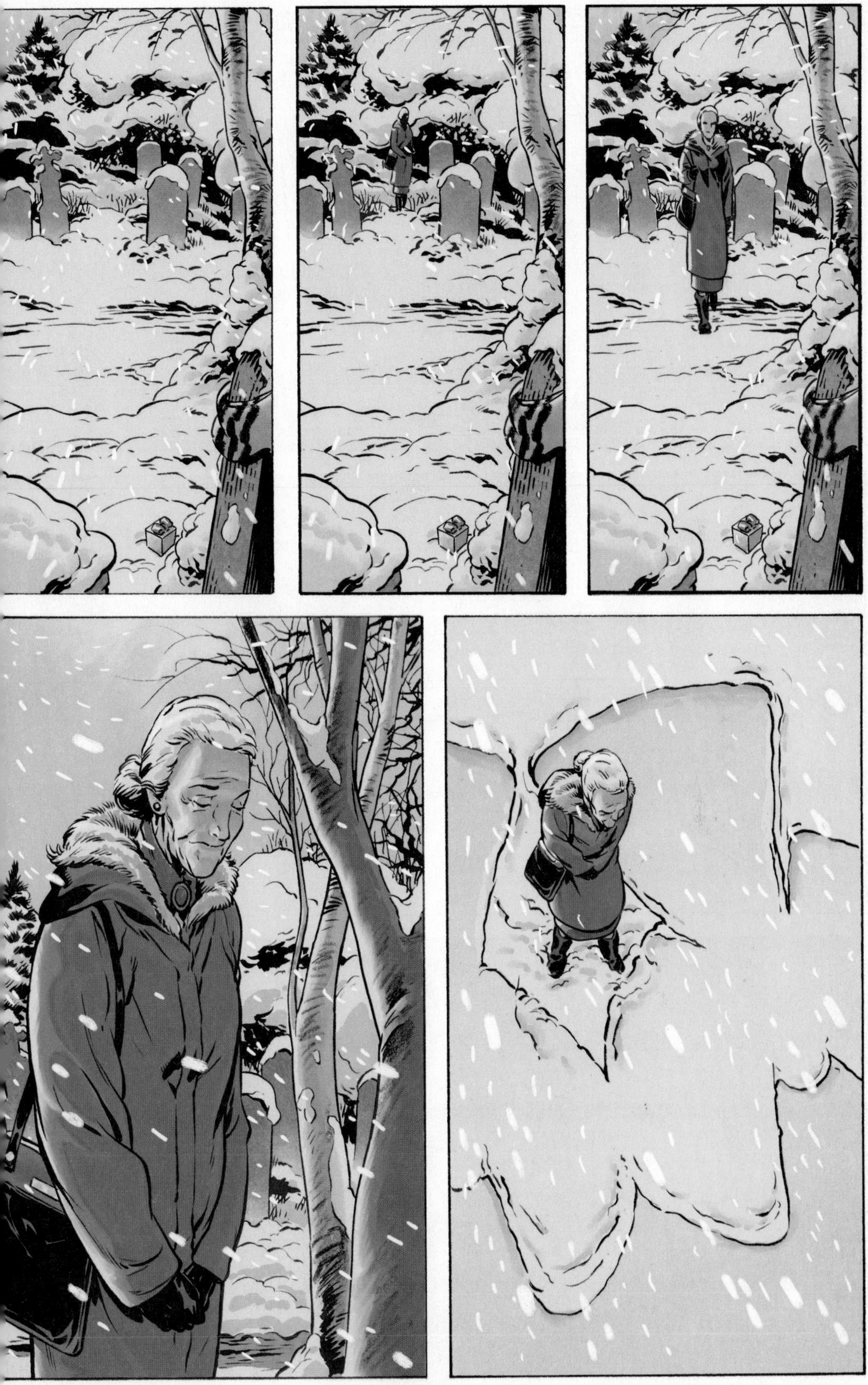

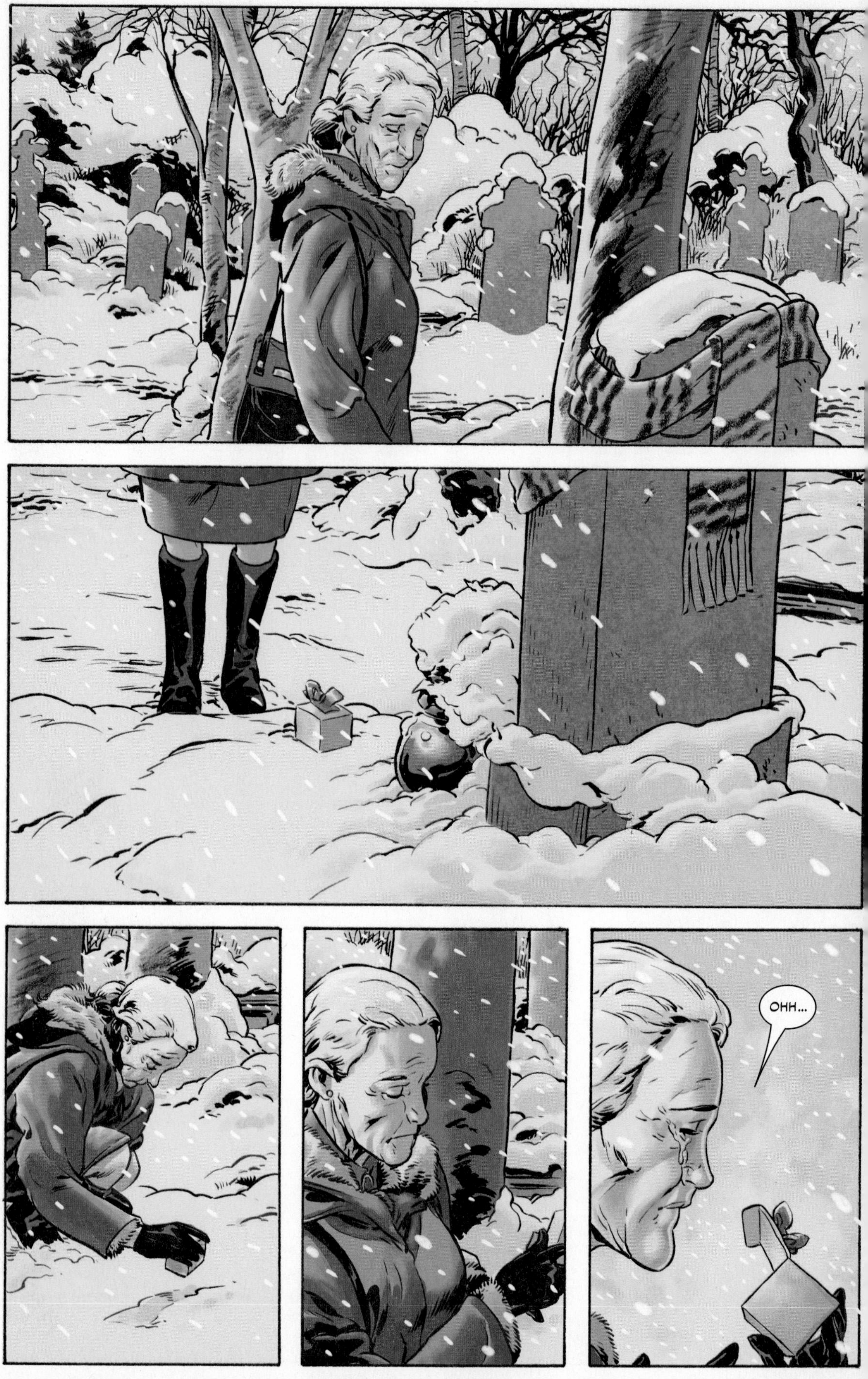
OHH...

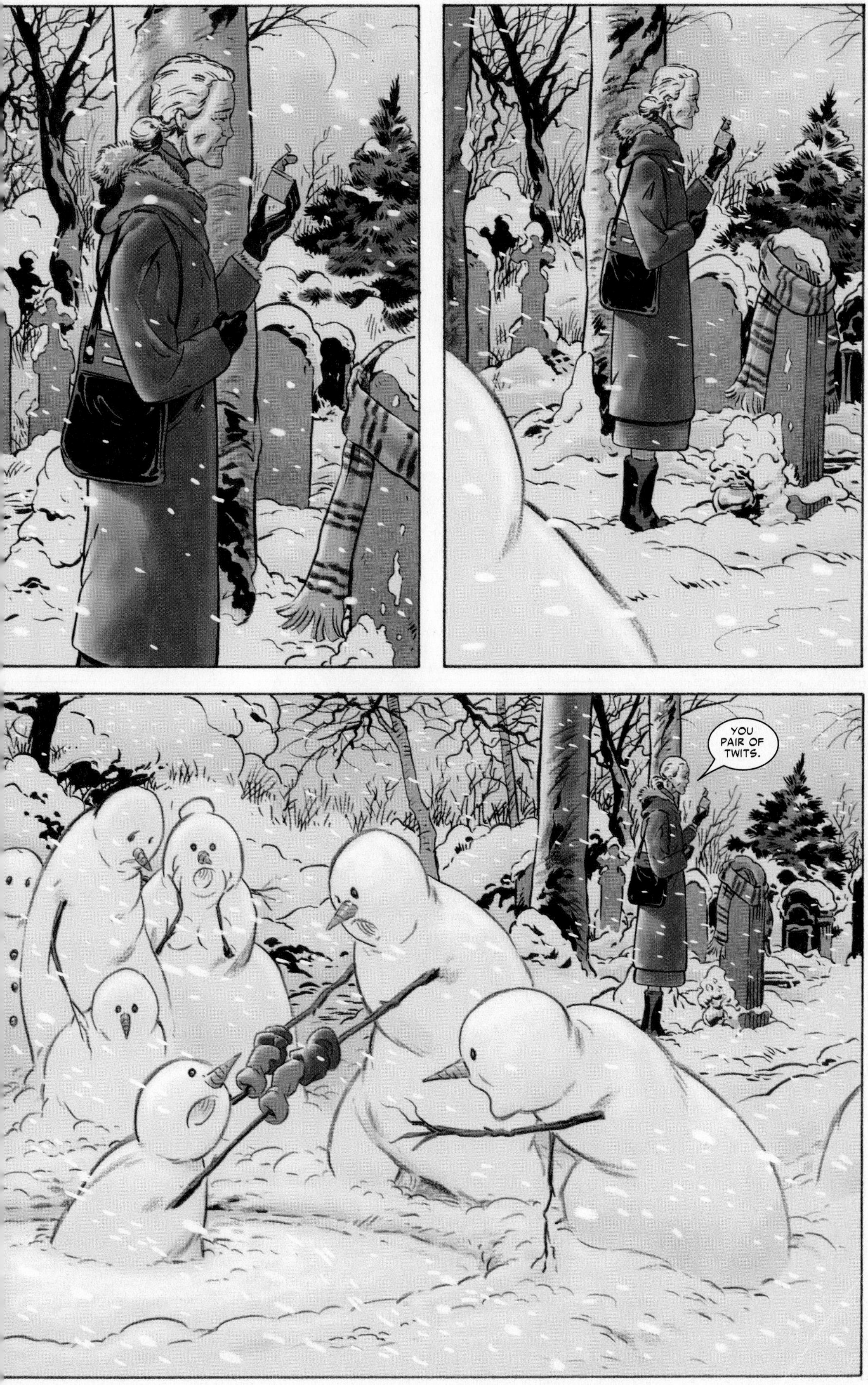
YOU PAIR OF TWITS.

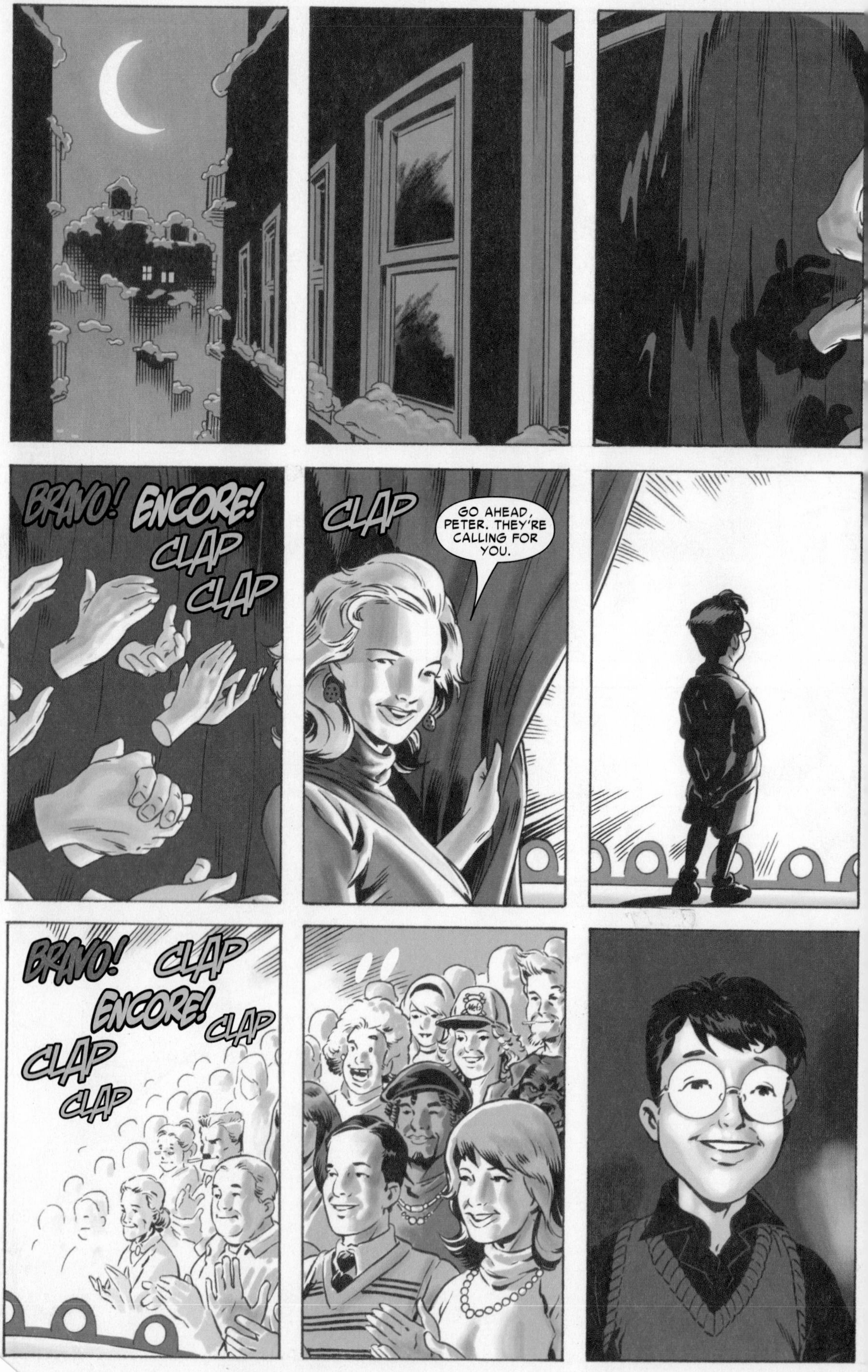
BRAVO! ENCORE!
CLAP
CLAP
CLAP
GO AHEAD, PETER. THEY'RE CALLING FOR YOU.
BRAVO! CLAP
ENCORE! CLAP
CLAP
CLAP

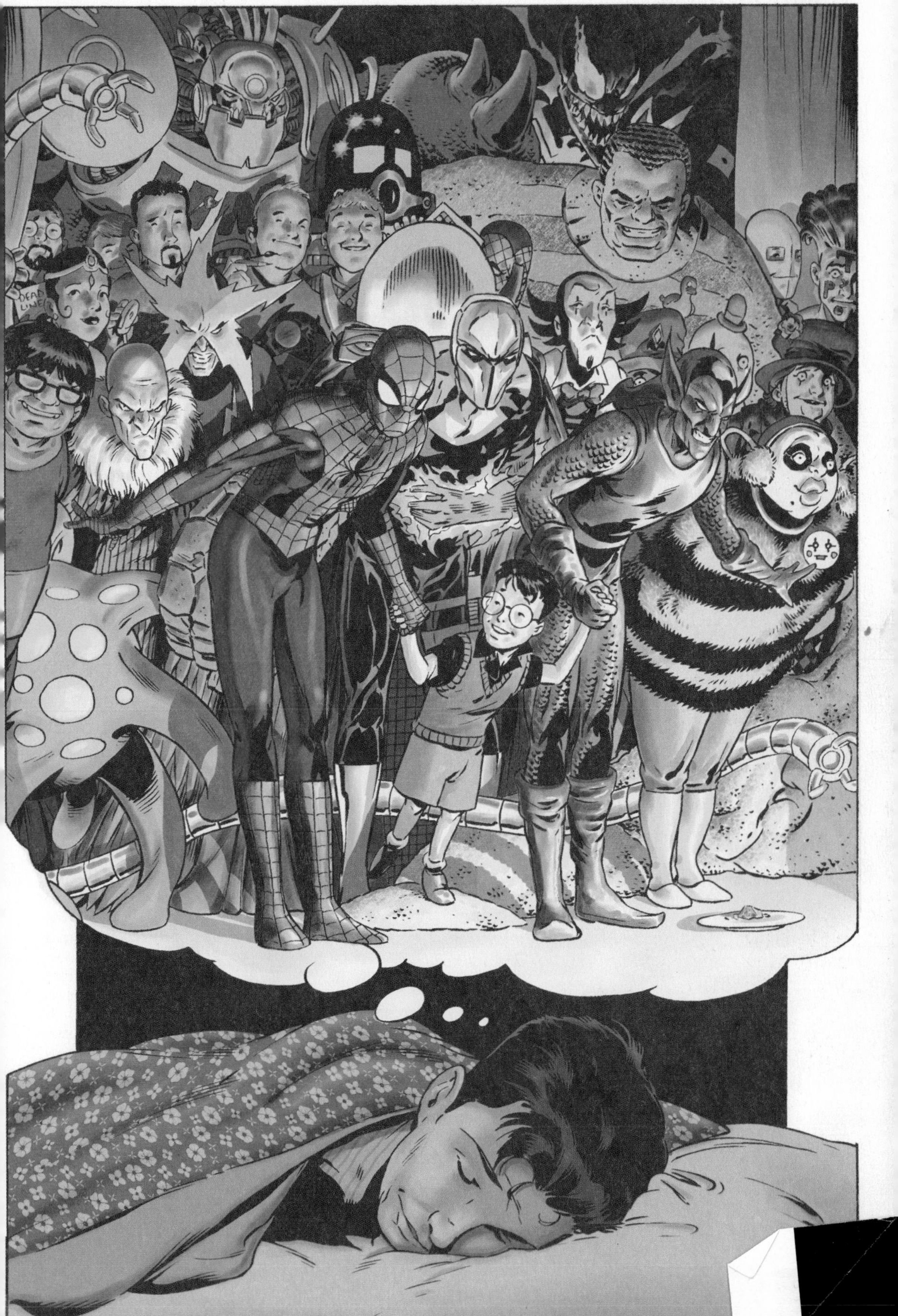

SPIDER-MAN

REAL NAME: Peter Benjamin Parker
ALIASES: "Spidey," "Wallcrawler," "Web-head," "Web-slinger," "Web-spinner," "Tiger," "Spider," "Scoopy," "the Bug," "Porker," "Porter," "Palmer," "Parkins," "Parsons," "Pearson," "Paul Porter," "Parkman," "Perkins," "Parkinson," "Palmer," Ben Reilly, "Amazing/Bombastic Bag-Man," "P," "Spider-Morphosis," Dusk, Hornet, Prodigy, Ricochet, Herbert Fillmore Smith, Scarlet Spider, "Octo-Spidey," Cartwright, "Spider-Hulk," Captain Universe, Mad Dog 336, "Man-Spider," Jay Jameson, Poindexter, "Spider-Lizard," "Kid Parker," "Puny Parker"; impersonated Challenger, Daredevil, Venom, others
IDENTITY: Secret
OCCUPATION: Adventurer, freelance photographer and NYC mayoral staff photographer; former licensed super hero, comic book store clerk, assistant high school coach, bartender, high school teacher, research scientist, college teaching assistant, performer, wrestler
CITIZENSHIP: USA
PLACE OF BIRTH: Forest Hills, Queens, New York
KNOWN RELATIVES: Richard & Mary Parker (parents, deceased), May Parker-Jameson (aunt), Ben Parker (uncle, deceased), Peter and Ann Parker (grandparents, deceased), Will Fitzpatrick (grandfather, deceased), Ben Reilly (clone, deceased), Kaine (clone), other deceased clones, Ben & May Parker's unborn child (cousin, deceased), J. Jonah Jameson Sr. (uncle), J. Jonah Jameson Jr., April Reilly, Jan Reilly, Sam & Diane Reilly, Roger Reilly, Harold Reilly, Julia, Amanda, Amy, Alexa (last names unrevealed) (relatives via extended family)

GROUP AFFILIATION: Avengers, Front Line staff; formerly "Secret Avengers," Initiative, Secret Defenders, Outlaws, Daily Bugle staff, Tri Corp Research, Defenders associate, Boy Scouts of America
EDUCATION: BS in physics, doctoral studies in biochemistry at ESU (incomplete)
FIRST APPEARANCE: (Spider-Man) Amazing Fantasy #15 (1962); ("Spider-Lizard") Peter Parker the Spectacular Spider-Man #39 (1980); (1st Man-Spider) Marvel Fanfare #2 (1982); (Captain Universe) Spectacular Spider-Man #158 (1989); ("Spider-Hulk") Web of Spider-Man #70 (1990); (Scarlet Spider) Spider-Man Unlimited #9 (1995); (Dusk) Peter Parker: Spider-Man #90 (1998); (Hornet) Sensational Spider-Man #27 (1998); (Prodigy) Spectacular Spider-Man #256 (1998); (Ricochet) Amazing Spider-Man #433 (1998); (2nd Man-Spider "Spider-Morphosis") Amazing Spider-Man #437 (1998); (3rd Man-Spider) Spectacular Spider-Man #17 (2004)

HISTORY: Once an ordinary teenager gifted with extraordinary powers, Peter Parker rose above poverty and personal tragedy to become one of New York's most uniquely celebrated and controversial crime-fighters: The wisecracking, web-slinging hard-luck hero called Spider-Man. The only child of secret government agents Richard and Mary Parker, Peter was orphaned as a baby when his parents infiltrated the criminal organization of the Red Skull (Albert Malik), who had them killed by the Finisher (Karl Fiers) after discovering the Parkers were double agents. Peter's elderly uncle and aunt, Ben and May Parker, unhesitatingly raised the boy as if he were their own son. Academically gifted, Peter soon proved to be a natural scientific genius. Socially, however, he was painfully shy and often mistreated by peers — especially after popular football star "Flash" Thompson joined Peter's class. An athletic, charismatic bully who scorned intelligence, Flash treated Peter shabbily and encouraged other students to do the same, until Peter had no friends left at school at all. Peter's uncle and aunt tried to compensate with their steadfast love, but they secretly worried about the fragile boy.

As a Midtown High School student, Peter attended a public exhibition of nuclear laboratory waste handling by Dr. Eric Schwinner of General Techtronics East. A spider, accidentally struck by an Isotope Genome Accelerator's particle beam during the demonstration,  fell onto Peter's hand and bit him. Apparently already mutated by prior exposure to certain radiation frequencies, the irradiated common house spider (Achaearanea tepidariorum) died of its final radiation dose shortly after biting Parker. The spider's bite transferred radioactive, complex mutagenic enzymes from its blood to Parker, triggering numerous bodywide mutagenic changes. His hand burning from the wound, Peter left the exhibition in a daze and walked into the path of an oncoming car. Without thinking, Peter jumped onto a nearby wall, sticking to it with his bare hands. Stunned, he realized he had acquired spider-like superhuman powers: Enhanced strength and agility, the ability to cling to almost any surface, and even a sixth sense that warned him of impending danger.

To test his new powers, Peter donned a makeshift mask and entered an all-comers wrestling match against Joe "Crusher" Hogan, winning easily. Spotted by talent scout Maxie Shiffman, who promised to arrange TV appearances, Peter hurried home and created a more elaborate costume, including unique web-shooters loaded with an adhesive chemical "webbing" of his own design based on an earlier science

ART BY PHIL JIMENEZ WITH STEVE McNIVEN (INSET)

WRESTLING COSTUME

ART BY LEE WEEKS

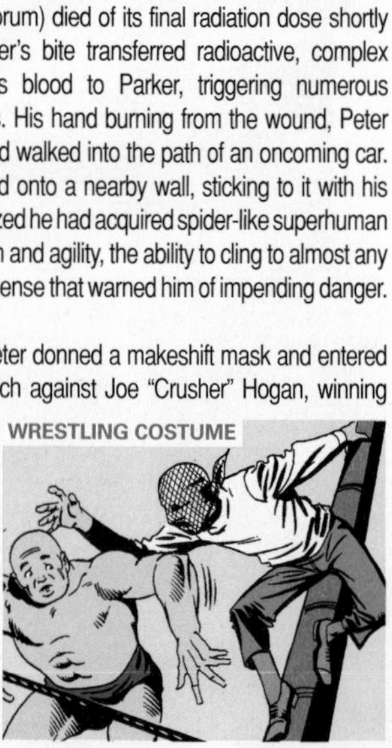

ART BY STEVE DITKO

project. Calling himself Spider-Man, he became an overnight sensation after appearing on television. Suddenly successful and powerful, Peter promised himself he would take care of Uncle Ben and Aunt May. However, he felt indifferent to the rest of the world that had so often mocked or ignored lonely misfit Peter Parker, so when a fleeing burglar ran past Spider-Man following a TV appearance, Peter did nothing to intervene. The burglar escaped and security guard Baxter Bigelow angrily berated Spider-Man, who arrogantly replied that catching criminals was Bigelow's job, not his.

Returning home one evening a few days later, Peter was horrified to learn an intruder had murdered Uncle Ben. Seeking justice, Peter left his home as Spider-Man, unaware that Mary Jane Watson, his next-door neighbor Anna Watson's niece, observed him. Capturing the killer in the old Acme Warehouse at the waterfront, Peter discovered it was the same burglar he had failed to stop just days before. Filled with remorse, Peter finally understood that with great power, there must also come great responsibility. Initially uncertain of how to fulfill that responsibility, Peter stumbled onto the ghoulish con man Undertaker (Conrad Eisenstadt) and his gang after one of them scammed Aunt May. When the criminals tried to kill him after he confronted them as Spider-Man, Peter overcame his fear and inexperience and captured the entire gang single-handedly. Thrilled by this victory and realizing he had found a way to atone for his uncle's death, Spider-Man began using his powers heroically on a regular basis, subduing petty crooks like muggers and rescuing people from fires and other threats. He also befriended fellow super-powered teenager Joey Pulaski until he learned she was using her powers for crime. Spider-Man reluctantly captured the unstable girl for the police, earning the notice of Joey's sometime employer, the Kingpin (Wilson Fisk).

Wanting to use his powers unselfishly, Spider-Man initially resisted Maxie Shiffman's efforts to lure him back into show business; however, Peter changed his mind after watching Aunt May struggle to pay their bills alone. Spider-Man reluctantly agreed to appear on the "It's Amazing!" television show, arranged by Shiffman. This last-minute booking forced the show to postpone its previously scheduled guest, astronaut John Jameson. John did not mind, but his father, Daily Bugle newspaper publisher J. Jonah Jameson Jr., considered it an outrageous slight; Jonah deemed Spider-Man a glory-hungry show off whose apparently selfless heroism had to be fake, sticking to that opinion even after Spider-Man rescued the Jamesons and the rest of the "It's Amazing!" studio audience from murderous super-powered fanatic Supercharger (Ronnie Hilliard). Feeling responsible for the battle's extensive damage to the studio, especially after Supercharger turned out to be a rogue Shiffman client, Spider-Man convinced Maxie to refund their appearance fee so the studio could rebuild. Still needing money, Peter agreed to further appearances on other shows, but these plans were abruptly canceled when J. Jonah Jameson's anti-Spider-Man editorials turned public opinion against Parker's alter ego. Even after Spider-Man rescued John Jameson from a malfunctioning space capsule, Jonah continued to publicly condemn Spider-Man as a menace. Spider-Man quickly became one of the city's most feared and mistrusted super heroes. Ironically, his most loyal defender was Spider-Man fan club founder Flash Thompson, though Flash continued to bully "Puny Parker" at school. Flash's girlfriend, the popular Liz Allan, soon complicated matters further by developing a crush on "Petey," making Flash jealous.

Trying and failing to find paid employment with the Fantastic Four, Spider-Man helped police capture the Chameleon (Dmitri Smerdyakov Kravinoff) after that master of disguise committed crimes while posing as Spider-Man. When J. Jonah Jameson offered a reward for photos of the elusive flying criminal Vulture (Adrian Toomes), Peter realized he could fulfill his debt to Uncle Ben by fighting crime, while selling photos of the action to pay his bills. Spider-Man soon battled a bizarre array of thieves, gangsters and megalomaniacs including armored flamethrower Scorcher (Steven Hudak), criminal inventor the Tinkerer (Phineas Mason), mechanical-tentacled megalomaniac Dr. Octopus (Otto Octavius), the granular-bodied Sandman (William Baker), Latverian tyrant Dr. Doom (Victor von Doom),

human powerhouse Electro (Max Dillon) and aristocratic thief Commanda (Catherine, Lady D'Antan). In Florida, he befriended Dr. Curtis Connors after reversing the scientist's transformation into the terrible Lizard. Though Spider-Man had many enemies, he also shared adventures with the Fantastic Four (including his rival, the Human Torch, Johnny Storm), the Avengers, the X-Men, Daredevil (Matt Murdock) and Dr. Stephen Strange. He also found a friend and his first love in Jonah's secretary, Betty Brant. The shy Betty was both excited and troubled by the apparent danger of Peter's Spider-Man photography. However, when one of Spider-Man's battles led to the death of Betty's brother Bennett Brant at mobster Blackie Gaxton's hands, Peter fully realized how much his dual identity endangered those he loved. Betty initially blamed Spider-Man for Bennett's death. Though she later forgave him, Spider-Man still reminded her of losing her brother, making Peter even more reluctant to confide in her. While Spider-Man faced mobster the Big Man (Bugle reporter Frederick Foswell) and the Enforcers, his Aunt May required an operation; though uncertain of the risks, Peter gave her a transfusion of his irradiated blood and May recovered. When a virus-stricken Spider-Man was unmasked by Dr. Octopus in front of Betty, Jonah and others, everyone assumed it was a trick and that the weakened Parker couldn't possibly be the real Spider-Man, saving Peter's secret again.

COLLEGE FRIENDS

ART BY SALVADOR LARROCA

More criminals clashed with Spider-Man, including the axe-wielding Headsman (Cleavon Twain), the bizarre mastermind Green Goblin (wealthy industrialist Norman Osborn), criminal genius the Wizard (Bentley Wittman, defeated during Spider-Man's first of many team-ups with the Human Torch), master illusionist Mysterio (Quentin Beck), rogue big game expert Kraven the Hunter (Sergei Kravinoff) and outlaw archer Hawkeye (Clint Barton, who soon reformed and joined the Avengers). At home, Aunt May suffered a heart attack, causing Spider-Man to abandon a fight with the Green Goblin, further tarnishing Spider-Man's reputation. May's fragile health and the Parkers' financial troubles would remain lingering concerns for Peter. Some of his leading foes soon joined forces as the Sinister Six, but Spider-Man defeated them all. Meanwhile, his romance with Betty crumbled as reporter Ned Leeds stole her heart. Taking his Spider-Man vendetta to a new level, Jonah paid Dr. Farley Stillwell to transform private detective Mac Gargan into the superhuman Scorpion to hunt Spider-Man. Driven mad by the process, Gargan soon turned on Jonah, whom Spider-Man rescued. After helping the Human Torch capture his armored enemy Beetle (Abe Jenkins), Spider-Man faced another Jameson-sponsored menace when Jonah rented the first of a series of robotic Spider Slayers invented by Dr. Spencer Smythe, though Parker escaped it.

While Aunt May tried repeatedly to introduce Peter to Mary Jane, Spider-Man tackled organized crime leaders the Crime-Master (Nick Lewis) and the Green Goblin, though Lewis was quickly brought down with the reformed Frederick Foswell's aid. Tired of Jonah's harassment, Peter tried selling pictures to the Daily Globe but gave up when the Globe's editor Barney Bushkin proved too curious about Peter's methods. After capturing Liz Allan's super-criminal stepbrother the Molten Man (Mark Raxton), Peter Parker graduated Midtown High with the highest scholastic average in the school's history, earning a science scholarship to Empire State University (ESU). Athletic scholarship winner Flash Thompson also went to ESU, where their new classmates included two Standard High graduates: Norman Osborn's troubled son Harry Osborn, and beauty queen Gwen Stacy. Peter, Harry, and Gwen shared freshman chemistry lab with Professor Miles Warren, who ran secret experiments on cloning at ESU, and became instantly infatuated with Gwen. Harry and Gwen considered Peter snobbish at first, unaware he was preoccupied by his aunt's latest hospitalization. Discovering she was slowly dying from the transfusion of Peter's radioactive blood, Spider-Man had Dr. Connors develop an antidote, but before Spider-Man could administer it, he was trapped under rubble in a battle with Dr. Octopus. Pushed to his mental and physical limits, Spider-Man freed himself in time to save Aunt May. With May recovering, a more relaxed Peter befriended Harry and Gwen and made peace with Flash, and the four close-knit friends became regulars at the Coffee Bean café. Soon after, the Green Goblin discovered Peter Parker was Spider-Man and kidnapped him, revealing himself to be Harry's father. Parker broke free and their battle ended with an accidental electrochemical shock that left Norman partially amnesiac, blocking his memories of being the Goblin.

The Avengers offered Spider-Man membership, but he failed his initiation test when the softhearted Parker could not bring himself to capture the tormented man-monster Hulk (Bruce Banner), later trying to convince himself he was a better off as a loner. Meanwhile, no longer able to avoid meeting Mary Jane, Peter was pleasantly stunned to discover she was both gorgeous and vivacious, while unaware she secretly knew about his alter ego. During their first date, they rode into the city on Peter's new motorcycle to photograph the super-criminal Rhino (Aleksei Sytsevich). After battles with the Lizard, new costumed thief the Shocker (Herman Schultz) and others, Peter moved into Harry's apartment, rent free — but happiness eluded him despite his newfound independence. Worn out by Jameson's editorials, the public's fear of him, Aunt May's fragile health, his slipping grades and a floundering love life, Peter abandoned his Spider-Man identity. While Parker enjoyed spending more time on school, friends and family, crime escalated as the Kingpin rose to the top of New York's criminal underworld. After Peter rescued a watchman resembling his Uncle Ben from two robbers, he renewed his vow to protect the innocent and resumed his Spider-Man identity, opposing Kingpin's plans. Fred Foswell briefly joined Kingpin's gang but ultimately sacrificed his life to help Spider-Man save Jonah from the Kingpin.

Spider-Man subsequently battled Dr. Octopus (who became Aunt May's boarder), a new Vulture (Blackie Drago) and many other menaces. Though Peter sometimes dated Mary Jane, he soon fell for the more serious-minded Gwen, causing tension between Harry and himself. Given two tickets to a science exposition by Miles Warren (now their biochemistry professor), Peter invited Gwen, and soon after Gwen became Peter's regular girlfriend, while Mary Jane became Harry's. During this time, Warren had his assistant, Anthony Serba, collect cell samples from his students (including Peter and Gwen) for experiments. Gwen's father, retired police Capt. George Stacy, studied Spider-Man and questioned Peter about him. When the Kingpin brainwashed Capt. Stacy into stealing police records, Peter published pictures exposing Stacy, and the Kingpin kidnapped George and Gwen. Spider-Man and Norman Osborn rescued them, but the Kingpin escaped. Feeling Peter had betrayed her father, Gwen stopped dating him. During this time, Gwen had a spontaneous affair with Norman Osborn, leaving her secretly pregnant with twins. Spider-Man soon became embroiled in the fight for possession of a legendary stone tablet inscribed with a youth formula, sought by criminals such as Kingpin, Shocker, Michael "Man-Mountain" Marko and Marko's aged gangster employer, Silvermane (Silvio Manfredi), who de-aged seemingly into nothingness after using the formula. Would-be super-criminal Prowler (Hobie Brown) later met a happier fate when a sympathetic Spider-Man captured him and set him free, convincing Brown to go straight.

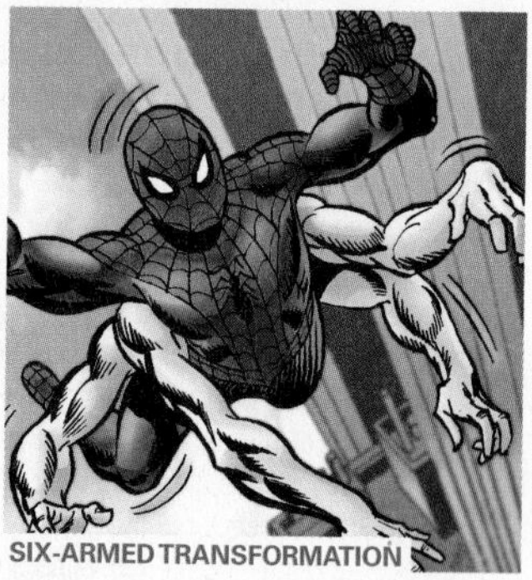
SIX-ARMED TRANSFORMATION

ART BY GIL KANE

Learning his parents had been framed for treason after their deaths, Peter went to Algeria, where he fought the Red Skull and uncovered evidence of his parents' double-agent status, clearing their names. Recovering from his brainwashing, Capt. Stacy exonerated Peter for photographing him; Gwen and Peter reunited. Though Peter's frequent, unexplained disappearances as Spider-Man caused friction with Gwen, she and Peter grew ever closer. Gwen's father observed approvingly, and he also became a staunch Spider-Man supporter. After Peter revealed his secret identity to his friends and Capt. Stacy while delirious with fever, he "disproved" this statement by having a wall-crawling Prowler appear in a Spider-Man costume near Peter and the others. Peter's deceptions left George unconvinced. When Captain Stacy was fatally wounded during a battle between Spider-Man and Dr. Octopus, the dying Stacy's last words made it clear he knew Peter's secret identity, as he entrusted his daughter to Spider-Man's care. The web-slinger had lost a great ally, and Gwen blamed Spider-Man for her father's death. Peter's conscience, already tormented by his many lies to Gwen, became even more troubled. He did not stop Gwen from going to Europe, where she secretly gave birth to her twins after an accelerated gestation before staying with her uncle in London. Yet love prevailed and Gwen returned to New York, hoping to share her secrets with Peter and marry him. While a distraught Harry became a drug addict, Peter briefly became a six-armed freak after an aborted attempt to remove his own powers. After clashing with the "living vampire" Michael Morbius, Peter and Gwen traveled to the Savage Land on assignment for the Daily Bugle. Aided by Ka-Zar (Kevin Plunder), Spider-Man saved Gwen from becoming Kraven the Hunter's queen. Spider-Man later traveled to Earth-6297's 23rd century with Iron Man (Tony Stark) to face Zarrko the Tomorrow Man and a robot simulacrum of Kang the Conqueror (Nathaniel Richards), stopping Zarrko's time bombs in the present with the Human Torch's aid.

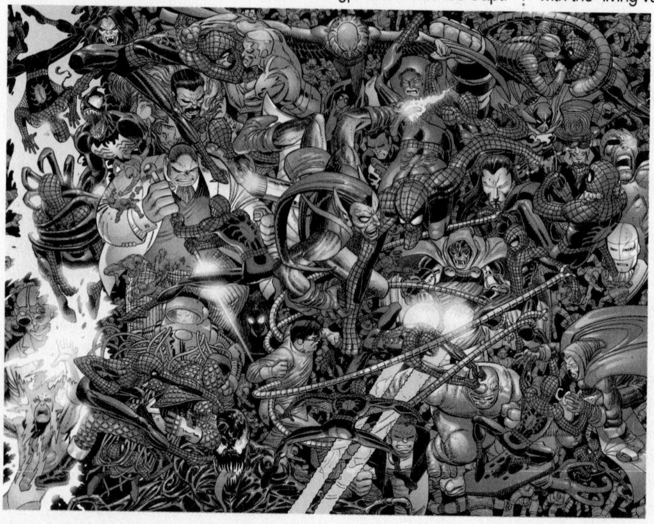
ART BY JOHN ROMITA JR.

Norman Osborn relapsed into his Green Goblin persona, blaming Spider-Man for Harry's drug abuse, and fighting with Gwen over custody of the twins. Kidnapping Gwen, the Goblin knocked her off the top of the Brooklyn Bridge. Spider-Man tried to save her with a webline but failed, snapping her neck during the rescue attempt. In the vicious battle that ensued, Norman was accidentally impaled by his own Goblin-glider. Harry covertly observed his father's seeming demise, swearing revenge on Spider-Man, while suspicious of Spider-Man's connection to Peter. Secretly surviving due to his regenerative powers, Norman fled into seclusion in Europe where he regained his strength, plotted revenge and secretly raised Gwen's twins, Gabriel and Sarah Stacy, who were aging rapidly due to the inherited effects of his Goblin formula. Norman told them Peter was both Gwen's killer and their biological father. Back in New York, Peter was devastated; like Uncle Ben's murder, Gwen's death would always haunt Peter.

Warren also blamed Spider-Man for Gwen's demise, and after suffering a breakdown, adopted the costumed Jackal identity. After Spider-Man helped the savage Man-Wolf (John Jameson) regain human form, the Jackal tricked the killer vigilante Punisher (Frank Castle) into briefly targeting Spider-Man. Meanwhile, a misguided Aunt May nearly married Dr. Octopus, though the interference of Spider-Man and mobster Hammerhead prevented it. Harry found Spider-Man's costume in Peter's room, confirmed his suspicions, and embraced his father's legacy by becoming the new Green Goblin. Booby-trapping Peter's apartment door with explosives, sending Mary Jane to the hospital, Harry destroyed their home. As the Goblin, he kidnapped Aunt May, Mary Jane, and Flash, but Spider-Man rescued his loved ones, sending Harry to a sanitarium. Homeless, Peter briefly moved in with Flash (encountering the Mindworm), before finding a new apartment in Manhattan's Chelsea district, where he befriended neighbor and aspiring model Glory Grant. By now, using the cell samples he collected earlier, the Jackal had succeeded in cloning Spider-Man and Gwen, thanks in part to funding and tech support from an enigmatic masked Scrier (Samuel Fox) — actually Norman Osborn's agent, unbeknownst to Warren. Romance had begun to grow between Peter and Mary Jane, but the appearance of Gwen Stacy's clone derailed their courtship and sent Aunt May to the hospital with another heart attack. While Spider-Man was distracted facing the Scorpion and South American terrorist Tarantula (Antonio Rodriguez), the Jackal's schemes reached fruition: Spider-Man was captured and forced to battle his clone in Shea Stadium. The fight ended with the seeming deaths of the Jackal (whose clone was killed in his place) and Spider-Man's clone (who also secretly survived). Gwen's clone fled to make a new life for herself, as did the Spider-Man clone, taking the new civilian identity of Ben Reilly. With their departures, Peter's life returned to relative normalcy.

While attending ESU, Peter teamed up with many of the world's greatest heroes, such as size-changing spouses Yellowjacket (Hank Pym) and Wasp (Janet Van Dyne), who gradually overcame her longstanding instinctive wariness of Spider-Man, and super-mercenaries Power Man (Luke Cage) and Iron Fist (Danny Rand). Meanwhile, Peter's closest friends began finding true love. Liz Allan dated a psychologically recovering Harry Osborn. Flash Thompson searched for a life after football and the army with his girlfriend, Sha Shan. Betty Brant married Ned Leeds, with Peter as best man. Peter helped Glory Grant replace Betty at the Bugle as Jonah's secretary. New enemies emerged, including Stegron the Dinosaur Man, the Fly (Rick Deacon), ethereal Will O' The Wisp, the skateboarding Rocket Racer (Robert Farrell) and a short-lived new Green Goblin (Harry's therapist Bart Hamilton). Shortly before his college graduation, Peter proposed to Mary Jane, but having seen so much pain in her own family, and unsure how she could handle being married to Spider-Man, she flippantly rejected him. Peter thought his luck was changing when he completed his final graduation requirements, but a dying Spencer Smythe ruined his celebrations by shackling Spider-Man and Jonah together with a bomb, though Spider-Man freed himself and Jameson. Later, while curing the Lizard using a portable Enervator apparatus, exposure to radioactive feedback transferred Connors' reptilian metamorphosis ability into an unwitting Spider-Man, though the power initially lay dormant. Soon after, Spidey encountered the costumed thief Black Cat (Felicia Hardy) when she liberated her father from jail so he could die at home. Meanwhile, having marriage troubles, newlywed Betty briefly tried to rekindle her romance with Peter, who soon began acting callously toward her, hoping to push her back to Ned.

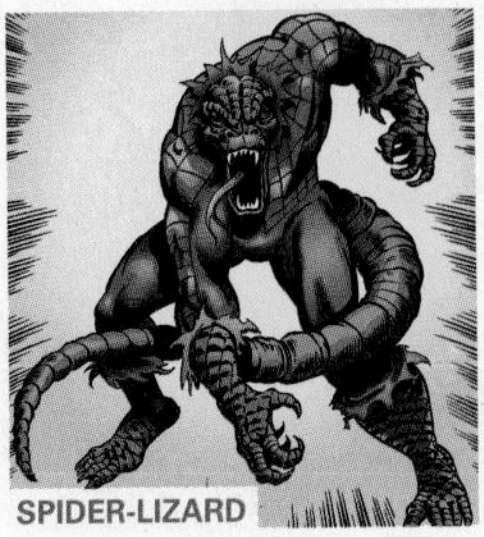

SPIDER-LIZARD

ART BY AL MILGROM

Already distraught after the Black Cat seemingly drowned while escaping him, Peter learned his beloved Aunt May had died, but this turned out to be one of Mysterio's illusions. Mysterio and the Burglar, Uncle Ben's killer, were seeking a long-lost treasure hidden in the Parker home. When the Burglar, holding May hostage, discovered that Spider-Man was Peter Parker, the terrified criminal suffered a fatal heart attack. May revealed that silverfish had eaten the sought-after treasure. After graduating from ESU, Peter pursued his graduate studies there, gaining a teaching assistantship in biochemistry while working as chief photographer at the Daily Globe, having been fired from the Daily Bugle by an increasingly irrational J. Jonah Jameson. Spider-Man contributed to Morbius' cure for a time when the Living Vampire was struck by lightning while drinking Peter's radioactive blood. After growing increasingly aggressive during a battle with the Schizoid Man (Chip Martin), Spider-Man transformed into the 6'6" "Spider-Lizard," and rampaged through the city. While SWAT teams were unable to drown the Spider-Lizard, Connors courageously administered an antidote, returning Peter to normal.

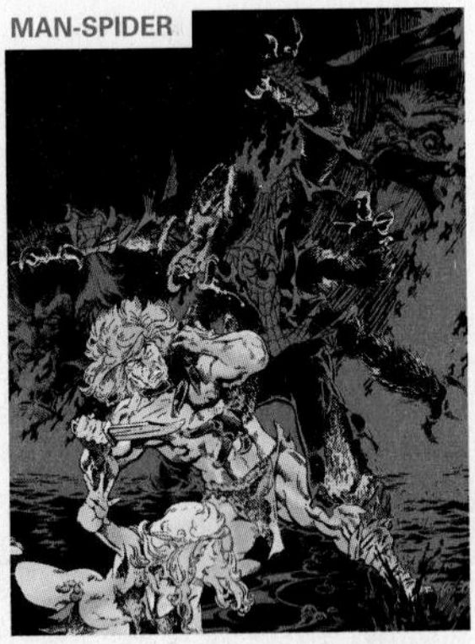

MAN-SPIDER

ART BY MICHAEL GOLDEN

After Mary Jane left to pursue a modeling career in Florida, Peter had several failed romances. He dated fellow student Cissy Ironwood, but she moved west after her father was killed. Undergraduate Dawn Starr tried to seduce Peter in order to steal a science exam. A beautiful new neighbor turned out to be a disguised Llyra of the criminal Frightful Four. Peter was attracted to aloof fellow teaching assistant Marcy Kane (never suspecting she was secretly alien Contraxian spy Kaina), but ended up asking out shy science department secretary Debra Whitman instead. Unfortunately, Peter's frequent date-breaking in order to web-swing only increased Deb's inferiority complex. At the Globe, Peter met and immediately disliked fellow photographer Lance Bannon; later, circulation manager Rupert Dockery's attempted murder of reclusive Globe owner K.J. Clayton resulted in suspension of the paper's publication. Jonah Jameson, having recovered from insanity induced by criminal scientist Jonas Harrow, soon offered Peter his old Bugle job.

While Aunt May got engaged to fellow nursing home resident Nathan Lubensky, Deb Whitman dumped the undependable Peter. Spider-Man continued teaming up with other heroes including Captain America (Steve Rogers), Dazzler (Alison Blaire), Wolverine (Logan/James Howlett), and Moon Knight (Marc Spector). An accidental merging of foes Sandman and Hydro-Man created the Mud-Thing, which so unsettled Sandman after the two villains separated that he went straight, becoming Spider-Man's ally. Newlyweds Harry Osborn and Liz Allan re-entered Peter's life, menaced by the Molten Man, whom Spider-Man defeated. Spider-Man met the ruthless vigilantes Cloak (Tyrone Johnson) and Dagger (Tandy Bowen) and became romantically entwined with the Black Cat, who renounced crime for Spider-Man's love. Briefly transformed into a man-spider by the Savage Land Mutates' Brainchild, Spider-Man later fought a seemingly hopeless fight against the virtually unstoppable Juggernaut (Cain Marko) until steering him into a wet concrete foundation. Overwhelmed by it all, Peter gave up his teaching assistantship, even as Amy Powell began pursuing him in order to make her boyfriend Lance

Bannon jealous. From the mundane to the cosmic, Spider-Man joined other heroes at the deathbed of Captain Marvel (Mar-Vell) on Saturn's moon, Titan, yet fled from the room, shaken that cancer could kill such a hero. Soon after, he helped a new Captain Marvel (Monica Rambeau) get her start with the Avengers.

Peter helped Aunt May move back into their Forest Hills home, which became a boarding house for Nathan and other Restwell residents. Learning that a mentally ill Deb Whitman had come to believe he was Spider-Man, Peter unmasked for her, but Deb thought he had merely rented a costume to shock her back to normal. Grateful, she returned to her Midwest hometown. Shortly thereafter, Spider-Man and the Black Cat were drawn into a war between Dr. Octopus and the Owl (Leland Owlsley), during which the Cat nearly died when shot by Octopus' men. At the Cat's hospital bedside, Spider-Man realized the depth of his feelings for her, and his police ally Captain Jean DeWolff arranged amnesty for the recovering Black Cat. Stumbling onto a hidden Green Goblin lair after Spider-Man quit his pursuit, bank robber George Hill passed its location on to corrupt fashion industry mogul Roderick Kingsley, who murdered Hill and used the Goblin's technology to become the super-criminal Hobgoblin. Initially physically outclassed by Spider-Man, Kingsley found the Goblin's strength-enhancing formula, testing it on disposable henchman Arnold "Lefty" Donovan before optimizing the serum for himself.

ART BY GREG LAROCQUE

ALIEN COSTUME

As Spider-Man's Black Cat romance deepened, Mary Jane returned to Peter's life. Still overwhelmed, Peter quit the ESU graduate program altogether. He took time out from his search for Hobgoblin to reveal his identity to Timothy Harrison, a nine-year-old Spider-Man fan dying of leukemia, and to the Black Cat, who reacted to unglamorous Peter Parker with horror, loving only Spider-Man. Blackmailed by Hobgoblin, Jonah Jameson publicly admitted his role in the Scorpion's creation and resigned as Bugle editor-in-chief. The Hobgoblin was nearly drowned battling Spider-Man, but fled to a hideout where he captured and hypnotized Ned Leeds into becoming a stand-in Hobgoblin. Blaming herself for Spider-Man's injuries in a battle with Cobra (Klaus Voorhees) and Mr. Hyde (Calvin Zabo), the Black Cat sought super-powers, eventually receiving "bad luck" abilities from the Kingpin. Spider-Man's later discovery of Felicia's deceit about her powers' source, and her distaste for his life as Peter Parker, began their relationship's dissolution. Soon after the Cat's power search, Spider-Man and other super-beings were drafted into the "Secret Wars" arranged by the near-omnipotent Beyonder on his patchwork planet Battleworld. There, Spider-Man received a globe from

ART BY TODD MCFARLANE

CLOTH BLACK COSTUME

a strange machine that became a black costume that responded to his mental commands. Later discovering the costume was a living alien symbiote feeding off his adrenalin, and leaving him exhausted by taking his body on nocturnal adventures while he slept, Peter had the symbiote forcibly removed and captured by Mr. Fantastic (Reed Richards). Lent a spare, maskless FF costume, Spider-Man returned home hiding his face in a paper bag, humiliated by Johnny Storm. As the Hobgoblin, Ned Leeds began partnering with the criminal Rose (the Kingpin's son Richard Fisk)

while sparring with Spider-Man and the Black Cat. Felicia made Spider-Man a new, black cloth costume, and for a time he alternated costumes, switching back and forth between his original outfit and the black one. Meanwhile Harry and Liz Osborn had a son "Normie."

Before the Black Cat could selflessly break up with Spider-Man (fearing her bad luck would ultimately kill her lover), Spider-Man instead broke up with her, tired of her recklessness, lies, and love only of his costumed identity. Immediately after, the alien symbiote fought to reattach itself to Peter, but was driven off by high intensity sound in a church bell tower. The symbiote sympathetically pulled a fallen Peter from harm's way and seemingly disintegrated, but secretly survived. Mary Jane grew closer to Peter, shocking him with her longtime knowledge of his dual identity, and sharing with him the secrets of her tragic, dysfunctional upbringing. Meanwhile, Jonah Jameson married Dr. Marla Madison after Spider-Man rescued her from the Scorpion. The Beyonder came to Earth, where Spider-Man provided lessons about being human. Spider-Man first met tenuous ally and international bounty hunter Silver Sable, and proved remarkably resilient in defeating the cosmic-powered Firelord. Tragedy struck Peter's life again when the insane serial killer Sin-Eater (police Sgt. Stan Carter) murdered Jean DeWolff. Daredevil helped Spider-Man catch the murderer and later told Spider-Man that he had discovered his secret identity as Parker, sharing his own secret identity with Peter as well. Spider-Man's capture of Carter ruined Daily Globe reporter Eddie Brock's reputation for his exclusives that identified the wrong man. Contemplating suicide, Eddie prayed at the same church where the symbiote was; the two bonded becoming Venom, knowing all of Peter's secrets via the symbiote's memories. In a contest with the Hell-lord demon Mephisto, the Beyonder tested humanity's worth, secretly choosing Spider-Man as humanity's champion; Spider-Man's virtues persuaded the Beyonder to allow all humanity to continue to exist. While Flash was framed and jailed as the Hobgoblin, Spider-Man was missing-in-action on assignment in Appalachia, foiling the nefarious plans of Magma (Jonathan Darque), but getting arrested (as "Jay Jameson") and returning home in tatters. Spider-Man, Silver Sable, and the Sandman joined forces to stop the Sinister Syndicate.

UNKNOWN SUPER HERO

ART BY RON FRENZ

Suffering bad luck from his prolonged exposure to the Black Cat, Spider-Man had Dr. Strange remove the curse, which eliminated Felicia's powers in mid-battle, resulting in her receiving a beating. Felicia briefly allied herself with the criminal mercenary Foreigner in retaliation. Following a citywide gang war in the Kingpin's absence, Jack O'Lantern (Jason Macendale) hired the Foreigner to murder Ned Leeds in Germany, believing Leeds was the true Hobgoblin, and Macendale usurped the Hobgoblin identity.

After a reignited romance, Peter Parker again proposed marriage to Mary Jane; this time she accepted, and the two married soon afterward, honeymooning in Calais, France thanks to a debt owed Peter by the Puma (Thomas Fireheart). Mary Jane learned quickly about super hero married life when Peter disappeared for two weeks, buried alive by Kraven, who took over Spider-Man's identity and defeated Vermin (Edward Whelan) — an opponent Spider-Man previously defeated only with help — before committing suicide. Things got worse when

SPIDER-HULK

ART BY ALEX SAVIUK

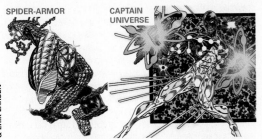

SPIDER-ARMOR

CAPTAIN UNIVERSE

ART BY ALEX SAVIUK & ERIK LARSEN

Venom introduced himself to the Parkers, and nearly killed Spider-Man at the church bell tower, though Peter survived by tricking his foe into exhausting himself. Venom's resemblance to Spider-Man so frightened Mary Jane that Peter promised to stop wearing his black costume. When Mary Jane's modeling career took off, the Parkers moved into the exclusive Bedford Towers apartments. The Gwen Stacy clone returned, but Miles Warren's former colleague the High Evolutionary misinformed Spider-Man that the clone was actually a woman infected with a genetic virus. Peter returned to school; meanwhile Wiltonbooks published "Webs," a collection of Parker's Spider-Man photos, sending him on a book tour that included a Tonight Show appearance. Unfortunately, Bedford Towers owner Jonathan Caesar, an obsessed Mary Jane fan, tried to kidnap her. After being jailed, Caesar retaliated by evicting the Parkers, forcing them to move back in with Aunt May, and used his influence to deprive Mary Jane of modeling assignments. During a demonic invasion of New York, Spider-Man faced the new Hobgoblin (Macendale), now merged with a demon.

In addition to his old enemies, Spider-Man faced new foes such as Skinhead (Edward Cross), Styx and Stone, lycanthropic mutants Carlos and Eduardo Lobo, and albino hitman Tombstone. Peter's heroic and private lives overlapped as his friend Bugle Editor-in-Chief Joe Robertson briefly went to jail for failing to report one of Tombstone's crimes years earlier; Thomas Fireheart took over ownership of the Daily Bugle; a jealous Black Cat dated Flash Thompson to spite Peter; and Nathan Lubensky died during a confrontation with the Vulture (Toomes). Meanwhile, the Parkers moved into a SoHo loft right above Harry and Liz Osborn, and Mary Jane was cast in the soap opera "Secret Hospital." After briefly wielding the cosmic Uni-Power as Captain Universe, Spider-Man was tricked by Chameleon into being stripped of all his powers, but the Black Cat helped restore Peter's abilities, sacrificing her own powers in the process. Accidentally acquiring the Hulk's powers through Armand Jones' Bio-Kinetic Energy Absorber, Peter became an 800 lb. rampaging "Spider-Hulk" until the transformation was reversed. Spider-Man's latest enemies included Hobgoblin's now separated demonic half Demogoblin, vigilante Cardiac, Spencer Smythe's son Alistaire and his new Spider Slayers, sociopath Shriek, the Jury's armored vigilantes, the six-armed Doppelganger and a youth-restored Vulture (Toomes). Spider-Man finally joined the Avengers after aiding the team against the space-pirate Nebula, but did not serve full-time before resigning; he briefly joined former foes Prowler, Sandman, Puma, Rocket Racer and Will O' The Wisp in an alliance that became Silver Sable's mercenary Outlaws, but Parker's longtime rivalry with Puma intensified to a mystical level and resulted in Puma degrading into a beast. The Venom symbiote's spawn bonded with serial killer Cletus Kasady to form the savage Carnage, who led fellow menaces in terrorizing New York City until Spider-Man, Black Cat, Venom and others stopped them. A clash with the New Enforcers, Blood Rose (Richard Fisk) and Gauntlet (Alfredo Morelli) drove Spider-Man to construct a bulletproof suit of armor, though it was soon destroyed by acid in battle.

OCTO-SPIDEY

ART BY STEWART JOHNSON

WITH CYBERNETICS

ART BY ERIK LARSEN

Spider-Man temporarily took on a cyborg-like appearance when he wore mechanical, healing-enhancing braces while foiling Dr. Octopus' latest plans. His sanity gradually slipping, Harry Osborn became the Green Goblin again, terrorizing the Parkers and his own family until an experimental Goblin formula seemingly killed him, though Norman Osborn had actually made elaborate arrangements with Mysterio to fake Harry's death while the younger Osborn physically and mentally recovered. Despite Harry's "death," plots he had initiated continued to torment Peter, including one whereby the Chameleon created android duplicates of Peter's deceased parents, supposedly still alive. Peter was devastated to discover the truth, and retreated into being only Spider-Man for a time. From Europe, Norman Osborn had Peter's Aunt May kidnapped and replaced by an ailing genetic duplicate. News of this May's failing health attracted Spider-Man's long-lost clone Ben Reilly back to New York. Developing his own costumed identity as the "Scarlet Spider," the clone befriended Peter; but Reilly was pursued by another Parker clone, the deformed Kaine, who killed Dr. Octopus. Spider-Man briefly became "Octo-Spidey" using Dr. Octopus' mechanical arms, teaming with Reilly and an unseen Kaine to defeat various villains seeking Dr. Octopus' technology. Peter and his allies would also face new threats such as mutant mentalist Judas Traveller, Kraven's son the Grim Hunter (Vladimir Kravinoff), and a female Dr. Octopus (Carolyn Trainer).

SCARLET SPIDER COSTUME

ART BY MARK BAGLEY

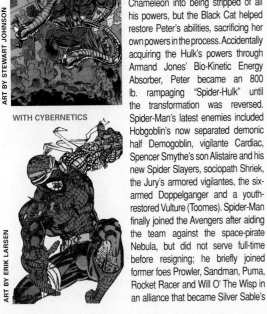

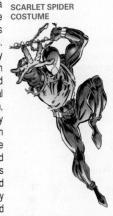

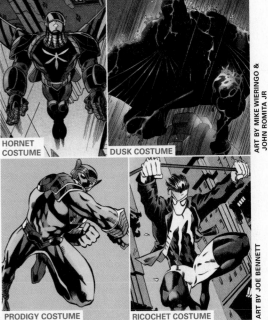

HORNET COSTUME

DUSK COSTUME

ART BY MIKE WIERINGO & JOHN ROMITA JR

PRODIGY COSTUME

RICOCHET COSTUME

ART BY JOE BENNETT

"ELECTRO-PROOF" COSTUME

ART BY STEVE SKROCE

NEGATIVE ZONE COSTUME

ART BY JOHN ROMITA JR

SPIDER-MORPHOSIS

ART BY RAFAEL KAYANAN

ART BY GRAHAM NOLAN

NANOTECH-ARMOR

Norman Osborn secretly deceived the Jackal into believing that Peter was the clone and Reilly was the original Parker, and the Jackal in turn convinced Peter and Ben of this too. After the Aunt May imposter died of natural causes, a grieving Peter was arrested for one of Kaine's murders. Ben took Peter's place in jail while Peter became the Scarlet Spider. Later, Kaine confessed, exonerating Peter. With the Jackal apparently killed and Mary Jane pregnant, Peter took a scientific job with the Seattle-based GARID (formerly General Techtronics West) under Dr. Eric Schwinner, and handed Ben the Spider-Man identity, with the Parkers relocating to the West Coast hoping for a normal family life. When Peter lost his powers, the couple returned home to raise their family in Aunt May's Forest Hills home. After nearly dying while his powers returned, Peter and Ben faced the psionic entity Onslaught's forces ravaging Manhattan. Norman Osborn returned to America, disgusted by how Peter adapted to every hardship. Now seeking vengeance more directly, Osborn had Mary Jane poisoned, causing an apparent miscarriage, and as the Green Goblin he killed Ben Reilly, whose subsequent disintegration confirmed he had been the clone all along.

Peter and Mary Jane returned to ESU, where they met Gwen's uncle Arthur and her cousins, Jill and Paul Stacy. Spider-Man helped Betty Brant expose Roderick Kingsley as the true Hobgoblin, finally clearing Ned Leeds' name. After Spider-Man defeated a super-charged Electro while wearing a special insulated costume, Dr. Octopus (Octavius) was resurrected through the ninja cult, the Hand. Norman Osborn bought the Daily Bugle and framed Spider-Man for murder while Spider-Man battled new gang leaders Don Fortunato, the Black Tarantula and the new Rose (former Bugle columnist Jacob Conover). Spider-Man leapt into the Negative Zone antimatter universe to rescue children from Blastaar, acquiring a monochromatic look while aiding a rebel leader disguised as his missing commander, Dusk. Returning with the children, Peter adopted the Dusk costume plus three other costumed identities — Hornet, Prodigy and Ricochet — to continue his crime-fighting until he finally cleared Spider-Man's name; several youths later adopted his four discarded alternate identities to become the heroic Slingers. Mutagenic pollen from Plantman (Sam Smithers) transformed Spider-Man into a man-spider ("Spider-Morphosis") for a second time, but Spider-Man and the similarly mutated Synch (Everett Thomas) forced Plantman to cure them. Discovering Aunt May was still alive, Spider-Man rescued her and defeated the delusional Norman Osborn, who was driven madder than ever by an arcane ritual. Trying to start a new chapter of their lives, Peter promised Mary Jane he would quit being Spider-Man, moved into an upscale apartment, left graduate school again, and worked at Tri Corp Research Foundation (formerly General Techtronics East) while Mary Jane resumed her modeling career and super-powered teenage girl Mattie Franklin began posing as the absent Spider-Man; however, Peter's sense of responsibility inevitably drove him back to heroics and into battles with the latest Sinister Six, a villainous Spider-Woman (Charlotte Witter) and the alien Z'nox. Franklin would become a new heroic Spider-Woman, but Peter lost another ally when the Wizard mind-warped Sandman into resuming his criminal career.

Harassed by a new stalker, Mary Jane seemingly died in a plane explosion but was secretly kidnapped by the stalker. A mourning Peter returned to the Negative Zone mysteriously outfitted in Spider-Man's nanotech-costume from Reality-751263's Counter-Earth where he rescued the true Dusk and helped him defeat Blastaar. Trying to accept Mary Jane's seeming death, Peter moved into a small apartment, later joined by Joe's son Randy Robertson. Spider-Man finally rescued Mary Jane from the Stalker, but she was now too traumatized to remain in Spider-Man's dangerous world. Mary Jane relocated to the West Coast, leaving Peter to struggle with a loss almost as painful as believing she died.

Peter began questioning the nature of his abilities when similarly spider-powered mystery man Ezekiel Sims claimed they derived from magic. Though he aided Spider-Man against the near-unstoppable vampiric Morlun, Ezekiel had mystically stolen his own powers and ultimately needed to sacrifice Spider-Man to keep them. Visiting unannounced, May found Peter asleep after his grueling victory over Morlun, bloodied and battered, his shredded costume near his bed. May was initially devastated to discover Peter's greatest secret, but she soon came to terms with it and became one of Spider-Man's strongest supporters, and the two grew closer than ever. May also prompted Peter to return to Midtown High as a science teacher. Peter assisted many students inside and outside the classroom — for instance, helping student Jennifer Hardesky find her missing brother, which pitted Spider-Man against the Shade (Jake Nash) on the astral plane, where Peter's curiosity may have attracted the notice of other mystical beings. Spider-Man subsequently fought Shathra, the manipulative mystical Spider-Wasp. Meanwhile, Peter and Mary Jane reunited, trying to make their marriage work. During this time, elite intelligence agency SHIELD's director Nick Fury drafted Spider-Man and other heroes into an unauthorized covert mission to help overthrow Latveria's prime minister Lucia von Bardas; after von Bardas' seeming demise, Fury erased the heroes' memories of this "Secret War." On his birthday, teaming up with Dr. Strange against Dormammu and the Mindless Ones, Spider-Man became disconnected from time and space, reliving his life and glimpsing a possible tragic future, before returning home, where Strange rewarded Peter with a five-minute

"SECRET WAR" IMPACT SUIT

ART BY GABRIELE DELL'OTTO

TRANSFORMED BY THE QUEEN

ART BY PACO MEDINA

visit by Uncle Ben's spirit. After defeating new villains including gamma-powered mobster-amalgam Digger, sorceress Morwen and amateur villain the Shaker, Peter discovered Ezekiel's true motives as the paranormal spider entity Gatekeeper bonded with him, explaining how the radioactive spider that gave him his powers chose him as a fellow hunter, using Peter's rage to turn from being the "prey" into the "predator." Ezekiel tried to have Spider-Man ritually sacrificed in a Peruvian temple to retain his own abilities, but when the ceremony joined their minds, Ezekiel realized he had squandered his powers and sacrificed himself instead.

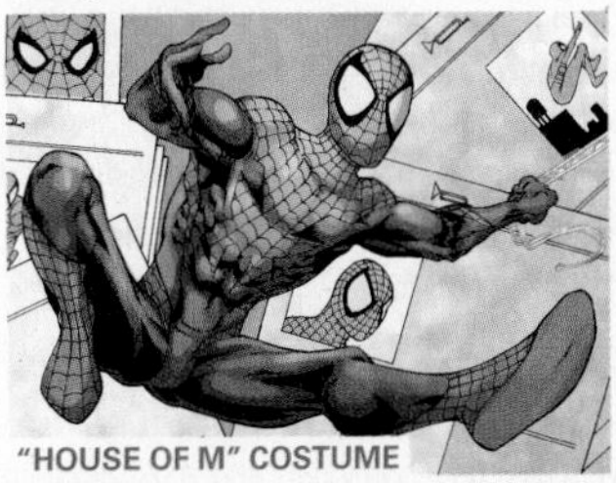
"HOUSE OF M" COSTUME

ART BY SALVADOR LARROCA

Back home, Spider-Man fought Gwen's now adult children, eventually making them realize who their mother's killer really was. Soon after, Peter's Forest Hills home was burned down by spiteful former classmate Charlie Weiderman, who became a new "molten man" but was defeated and immobilized. Spider-Man and the other heroes from Fury's "Secret War" regained their memories while helping Fury, his protégée SHIELD agent Daisy Johnson and others foil von Bardas' retaliatory assault on the USA, estranging Fury from the heroes and leading to his removal as SHIELD director. After being publicly exposed as the Green Goblin and jailed for murdering journalist Terri Kidder, Norman Osborn disclosed Spider-Man's identity to the Scorpion and had him kidnap Aunt May. Osborn knew big businesses had been conspiring since the 1950s to create super villains and, as a potential whistle-blower, he was an easy target in prison. Osborn blackmailed Peter into breaking him out in return for May's freedom, but when Peter did so, Osborn reneged on the deal, deploying his new Sinister Twelve — including Gargan, who bonded with Brock's alien symbiote as the new Venom. The Twelve were defeated, May was rescued and Osborn was ultimately recaptured. Around this time, Spider-Man met the Queen (Ana Soria), who could control the world's insects (and arthropods to a lesser degree), eventually causing Spider-Man to mutate from a man-spider into a giant spider. She planned to detonate a bomb that would kill everyone except those with the insect gene, but Peter returned to his human form, albeit with enhanced powers, and stopped her.

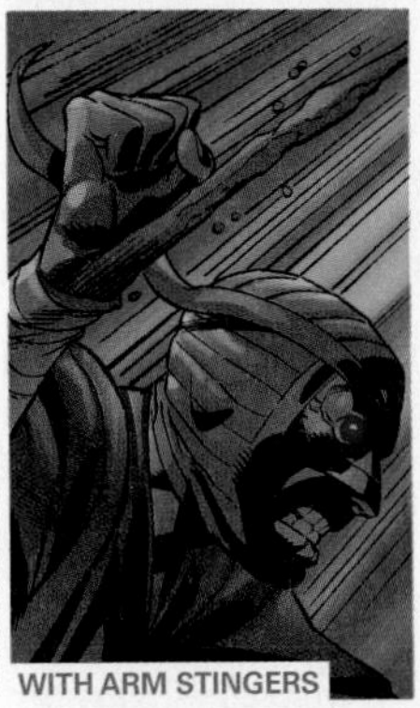
WITH ARM STINGERS

ART BY MIKE WIERINGO

After the Avengers' mutant mystic Scarlet Witch (Wanda Maximoff) had a nervous breakdown, she transformed the world into the "House of M" (Reality-58163) wherein mutants ruled. Pretending to be a mutant, Spider-Man was a successful businessman and entertainer in this world, and had a son, Ritchie, with his wife, Gwen Stacy, while his Uncle Ben and father-in-law George Stacy both still lived. Guilt-ridden by nightmares of his tragic past in conventional reality (Reality-616), Peter sabotaged his own life, becoming the Green Goblin and allowing his publicist, J. Jonah Jameson Jr., to discover his journals and expose him. A fugitive, Peter faked his own death and fled with his family to the country until Layla Miller fully restored his previous life's memories, after which the Scarlet Witch restored Reality-616.

Rejoining the newly reorganized Avengers as a full-time member, Spider-Man moved into the team's luxurious Stark Tower along with Mary Jane and Aunt May. He began to trust his super-heroic peers, sharing his secret identity with the Fantastic Four and his fellow Avengers. Tony Stark grew fond of Peter, viewing him as a protégé. After dealing with clandestine Skrull operations, the global subversive group Hydra and the sentient robot Tracer, Peter developed a mysterious terminal illness, baffling his colleagues. Already weakened, he was ill-prepared for the return of Morlun, who savagely beat Spider-Man, ripping an eye out and consuming it. Morlun returned to finish the kill, but when he threatened Mary Jane, venomous stingers surprisingly sprang from the hospitalized Spider-Man's arms, and he used his remaining strength to stab and kill Morlun, then died. A rejuvenated Peter emerged from his own corpse, cocooned himself and returned with new powers, enhanced abilities and miraculously healed injuries, having embraced the totemic forces of the spider via the spider god, the Great Weaver. A new creature also emerged from the corpse, Spider-Man's counterpoint Ero, who fled and also entered a cocoon.

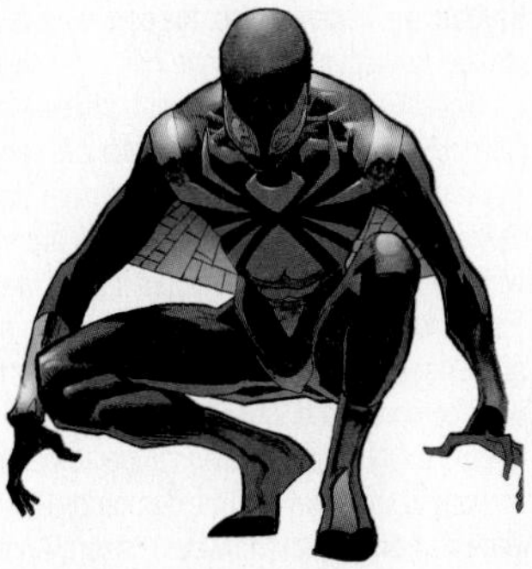
"IRON-SPIDER-MAN" ARMOR

ART BY RON GARNEY

As a "rebirth" present, Tony Stark built Peter a high-tech armored Spider-Man costume (the Spider-Man Armored Fighting Suit or "Iron Spider-Man" costume). When the villain Nitro killed hundreds of civilians (including many schoolchildren) while battling the New Warriors in Stamford, Connecticut, the US government fast-tracked the Superhuman Registration Act requiring super heroes to register themselves and reveal their identities to the government. Tony Stark led the pro-registration movement while Captain America led his outlaw "Secret Avengers" in opposing the Act. To support Iron Man, and perhaps seeking ever-elusive public respect, Spider-Man registered as part of the government's new Initiative super-army and made the difficult decision (with May and Mary Jane's support) to reveal his identity to the world during a press conference. Facing the dangers of public exposure imposed upon his family and loved ones, and the prospect of having to capture his renegade anti-registration friends in what had become an all-out "civil war" among super heroes, Peter soon regretted his decision. After witnessing rebel hero Goliath (Bill Foster)'s death and the establishment of a horrific Negative Zone prison for captured anti-registration heroes, Parker abandoned the registration movement with his family, battling Iron Man during his exit.

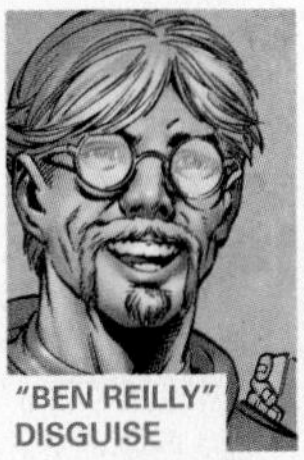
"BEN REILLY" DISGUISE

ART BY SCOT EATON

Now a fugitive, Spider-Man was nearly captured by government-backed Thunderbolts agents Jester (Jody Putt) and Jack O'Lantern (Steve Levins) until the Punisher apparently slew them. Punisher brought the wounded Peter to Captain America's hideout, where a contrite Spider-Man joined the rebellion. He soon publicly admitted his mistake in registering, and vowed to fight the law. On the run, living in a run-down motel with May and Mary Jane, Parker faced some of his darkest days. Some friends, like Betty Brant, remained loyal; his enemies used others, like Liz Osborn, as pawns; longtime employer J. Jonah Jameson now hated him as both Spider-Man and Peter Parker. Reality-6078's Ben Parker walked the streets thanks to the Hobgoblin of Earth-9500's 2211 AD. The Chameleon of 2211 AD killed this Uncle Ben and assumed Ben's identity until Spider-Man defeated him. Ero, posing as school nurse Miss Arrow, revealed her intention to mate with and kill Flash Thompson to give birth to thousands of entities like her; aided by Betty Brant, Spider-Man ended her threat.

Jake Martino, one of the Kingpin's snipers, shot Aunt May, leaving her comatose and hospitalized under an alias. Anguished and embittered by this tragedy and his new fugitive life in general, Spider-Man returned to his black cloth costume, reflective of his dark and troubled life. Though Martino died fleeing from Spider-Man and Parker left Kingpin battered and humiliated in prison, Spider-Man felt little relief. Speaking through Peter's psychic ally Madame Web, the comatose Aunt May urged Peter to let her die, but he kept trying to save her, even giving her another transfusion of his blood. Outside May's hospital, Spider-Man helped the Initiative's three Scarlet Spiders (clones of MVP/Michael van Patrick wearing Stark's "Iron Spider-Man" armor) capture the criminal Vulturions. Grateful, the Scarlet Spiders each mimicked Peter Parker, allowing Peter to escape capture, while causing the public to doubt if Peter was ever truly Spider-Man. Still, Peter's fugitive lifestyle worsened when he struck a police officer, stole an ambulance and transferred May to another hospital before their identities were compromised. Despite money from a sympathetic Tony Stark, and tapping every paranormal and superhuman resource, Peter could not find any way to save May until the demon lord Mephisto offered Peter and Mary Jane a choice. Mephisto would restore Aunt May if the couple sacrificed their marriage, erasing it from history and losing all memory of it ever having occurred. Knowing Peter would never forgive himself for allowing Aunt May to die so that he could remain happily married, Mary Jane agreed, followed by Peter.

Thus, the couple's marriage was pulled from the timeline and Mary Jane never became pregnant, though all other events in Spider-Man's life still happened. For reasons unrevealed, Spider-Man returned to using his web-shooters, and the world was made unaware of Peter Parker's secret identity, except apparently Mary Jane. Mental blocks were placed obfuscating any person trying to connect Peter to Spider-Man. After years of dating instead of being married, Peter and Mary Jane had broken up; Mary Jane went to California to continue her acting career. Harry Osborn surprised everyone by returning to New York alive. Using his wealth, he restored the Parkers' home in Forest Hills, where Peter lived with Aunt May while searching for work. Harry introduced Peter to his girlfriend Lily Hollister and her best friend, forensic detective Carlie Cooper. While New York City enjoyed a lull in crime, Spider-Man took time off for roughly 100 days, though he made an exception by capturing technological villain Overdrive while encountering red-headed rookie heroine Jackpot (Alana Jobson), whom Peter feared was secretly Mary Jane. Spider-Man soon returned to full-time heroics, protecting the Karnelli mobsters' families from dual-natured Chinatown gangster Mr. Negative (secretly Aunt May's boss at the FEAST homeless shelters in his civilian guise as "Martin Li"). When Jonah's heart attack prompted his wife to sell the Bugle to Dexter Bennett, changes at the new "DB!" meant bigger paychecks for Peter, but the more generous Bennett soon proved to be erratic, ruthless and unethical. During a hot political race for New York mayor, Lily's father Bill replaced candidate Lisa Parfrey, who had been accidentally slain by the Goblin-like political terrorist Menace — secretly Lily, who had stumbled onto one of Norman's Green Goblin caches and accidentally exposed herself to an experimental Goblin formula. While Menace manipulated the election to favor her father, Spider-Man clashed with the infinitely adaptive mutated drug addict Freak. Wearing a Spider-Man mask, the "Spider-Mugger" (Sean Boyle) robbed Peter, taking his web-shooter. Peter recovered it after Boyle was murdered by his fence, Dooley. Rogue police later planted a Spider-Tracer on Boyle's corpse as part of an anti-vigilante conspiracy to frame Spider-Man.

AS CHALLENGER

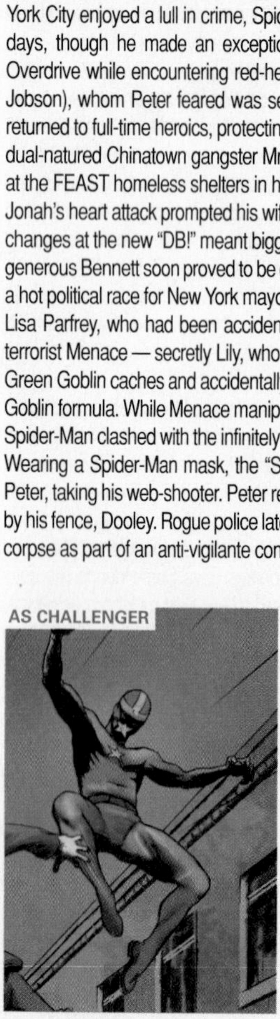

ART BY STEVE SADOWSKI

After teaming with homeless men to stop power-hungry Dr. Benjamin Rabin, who had summoned the ancient Mayan Wayep deity, Peter moved into a new Manhattan apartment with Carlie's friend police officer Vin Gonzales, secretly part of the Spider-Tracer conspiracy. Following an embarrassing chase after the acrobatic parkour master Screwball, Peter was lured by Dexter Bennett into becoming a paparazzo. Pursuing a million dollar reward for a picture of actor Bobby Carr's secret girlfriend, Peter photographed Carr violently dismissing waitress Edith Harper, making headlines. Harper tried to exploit the situation, but was murdered by Carr's insanely jealous fan, the two-dimensional Paper Doll (Piper Dali). At Carr's Hamptons estate Spider-Man rescued Carr from Paper Doll and obtained a photograph of Carr's girlfriend, unaware that it was Mary Jane. Disgusted with his ethical decline, Peter destroyed his camera's memory card, forfeiting the reward and his job at the DB! At the super villains' "Bar with No Name," the Bookie (Johnny LaDue) placed bets on the outcome of super-hero fights. Caught rigging a fight using Screwball disguised as Spider-Man, the Bookie was rescued from the Enforcers by Spider-Man. A new Kraven, the teenaged Ana Kravinoff (allegedly Sergei Kravinoff's daughter), mistakenly concluded Vin was Spider-Man, destroyed his personal life and kidnapped him, dressing him in a Spider-Man costume found in Peter's apartment. Peter, borrowing Daredevil's costume, rescued Vin from Ana and Vermin.

The super-hero "Civil War" over registration had long since ended after Captain America surrendered to the authorities and seemingly died in custody. The "Secret Avengers" had disbanded and most of them registered, but Spider-Man, Luke Cage and a few other anti-registration heroes had stayed together as an outlaw faction of the Avengers, battling threats such as ninja cult the Hand and the Red Skull (Johann Shmidt) of Reality-93198's year 1944, where Peter posed as 1940s hero Challenger (Bill Waring) while helping undo that Skull-dominated alternate reality. Meanwhile, near-undetectable shape-shifting alien Skrulls had been secretly invading Earth — for instance, the Skrull Queen Veranke had long posed as Spider-Man's Avengers teammate Spider-Woman (Jessica Drew). Spider-Man's outlaw Avengers, Iron Man's registered Avengers and many other heroes ultimately exposed and defeated the alien invaders, but the victory had dark consequences. Norman Osborn, who had been pardoned and appointed as head of the Thunderbolts during the civil war, killed Veranke with a random lucky shot during the Skrulls' final defeat. Blaming Stark technology for failing to detect the Skrulls, Osborn gained massive political and public support after the Skrull conflict.

Peter and Joe Robertson joined Ben Urich's small but ethical Front Line newspaper. As a cancer-stricken Eddie Brock was cured and transformed into Anti-Venom by Mr. Negative, Norman and his Thunderbolts, which included Venom, hunted Spider-Man. Anti-Venom discovered his touch burned away the Venom symbiote from Gargan, and all vestiges of the symbiote from Spider-Man's blood, but Brock's presence also negated Spider-Man's powers. Discovering how Spider-Man's automatic camera had been modified to automatically take pictures centered on a tracking chip in his costume's chest emblem, Norman had his Thunderbolts forces use the chip to track Spider-Man until Peter discarded it. Meanwhile, Norman used Freak's adaptive ability to create a counter-measure to Anti-Venom, healing Venom. At Oscorp in Jersey City, Spider-Man and Harry confronted Norman, who fought back as the Green Goblin. Spider-Man discovered Oscorp housed human test subjects for the "Promethean Trials," experiments Harry was secretly conducting to cure his former brother-in-law Molten Man, of his unstable powers; Harry appeared surprised and horrified by this new round of human testing, having already perfected Raxton's treatment using earlier voluntary test subject Charlie Weiderman, curing him of his similar condition. Spider-Man rescued the new test subjects before the Goblin blew up the Oscorp building.

Spider-Man and Jackpot failed to stop new villain Blindside (Nick Chernin) from a bank robbery. Investigating Jackpot, Spider-Man discovered her secret identity and how she derived her powers from illegal drugs. Ignoring warnings to quit, Jackpot died battling Blindside and Commanda when the drugs in her system lethally interacted with Blindside's neurotoxin. Spider-Man blamed superhuman Initiative dropout Sara Ehret for irresponsibly selling her Jackpot identity to Jobson. After Spider-Man protected children in a Bronx gang from an enhanced Hammerhead, he helped Punisher prevent Moses Magnum from obtaining gamma-enhanced MGH drugs. Later, Spider-Man befriended J. Jonah Jameson Sr. — Jonah's father —

AS VENOM

ART BY MARCO CHECHETTO

when the Shocker trapped them and others in a subway car until Spider-Man freed them all. While Spider-Man captured slippery robber the Blank for the police, Flash Thompson performed his own heroics as an army reservist in Iraq. Inspired by Spider-Man, Flash saved a fellow soldier but lost his legs. Harry and Peter visited Harry's estranged wife and son Liz and Normie in New Jersey, where Spider-Man helped Harry make amends with Liz by using Prometheus X-90 to cure the physically deteriorating Molten Man. After Harry proposed to Lily, Menace beat Spider-Man, enabling his arrest and swinging more votes towards anti-vigilante candidate Bill Hollister. Afterwards, Lily revealed her Menace identity to Harry and Carlie's investigations of the "Spider-Tracer Killer" led to Vin, where she learned of the whole police conspiracy. Vin was arrested, set up to take the blame with Carlie for the conspiracy. Matt Murdock defended Spider-Man in court, helping him dodge a civil suit with the assistance of heroes, both registered and unregistered, impersonating Spider-Man to prove a legal point, and also helping Spider-Man escape custody (with the Black Cat's aid), and rescue Vin from his fellow prison inmates. When Bill Hollister was elected as New York's mayor, Harry exposed Lily as Menace on live television with Spider-Man's help; Hollister refused office, while Vin went into protective custody after he arrested the police conspiracy's leader, Sgt. Quentin Palone.

During a mission to the Macroverse with the Fantastic Four, Spider-Man helped the FF secure peace between the warring Kort and Dregan peoples, but Johnny Storm was disturbed to realize he could not recall Spider-Man's unmasked face from a previous Macroverse adventure they had shared. On the trip home, Spider-Man unmasked for the Fantastic Four, dispelling the "psychic blindspot" that prevented their recollection of his identity. At the insistence of the outlaw Avengers' new leader Ronin (Clint Barton), Spider-Man soon shared his secret identity with his fellow Avengers as well, which became awkward when Luke Cage's wife Jessica Jones turned out to be an old high school classmate who had a crush on Peter in their teens. Meanwhile, Peter discovered that differing flows of time between dimensions meant that two months had elapsed on Earth during his hours-long Macroverse mission. In Peter's absence during these two lost months, J. Jonah Jameson Jr. became New York's mayor, Harry relapsed into drinking, Aunt May and Jay Jameson Sr. began dating and Vin's sister Michele moved into Peter's apartment. Worst of all, Norman Osborn had used his new influence to replace a discredited Stark as head of the Initiative, the registered Avengers and SHIELD (which Osborn disbanded and replaced with his new HAMMER agency). Wearing Stark-derived armor as the Iron Patriot, Osborn now led the registered Avengers, whose newly revamped ranks included corrupt Osborn cronies such as a new Spider-Man (Mac Gargan). With Mayor Jameson forming an "Anti-Spider Squad" to take down the wall-crawler, Spider-Man performed heroics night and day trying to win over the public, though he angered baseball fans by interrupting a Yankee Stadium game while subduing a horrific new acid-spewing Vulture. May and Jay Jameson became

CORRUPTED BY MR. NEGATIVE

ART BY GIANLUCA GUGLIOTTA

engaged while Spider-Man fruitlessly sought some means of bringing down the corrupt Norman Osborn. After Spider-Man gave Norman a futile beating, Harry accepted a job with his father to be close to Lily, who was pregnant and living under Norman's care. Norman transformed Harry into the armored American Son, grooming him for Avengers membership. Disguised as his imitator Gargan, Spider-Man infiltrated Avengers Tower seeking to help Harry, but was caught and tortured. Once Harry learned Lily was pregnant with Norman's child and not his, Harry rebelled and freed Spider-Man, who helped Harry walk away from Norman, albeit powerless and cut off from the Osborn millions.

In Boston, Peter discovered many new relatives on May's side of the family during an engagement party. There, he clashed with the vengeful Raptor (Damon Ryder), who mistook Peter for Ben Reilly, blaming Ben for killing his family. Right before May married Jay, Spider-Man and the Human Torch waged war against "New York City" as a dying Dr. Octopus took control of the city's technology. At May's wedding, Mary Jane returned to catch the bouquet, flustering Peter, and leading to an intoxicated romantic liaison between Peter and Michele Gonzales. Taking a job as Mayor Jameson's staff photographer under Press Secretary Glory Grant, Peter was targeted by the Chameleon, seeking access to the city's security system to plant a dirty bomb. Abducting and replacing Parker, the Chameleon meddled in Peter's life before Spider-Man thwarted his plans. Spider-Man turned vicious, corrupted by Mr. Negative while interfering in gang disputes; his love for his friend, Betty Brant, stopped him from killing her and reversed the corruption. Mistakenly believing he found Ben Reilly in New York City, Raptor violently confronted Peter at the Front Line office, while Kaine reappeared, seeking Ryder for a cure to his deteriorating condition. Spider-Man stopped Raptor from killing Aunt May's nieces and Harry Osborn. With Jonah now Aunt May's son-in-law, Mary Jane back in his life, and the Black Cat showing renewed romantic interest in him, Spider-Man's life remains as complicated as it is dangerous.

NOTE: Cosmic entities Lord Chaos and Master Order claim to have orchestrated Spider-Man's origin so that Spider-Man would later release Adam Warlock from his Soul Gem to defeat Thanos of Titan at a precise moment.

INSTALLING WEB-FLUID CARTRIDGE

STRAND

PASTE

NETTING

ART BY JOHN ROMITA SR.

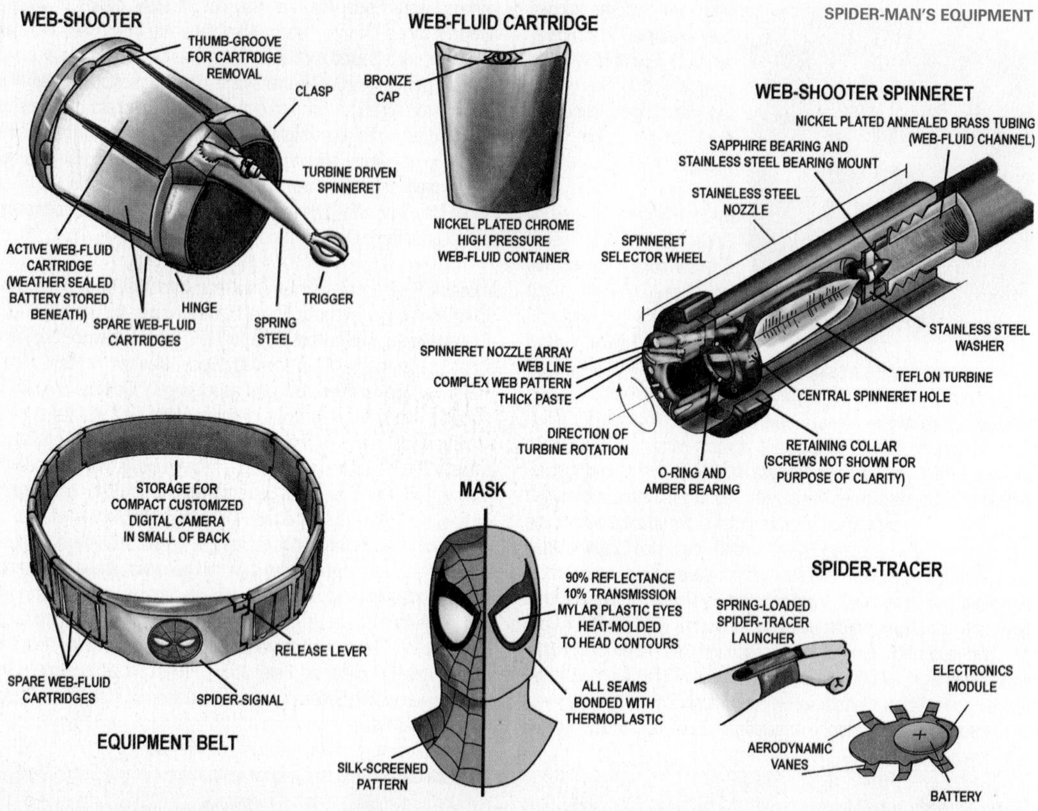
SPIDER-MAN'S EQUIPMENT
WEB-SHOOTER
THUMB-GROOVE FOR CARTRDIGE REMOVAL
CLASP
TURBINE DRIVEN SPINNERET
ACTIVE WEB-FLUID CARTRIDGE (WEATHER SEALED BATTERY STORED BENEATH)
HINGE
SPARE WEB-FLUID CARTRIDGES
SPRING STEEL
TRIGGER
WEB-FLUID CARTRIDGE
BRONZE CAP
NICKEL PLATED CHROME HIGH PRESSURE WEB-FLUID CONTAINER
WEB-SHOOTER SPINNERET
NICKEL PLATED ANNEALED BRASS TUBING (WEB-FLUID CHANNEL)
SAPPHIRE BEARING AND STAINLESS STEEL BEARING MOUNT
STAINELESS STEEL NOZZLE
SPINNERET SELECTOR WHEEL
STAINLESS STEEL WASHER
SPINNERET NOZZLE ARRAY
WEB LINE
COMPLEX WEB PATTERN
THICK PASTE
TEFLON TURBINE
CENTRAL SPINNERET HOLE
DIRECTION OF TURBINE ROTATION
O-RING AND AMBER BEARING
RETAINING COLLAR (SCREWS NOT SHOWN FOR PURPOSE OF CLARITY)
STORAGE FOR COMPACT CUSTOMIZED DIGITAL CAMERA IN SMALL OF BACK
SPARE WEB-FLUID CARTRIDGES
RELEASE LEVER
SPIDER-SIGNAL
EQUIPMENT BELT
MASK
90% REFLECTANCE 10% TRANSMISSION MYLAR PLASTIC EYES HEAT-MOLDED TO HEAD CONTOURS
ALL SEAMS BONDED WITH THERMOPLASTIC
SILK-SCREENED PATTERN
SPIDER-TRACER
SPRING-LOADED SPIDER-TRACER LAUNCHER
ELECTRONICS MODULE
AERODYNAMIC VANES
BATTERY

ART BY ELIOT R. BROWN & MIKE FICHERA

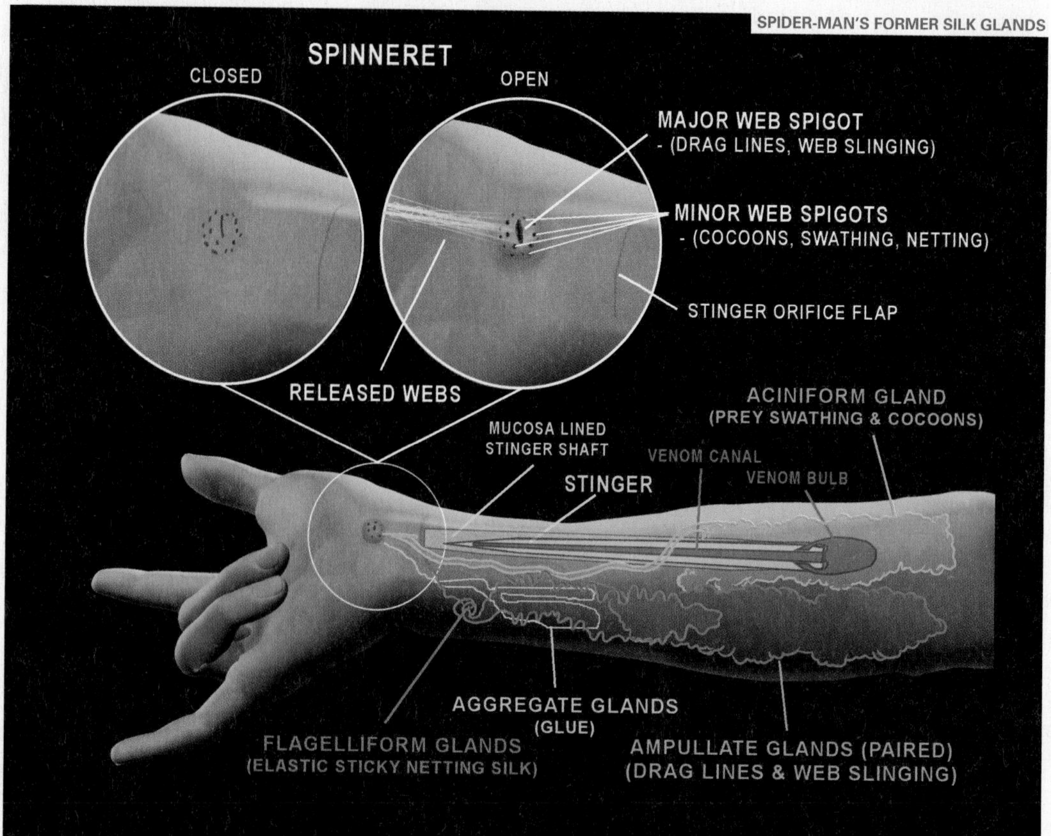
SPIDER-MAN'S FORMER SILK GLANDS
SPINNERET
CLOSED
OPEN
MAJOR WEB SPIGOT
- (DRAG LINES, WEB SLINGING)
MINOR WEB SPIGOTS
- (COCOONS, SWATHING, NETTING)
STINGER ORIFICE FLAP
RELEASED WEBS
ACINIFORM GLAND
(PREY SWATHING & COCOONS)
MUCOSA LINED STINGER SHAFT
VENOM CANAL
VENOM BULB
STINGER
AGGREGATE GLANDS
(GLUE)
FLAGELLIFORM GLANDS
(ELASTIC STICKY NETTING SILK)
AMPULLATE GLANDS (PAIRED)
(DRAG LINES & WEB SLINGING)

ART BY MIKE FICHERA

HEIGHT: 5'10"
EYES: Hazel

WEIGHT: 167 lbs.
HAIR: Brown

ABILITIES/ACCESSORIES: Spider-Man has superhuman strength (lifting at least 10 tons), speed, reflexes (at least 15 times faster than an average human, enabling him to dodge bullets if he is far enough away), endurance (able to fight for hours without rest) and equilibrium. Parker's superhuman metabolism heals his injuries rapidly. His skeleton, interconnective tissues, muscles and nervous system are all enhanced. Extraordinarily limber, he has tendons and connective tissue twice as elastic as an average human being's, despite his enhanced strength. Spider-Man can mentally control the inter-atomic attraction between molecular boundary layers. This ability to affect the attraction between surfaces is limited to his body and another object, with an upper limit of several tons per finger. This attraction is concentrated in his palms and soles, enabling him to cling to or crawl across most surfaces.

Spider-Man's "spider-sense" alerts him to imminent danger via a tingling sensation in the back of his skull. This sense is linked with his superhuman kinesthetics, incorporated into his fighting style, enabling him to evade most any injury unless he cognitively overrides his autonomic reflexes. He can discern the danger's severity by the magnitude of the tingling sensation, and can experience a more vague general response to threats up to several minutes away. On occasion, Spider-Man has used his spider-sense for ascertaining non-threatening information, such as detecting loved ones' concealed presence or for receiving broadcasts from his Spider-Tracer devices attuned to his spider-sense.

Spider-Man has developed a unique fighting style that exploits his agility, speed, strength and equilibrium, as well his subconscious spider-sense. He typically uses a combination of acrobatic leaps and web-slinging to travel rapidly. Parker is a gifted scientist, skilled photographer, self-taught inventor and naturally talented teacher. His greatest personal assets include his fierce willpower and determination.

Spider-Man's web-shooters are twin devices worn on his wrists that can shoot thin strands of special "web fluid" at high pressure. The web fluid is a shear-thinning liquid (virtually solid until a shearing force is applied to it, rendering it fluid) of unrevealed formulation, related to nylon. On contact with air, the long-chain polymer knits and forms an extremely tough, flexible fiber with extraordinary adhesive properties. The web fluid's adhesive quality diminishes rapidly with exposure to air (where it does not make contact with air, such as the web-shooter's attachment disk, it remains very adhesive). After about one to two hours, certain imbibed esters cause the web fluid's solid form to dissolve into a powder. Because components of the fluid almost instantly sublimate from solid to gas when under shear pressure, and it is not adhesive in its anaerobic liquid/solid phase transition point, there is no clogging of the web-shooter's parts. The web-shooter's spinneret mechanism is machined from stainless steel, except for the turbine component that is machined out of a Teflon block and the two turbine bearings that are made of amber and artificial sapphire. The wristlets and web fluid cartridges are mainly nickel-plated annealed brass. The cartridges are pressurized to 300 pounds per square inch and sealed with a bronze cap, which is silver soldered closed. The wristlets have sharp steel nipples that pierce the bronze caps when the cartridges are tightly wedged into their positions. The hand-wound solenoid needle valve is actuated by a palm switch that is protected by a spring-steel band that requires 65 pounds of pressure to trigger. The switch is situated high on the palm to avoid most unwanted firings. A rubber seal protects the small battery compartment. The effect of the very small turbine pump vanes is to compress (shear) the web fluid and then force it, under pressure, through the spinneret holes, which cold-draws it (stretches it: the process wherein nylon gains a four-fold increase in tensile strength), then extrudes it through the air where it solidifies. As the web fluid exits the spinneret holes, it is attracted to itself electrostatically and thus can form complex shapes. The spinneret holes have three sets of adjustable, staggered openings around the turbine that permit a single web line, a more complex, spun web line, and a thick stream. The web line's tensile strength is estimated

to be 120 pounds per square millimeter of cross section. The 300 psi pressure in each cartridge is sufficient to force a stream of the complex web pattern an estimated 60 feet (significantly farther if shot in a ballistic parabolic arc). On later models of his web-shooters, Parker has added a sensor to indicate when web fluid levels are low. Spider-Man has made a plastic version of his web-shooters to evade metal detectors. Spider-Man's web cartridge belt is made out of brass and light leather, and different versions have held from 21 to 30 web cartridges. Spider-Man's belt also contains the Spider-Signal, a high intensity red-tinted light that projects Spider-Man's visage, and can house his compact customized digital camera. For a time, his automatic camera could track a chip embedded in Spider-Man's costume's emblem. Spider-Man's mask contains "one way" (90% reflectance) Mylar plastic lenses over the eyes, heat-molded to the head contours.

Parker's self-designed and constructed Spider-Tracers are tiny tracking devices that can transmit a signal at short-to-medium range. Each micro radio transmitter is embedded in a tiny, spider-styled casing. The casing's legs are actually aerodynamically shaped fins that aid in throwing and placement. The coded signal sent by the original tracers required a separate, portable unit to track. This somewhat bulky battery-powered tracking unit had a limited operational period and range. Through experimentation and analysis, Parker modified the tracers to transmit on a coding and frequency his spider-sense could detect without requiring the tracking unit. The tracers can be placed or thrown. Parker developed a wrist-launcher to fire tracers at high velocity. The tracers are coated in a sticky substance to keep them firmly attached to their targets. Spider-Man has given tracers to friends and allies for activation should they require his aid.

Spider-Man's powers underwent augmentations and alterations after his transformation by the Queen and subsequent rebirth. After the Queen's transformation, Parker could produce silk from glands within his forearms, limited by his body's health and nutrition. These organic webs had many similar properties to his artificial webbing, though they required a week to decay rather than decomposing within two hours. The silk was released through a spinneret near each wrist containing a central web spigot orifice used for web-slinging and drag lines, supplemented by several radial minor spigots for other types of webs (sticky nets, cocoons, prey swathing, etc.) connected to specialized glands. Each arm also contained a concealed stinger that could eject and release polyamine venom, causing direct trauma and/or flaccid paralysis via interference with nerve impulse transmission. While a typical injection might have paralyzed a normal adult human for several hours, the impalement proved fatal to the nigh-invulnerable Morlun. How it pierced Morlun's skin is yet unrevealed, and may have involved mystical factors. Parker subconsciously extended his stingers in response to stress. In addition to the silk glands and stingers, the Queen's transformation provided increased strength (lifting 15 tons) and an enhanced spider-sense, including a stronger psychic alignment with his environment, especially with other arachnids and insects. Spider-Man also had the ability to recover from death, emerging with a new body from his corpse. In this new body, Parker had even greater strength (lifting 20 tons), agility, healing and control over somatic molecular attraction. He also gained night vision and increased sensory awareness via tactile interpretation of vibratory patterns transmitted over his web lines and via superhuman awareness of air movements across his body hairs. Whether Parker has lost all these enhancements and new abilities is unrevealed.

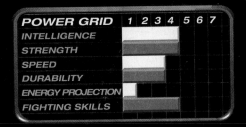

POWER GRID	1	2	3	4	5	6	7
INTELLIGENCE							
STRENGTH							
SPEED							
DURABILITY							
ENERGY PROJECTION							
FIGHTING SKILLS							

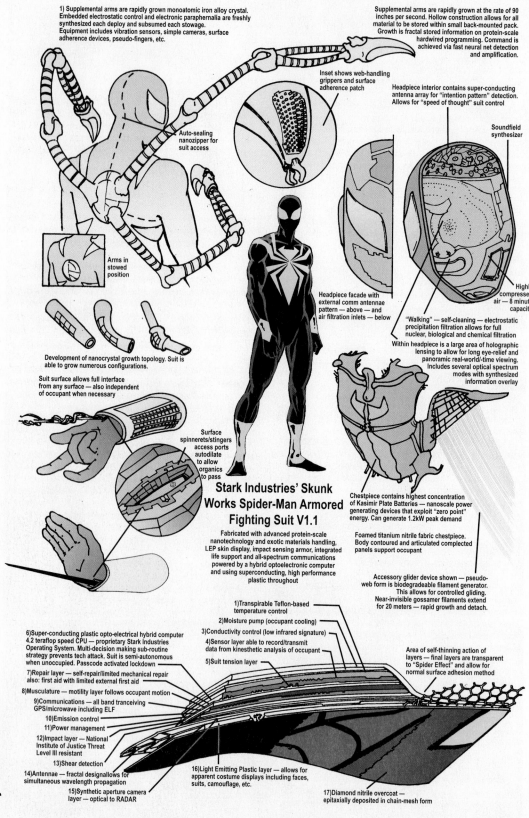

1) Supplemental arms are rapidly grown monoatomic iron alloy crystal. Embedded electrostatic control and electronic paraphernalia are freshly synthesized each deploy and subsumed each stowage. Equipment includes vibration sensors, simple cameras, surface adherence devices, pseudo-fingers, etc.

Supplemental arms are rapidly grown at the rate of 90 inches per second. Hollow construction allows for all material to be stored within small back-mounted pack. Growth is fractal stored information on protein-scale hardwired programming. Command is achieved via fast neural net detection and amplification.

Inset shows web-handling grippers and surface adherence patch

Headpiece interior contains super-conducting antenna array for "intention pattern" detection. Allows for "speed of thought" suit control

Soundfield synthesizer

Auto-sealing nanozipper for suit access

Arms in stowed position

Highly compressed air — 8 minute capacity

Headpiece facade with external comm antennae pattern — above — and air filtration inlets — below

"Walking" — self-cleaning — electrostatic precipitation filtration allows for full nuclear, biological and chemical filtration

Development of nanocrystal growth topology. Suit is able to grow numerous configurations.

Within headpiece is a large area of holographic lensing to allow for long eye-relief and panoramic real-world-/time viewing. Includes several optical spectrum modes with synthesized information overlay

Suit surface allows full interface from any surface — also independent of occupant when necessary

Surface spinnerets/stingers access ports autodilate to allow organics to pass

Stark Industries' Skunk Works Spider-Man Armored Fighting Suit V1.1

Fabricated with advanced protein-scale nanotechnology and exotic materials handling, LEP skin display, impact sensing armor, integrated life support and all-spectrum communications powered by a hybrid optoelectronic computer and using superconducting, high performance plastic throughout

Chestpiece contains highest concentration of Kasimir Plate Batteries — nanoscale power generating devices that exploit "zero point" energy. Can generate 1.2kW peak demand

Foamed titanium nitrile chestpiece. Body contoured and articulated completed panels support occupant

Accessory glider device shown — pseudo-web form is biodegradeable filament generator. This allows for controlled gliding. Near-invisible gossamer filaments extend for 20 meters — rapid growth and detach.

1) Transpirable Teflon-based temperature control

2) Moisture pump (occupant cooling)

6) Super-conducting plastic opto-electrical hybrid computer 4.2 teraflop speed CPU — proprietary Stark Industries Operating System. Multi-decision making sub-routine strategy prevents tech attack. Suit is semi-autonomous when unoccupied. Passcode activated lockdown

3) Conductivity control (low infrared signature)

4) Sensor layer able to record/transmit data from kinesthetic analysis of occupant

5) Suit tension layer

Area of self-thinning action of layers — final layers are transparent to "Spider Effect" and allow for normal surface adhesion method

7) Repair layer — self-repair/limited mechanical repair also: first aid with limited external first aid

8) Musculature — motility layer follows occupant motion

9) Communications — all band tranceiving GPS/microwave including ELF

10) Emission control

11) Power management

12) Impact layer — National Institute of Justice Threat Level III resistant

13) Shear detection

14) Antennae — fractal designallows for simultaneous wavelength propagation

15) Synthetic aperture camera layer — optical to RADAR

16) Light Emitting Plastic layer — allows for apparent costume displays including faces, suits, camouflage, etc.

17) Diamond nitrile overcoat — epitaxially deposited in chain-mesh form

Art by Eliot R. Brown

LIZARD

REAL NAME: Dr. Curtis Connors
ALIASES: None
IDENTITY: Known to authorities
OCCUPATION: Leading researcher in biogenetics, college professor
CITIZENSHIP: USA
PLACE OF BIRTH: Coral Gables, Florida
KNOWN RELATIVES: Martha Connors (wife, deceased), William Connors (son), unidentified sister-in-law
GROUP AFFILIATION: None; formerly Sinister Twelve
EDUCATION: Medical school graduate, later earned twin doctorates in biology and biochemistry (mutagenics)
FIRST APPEARANCE: Amazing Spider-Man #6 (1963)

HISTORY: Dr. Curt Connors was a gifted surgeon and biologist who went to war when his country called. He served as a battlefield medic until his arm was wounded in an explosion and was ultimately amputated. His surgical career brought to an abrupt end, Curt returned to his Florida laboratory. Inspired by a reptile's ability to regenerate lost limbs, he pursued a revolutionary study of reptilian molecular biology and DNA manipulation to replicate the process in humans. Curt then drank his untested formula; within seconds, his lost arm miraculously regenerated.

Although the serum worked as predicted, it was more powerful than Curt had expected. The chemical mix transformed him into a human lizard. Overwhelmed by his new reptilian nature, he fled into the dense Florida swamps. From his jungle sanctuary, the Lizard built an army of cold-blooded creatures — aiming to destroy humankind. Rumors of a "giant lizard" soon spread, drawing the attention of New York's *Daily Bugle*. Viewing the creature as a public menace, J. Jonah Jameson brazenly challenged Spider-Man to face the Lizard.

As a photographer for the Bugle, Peter Parker traveled to Florida. Tracking down Curt's wife, Martha, and young son, Billy, Spider-Man learned the truth. Using Curt's lab notes and equipment, as well as his own scientific knowledge, he was able to concoct an antidote. Battling the Lizard to a standstill, Spider-Man forced the creature to swallow the solution and revert to human form — minus his newly regenerated arm. Spider-Man's aid earned him Curt's undying gratitude, as well as the enmity of his reptilian alter ego.

Curt would soon have the opportunity to repay the favor. When Peter gave his ailing aunt, May Parker, a transfusion, his radioactive blood put her in deadly peril. With doctors powerless, a desperate Spider-Man brought his friend a sample of May's blood. Curt helped the hero develop a formula to save May's life. However, Curt remained unaware of Spider-Man's secret identity.

Shortly thereafter, Curt and Spider-Man again worked jointly to create a solution that would soften the Rhino's hide. Unfortunately, the chemicals in that solution caused Curt to revert to reptilian form once more. Knowing a cold-blooded creature cannot regulate its internal temperature, Spider-Man trapped the Lizard in a refrigerated train carriage.

For a while, Curt split his time between Florida and New York. A research grant at Empire State University established him for a time in Manhattan, where Peter worked as his teaching assistant. Yet Curt could not escape the Lizard's shadow. More and more frequently, extreme stress or exposure to chemicals would transform him into the horrific creature. Connors and many heroes and villains were transported off Earth to the so-called "Secret Wars" orchestrated by the near-omnipotent Beyonder. There on "Battleworld," though grouped with the villains, the Lizard tried to remain neutral after sustaining an injury, and befriended the Wasp. Upon returning to Earth in tatters, Martha took Billy and left him, unable to deal with the toll of her husband's relapses. Though distraught by

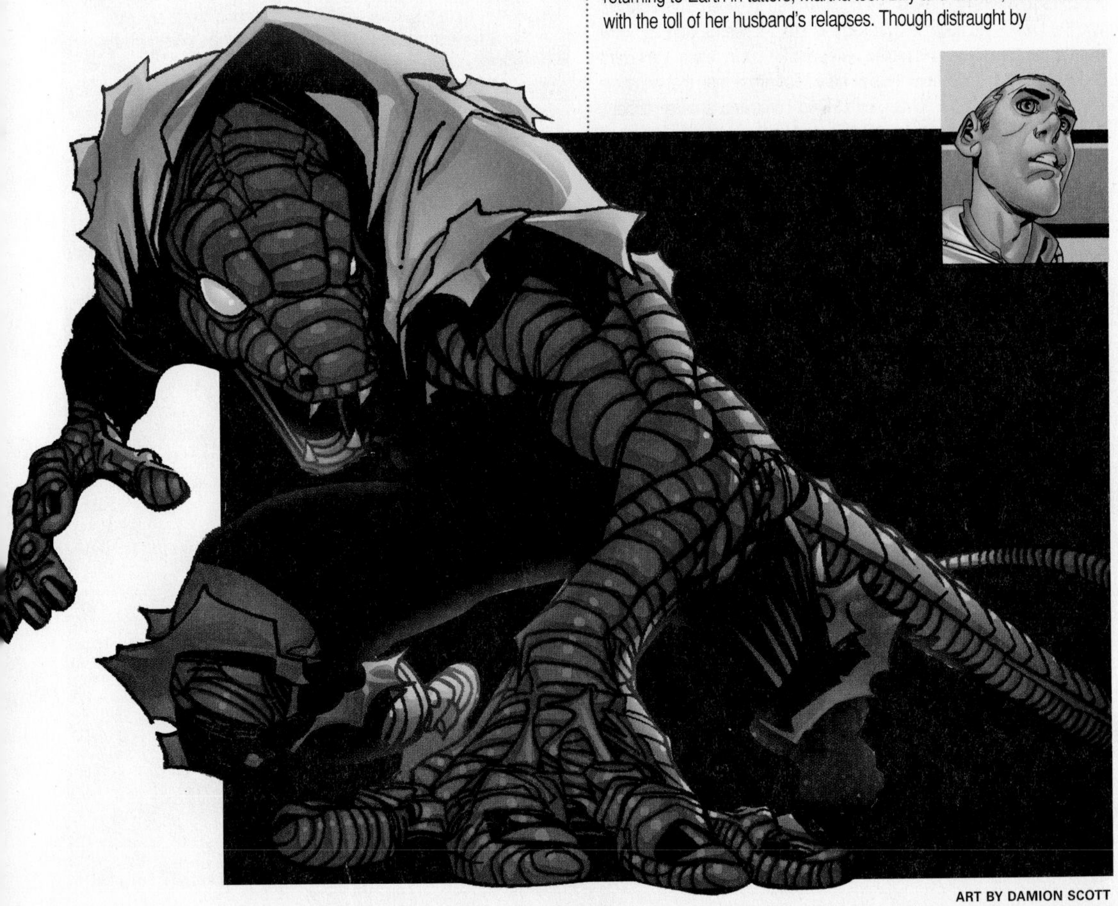

ART BY DAMION SCOTT

the separation, Connors managed to gain some control over his Lizard persona and helped rescue his family, kidnapped by the Owl. This control was short lived, as a demonic invasion of New York called the "Inferno" turned the Lizard savage again. Calypso used her voodoo powers to usurp control of the Lizard's mind in pursuit of her own deadly vendetta against Spider-Man, after the death of her lover, Kraven the Hunter (Sergei Kravinoff). The Lizard was captured after an explosion at Kraven the Hunter's mansion. Calypso infiltrated the Vault prison to liberate the Lizard but, after training to resist her charms, the Lizard instead slaughtered her.

In the wake of Calypso's defeat, Curt embarked on a search for a permanent cure to his condition. To that end, he created a modified version of his original regeneration formula. Connors' assistant, Aldo Quadrini, injected this new serum into a severed fragment of the Lizard's tail, with disastrous effects. The tail grew into a completely new Lizard, devoid of any shred of humanity. Curt was forced to trigger his transformation to protect his wife and son.

Following her husband's brave sacrifice, Martha returned to Curt. With his missing arm miraculously restored by Hammerhead, a happy ending for the Connors family seemed assured. However, the cellular structure of Curt's new arm proved unstable, and it soon became useless. A short time later, Martha and Billy were diagnosed with cancer, a result of pollution from an industrial lab near the Connors' Florida home. The combined efforts of Curt, his reptilian alter ego and Spider-Man were enough to persuade a Monnano Corporation employee to expose the company's misdeeds — but it was too late. Martha's cancer was inoperable, and Curt's long-suffering wife died.

Billy survived, and unwillingly holds his father partly responsible for the tragedies which befell them both. Under the strain of his wife's death and his son's resentment, the line that once existed between Curt Connors and the Lizard has become ever more blurred. It seems Curt can now exert some control over his reptilian alter ego — but in return, the Lizard is ever waiting for those moments of weakness in the man that will allow him to take over Curt's human form. Curt commited a bank robbery, deliberately allowing himself to be imprisoned for the protection of himself and those he loved.

Free from prison, the Lizard was given a power upgrade by Norman Osborn, enabling him to radiate aggression through pheromones. In return, the Lizard joined Osborn's short-lived Sinister Twelve team to greet Spider-Man once the wall-crawler was coerced into liberating Osborn from prison; the Twelve were defeated by Spider-Man and his heroic allies. Later, Connors returned to research, but was driven feral by Stegron's use of the ancient Rock of Life, which de-evolved animalistic beings. In this crazed state, the Lizard injected his biorestorative serum into his son, causing Billy to become a lizard-man as well. Billy was treated by Mr. Fantastic, while the Lizard raged against Vermin until Spider-Man defeated Stegron. Connors' research inadvertently gave superhuman powers to a drug-addicted intruder in his lab, transforming him to become the super-adaptive monster known as Freak. One of Connors' graduate students, Melati Kusama, stole the Lizard formula and perfected it for her own DNA, enabling her to transform into a lizard-like form. Calling herself Komodo,

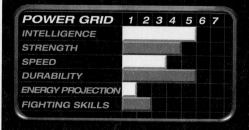

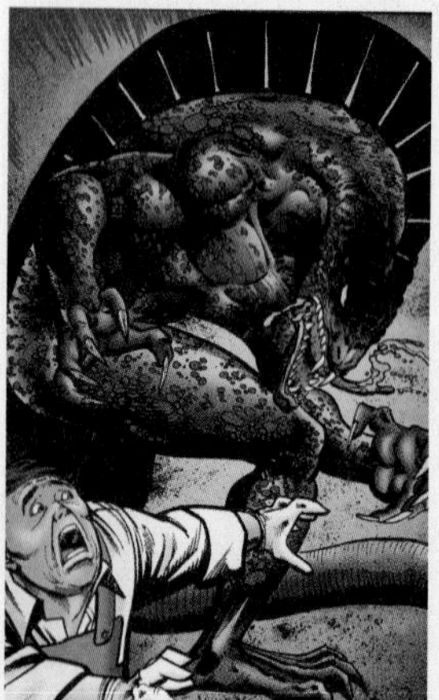

LIZARD'S TAIL LIZARDMAN
AND ALDO QUADRINI

Kusama gained a tail and regenerative abiliities, however unlike Connors, she could control her transformations and maintained her human mentalitiy while in lizard form. Connors recommended Komodo for the Initiative.

HEIGHT: (Connors) 5'11"; (Lizard) 6'8" (variable)
WEIGHT: (Connors) 175 lbs.; (Lizard) 550 lbs. (variable)
EYES: (Connors) Blue; (Lizard) Red pupils
HAIR: (Connors) Brown; (Lizard) None

ABILITIES/ACCESSORIES: The Lizard possesses a number of superhuman powers endowed by his reptilian form, including the ability to regenerate missing limbs, release pheromones to produce violent behaviors in people, and superhuman strength (able to lift 12 tons). His powerful leg muscles enable him to clear 12 feet in a standing high jump and 18 feet in a standing broad jump. His alligator-like hide is tougher than human skin and is capable of resisting the penetration of small-caliber bullets. His reaction time is about twice that of the normal human being and he can run at speeds of up to 45 miles per hour.

The Lizard possesses a 6.5-foot tail that he can whip at speeds up to 70 miles per hour. Like a Gegku lizard, his hands and feet have retractable 1-inch hooks growing from the base of his palm and the ball of his foot, and his fingers and toes are covered with scores of tiny claws to create adhesive pads. As a result, the Lizard can support his weight climbing up and down normally intractable surfaces.

When the Lizard emerges, the R-complex of Connors' brain (the most primitive region of the human brain containing the most bestial drives) takes over the cerebellum, causing Connors' mind to become progressively inhuman. The Lizard gains a quasi-telepathic ability to communicate with and command all reptiles within about a one-mile radius of himself.

In his human form, Dr. Curtis Connors is a brilliant biologist and biochemist, and is a leading herpetologist (a scientist who studies reptiles).

POWER GRID	1	2	3	4	5	6	7
INTELLIGENCE							
STRENGTH							
SPEED							
DURABILITY							
ENERGY PROJECTION							
FIGHTING SKILLS							

FLASH THOMPSON

REAL NAME: Eugene "Flash" Thompson
ALIASES: Lightning Three; has impersonated Stilt-Man, Hobgoblin, Spider-Man
IDENTITY: No dual identity
OCCUPATION: Corporal in the US Army reserves, special advisor to the Mayor's Office of Veterans Affairs; former combat soldier, gym teacher, Oscorp employee, college football player
CITIZENSHIP: USA with a criminal record
PLACE OF BIRTH: Forest Hills, Queens, New York
KNOWN RELATIVES: Harrison & Rosie (parents), Jessie (sister)
GROUP AFFILIATION: US Army reserves, Alcoholics Anonymous; formerly Oscorp staff, Spider-Man Fan Club
EDUCATION: High school graduate, some college courses and military training
FIRST APPEARANCE: Amazing Fantasy #15 (1962)

HISTORY: Handsome and naturally athletic, young Eugene Thompson seemed to have a bright future ahead of him, but hidden darkness in his family set the stage for a life of largely wasted potential. His father, popular policeman Harrison Thompson, had a secret drinking problem, and it was all the Thompson family could do to hold him together at times. Alternating between anger and despair, the self-loathing Harrison took out his frustrations on his family, often verbally and physically abusing Eugene. Eugene, in turn, became a neighborhood bully, taking out his own frustrations on weaker and less popular children. One of his earliest and longest-running targets was Peter Parker, a bookish boy who later became the masked adventurer Spider-Man.

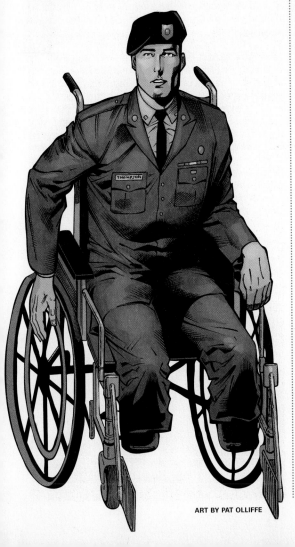

ART BY PAT OLLIFFE

Despite his often-obnoxious personality, football prodigy Eugene became one of the most popular (and most conceited) students at Midtown High School, where his speed on the football field earned him the lifelong nickname "Flash." His wide circle of friends included Tiny McKeever, Jason Ionello, Seymour O'Reilly, Charlie Murphy and numerous female admirers such as Sally Avril and Liz Allan, who was Flash's steady girlfriend for some time. The more popular Flash became, the more he mocked the shy Peter Parker; however, as Parker (secretly emboldened by his new spider-powers) became more confident, he began to stand up to Flash more often, and even took on Flash in a boxing match that ended with Flash being kayoed by a spider-strength jab that most onlookers misinterpreted as a lucky sucker punch. Flash continued to ride Peter despite this setback, and Peter generally tolerated Flash's abuse rather than risk revealing his super-powers or seriously injuring Thompson.

Flash considered himself Spider-Man's biggest fan, never dreaming that his hero was the same "Puny Parker" he so often tormented. As annoyed as Peter was by Flash in general, he was secretly touched and impressed by Thompson's enduring loyalty to Spider-Man. Flash founded the Forest Hills chapter of the Spider-Man fan club and took it upon himself to defend the oft-maligned Spider-Man's reputation, sometimes in reckless and foolish ways. When he impersonated Spider-Man in an attempt to teach Parker to respect the hero, Flash was mistaken for the real thing and imprisoned by Dr. Doom (Victor von Doom) until the true Spider-Man rescued him. Later, when a humiliating encounter with the Green Goblin (wealthy industrialist Norman Osborn) had the whole city calling Spider-Man a coward, Thompson donned a Spider-Man costume again and tackled some cheap crooks in an effort to restore Spidey's reputation, but all he got for his trouble was a beating. Shortly thereafter, when another Spider-Man impersonator tried to tarnish the hero's name with a string of petty crimes, Flash unmasked the culprit as his own friend Jason Ionello, who wrongly blamed Spider-Man for the recent death of their mutual friend Sally Avril during Spider-Man's battle with the Black Knight (Nathan Garrett). Flash also repeatedly denounced the many anti-Spider-Man tirades by Daily Bugle publisher J. Jonah Jameson, and one angry confrontation between Thompson and Jameson caused the unwitting pair to foil a plot against Spider-Man by Mysterio (Quentin Beck).

Gradually impressed by Peter's maturity and sick of Flash's bullying, Liz dumped Flash and began showing strong romantic interest in Peter, which only made Thompson hate Parker all the more. When Flash and Peter graduated from Midtown High, both were awarded full scholarships to Empire State University (for athletic and academic achievement, respectively). By this time, relations between the two had begun to thaw ever so slightly, and they soon became part of a close-knit social circle that included fellow students Gwen Stacy, Harry Osborn (son of Norman) and Mary Jane Watson. By the time Flash left college to join the army, he and Peter parted as friends.

Stationed in Southeast Asia, Flash stumbled across a hidden temple whose residents — notably the beautiful Sha Shan — nursed a wounded Flash back to health; however, after American forces mistakenly shelled the temple despite Flash's efforts to protect it, Flash left the army to return to America, where temple survivors who mistakenly blamed him for the tragedy made attempts on his life. With Spider-Man's aid, Flash survived long enough to convince the temple survivors of his innocence, and was briefly reunited with Sha Shan. Later, Sha Shan returned to America as Sister Sun, the reluctant bride of cult leader Brother Power (Achmed Korba), himself a pawn of the evil Man-Beast; but Sha Shan ultimately turned on Korba, and the Man-Beast was thwarted through the combined efforts of Spider-Man, Razorback and Flash. Korba having died in the battle, Sha Shan became Flash's lover and lived with him for some time.

Later, when Flash's old friend Betty Brant was struggling to cope with her failing marriage to reporter Ned Leeds, who had secretly been

ART BY STEVE DITKO

brainwashed into serving as a pawn and occasional stand-in for the criminal Hobgoblin (Roderick Kingsley), Betty sought comfort in Flash's arms, and soon the two began a secret affair. Sha Shan realized this and walked out on Flash after a violent argument. The unstable Ned suspected the truth as well, and Flash unwittingly provoked matters further when he insulted the Hobgoblin on television. Kingsley responded by framing Flash as the supposed Hobgoblin, sending Flash to prison, where the vigilante Scourge would have killed him if not for Spider-Man's intervention. Escaping jail, Flash sought refuge with Betty but was attacked by the Hobgoblin (Leeds), who fled after Betty saw him unmasked as Ned. Shortly thereafter, word of Ned's double identity leaked out, and assassins hired by Hobgoblin's mercenary rival Jason Macendale murdered Leeds; Macendale then used Ned's gear to become the new Hobgoblin. Aiding Spider-Man in battle with the new Hobgoblin, Flash suffered an arm injury that ended any hope of restarting his old sports career, but he was cleared of all charges related to the Hobgoblin case and set free.

Ned's death sent Betty into a nervous breakdown, and she fell under the influence of the sinister Students of Love cult. Flash, Spider-Man and Reverend Tolliver joined forces to liberate Betty and deprogram her. Having lost all her worldly possessions to the cult (which was destroyed in a fire), Betty lived with Thompson until the demonic Inferno invasion of New York, when demons posing as Spider-Man and the late Ned attacked Flash's home; the demons were defeated, but Thompson's home was destroyed in the process. Shortly thereafter, Betty and Flash decided they were better off as friends rather than lovers, and parted amicably. By now, Peter Parker had married Mary Jane Watson, and Harry Osborn had married Flash's old flame Liz Allan, and odd-man-out Flash was determined to find a new love of his own. For a while, he dated the glamorous adventurer Felicia Hardy, alias the Black Cat. Formerly Spider-Man's lover and partner, Felicia dated Flash mostly to irritate Peter at first, but found herself genuinely falling for Thompson over time; however, Flash ultimately broke up with her, feeling he could never fit into her exotic lifestyle.

Directionless, lonely and increasingly bitter, Flash developed a drinking problem like his father before him, leading to a car crash that got Flash arrested again and cost him his job as a school gym teacher. By this time, Flash had begun blaming much of his troubles on his family in general and his father in particular, but a violent confrontation with his father finally forced Flash to realize that he had become the same sort of self-deluded wreck his father was, and that only he could take responsibility for fixing his life. Flash sobered up and started trying to turn his life around, though without much success in terms of either romance or career. His luck seemed to change when Norman Osborn offered him a good job with his Oscorp company, but Osborn had actually done this as part of an elaborate plot against his enemy Peter Parker. Osborn hoped to turn Flash against Spider-Man, but Thompson remained loyal to his boyhood idol despite Osborn's influence. Later, when Osborn stepped up his attacks on Parker, he staged a car crash that sent an Oscorp truck smashing into Midtown High with Thompson at the wheel, and made it look as if Flash had been driving drunk. Rendered comatose by the accident, Flash eventually revived but was broken in mind and body, wheelchair-bound and trapped in a stupor. He was regularly visited by old friends such as Peter, Betty and Liz Allan, whose wealth provided Flash's housing and medical care.

ART BY DALE EAGLESHAM

Comatose again for a time, Flash eventually recovered, though slight brain damage had left him partially amnesiac regarding much of his adult life. Becoming Midtown High's new athletics coach, Flash fell back into his old adversarial relationship with Peter Parker, now a teacher there, since Thompson no longer remembered their friendship. Flash also developed a romantic interest in school nurse Miss Arrow, unaware she was secretly the supernatural spider-predator Ero. When Spider-Man's real identity became public knowledge, Flash initially disbelieved the news, then resented it, but finally accepting it he became one of Peter's most supportive friends in his newly public double life. He aided Spidey against foes such as Mysterio (Francis Klum) and Vulture (Adrian Toomes), denounced Deb Whitman's tell-all book about her former relationship with Peter, and even allowed Peter to hide out in his apartment during a period when Spider-Man was declared an outlaw. Flash also started dating Betty Brant again, prompting a series of attacks on Betty by a jealous Ero. When Ero tried to make Flash the host body for her eggs (a process that would have killed him), Spider-Man and Betty came to his rescue and Ero was destroyed. Knowledge of Spider-Man's dual identity was eventually wiped from most of the public's minds, including Flash's, but he and Peter have remained friends regardless.

As an army reservist called back into service in Iraq, Flash was participating in a cordon-and-search mission in Mosul when insurgents ambushed his squad. During the battle, Flash freed himself and his squad from an overturned Stryker ICV transport, killed or fought off seven insurgents single-handedly to save fellow soldier Santos, then carried the wounded Santos to safety; by the time Flash finally sought medical attention for his own wounds, blood loss and tissue damage forced the doctors to amputate both his legs at the knee. Sent home with the Medal of Honor, Thompson has done his best to adjust to his new situation with the aid of supportive friends such as Peter, Betty and Harry Osborn, becoming an avid wheelchair athlete and a special advisor to New York City's new mayor, Flash's old nemesis J. Jonah Jameson; however, when the criminal Chameleon posing as Peter Parker mocked Flash's disability, a shaken Thompson started drinking again.

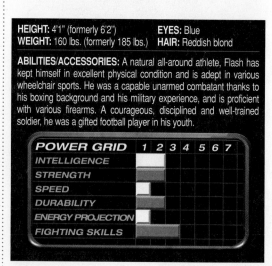

HEIGHT: 4'1" (formerly 6'2") **EYES:** Blue
WEIGHT: 160 lbs. (formerly 185 lbs.) **HAIR:** Reddish blond

ABILITIES/ACCESSORIES: A natural all-around athlete, Flash has kept himself in excellent physical condition and is adept in various wheelchair sports. He was a capable unarmed combatant thanks to his boxing background and his military experience, and is proficient with various firearms. A courageous, disciplined and well-trained soldier, he was a gifted football player in his youth.

POWER GRID	1	2	3	4	5	6	7
INTELLIGENCE	■	■					
STRENGTH	■	■					
SPEED	■						
DURABILITY	■	■					
ENERGY PROJECTION	■						
FIGHTING SKILLS	■	■	■				

GWEN STACY

HISTORY: Gwen Stacy was Peter Parker's first great love. Next to the death of his Uncle Ben, no death has weighed as heavily upon Spider-Man as her passing.

Gwen grew up in New York City, close friends with her cousins Paul and Jill Stacy, children of her Uncle Arthur and Aunt Nancy. At some point before starting college, her cousins moved away and she lost her mother, Helen. Gwen came to Empire State University (ESU) from Standard High School, where she had been the resident "beauty queen" and friends with Harry Osborn. As a freshman, she and Harry befriended athlete Eugene "Flash" Thompson. Flash tried to introduce Harry and Gwen to his high school classmate Peter during their first chemistry lab. When Peter unintentionally ignored Flash and his new peers, the popular Gwen and wealthy Harry resented the perceived snub, unaware of the many concerns that preoccupied Peter. His aunt May Parker was recovering from radiation poisoning; he was still recovering from recent battles as Spider-Man against Kraven the Hunter (Sergei Kravinoff) and the Green Goblin (Norman Osborn, Harry's father); and he had just broken up with girlfriend Betty Brant. Over time, though, Peter built friendships with Gwen, Harry and Flash. Gwen and Peter eventually noticed each other romantically the day Peter arrived at ESU on his new motorcycle brimming with confidence, secretly elated following victories over the Green Goblin and the Rhino (Aleksei Sytsevich). Peter intrigued Gwen, but their potential romance was sidetracked by Peter's long delayed initial meeting with Mary Jane Watson, the spunky, glamorous niece of Aunt May's best friend Anna Watson. Peter dated Mary Jane while a jealous Gwen dated Harry. Unaware she was watching Peter, Gwen first saw Spider-Man in action when he saved Harry and Norman Osborn from Kraven the Hunter, a then-amnesiac Norman having forgotten his Green Goblin identity and past dealings with Kraven.

Despite dating Harry, Gwen still secretly held a torch for Peter; finally, Peter invited Gwen to a science exposition after their biochemistry professor Miles Warren gave him two tickets. Gwen and Mary Jane became rivals for Peter's affections until Gwen became Peter's regular girlfriend, while Mary Jane became Harry's. Peter and Gwen fell deeply in love with each other. Gwen's wise father, retired police captain George Stacy, warmly approved of Peter and respected Spider-Man, though he was curious to learn more about the hero. At some point, Prof. Warren also fell in love with Gwen to the point of obsession, and obtained cell samples of her and other students for secret cloning experiments.

When Dr. Octopus (Otto Octavius)' stolen Nullifier gave Spider-Man amnesia, Gwen first met Spider-Man and accused him of causing Peter's unexplained absence; she was overjoyed when Parker finally reappeared. Later, Wilson Fisk, the Kingpin of Crime, brainwashed Capt. Stacy into stealing police records. After Peter appeared to have attacked Capt. Stacy and later took front page photographs exposing the captain's attempted theft, Gwen felt betrayed by Peter. George and Gwen tried to flee, but the Kingpin kidnapped them and imprisoned the Stacys at an Osborn Chemical research lab; Spider-Man and Norman Osborn rescued the two, though the Kingpin escaped. Gwen was now appreciative of Spider-Man, but wanted nothing to do with Peter Parker. Gwen subsequently visited Norman to thank him for saving her and her father's lives. She found Norman despondent yet charismatic, feeling both sympathetic and attracted to him. A brief spontaneous affair between the two ensued, leaving Gwen pregnant with twins.

After a period of separation between Peter and Gwen, Capt. Stacy fully recovered from his brainwashing and explained to Gwen how Peter had actually tried to help him; Gwen and Peter reconciled, with Gwen deciding not to tell Peter of her fling with Norman. Though Spider-Man helped the Stacys again, rescuing Capt. Stacy from prison inmates who had taken him captive, Peter's double life eroded his relationship. Gwen grew frustrated with Peter's disappearances and secrets. Questioning Peter's bravery herself, she once struck an ESU student who accused Peter of

REAL NAME: Gwendolyne Stacy
ALIASES: "Gwendy"
IDENTITY: No dual identity
OCCUPATION: Student, model
CITIZENSHIP: USA
PLACE OF BIRTH: Presumably New York City, New York
KNOWN RELATIVES: Gabriel Stacy (Gray Goblin, son), Sarah Stacy (daughter), George & Helen Stacy (parents, deceased), Arthur Stacy (uncle), Nancy Jean Stacy (aunt, deceased), Paul & Jill Stacy (cousins), Gwen Miles and other Gwen Stacy clones (clones, some deceased)
GROUP AFFILIATION: None
EDUCATION: College educated (biochemistry major, incomplete)
FIRST APPEARANCE: Amazing Spider-Man #31 (1965)

cowardice for his absence at a school protest. Peter mistakenly thought Gwen had left him for Flash Thompson, but Gwen was only seeking advice from Flash about Peter's mysterious behavior. Later, Peter secretly used his superhuman strength to save Gwen from a toppling truck. Capt. Stacy suspected a connection between Spider-Man and Parker, who continually succeeded in getting action photographs of the crimefighter for the Daily Bugle. When Gwen and George questioned Peter in his apartment, Peter excused himself to his darkroom while returning through a window as Spider-Man, pretending Peter owed him a share of the profits from photographing him in action. Though Gwen felt relieved by this explanation of Peter's odd behavior, she feared the risks Peter

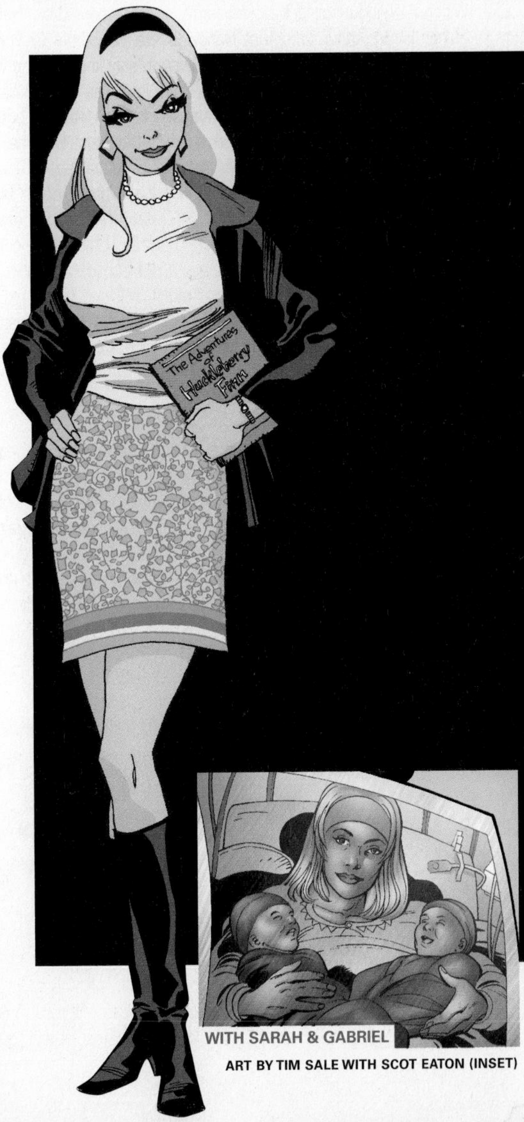
The Adventures of Huckleberry Finn

WITH SARAH & GABRIEL

ART BY TIM SALE WITH SCOT EATON (INSET)

took were too great, and insisted he promise to discontinue his supposed collusion with Spider-Man. Later, while delirious from the flu, Peter confessed in front of the Stacys and other friends that he was Spider-Man. Upon recovering, Spider-Man had his ally the Prowler (Hobie Brown) appear dressed as Spider-Man simultaneously with Peter. Gwen believed the ruse, but her father was apparently not fooled.

Tragically, Gwen's father was fatally injured protecting an innocent child during a battle between Spider-Man and Dr. Octopus. Calling him Peter, George asked Spider-Man to look after Gwen, and then died in his arms. A bereaved Gwen blamed the hero for her father's death. Peter withdrew while Gwen raged against his alter ego. With Gwen seeking a candidate tough on crime to bring Spider-Man to justice, corrupt and bigoted New York district attorney candidate Sam Bullit acquired Gwen's endorsement, certain support from the Stacy name would capture more liberal voters. Later, Spider-Man and Iceman (Bobby Drake) exposed Bullit's attempt to kill Bugle editor Joe Robertson, resulting in Bullit's arrest.

With her life in turmoil, and lacking family, Gwen accepted the invitation of her Uncle Arthur and Aunt Nancy to live with them in London. Unable to reconcile how to convince Gwen to stay knowing she would ultimately find out he was Spider-Man, Peter let Gwen leave, while she silently hoped Peter would propose marriage to her. Unable to bear the separation, Peter soon flew to London on assignment with the Daily Bugle to convince Gwen to return, but a subsequent appearance by Spider-Man made the local papers, and Peter returned home fearing an obvious connection would be made. Despite his failed attempt to see Gwen, his heroic deeds convinced Arthur that Spider-Man couldn't be responsible for his brother's death. Listening to her uncle, and realizing she may have expected too much of Peter, Gwen returned home again, certain she could salvage her relationship. She was met by Peter's welcoming arms. During her absence, Norman became the Green Goblin again and Harry turned to LSD while Mary Jane, Harry's supposed girlfriend, blatantly flirted with Peter.

Peter hinted at marriage to Gwen despite the constant trouble of leading a double-life — including secretly growing four extra arms for a time. Peter took Gwen with him on an expedition and photo shoot of the Savage Land in Antarctica, where Gwen acted as a model. The pair had an exciting adventure, encountering the colossal Tsiln alien Gog, which took Gwen back to its master, Kraven the Hunter, to be Kraven's queen. Kraven and Gog were defeated by Spider-Man and jungle adventurer Ka-Zar (Kevin Plunder).

Having recovered his memory of Peter's secret identity, Norman Osborn burned with insane hatred for Spider-Man. Gwen, now aware of her pregnancy, fled to Europe where she secretly carried the twins to full term after an abnormally swift gestation, giving birth to Gabriel and Sarah. Osborn arranged to provide for the twins in Paris while Gwen returned home and reunited with Peter. Gwen argued with Norman that she should raise the children, assuming that Peter's love would enable him to overlook her infidelity and they would marry. Gwen confided only in Mary Jane, who had overheard the argument and promised to keep her secret. Osborn planned to raise the children to be the heirs to the Goblin legacy. Deciding to hit the wall-crawler where it would hurt most and rid himself of the young nuisance, the Goblin kidnapped Gwen and carried her to the top of the Brooklyn Bridge. A horrified Spider-Man arrived and fought fiercely to free her, but his ferocity could not to prevent the Goblin from pushing Gwen off the bridge. Trying desperately to save his beloved, Spider-Man fired a slender web-line that caught Gwen by her ankle, stopping her fall before she hit the water. Her neck snapped. Raising her up, Spider-Man discovered she was already dead. A taunting Goblin gloated that the shock of the fall had already killed her.

Even though Spider-Man's subsequent confrontation with the Green Goblin ended in Norman's seeming demise, impaled by his own remote-controlled Goblin-glider, Peter's anguish did not die so readily. Even now, years after Gwen's death, Peter is tormented by nightmares and agonizes over how he might have saved her if he had done something differently. Peter's love for Gwen also lives on, in his memories and deep within his heart. When Spider-Man was paid to protect mob boss Morris Forelli from the monstrous radioactive undead Digger, Peter used the money to establish a memorial library in Gwen Stacy's name. Later, the alleged spirit of Gwen Stacy helped Dead Girl and Dr. Stephen Strange stop the souls of the Pitiful One and other villains from escaping confinement in hell.

Using the cell samples he obtained previously, Prof. Warren (who became the super-criminal Jackal) later created clones of Peter and Gwen, assisted (unbeknownst to Warren) by Norman Osborn, who dispatched Scrier cultist Samuel Fox to work with Warren; many were genetically unstable, but a stable Gwen clone eventually approached Peter some months after Gwen died. The clone ultimately opted to have nothing to do with Peter Parker's life. Married to a clone of Miles Warren, the Gwen clone (named Gwen Miles) tried to live a peaceful life in suburban New Jersey until her husband died in a car accident after recklessly fleeing from Peter's clone, Ben Reilly. A genetically mutated Jackal resurfaced and created several other clones of Gwen, but they lacked Gwen Miles' stability, decomposing after a short time. During a conflict upon the Daily Bugle's roof, Gwen Miles had an opportunity to kill the Jackal, but she lacked the resolve. After the Jackal was apparently killed, falling from the rooftop, Gwen Miles slipped away; her current whereabouts are unrevealed.

HEIGHT: 5'7"	EYES: Blue
WEIGHT: 130 lbs.	HAIR: Blonde

ABILITIES/ACCESSORIES: Gwen Stacy was a gifted scholar in the field of biochemistry.

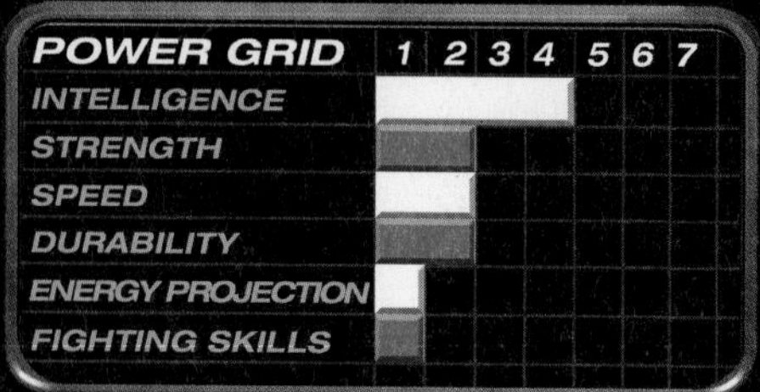

POWER GRID	1	2	3	4	5	6	7
INTELLIGENCE							
STRENGTH							
SPEED							
DURABILITY							
ENERGY PROJECTION							
FIGHTING SKILLS							

GEORGE STACY

REAL NAME: George Stacy
ALIASES: None
IDENTITY: No dual identity
OCCUPATION: Retired; former police captain
CITIZENSHIP: USA
PLACE OF BIRTH: Unrevealed, presumably New York City
KNOWN RELATIVES: Gwen Stacy (daughter), Helen Stacy (wife, deceased), Arthur Stacy (brother), Nancy Jean Stacy (sister-in-law, deceased), Gabriel Stacy (Gray Goblin, grandson), Sarah Stacy (granddaughter), Jill Stacy (niece), Paul Stacy (nephew)
GROUP AFFILIATION: New York Police Department, Century Club (for Midtown Business Executives)
EDUCATION: B.S. in Criminal Justice
FIRST APPEARANCE: Amazing Spider-Man #56 (1968)

HISTORY: Early in his police career, George Stacy, with his brother Arthur (head of security for Norman Osborn) investigated a break-in at an Osborn Chemical plant. Osborn feigned innocence to the Stacy brothers when attacked by disfigured employee Nels Van Adder (later dubbed the Proto-Goblin), whom Osborn had secretly experimented upon for strength-enhancement research. George rose in the ranks in the police force, retiring as a respected police captain. While losing his wife, Helen, George raised his daughter Gwendolyne, who grew to become an intelligent headstrong student at Empire State University. There, Gwen met and fell in love with Peter Parker, secretly the super hero Spider-Man, whose activities interested the retired captain.

It wasn't long before Col. John Jameson called Captain Stacy out of retirement to assist in the return of a device called the Nullifier – which could render any electrical or mechanical apparatus inoperative – that Doctor Octopus had tricked an amnesiac Spider-Man into stealing. After safely securing the weapon, Captain Stacy interviewed Peter Parker, believed to have been held captive by Doc Ock and Spider-Man.

During the interview Captain Stacy revealed to Peter that he had spent time studying the career of Spider-Man, and that he was glad to have met Peter, known for photographing the wall-crawler on numerous occasions. Identifying himself as a strong supporter of Spider-Man, Captain Stacy wished to see the wall-crawler redeemed in the public eye. He also took an instant liking to Peter, and openly encouraged the growing bond between the youngster and his daughter, Gwen.

Receiving a special invitation to the Gloom Room A-Go-Go dance club, George was hypnotized unwittingly by hired dancer, Mary Jane Watson, through her camera rigged by Norman Osborn's researcher, Dr. Gerhard Winkler, on behalf of the "Brainwasher," Wilson Fisk (the Kingpin of Crime). After further brainwashing by Winkler, George, a regular advisor to the police in his retirement, used his privileges to steal top-secret police files, but was stopped by Spider-Man. Peter Parker's front page headline photos of the incident made George and Gwen become fugitives. The Kingpin kidnapped the Stacys, taking them to Winkler's lab at Osborn Chemicals. There, they were rescued by Spider-Man and Norman Osborn, but Gwen was left feeling betrayed by Peter. When the effects of the brainwashing subsided, George exonerated Peter from wrong-doing, much to Gwen's relief. Later, Spider-Man rescued Capt. Stacy from prison inmates who had taken George hostage. After several more encounters with Spider-Man and Peter, Captain Stacy started to suspect the two were one. Wary of anyone making the connection, Peter began taking increasingly drastic measures to throw Captain Stacy off the trail, even pretending Spider-Man and Peter Parker had an arrangement to split the profits of his newspaper photos. Delirious from the flu, Peter admitted he was Spider-Man before George and his friends. Later, Spider-Man arranged for the Prowler (Hobie Brown) to dress as Spider-Man and appear simultaneously with Peter Parker before his friends. George was apparently not deceived by Parker's trick.

Called into action one night, Captain Stacy watched Spider-Man battle Doctor Octopus on a rooftop high above the city. A crowd had gathered nearby to watch the confrontation. When Spider-Man caused Dr. Octopus to lose control of his mechanical arms, chunks of concrete were dislodged from the roof and rained on the spectators below. Spotting a child standing under the trajectory of falling masonry, Captain Stacy leapt to cover the boy — and paid for his act of heroism with his own life. Abandoning the fight, Spider-Man swung down in time to hear Captain Stacy's final words. Calling Spider-Man, "Peter," George asked him to take care of Gwen once he was gone.

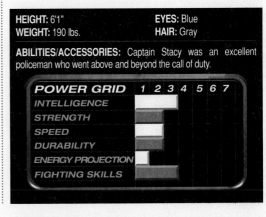

HEIGHT: 6'1"
WEIGHT: 190 lbs.
EYES: Blue
HAIR: Gray

ABILITIES/ACCESSORIES: Captain Stacy was an excellent policeman who went above and beyond the call of duty.

POWER GRID	1	2	3	4	5	6	7
INTELLIGENCE							
STRENGTH							
SPEED							
DURABILITY							
ENERGY PROJECTION							
FIGHTING SKILLS							

ART BY JOHN ROMITA SR.

MAY PARKER

HISTORY: May Reilly was a strikingly beautiful but naïve young woman who lived with her parents in Brooklyn during a nationwide depression. When May's father walked out, her mother raised her begrudgingly — not bothering to conceal the fact that she saw May as nothing more than an unwelcome burden.

When May was a young woman, two men vied for her affection. One was a flashy, wealthy man named Johnny Jerome; the other, a carnival barker named Ben Parker. May believed she was in love with Johnny, whom she thought offered her more promise during the time of economic hardship than did Ben. Ben warned May that Johnny was actually a criminal, but she dismissed Ben's warnings as jealous slander. One day, however, Johnny unexpectedly proposed to May, saying he wanted them to leave together right away. May heard the police on the street, and realized something was wrong. Ben stormed in, telling May that Johnny had just robbed a jewelry store, and had shot a man who tried to call for help. May then realized Johnny was indeed a criminal, and rejected his proposal. Johnny was captured by the police and convicted for murder and burglary.

May Reilly set aside her fantasies about marrying someone well-to-do financially and began to make decisions about the direction of her life. Coming to appreciate Ben Parker, and his devotion to her, May fell in love with him. She married Ben, and their life together was peaceful and happy.

During their time dating, they were often saddled with Ben's much younger brother, Richard. So after Ben and May married, they chose to remain childless — free from the worries youngsters can bring. Richard and his wife, Mary, however, brought a son into the world named Peter.

Unexpectedly, Ben and May doted on their nephew; the young boy particularly captivated Ben. When Richard and Mary — secretly government agents — were called overseas on an assignment, May and Ben happily took Peter into their home until his parents could return. When word arrived that Richard and Mary had been killed in a plane crash in Algeria, they were designated as Peter's legal guardians. Since Richard and Mary were secret agents, Peter was temporarily held while Ben and May's backgrounds were thoroughly investigated; they were given full custody of Peter at the memorial service for Peter's parents. At first May was overwhelmed with the responsibility, even angry with Richard and Mary for dying and leaving her and Ben with the challenge of bringing up Peter at such a late stage in their life. Yet her heart could not help but be touched by how kind and thoughtful Peter grew to be. May became like an overprotective mother to sensitive Peter and together, the three became a true family.

As he matured into his teens, little did May or Ben realize that the science-loving, socially awkward Peter had, by way of a radioactive spider-bite, become the daring and colorful Spider-Man they watched on television. As Spider-Man, Peter had become an overnight sensation in the entertainment world. After a television appearance, Spider-Man saw a guard chasing a thief in the studio building. Though the guard asked Spider-Man for help, the costumed youth ignored him and allowed the burglar to get away.

One fateful night at the Parker residence in suburban Forest Hills, Queens, that same burglar came seeking hidden assets worth millions of dollars belonging to a previous owner of the Parker home, gangster "Dutch" Mallone. While in jail, the burglar had been a cellmate of the elderly Mallone, and learned of the treasure from Mallone's mumbling while he slept. Ben and May had a small quarrel that night, and Ben left the house to take a walk, leaving the front door unlocked. In his absence, the burglar easily entered the Parker home. Ben returned home and discovered the burglar, who manhandled May for the exact location of the cache. When Ben furiously ordered the burglar to unhand her, the burglar panicked, fatally shot Ben, and fled to a warehouse where he was ultimately caught

REAL NAME: May Reilly Parker
ALIASES: formerly May Morgan, May Reilly
IDENTITY: No dual identity
OCCUPATION: Homeless shelter volunteer
CITIZENSHIP: USA
PLACE OF BIRTH: Brooklyn, New York
KNOWN RELATIVES: Ben Parker (husband, deceased), Albert and Claire Reilly (parents, deceased), Peter Parker (Spider-Man, nephew), Richard and Mary Parker (brother-in-law and sister-in law, deceased), Horace Reilly (paternal uncle, deceased)
GROUP AFFILIATION: FEAST Project, Forest Hills Public Library; formerly Gray Panthers
EDUCATION: High school graduate
FIRST APPEARANCE: Amazing Fantasy #15 (1962)

YOUNG MAY

ART BY JOHN ROMITA JR. WITH KERRY GAMMILL (INSET)

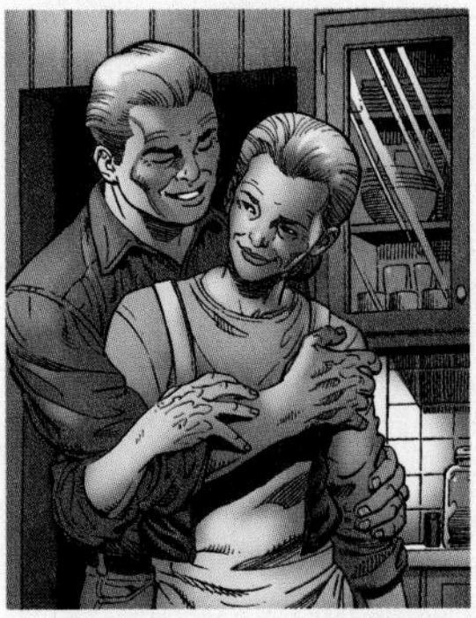

ART BY SEAN CHEN

by Spider-Man. Before May could call for an ambulance, Ben told May he loved her and died. It was this incident which initially aggravated May Parker's weak heart condition which has caused her serious health problems over the years. Guilt-ridden for previously allowing the burglar to pass, Peter's attitude towards life and his superhuman abilities radically changed after that night, devoting his life to selfless heroics. For years afterwards, May too harbored guilt thinking had she not argued with Ben, perhaps her husband would still be alive.

May was left to continue her life without Ben's strength — a life further complicated by financial woes, her own ever-failing health and the strange new secrecy with which Peter conducted his affairs. To help his aunt pay the bills, including the escalating costs of her various medications, Peter took a job photographing himself as Spider-Man for the Daily Bugle. May was worried about her fragile nephew, taking pictures so close to the most dangerous of super-powered battles. For Peter, lying to his aunt became a painful — yet seemingly necessary — way of life.

Merely by being in the company of Daily Bugle secretary Betty Brant, May was kidnapped by Dr. Octopus (Otto Octavius) during the first attack of the Sinister Six. Though Betty was Doc Ock's intended target, he treated May so well she never realized the charming scientist was actually a deadly villain.

Soon after Ben's death, May became seriously ill and was hospitalized, requiring a blood transfusion. Though not a blood relative, Peter was a suitable match for May; after a moment of hesitation, uncertain what his radioactive blood would do to his aunt, Peter agreed to give May the transfusion. May was restored to health, and recuperated in Florida. Sometime later, the radioactivity in her bloodstream began to kill May. Aided by Dr. Curt Connors, Peter overcame many obstacles through the underwater headquarters of Dr. Octopus in order to deliver a serum, ISO-36, which stopped her blood from deteriorating, and saved her life.

For a long time, May's neighbor and best friend, Anna Watson, conspired with May to introduce Anna's niece, Mary Jane Watson, to Peter, but both teenagers resisted. Finally, Peter could put off meeting Mary Jane no longer, and was attracted to her at first sight. Thus began the courtship of Peter and Mary Jane.

Peter greatly reduced his need to deceive his aunt when he relocated to an apartment in Manhattan, while Anna Watson moved in with May. Though Peter and May now lived farther apart, many of Spider-Man's battles still took place dangerously close to May. The wall-crawler's web seemed to be inextricably woven into May's life. The Beetle (Abner Jenkins) took May as a random hostage, and Spider-Man again rescued her.

Just when life had begun to quiet down, May inherited a Canadian island that was the site of a uranium mine and small commercial reactor. Dr. Octopus charmed May into a sudden wedding, with the aim of acquiring the island's valuable atomic resources for his own nefarious ends. But the intervention of Hammerhead resulted in the destruction of the island and the apparent death of May's groom-to-be. Later, the Green Goblin (Harry Osborn) captured a confused May after he uncovered Spider-Man's secret identity, but May was rescued unharmed, none the wiser as to her nephew's exploits.

The shock of seeing the apparent return of Peter's murdered girlfriend, Gwen Stacy (actually a clone created by Professor Miles Warren, the Jackal) sent May back to the hospital. There she was confronted by the Scorpion (Mac Gargan) whom the Jackal, knowing Spider-Man's identity, directed to May; May indignantly scolded the Scorpion after Spider-Man defeated him. While Peter and Mary Jane grew closer than ever during this time, the apparent return of "Gwen" derailed their romance. May supported Mary Jane, encouraging her to fight for her man, much the way May had to be assertive while dating shy Ben Parker to bring about their engagement. Mary Jane, however, later rejected Peter when he proposed to her, and moved to Florida.

Despite her nagging ill health, May maintained an iron will. However, while taking part in a rally at City Hall with senior citizen activist group, the Gray Panthers, she suffered a mild heart attack and was sent to Newhope Memorial Hospital. As she continued her convalescence at the Restwell Nursing Home, the burglar who had killed her husband was freed from prison. Still seeking the treasure hidden in the Parkers' home, the burglar forced the head of the nursing home (Mysterio posing as Dr. Ludwig Rinehart) to fake Aunt May's death so she could be interrogated without the interference of her doting nephew. When Peter discovered the truth, his fury was so terrifying that the burglar died of a heart attack. More tragic was the fact that all May's suffering was over nothing: silverfish had long since eaten the treasure.

May returned to Forest Hills after recovering sufficiently and set up her home as a boarding house, taking in half a dozen paying houseguests. During this time, Peter and May's relationship hit a low point. When Peter decided to drop out of his graduate studies at Empire State University, May was so upset she stopped speaking to him for a time, but the two eventually reconciled. Among May's boarders was Nathan Lubensky — a charming, wheelchair-bound gentleman she had met at the nursing home. The two were engaged until May witnessed a cold, cruel side to Nathan who caused the death of a mugger who had invaded their house after Spider-Man had already webbed the crook; May called off the wedding. Despite this, Nathan's final act proved his affection for May: he died to prevent her from becoming a hostage of the Vulture (Adrian Toomes).

Mary Jane returned to New York, and May was overjoyed when she and Peter were married. While the newlyweds lived in Manhattan, May decided to close the boarding house and live alone. She shared a few dates with mailman Willie Lumpkin during this time. May was astonished to be reunited with Richard and Mary Parker, Peter's parents. While they were convincing to Peter, May's doubts were confirmed; they were actually replicoid duplicates, created by the Chameleon as part of Harry Osborn's complex revenge schemes.

Shortly thereafter, Peter believed he had lost his aunt when she seemingly died of old age. However, he was unaware of the depths to

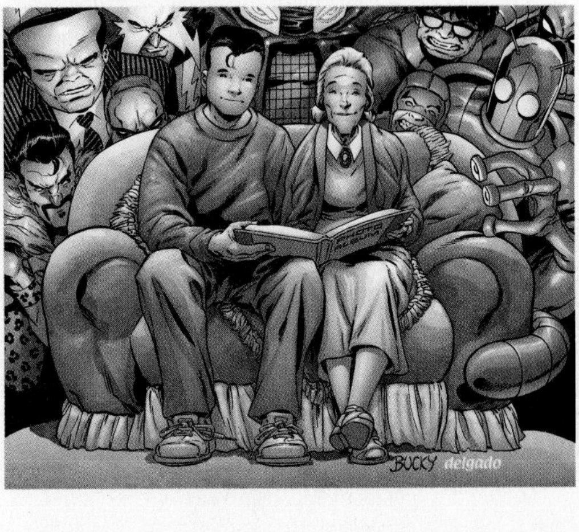
BUCKY
delgado

ART BY MARK BUCKINGHAM

which the original Green Goblin, Norman Osborn, had sunk. Norman had kidnapped May and replaced her with a genetically adapted actress. While Norman lost what remained of his sanity — taking part in the mystical ceremony, the Gathering of Five — his former agent, Alison Mongrain, aided by Joseph "Robbie" Robertson, revealed May's location to Peter. Peter rescued his aunt and defeated the crazed Green Goblin, whose plans for the real May were never fully revealed.

After May returned, she struggled to regain her place in Peter's life. It was with Mary Jane's reported death (though secretly kidnapped by the mysterious "Stalker") that Peter again realized the strength he and May could give to each other. Though Mary Jane was rescued, she and Peter separated for a time; Peter relied on May to help him through the difficult times of loss — as they had helped each other many years before.

Arriving at Peter's apartment one afternoon, May finally learned the truth her nephew had so long concealed. Battered and bruised, Peter was asleep in bed with his Spider-Man costume and equipment tossed on the floor. After spending a whole day dealing with her newfound knowledge, May finally confronted Peter and began to break through a lifetime of deception. Seemingly stronger than ever, May was driven to improve Spider-Man's public image and determined to understand Peter's alter ego. With the lies behind them, May and Peter's relationship deepened like never before — reborn through a new level of honesty and trust. Mary Jane returned to Peter, and she and May were partners in caring for Spider-Man.

When Norman Osborn was finally jailed, publicly revealed to be the Green Goblin, he had May captured by the Scorpion and buried in a sleep-like state as ransom for his liberation from jail. Spider-Man complied, freeing Osborn and rescuing May. More tragedy struck May as her home in Forest Hills was burned down by Charlie Weiderman, a vengeful former classmate of Peter's. While Spider-Man joined the Avengers, May was invited to move into the luxurious Stark Tower to live with Peter and Mary Jane. There she befriended and began dating whom she believed was Edwin Jarvis, the Avenger's butler (secretly an alien Skrull infiltrating the Avengers). During a date with "Edwin," her beloved husband reappeared. This Ben Parker was, in fact, taken from an alternate universe (Earth-6078) by the Hobgoblin (Robin Borne) of an alternate Earth in the year 2211. Rejected by the horrified May, Ben fled and was ultimately killed.

May supported Peter's decision to publicly unmask for the sake of Tony Stark and the Superhuman Registration Act. Peter later regretted his decision, and withdrew his support for Stark. A fugitive from the law, Peter moved into a seedy motel with May and Mary Jane. When the incarcerated Kingpin (Wilson Fisk) learned of Spider-Man's identity, he dispatched a sniper to the motel. Peter saved Mary Jane from the sniper's bullet, but May was struck instead. In a coma, May was hospitalized under her maiden name. In the same hospital as the cancer-stricken Eddie Brock (formerly Venom), May was nearly murdered by the deranged Brock. With May still in a coma, Peter discreetly offered May another transfusion of his blood, but the effort failed. Hoping to revive his aunt, Peter contacted the comatose May via the psychic Madame Web, but May seemed complacent about her fate. As the police investigated the suspicious nature of May's gunshot injury, Peter and Mary Jane were forced to break the law to move May to another hospital. After Peter violently demanded Tony Stark help pay for May's hospital bills, Stark remorsefully sent "Jarvis" to deliver two million dollars. Still, May's doctor offered little hope for her recovery. Peter frantically searched to save the life of his precious aunt. Out of options, he and Mary Jane painfully consented to a deal with Mephisto, who offered to restore May in exchange for eliminating their marriage from ever occurring in history. Subsequently, May returned in full health to her home in Forest Hills, rebuilt by Harry Osborn (who had returned after faking his death). No longer aware of Peter's alter ego (through unrevealed means), May temporarily housed her nephew until he found a new apartment. She has been volunteering at the FEAST Project (Food, Emergency Aid, Shelter, and Training) homeless shelter under the management of Martin Li (secretly Mr. Negative). She was present but unharmed during a bank robbery performed by the elusive Blank. May was temporarily transferred to a Coney Island branch of FEAST, where she ran into trouble with local gangsters. May has begun a romantic relationship with J. Jonah Jameson's father, J. Jonah Sr.

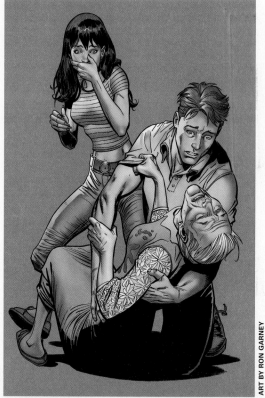

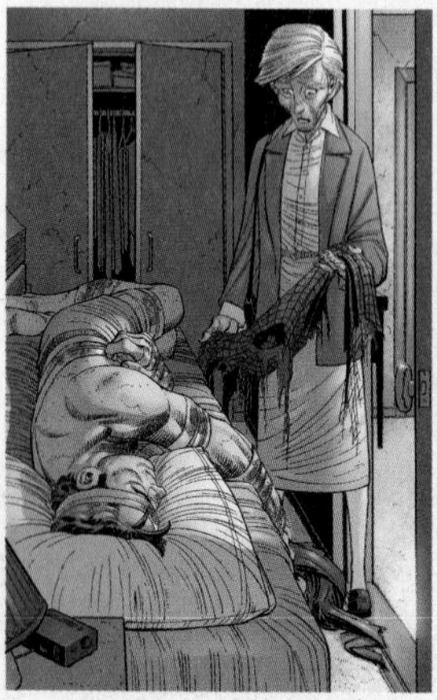

ART BY RON GARNEY

ART BY JOHN ROMITA JR.

| HEIGHT: 5'5" | EYES: Blue |
| WEIGHT: 110 lbs. | HAIR: White (formerly blonde) |

ABILITIES/ACCESSORIES: May Parker typically possesses the normal human strength of a woman her age, height and build who engages in occasional mild exercise.

POWER GRID	1	2	3	4	5	6	7
INTELLIGENCE							
STRENGTH							
SPEED							
DURABILITY							
ENERGY PROJECTION							
FIGHTING SKILLS							

BEN PARKER

REAL NAME: Benjamin Parker
ALIASES: None
IDENTITY: No dual identity
OCCUPATION: Retired; former textile worker, carnival barker
CITIZENSHIP: USA
PLACE OF BIRTH: Brooklyn, New York
KNOWN RELATIVES: May Parker (wife), Richard Parker (brother), Mary Parker (sister-in-law), Peter Parker (Spider-Man, nephew)
GROUP AFFILIATION: None
EDUCATION: High school graduate
FIRST APPEARANCE: Amazing Fantasy #15 (1962)

HISTORY: In his youth, Ben Parker worked as a carnival barker at New York's Coney Island. During his tenure at the carnival, Ben became attracted to May Reilly, a beautiful but naïve woman who lived with her parents in Ben's Brooklyn neighborhood. May, however, had taken a shine to the confident, flashy Johnny Jerome — who always seemed to have plenty of money, even during terrible financial times. Ben Parker did his best to warn May that Jerome was surely up to no good, but she listened only to her own foolish dreams.

One night, Jerome came to May, anxiously asking her to elope with him. While May struggled to decide, Ben Parker informed her that Johnny had just robbed a jewelry store. When the police arrived, it all hit home for May — and she gave her heart that night to the wise and trustworthy Ben.

After Ben and May married, Ben's younger brother and sister-in-law, Richard and Mary Parker — both government agents — were assigned to an undercover mission. Entrusting the care of their only child, Peter, to Ben and May, Richard and Mary left the country. They never returned.

After receiving word of Richard and Mary's deaths, Ben and May adopted Peter and raised him in suburban Forest Hills, Queens, providing the boy who would one day become Spider-Man with unconditional love and unwavering emotional support. Much older than most parents, the Parkers got by, scrimping and saving as best they could. Ben became his nephew's best friend, and the two were inseparable. As he struggled to find ways to boost the shy, friendless Peter's self-esteem, Ben came upon an old box of Golden Age super-hero comics in the attic and gave them to the young man, overriding May's concerns regarding the effect the books' violence might have on the sensitive boy. Ben would never know he had inspired the creation of Spider-Man. One fateful night, a burglar seemingly stumbled on the Parker household — and though he shot Ben dead, he could not kill Ben's influence on the teenaged Peter. Even in death, Ben instilled in Peter one overarching lesson: With great power, there must also come great responsibility.

After becoming the superhuman celebrity Spider-Man, Peter once allowed a fleeing burglar to pass unobstructed. One fateful night at the Parker residence, that same burglar came seeking hidden assets worth millions belonging to a previous owner of the Parker home, his former cellmate, gangster "Dutch" Mallone. After a small quarrel with May that night, Ben left the house to take a walk, leaving the front door unlocked. In his absence, the burglar easily entered the Parker home. Ben returned home and discovered the burglar, who manhandled May for the exact location of the cache. When Ben furiously ordered the burglar to unhand her, the burglar panicked, fatally shot Ben, and fled to a warehouse where he was ultimately caught by Spider-Man. Before May could call for an ambulance, Ben told May he loved her and died. From that day forward, Spider-Man became a devoted crime fighter as Ben's death taught Peter about the responsibility that comes from having great power.

HEIGHT: 5'9"
WEIGHT: 175 lbs.
EYES: Blue
HAIR: White (formerly brown)

ABILITIES/ACCESSORIES: Ben Parker was a good parent and a loving husband.

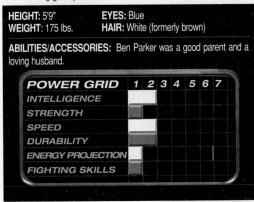

POWER GRID	1	2	3	4	5	6	7
INTELLIGENCE							
STRENGTH							
SPEED							
DURABILITY							
ENERGY PROJECTION							
FIGHTING SKILLS							

ART BY PAUL RYAN

YOUNG BEN

RICHARD AND MARY PARKER

REAL NAME: Richard "Ray" Laurence Parker; Mary Teresa Fitzpatrick Parker

ALIASES: (Richard) No. 7Y6834-R; both Parkers used various aliases as spies

IDENTITY: No dual identities; their CIA careers are not general knowledge

OCCUPATION: (Both) CIA agents, couriers; (Richard) former Special Forces operative; (Mary) translator

CITIZENSHIP: (Both) USA

PLACE OF BIRTH: (Both) Unrevealed

KNOWN RELATIVES: (Richard) Mary (wife, deceased), Peter (Spider-Man, son), Ben (brother, deceased), May (sister-in-law); (Mary) Richard (husband, deceased), Peter (Spider-Man, son), William "Wild Bill" Fitzpatrick (father, deceased), unidentified mother (deceased), Ben (brother-in-law, deceased), May (sister-in-law)

GROUP AFFILIATION: (Both) CIA, Red Skull (Albert Malik's) organization (as double agents); (Richard) formerly US Army Special Forces

EDUCATION: (Richard) High school dropout, Special Forces training; (Mary) college graduate; (both) extensive government training

FIRST APPEARANCE: (Both) Amazing Spider-Man Annual #5 (1968)

HISTORY: About three decades ago, Richard Parker and his best friend, "Big" Mike Callahan, lied about their ages and joined the US Army; sharing his older brother Ben's strength of character, Richard went on to Special Forces service. After that tour of duty, Nick Fury recruited him for a special CIA cell. There he fell in love with translator Mary Fitzpatrick, daughter of legendary OSS agent "Wild Bill" Fitzpatrick, who had worked with the Invaders during World War II. Richard used his influence to help Mary earn a field operative position like his own, and they soon married. Known only as government couriers to the general public, including Ben and his wife May, Richard and Mary secretly undertook dangerous espionage assignments under Fury's command. During one such assignment, they learned that communist operative Deadmaker (Gregori Anatolovich) was a Hydra double agent, a revelation that freed three imprisoned US agents and caused Deadmaker's death.

On vacation in the Riviera, the Parkers encountered neo-Nazi sympathizer Baroness Adelicia von Krupp, whom they discovered was working with enemy agents to interrogate the Canadian Agent Ten, aka Wolverine (Logan/James Howlett). Going undercover in India, the Parkers were captured by Hydra's Baron Strucker but quickly freed Agent Ten and escaped with him. Receiving medical attention shortly afterward, Mary learned she was pregnant. Eight months later she gave birth to baby Peter, adored not only by his parents but by his Uncle Ben and Aunt May as well. While Peter was still a toddler, Richard and Mary infiltrated the spy network of the communist Red Skull (Albert Malik) alongside FBI agent Charlie Shaddock, leaving Peter with Ben and May. While stationed in Algeria, their double agent status was uncovered by the freelance terrorist Gustav Fiers. Malik's right-hand man, the Finisher (Karl Fiers), tampered with their private plane, resulting in their deaths in a crash. Another Malik operative planted evidence framing the Parkers for treason against the US. Peter grew up with Ben and May, not knowing the truth about his parents; following Ben's murder, the teenaged Peter became the heroic Spider-Man.

Over a decade after the Parkers' deaths, Fury's CIA cell was among the government resources combined to form SHIELD, sometimes allied with Spider-Man. Learning of the allegations against his parents, Spider-Man investigated, clashing with Malik and uncovering evidence of the Parkers' double-agent status, clearing their names. The true Red Skull (Johann Shmidt) had Malik slain years later. The Chameleon, as part of a complex vengeance scheme by the Green Goblin (Harry Osborn), created replicoid duplicates of Richard and Mary to insinuate themselves into Peter's life, but when he set them against Spider-Man, they ultimately sacrificed themselves in imitation of the heroic parents they impersonated.

(Richard)
HEIGHT: 5'11"   **EYES:** Brown
WEIGHT: 175 lbs.   **HAIR:** Brown
(Mary)
HEIGHT: 5'6"   **EYES:** Hazel
WEIGHT: 114 lbs.   **HAIR:** Brown

ABILITIES/ACCESSORIES: Richard and Mary Parker were accomplished espionage agents, hand-to-hand combatants, athletes and firearms users; Richard received advanced training in US Army Special Forces, while Mary spoke several languages fluently. Both had access to advanced government equipment.

POWER GRID	1	2	3	4	5	6	7
INTELLIGENCE *							
STRENGTH							
SPEED							
DURABILITY							
ENERGY PROJECTION							
FIGHTING SKILLS							

* YELLOW BAR INDICATES MARY'S INTELLIGENCE RATING

ART BY JOHN ROMITA SR.